THE MIND OF GOD AND
THE WORKS OF MAN

The Mind of God and the Works of Man

EDWARD CRAIG

CLARENDON PRESS · OXFORD
1987

Oxford University Press, Walton Street, Oxford OX2 6DP

Oxford New York Toronto Melbourne Auckland
Delhi Bombay Calcutta Madras Karachi
Petaling Jaya Singapore Hong Kong Tokyo
Nairobi Dar es Salaam Cape Town

Associated companies in Beirut Berlin Ibadan Nicosia

Oxford is a trade mark of Oxford University Press

Published in the United States
by Oxford University Press, New York

British Library Cataloguing in Publication Data
Craig, Edward
The mind of God and the works of man.
1. Philosophy, Modern
I. Title
109   B791
ISBN 0-19-824933-0

Library of Congress Cataloging in Publication Data
Craig, Edward
The mind of God and the works of man.
1. Philosophy, Modern.   I. Title.
B791.C73   1986   190   87-1514
ISBN 0-19-824933-0

Set by Pentacor Ltd.
Printed in Great Britain
at the University Printing House, Oxford
by David Stanford
Printer to the University

FOR

E

AND

C

ACKNOWLEDGEMENTS

Many friends have helped me with comments, discussion and encouragement—even though it means leaving out the others there are some who must be mentioned: Tom Baldwin, Simon Blackburn, Ronald Gray, Martin Hollis, Christopher Hookway, Philip Pettit, Bob Stern and Crispin Wright.

Even warmer thanks are due to my two principal teachers: Casimir Lewy, whose inspiring help first shaped my interest in the subject; and Jonathan Bennett, who introduced me to the study of its history. This book, I am sorry to say, may not be wholly to the taste of either. But the discerning reader will see their influence on nearly every page; the less discerning must be prepared to take the author's word for it.

Finally, my thanks to the Master and Fellows of Churchill College for understanding and generosity during the latter stages of composition. Books used to be written, now they are processed—which sufficiently indicates one, but only one, of the ways in which my college has been of the greatest assistance. In particular, Andrew Tristram and Graham Dixon have been unstinting with their time and expertise. One learns a lot of philosophy from writing a philosophy book; as a bonus, I can now also tell a bit from a byte.

E.J.C.

Churchill College, Cambridge
July 1986

CONTENTS

INTRODUCTION

This book has grown out of a series of three radio talks first broadcast in January 1981; without much distortion it can be thought of simply as an expansion of them. An edited version of the talks was published in *Philosophy* in April 1983, and a quick run through that article still provides a good introduction. Another introduction is nevertheless called for, and that not just for reasons of accessibility. Since this is a book which different readers may best read different parts of, or in a different order, they may be helped by a brief guide to its structure. As well as that, something should be said in defence, or at least in evaluation, of the conception of philosophy that emerges from it, a matter about which the original talks said little.

The talks were directed to an audience supposedly puzzled about the relationship between philosophy, the subject currently practised, taught and studied in most universities of the English-speaking world, and what I called 'Philosophies', those sweeping maps of reality which the traditional philosopher figure of the popular intellectual image used to provide for our guidance in thought and behaviour. Had the connection been entirely lost?

There can be no doubt that there were many, and probably still are a few, who felt that it had not so much been lost as sloughed off, and that it was one of the great advantages of modern philosophical practice to have got rid of it. These were people who believed that to be intellectually reputable was to be quasi-scientific, and were aware that few *Weltbilder* are generated by anything approaching scientific methods, even if they sometimes incorporate the results of the natural sciences or take them as a starting-point. They accordingly preferred to limit their thought to such questions as they took to be amenable to rigorous treatment; their view of the history of metaphysics was sufficiently pessimistic (some will say sufficiently unsentimental) for this area to be fairly small, and to exclude most of the large, perennial questions which had formed the philosopher's traditional preserve. Philosophers now defined a job for themselves and got on with doing it, putting all else out of their minds; in other words, they became professional. But, being philosophers, they could not *just* put things from their minds, and so, within their philosophy— usually, it was within their theory of meaning—reasons grew up justifying this exclusion.

The grand questions, however, did not disappear. They merely became disreputable, an attitude which did nothing to endear the profession to those outside it (and one or two within) who still hankered after world-views. It is one contention of this book that these 'outsiders' had an important truth on their side. Not just that the reasons given for excluding the grand questions were poor ones—even if they were, why shouldn't one shelve certain questions simply in order to concentrate the mind on others more likely to prove answerable?—but that professional practice turns out to show every sign of itself standing in the service of a particular, and particularly pervasive, *Weltbild*.

One aim of this book, then, is to make a case for the link between philosophy and philosophies. Philosophical thought, so the idea runs, has always had the function of articulating certain very general pictures of the real, even if there have been times, like our own, when it has itself denied it. These pictures are such as to have a wide and deep emotional appeal, at the sources of which one can sometimes make vague and speculative, but not wholly implausible, guesses. The philosopher then fills them in with what one might call, allowing a broad sense of the term, logical detail; he hopes thereby to produce a structure capable of satisfying not only the emotions but the intellect as well, the latter by virtue of logical coherence, the former by virtue of being an em- bodiment of an attractive metaphysic. The expressions 'articulate' and 'fill in' are intended to contrast with 'prove', 'demonstrate', and such terms as imply that the metaphysic is solidly established by arguments starting from a neutral position. Philosophers, it need hardly be said, do character- istically claim to have found such arguments, but the evidence is that this claim is never borne out by careful analysis. On the contrary, it is repeatedly found that content smuggled in from the *Weltbild* itself is somehow assisting the passage to the conclusion. There is more than one way in which it can do so. One is by the more or less straightforward provision of a suppressed premiss; another is by helping a thinker to overlook an alternative which, once seen, is damaging to the cogency of his line of thought; a third is by conferring on certain key concepts a kind of aura which inhibits close inspection of their nature and logical connections. (The concept 'idea' enjoyed this kind of protection in the seventeenth-century; 'practice' has enjoyed it in our own.) I should add that if such an underlying metaphysic or philosophy can attract, it can also repel; and knowing what is repelling a philosopher can be as illuminating as knowing what is attracting him.

All this is to be illustrated by selections from the philosophy of the last four centuries. I also argue for a much stronger thesis. It is not only that we find the work of various philosophers to be infused with a metaphysical picture which performs the functions I have just described; we also find that two such pictures cover between them a very large proportion of the philosophy written since the time of Descartes. To sound sensational: modern philosophy consists of just two philosophies in various realisations. But before I am politely requested to pull the other one, I should quickly say that like most sensations, inspection reveals this one to be an exaggeration of truths rather less sensational. Were we to aim at completeness, we would immediately have to add (for instance) the vision of man as a part of nature, an idea which has had a long tradition and is represented as strongly as ever today. But that is a study for another occasion—in what follows I have touched on it only where it crosses the tracks of my favoured pair. Moreover, when I speak of two philosophies, the reader should be aware that the scope for variation, especially in the case of the second, is very wide indeed.

It need scarcely be said that in such a matter completeness would not be a very intelligent aim. This is a book about some of the more general formative influences on modern European philosophy, its goals and inspirations. The most a writer can hope for is to hit on a perspective which reveals a little bit of truth. However far he may go, he can hardly deny that other groupings of the subject-matter, and other explanatory principles, may reveal a little bit more. And why should he want to deny it? There is no reason to think that other perspectives will necessarily be incompatible with his own; the minds of the philosophers who wrote his raw material can safely be presumed sufficiently complex for many currents to have flowed in them at once.

To return: if we can see philosophy as thus articulating philosophies—even if the historical detail of my account be questionable—there will be various consequences which I should like to encourage. One will be an increased sympathy for the idea that philosophy may occur in a variety of media. There may be a number of ways of giving expression and substance to such an underlying picture: a novelist may give it force and content by embodying it in a narrative, a poet with imagery; but it could still be a very similar picture to the one which the philosopher fills out with what in a generous sense we may call logic. So this kind of comparison may help us to see the continuity between areas often thought of (at any rate by recent philosophers) as distinct, and so to understand why there is such a thing as philosophical literature and literary philosophy without having to resort to the implausible old dodge of saying that the word 'philosophy' is ambiguous.

A second effect which I would hope for is a greater appreciation of the historically variable factors in philosophy. Much criticism has recently been levelled at the attitude of 'analytic' philosophy towards the history of the subject. Critics have identified in some a tendency simply to neglect it, in others a tendency to treat it as if it contained nothing but embryonic and fumbling attempts to solve twentieth-century philosophical problems. That problems might alter, or that the boundary conditions for their solution might change, so that what is nowadays an acceptable response might to another age not seem worth a moment's consideration, is an idea outside the scope of the analytic 'historian of philosophy' of the last fifty years. There is certainly something in these accusations, though for two reasons I think it possible to press them too hard. Thinking that one has arrived at the truth, or at least discovered a method for arriving at it, is not a monopoly of analytic philosophy or indeed of any other school. And it is quite understandable that someone in that condition should regard the history of philosophy much as one would expect a physicist to regard the history of physics: either as a waste of good time that ought to be spent doing physics, or as a diverting story about early attempts to do what we now do a great deal better, the story of how *we* got *here*.

Another reason for not pressing this charge too hard is that to do so may give an exaggerated impression of the historical mobility of philosophical problems and methods. It is a striking fact about the history of philosophy, and one that we should not lose sight of, that it is not more incomprehensible to us than is actually the case. Many texts, in fact, are sufficiently comprehensible to nourish the illusion that there is nothing about them that we cannot understand without making the effort to get outside our current perspective. The *prima facie* case for supposing that many elements of philosophical thought are diachronically stable, stable enough to be found unchanged through hundreds, perhaps thousands, of years, is a very compelling one. That being so, there may well be a great deal of value that a contemporary philosopher can say about a historical text whilst still approaching it as if it had been written yesterday; no blanket theoretical considerations have ever been adduced that rule that out, nor are any likely to be. One thing this book does is present materials which might help us to form a discussible view as to which aspects of the philosophical scene are changing, and which are for all practical purposes abiding, features of the landscape; in that way we might also get an inkling of the types of historical misunderstanding, and more importantly of self-misunderstanding, against which to be most on our guard.

These are my hopes for the book. I also have certain fears. One is that careless reading of it may encourage the inflated historical perspectivism about understanding of which I have just spoken, and make a hermeneutic mountain out of what may well be only a hermeneutic molehill; but I can say little more to ward off that danger than what I have already said. Another is that it may be thought to be part of a movement which would insinuate the substitution of the study of the history of philosophy for the first-order activity itself. If so, I shall have been misunderstood; but some explanation is called for. Two lines of thought, one rather more subtle and enticing than the other, could lead in that direction. One would be the idea that to take present philosophical practice as the object of quasi-historical study—which I will be felt to invite the reader to do— was incompatible with an engagement in the practice itself, or at least implied a certain reserve which must make a whole-hearted commitment to it impossible. Put as crudely as that, it is no more impressive than the argument that someone writing a book on the sociology of golf could not at the same time be a keen and active golfer. But something a little more sophisticated is in the offing. Our golfing sociologist is not necessarily involved, whilst playing golf, in pursuing any aim which his sociology declares to be unattainable, whereas the corresponding philosopher may be, if he takes the sort of view of philosophy which this book recommends. For when he does philosophy he aims to acquire knowledge of the truth, whereas his theory about philosophy tells him to see his activity as logical embroidery upon a given design. Into the origins of this design he has very little insight, and what little he has gives him no grounds for regarding it as anything other than a historically determined preference. So this theory of the nature of philosophy is incompatible with the sincere pursuit of the first-order activity, as any thoroughgoing relativism about truth is in conflict with a sincere commitment to investigation.

Unlike its predecessor, this is a weighty argument. There are ways of evading it, but to refute it looks as if it calls for either an adjustment to the notion of truth or a reappraisal of the aims of philosophy. How, to start with, might one evade it? A possibility would be to run away into those reaches of philosophy which border very closely on mathematics, or on natural sciences such as linguistics. Another would be to work as it were in the conditional mood, pointing out inconsistencies in given doctrines, exposing inadequacies in the arguments advanced to support them, in general terms busying oneself with the logical relationships between philosophical positions and their components, and leaving it to others to commit themselves to their truth or falsity. The former method would give the impression, outside philosophy departments, that, however much might be going on, *philosophy* had stopped. The latter, whilst it would at least leave philosophers manifestly still talking about philosophy, could hardly become the universally accepted approach without stifling its own motivation. To investigate the inner logic of positions which everyone studiously held back from actually occupying, and mapping out their interrelationships, would be a strange enterprise to keep up for long. One would find oneself pushed towards the view, which has been held by many in recent times, that philosophy is a propaedeutic exercise, a kind of conceptual training-schedule; though to what Olympiad it is directed, and why other disciplines could not do the same job equally well, it might continue to prove difficult to say.

If these evasions prove unsatisfactory in one way or another, what does it cost to meet the argument head on? One resort, as I have said, would be to adjust the notion of truth in the style of the pragmatists, ascribing it to such systems as produce a coherent structure of beliefs satisfying both to thought and to feeling. Truth, on this account of it, would then be exactly what philosophers aimed at, on this account of philosophy; the suggestion of incompatibility between practice and theory would disappear. But it would be better, because more direct, to say straight out that the aim of philosophy was to give emotional and intellectual satisfaction by bringing the services of logic to the elaboration of a favoured (and perhaps needed) *Weltbild*, leaving untouched the question as to how the word 'truth' is to be allocated. Such a response takes the full force of the argument, but then goes on to say that the task which is left for philosophy to perform is a prestigious one, fulfilling a need of man hallowed by, if not strictly rational grounds, at any rate some thousands of years of cultural history, a task therefore of which no one need be ashamed, or make excuses for committing himself to.

At the time when the material which appeared in the radio talks was forming I hoped that a clearer perception of the links between philosophy, the discipline encountered in university courses and in the texts of those regarded, for the purpose of such courses, as great philosophers, and Philosophies, the great creeds of the history of thought, would result in an advancement of the public status of the former. So I think it should, but given the way in which the picture of these links develops some may feel that the price to be paid for the improvement is rather high. Philosophy, they will say, has always purported to be an investigation into the nature of reality, and optimism about the eventual outcome of that investigation has been a vital part of its motivation. Even those whose philosophy would impose limits on our ability to know have believed themselves to be straightforwardly right about these limits; they did not think that they were merely giving expression, in the mode of conceptual thought, to their 'feelings' about the universe. How sure is it that the sincere engagement with philosophical problems will survive this change in self-image? Is there not a danger that from this perspective the harder part of philosophy, the search for demonstration and harmony of logical detail, will come to be seen as so much effort wasted in pursuit of an illusion? Why, if we are in any case just expanding on our preferred meta-physic, should we not prefer to do so in a style less uncomfortable for both author and reader?

I shall return to that question. First a parenthesis: the idea that philosophical systems, and indeed philosophical points, may embody philosophies in the way I argue, does not by itself lead to the conclusion that philosophical truth is historically relative. On the contrary, it leaves open the possibility that one (or some) of these philosophies might be absolutely, even demonstrably, true, and so confer compar-able status on the philosophical systems which incorporate it. What speaks against that possibility is another, independent, point: that close inspection of philosophers' arguments shows so many of them to rely, in one way or another, on the tacit importation of material drawn from the very vision of reality which they were meant to support. And this does suggest— admittedly the evidence is inductive, but there is quite a lot of it—that attempts to demonstrate the truth of philosophical positions from a neutral starting-point cannot succeed. Which, if it is true, brings us right back to face the question from the end of the previous paragraph. But although there is no avoiding it, it is very far from being settled. At least two responses still have a great deal of life left in them, and they are such as to appeal to very different, indeed opposed, philosophical temperaments.

The first of them may be put like this: some set greater store by the achievement of intellectual satisfaction than others, and are prepared to go to greater lengths to get it. These, in the European tradition at least, are the natural philosophers. Whether their enthusiasm for this style of inquiry would survive the widespread and conscious acceptance of the general doctrine about the nature of their activity which this book suggests is a matter for guesswork. My own guess, for what it is worth, is that it would. But it seems that one concession, and many will feel it to be a large one, will be very hard to avoid: on what grounds are we to accord the rigorous, argumentative style of philosophy any preference (other than of a purely personal kind) over the more discursive, or more overtly psychological, or more poetic, or any of the other ways in which a metaphysical vision might be conveyed and enlivened? Perhaps, however, it would be no bad thing at this juncture if we leave that question unanswered (whether from choice or necessity) and allow our sympathies and interests to broaden.

The second possible response has more the nature of a counterattack. I have implied that there is 'quite a lot of evidence' for thinking that the acceptance of the philosophies which underlie philosophy is a prerational matter, and that we are consequently in no position to treat them as being true or false. But is this really so? After all, I have only spoken of two such philosophies, and is this enough to establish so sweeping a point of principle? Let us suppose (not wholly uncontroversially, be it said) that it is at any rate true of these two. The fact doesn't begin to exclude the possibility that there may be any number of such 'mottos' which there could be excellent reason to take for true, pure and simple, so that philosophical systems which embodied them would be objectively preferable to those that did not embody them, but rather embodied others less favoured by the evidence. A philosophy which elaborated on the thought that man is continuous with the rest of nature, for instance, might be one

such, because its 'motto' might be supported by everything
that was known to and being discovered by the physical and
biological sciences—that support could in time grow so strong
that any disagreement became more confirmative of the
continued existence of cranks than of the truth of relativism.
Some would happily say that the point had already been
reached. Hence the current interest in the view that naturalism, if comprehensive, is not selfconsistent, and, if selfconsistent, is not comprehensive; for it is apparent that a
comprehensive and consistent form of naturalism, could it be
devised, would even now have a very strong claim on our
belief. I shall not at present pursue this line of thought further;
I say only that those attracted to realist views about
philosophical truth do not necessarily have to choose between
them and what follows—a considerable measure of realism is
compatible with all that I shall say.

Besides, this somewhat bolder reply permits an answer to
our unanswered question, why special status should be
granted to logic and argument as the medium in which to
articulate a philosophy, as compared with other media less
directly tuned to the discovery and transmission of truths. For
the more objectivist one's view of philosophical activity and its
goals, the easier will it be to justify the use of those techniques
which have led, in mathematics and the sciences, to cognitive
success; and the less appropriate, conversely, will other forms,
such as literary narrative, appear.

It may help the reader to have a brief description of the
book's shape. It can be thought of as falling into three parts,
each consisting of two chapters. In the first chapter of each
pair I describe a philosophy, and illustrate it by reference to
writers who subscribe to it in a greater or lesser degree. Thus
Chapter 1 is concerned with the dominant philosophy of the
seventeenth and early eighteenth centuries—what I call the
'Image of God' doctrine; Chapter 5 portrays the 'Practice
Ideal' or 'Agency Theory', the metaphysic which I claim to
have been one of the most potent forces not only in the
nineteenth but in the twentieth century as well. It will at once
occur to the reader to wonder how, since I have advertised
just two principal *Weltbilder*, there can then be three parts to

the book. The answer is that there is no need to regard the subject matter of Chapter 3 (entitled 'The Metaphysic of the Romantic Era') as a distinct philosophy; it can be seen rather as a bridge, in which the chief characteristics of the flanking epochs were for a time closely united. But like most bridges, it does have a definite stamp of its own as well as that which it draws from the two banks.

In the second chapter of each pair I take a closer look at selected texts, hoping to show that reading them against the background provided by the previous chapter is rewarding, in that more satisfactory interpretations are suggested, or that connections appear which illuminate one's view of a whole period of philosophical endeavour. (I choose the first of these formulations with Chapter 2, on the understanding of Hume, primarily in mind, the second with an eye primarily to Chapter 6, on the understanding of our own century.) The even-numbered chapters, in consequence, demand a slightly higher level of knowledge and expertise than do the odd-numbered. The latter, if I have not made a misjudgement, should be accessible to any intelligent reader with a smattering of the history of modern philosophy, and I hope that such persons can get interest and enjoyment from Chapters 1, 3 and 5 taken alone.

It will be clear that I have also entertained various subsidiary, and more specific, aims. One, obviously enough, is to give us a better sight of Hume. There seems to have been in recent years an almost ubiquitous tendency to treat the great, dead philosophers as if they were our contemporaries; a practice which, by wrenching their work away from its native *Weltbild* and viewing it against the (often unconscious) background of another—our own—can seriously distort our understanding of it. In the case of Hume, who stands in many respects genuinely close to us, the tendency has proved almost irresistible—at least, that is what one would have to say if one were sure that any serious attempt had been made to resist it. Another aim has been to provide prologomena to the study of Hegel. I hope that this section will help to make Hegel's work and career more comprehensible as a historical phenomenon, and so do something to liberate us from the compulsion obviously felt by certain recent commentators to render Hegel acceptable by presenting his thought as more akin to our own than it really is.

In attempting a work with such a ground-plan an author must run one or other of two risks. On the one hand lies the danger of superficiality in respect of his knowledge, let alone his presentation, of at least some of the range of material involved. On the other lies the threat that the enterprise will turn into an obsessional life's work, culminating in a book which, having first devoured its author, then sets to work exhausting its tiny circle of readers. I need hardly say which of these alternatives I have embraced. It may also be thought that what I have said suggests a further book, one which would trace the naturalistic philosophy of man and delve for its less obvious effects. I agree, but I do not promise to write it. Nor do I promise not to.

1

THE MIND OF GOD

1. *The image of God*

My first aim is to describe and document one very deep and pervasive feature of the thought of the seventeenth and early eighteenth centuries, something which can clearly be seen as a central concern of nearly all the major philosophers of that period, even though they concerned themselves with it for different purposes and reacted to it in widely varying ways. If anything can properly be called the 'dominant philosophy' of these hundred or so years, this is it. But I shall also begin the pursuit of a second aim, the illustration of a thesis that I have already mentioned: that commentators to whom this dominant philosophy has, for historical reasons, ceased to mean anything, frequently fail to recognise its role in the thought of those whose works they discuss, and that the failure can and does lead to serious superficiality and distortion.

The word 'philosophy' should not here be taken in the sense of a worked-out system of related thoughts, otherwise the expression 'dominant philosophy' will be felt to be a misnomer for the idea that forms the basic theme of this chapter. In its least articulate form this philosophy was less an idea than an attitude, an attitude of confidence in the human individual and his powers. Our interest in it begins, however, at the point where it reaches verbal expression in what we might call the philosophical motto or slogan that man was made in the image of God. It is to be noted at once that, whatever emotional chords this motto may touch, its conceptual content could hardly be less determinate. To say that man is like God implies, apart from the existence of each, virtually nothing; any feeling that it has content arises because one has in mind some particular theology or philosophy which provides the dimensions of similarity. A particular system of thought, if it includes theses about the nature of the deity and of human beings, can indeed give it content to a high degree of precision; to show how this was done by philosophers from Galileo to Berkeley, and to exhibit the repercussions in metaphysics, epistemology and ethics is exactly the theme of this chapter.

With the origins of the doctrine that man was made in God's image (or, as for the sake of variation I shall sometimes call it, the Similarity Thesis) I shall not be much concerned—rather with its development and ramifications. But perhaps I may be allowed some very brief and uncertain speculations about the factors which may have supported and encouraged it. Obviously, it has deep roots in Christianity, and one central Christian dogma, that of the incarnation, almost *requires* it: if God could take upon himself not just outward human shape, but humanity, and yet without loss of divinity, then only total mysticism can avoid the consequence that the human and the divine natures must to a considerable extent overlap; and many who do not draw that conclusion consciously as a matter of logic will still find it more or less consciously present in their reaction to the doctrine.

Again, the 'children of God' metaphor, the emotional attraction of which is surely active well beyond the reaches of Christianity in such cultural phenomena as ancestor-worship, feeds the Similarity Thesis—nobody is unaware that children are of one species with their parents. But it may also have been nourished from another source by no means exclusive to the Judaeo-Christian tradition, namely the idea of the 'Great Chain of Being', whose history Arthur Lovejoy learnedly and brilliantly traced. For if we are encouraged to see all natural forms as ranged in a continuum of overlapping properties, and if the human race then finds in itself the highest known natural form, it is only a short step (and all the shorter for being welcome) to thinking that in many respects there cannot be much farther to climb up the ladder that leads to the highest form of all; and that amounts to thinking that human beings must at least in those respects bear quite a close resemblance to God.

None of these factors, however, does anything to explain why the philosophers of the seventeenth and eighteenth centuries should have turned with unique enthusiasm to the

doctrine of the Image of God and pursued it with such
intellectual intensity. It is not, in fact, an essential part of the
case which I shall be making in the first part of this book that
they were in this regard *unique*; but if, as I believe, they were,
then three points may make it more easily understandable,
and in any case they may serve to explain their indubitable
enthusiasm.

One of these was the rise of protestantism, tending as it did
to emphasise the closeness between God and the individual
human being. In so far as this was taken to mean *all* human
beings it must have bolstered the thought that the closeness
was a matter of human nature rather than of some special
status superadded to human nature by the fact of being, for
example, the elected representative of the church. But we
must not expect too much of this point; after all, the Image of
God doctrine was not the exclusive property of protestant
philosophers, nor even, as we shall see, of Christians. More
important, one may safely assume, was the effect of the new
and quite spectacular penetration which the scientists of this
period were achieving into the workings of the universe, the
message of the 'book of nature', thus providing startling
evidence of an affinity between their minds and the mind of its
author.

To this one ought to add the impact of some of the
particular discoveries which those scientists were making. The
rejection of the geocentric cosmology removed, admittedly,
only the mud we stand on from the centre of the universe, and,
as Lovejoy argued, the centre may not have appeared such a
univocally desirable place as some writers have assumed. But
in removing the Earth from what was at any rate a unique
position in a huge but countable system and making it one
amongst several, possibly amongst millions or even infinitely
many others, it invited the thought that man is perhaps very
far from being the sole rational, or even the most rational,
inhabitant of the cosmos. The invitation was seized upon in
most entertaining style by Bernard de Fontenelle in his
Conversations on the Plurality of Worlds:

'Twas well done of him [Copernicus], said I, to abate the Vanity of
Mankind, who had taken up the best place in the Universe.

To this one might react in two ways: either with relief at the removal of a burden, as does the imaginary philosopher in Fontenelle's *Conversations*, or with alarm and a feeling of lostness, as does his partner the countess:

You have made the universe so large, says she, that I know not where I am, or what will become of me.[1]

Either of these reactions may, to judge from the casual observation of human psychology, be considered very natural. What I want to suggest is that a concentration on the second might help to trigger the Image of God doctrine as a readily available form of defence mechanism against the vision of oneself as not unique in any way that mattered, a speck of dust in the encompassing vastness, insignificant in both quantity and quality. Significance of quality, it could easily be felt, could be maintained like this. To see the philosophers of the period as centrally concerned with the Similarity Thesis is to see them as, amongst other things, fighting a defensive action against the cultural effects of the new science. It does not of course conflict with this perspective that both endeavours are frequently found in the same individual; it would be surprising if it were not so.

Even if a certain speculative licence is permissible here, one gap must nevertheless be plugged. My story will begin with Galileo and Descartes. Can one speak of the impact on *them* of the discoveries of the new science without an uncomfortable feeling that the cart is overtaking the horse? It will help us here to think of the phenomenon in slightly broader terms. Such men were trying to achieve an independence for the human intellect; they sought emancipation from the tradition of reliance on authorities, those being principally Aristotle, as then understood, and God via the church as his earthly mouthpiece. How were they to forge the concept of the independent human thinker without losing all contact with that tradition in which most of their audience, and probably at times they themselves, still felt largely at home? Presumably just as such things are usually done: by taking recognisable materials from the earlier modes of thought and

[1] Bernard de Fontenelle: *Conversations on the Plurality of Worlds*, trans. John Glanvill (Nonesuch Press 1929) p. 114; previous quotation p. 25.

bending them to new uses. So if man is to be capable of acting as his own authority, what more likely to attract the conviction of both author and reader than to present him as having a marked resemblance to the authorities previously accepted? Forgetting for the moment the Image of God doctrine, it is worth noting that Galileo's spokesman in the *Dialogue Concerning the Two Chief World Systems* repeatedly claims that he, by insisting on accurate judgement based on accurate observation, is following the model of Aristotle much more closely than are his 'Aristotelian' opponents. The individual inquirer is to be more truly Aristotelian, and more truly godlike; he can be an authority precisely because the sources of the standard authorities' authority are present to some degree in him.

We should now leave these speculations in order to look at the phenomenon they are intended to explain, the popularity of the Image of God doctrine amongst the philosophers of the seventeenth century; but first I should emphasise a point which might otherwise be buried by what follows. From now on I shall focus all attention on the Similarity Thesis and its ramifications. But I am not claiming that this metaphysic so dominated thought that its humbler antagonist—we may call it the 'speck of dust' view of mankind—disappeared for a hundred and fifty years from men's minds. It quite certainly did not, and even without the impetus given to it by the advance of cosmology it almost certainly would not have done so. Self-abasement and self-congratulation are tendencies both of which have a firm foothold in normal Christian belief. Nowhere in this period are they more forcefully presented side by side than in the *Pensées* of Pascal—the paradoxical nature of man, his simultaneous grandeur and wretchedness. And many of those who did not bring anything like Pascal's passionate rhetoric to the subject, or his pessimism about the potential of unaided human nature, still paid service to both components of his paradox. Taking a more exalted view of human reason than did Pascal, however, they had no wish to make human nature appear intrinsically incomprehensible to man, and so generally took care to present the opposition in non-paradoxical form: the favourite device was to exploit the two dimensions of quality and quantity, restrict the similarity

between man and God to the former and allow an unbridgeable gap in respect of the latter. What this amounted to will
become clear in the course of the chapter.

It would be wrong, however, if the reader were to start off
with the idea that I propose to single out for treatment one of
two contrary themes which find equally powerful expression
in the philosophical writings of the seventeenth and early
eighteenth centuries; that there is also a 'Dissimilarity Thesis'
of comparable weight, and that I have simply chosen not to
talk about it. On the contrary, I shall talk about it; but it does
not have comparable weight, not in the letter of these writings,
and quite certainly not in their spirit. It is a striking feature of
this period, and of its impact on its successors, that in the
works of those whom we now regard as its great philosophers
the one theme, the proud vision of ourselves as made in the
image of God, predominates heavily.

2. *Insight and freedom: Galileo and Descartes*

The remarks of the last two paragraphs are excellently
illustrated by the closing pages of the *First Day* of Galileo's
Dialogue Concerning the Two Chief World Systems. The characters
are expatiating on the subject of the vast, indeed infinite, gap
between the divine understanding and power and that of man,
even of the most gifted men such as Socrates and Michel-
angelo. After a while this moves Simplicio to wonder whether
Salviato—who speaks for Galileo—has not committed himself to a contradictory position. Has he not just expressed
agreement with the remark of Socrates, that his own
knowledge was as nothing compared to the infinity of
knowledge which he lacked? And yet, Salviato,

Among your greatest encomiums, if not indeed the greatest of all, is
your praise for the understanding which you attribute to natural
man.[2]

But Salviato sees no difficulty in combining these two views.
Any appearance of contradiction fades if we distinguish
between the *intensive* and the *extensive* aspects of human
knowledge. The latter relates to the question of quantity: how

---

[2] Galileo: *Dialogue Concerning the Two Chief World Systems*, trans. Drake (University
of California Press 1953) p. 102.

much do we know? It is with reference to this question that we
have to agree with Socrates' self-estimate, for the number of
truths is infinite, and those known to us do indeed vanish
when compared with them. But when we think of human
knowledge as it is *intensively*, when we think, that is, of the
quality of our grasp of those truths which we see most clearly
and know most certainly: here one may speak of a perfection
in cognition upon which not even God can improve. God
knows infinitely more than we do; but as regards the depth of
the mind's penetration into particular truths, our best
efforts—which Salviato confines to the fields of geometry and
arithmetic—are on the same level as his:

> But with regard to those few which the human intellect does
> understand, I believe that its knowledge equals the divine in
> objective certainty, for here it succeeds in understanding necessity,
> beyond which there can be no greater sureness.[3]

Here we have it: the clash between the speck of dust and the
image of God, and its resolution by appeal to a distinction
between quantity and quality. But the interest of the passage
is not yet exhausted. Simplicio is unhappy about the reply he
has received; perhaps he did not expect Salviato to go quite so
far in his praise for the understanding of man as to make a
direct equation with aspects of the cognitive powers of the
deity. Is this not 'very bold and daring'? Salviato first makes
to defend himself and then, like a man who knows very well
that he is at the edge of the tolerable, turns conciliatory: even
if the little knowledge we have within the mathematical
sciences is the same kind of knowledge as that which God has,
it remains that the way in which God comes to this knowledge
is 'exceedingly more excellent than ours'. For what we learn
by slow and laborious passage from premisses to conclusions,
he grasps effortlessly and instantaneously in a single intuitive
act. But again, like a man determined to remain at the edge of
the tolerable and even hoping to push it back a little, Salviato
now gives his conciliatory offer a twist back in the other
direction: this immediate intuitive apprehension is not wholly
foreign to the human mind—we can approximate to it more
and more closely, as when we become very familiar with the

---

[3] Ibid. p. 103.

steps of a simple proof and can follow it as rapidly as we can bring the relevant thoughts to mind. There follows a cautious summing up, in which Salviato half appears to retract again, though significantly without proposing any new grounds for doing so, and with that he is allowed to have the last word on the question. Simplicio falls silent, Sagredo supports Salviato in discursive style; and a gondola ride is proposed. The attentive reader can be in no real doubt as to which way Galileo is facing; this is not the writing of a proponent of the 'speck of dust' doctrine from whom certain grudging concessions are being wrung.

Before leaving Galileo, we can take a first sighting of some themes which will gradually loom larger as we go on. One of these is the status of mathematical method in seventeenth-century thought. Obviously enough, it was very high: philosophers showed a strong tendency to present their own procedures as approximating, at the least, to those of the mathematicians, to set quasi-mathematical standards in their epistemology, to give, as we have just seen Galileo doing, mathematical examples as illustrative of the highest type of human knowledge. And many later readers, most especially recent ones, have registered this fact and spoken of it as if it were just a brute fact about seventeenth-century intellectual taste. The last few pages of the *First Day* of Galileo's *Dialogue* raise the suspicion that the fact is not so brute after all; perhaps the fascination with mathematics was not wholly for its own sake, but instead had something to do with the opportunity it gave for a detailed articulation of the Similarity Thesis. That task can only be carried out, after all, if the philosopher can find to hand something human which will stand comparison with God as he conceives him. It remains true, of course, that unless mathematical knowledge seemed to have in itself certain extraordinary properties it could not have been used for that purpose; but that is perfectly compatible with its not having been the properties in themselves which attracted the fuss so much as the end for which they made mathematical knowledge suitable. The impression that the mathematical sciences are being prized because they conform, or of all our knowledge most nearly conform, to some *external* standard, is at its strongest in the latter half of Salviato's final speech.[4] God, it has been decided, sees all truths instantaneously; Salviato's plea is that mathematical knowledge does not always fall too far short of that mark.

Whether that plea be accepted or not, it might be thought that by the time he makes it Salviato has already twisted mathematical knowledge somewhat out of shape in the attempt to make it do the sort of work that the Similarity Thesis demands. What reason did he give for the contention that our best acts of knowledge are *intensively* the equal of God's? It was that in these cases the human understanding grasps the necessity of the truth in question, not merely that it is true but that it must be true and could not possibly be otherwise; and since beyond necessity 'there is no greater sureness' we have thereby reached a limit which even God cannot surpass, simply because there is no further to go.

If that is a correct account of his thought, Galileo has fudged the issue. Let us accept that in mathematics, for instance, we can recognise not just the truth but the necessity of certain statements; that does not mean that we have a cognitive faculty which is not subject to the possibility of error. Indeed, if it did mean that we would have no other option than to drop the claim that we can recognise necessity, since nothing is more obvious than that we sometimes make mistakes in mathematics and so take things for true, and necessarily true, when they are not; we miscalculate, we take invalid proofs for valid. Even if we allow ourselves infallible insight into the individual steps of a proof or calculation whilst they are present to the mind, there is still the question of whether the memory might play us false during the operation. Descartes knew that, and was worried by it; Galileo knew the facts of mathematical practice and mispractice as well as anyone, but he hops over them. No doubt it is oversight, not intent. But we have just seen how important it is to the Image of God philosophy that mathematical knowledge turn out to have the 'right' properties. In his treatment of it, Galileo is at a crux; and as I have already hinted in the Introduction, in the immediate vicinity of a dominant philosophy the line between simple mistake and the beginnings of self-deception is

[4] Ibid. p. 104.

very hard to draw. We shall meet many more such cases.

A third theme that will reappear can be observed in Galileo's writings. When, as in the passage we have just been looking at, man is compared to God in point of his ability to acquire a certain type of knowledge, the thought very naturally follows that its acquisition is itself a moral value, something that we have an obligation to pursue. In doing so we ourselves approach more nearly to perfection; for since it is such items of knowledge that, amongst other things, compose the mind of God, it follows that in acquiring them we approach more nearly the divine state, the summit of all good. So that when the Image of God doctrine is worked out in terms of our cognitive faculties, the result readily supports a contemplative or scientific ethic in which knowledge, or the most prized kind of knowledge, appears as a good in itself and does not have to be justified in terms of its applications. We shall encounter a most vigorous expression of this attitude in Leibniz; here is Galileo's version:

He who looks the higher is the more highly distinguished, and turning over the great book of nature (which is the proper object of philosophy) is the way to elevate one's gaze.[5]

No mention is made of how we act or what we do. It is where we *look*, what we *see*, which makes up our worth. One has heard it said that the philosophers of the seventeenth and early eighteenth centuries saw themselves as spectators, inquirers into nature and reality, and were not much interested in action or practice. Put in those words, that is a crude exaggeration, but there is (indeed, it is one of the main themes of this book as a whole) a deep truth behind it. What we have seen here is one of its early manifestations, and a hint as to what its philosophical underpinnings might be.

It would be reasonable to expect to find in Descartes a particularly rich source of material for our topic. Nobody ever championed more explicitly than he the individual's claim to be his own authority, with his attempt to banish false belief, in fact to banish all doubt, by his own unaided reflective efforts. His aim was complete certainty, just that (alleged) property of mathematical beliefs which Galileo seized upon to draw

[5] Ibid. Author's Dedication.

parallels with the knowledge that God has. Relying solely on his own powers of thought, he would build up a system of completely reliable beliefs, taking as his starting-point totally transparent truths over which there was no possibility of error, and proceeding from them to other beliefs by a series of steps each of which carried a similar guarantee. Even with this limitation imposed upon his method, he clearly expected to be able to reach a good many beliefs, enough at any rate to carry him some way into theology, metaphysics and science. Some of his original beliefs would not, of course, be certifiable by this procedure, since presumably some of them were in fact false; some again might be unattainable as lying outside human scope, and so being matters reserved for faith and revelation. But a substantial part of our corpus of beliefs he did expect to secure by this type of investigation.

The route he took is extremely well known, most notably from the *Meditations*. Seeking for the indubitable basis, he was led to find his first certainty in the belief in his own existence as a thinking being, for this was a truth which any attempt to deceive him had to presuppose. Next he felt himself able to demonstrate the existence of God as his creator, and this licensed a conclusion about his cognitive faculties: that they could not be *in principle* deceitful—if he was deceived by them, it could only be the outcome of his precipitately rushing into belief before they had been given the opportunity to function to the best of their ability. It followed that any belief based on the best evidence we could possibly have for it was true.

Even that sketchiest of sketches reveals Descartes' reliance on a feature that throughout the Christian tradition has contributed to the articulation of the Image of God doctrine. The premiss that 'God is no deceiver', without which his salvage of knowledge fails *in limine*, is plucked out of the air, a product of the unthinking assumption that God's ways are our ways, that we resemble him in point of moral values—this is the response which Nietzsche was later to make with some trenchancy.[6] The expectation that the Similarity Thesis will be found at work in Descartes' thought is confirmed, though not quite from the direction in which the reading of Galileo

---

[6] See for instance Nietzsche: *The Will to Power*, ed. Kaufmann, trans. Kaufmann and Hollingdale (Vintage Books 1968) para. 436.

would point. And it is heightened by a wholly explicit passage at the end of the third *Meditation*:

From the mere fact of my creation by God, it is highly worthy of belief that I am made in his image and likeness . . .

The stage seems admirably set for a Galileo-like declaration of the divine qualities of human cognition. But no such declaration is found in Descartes' writings; not, that is to say, explicitly, and the passages in which a partisan reader might claim to find them implicit are quite unconvincing. All the more are they unconvincing for the fact that we undoubtedly do find a doctrine with a strong contrary pull: the 'eternal' truths depend on the will of God; God did not *see* that two plus two is four, rather his fiat made it so. That is, to say the least, a severe setback for the claim that our relationship to propositions of mathematics is the same as that of God. Leibniz, as we shall see the most outspoken adherent of the Similarity Thesis and the philosopher who presented it in its most highly developed form, was careful to issue an un-equivocal denial:

That is why I find altogether strange the expression of certain other philosophers who say that the eternal truths of metaphysics and of geometry and consequently also the rules of goodness, of justice and of perfection, are only the effects of God's will, whereas it seems to me that they are only consequences of his understanding, which assuredly no more depends on his will than does his essence.[7]

There are, however, other ways to develop the Image of God doctrine than the epistemological one favoured by Galileo. Descartes, although he did not take the matter very far compared to some of his successors, was not content to leave our quotation from the end of the third *Meditation* lying about as a detached piece of Christian piety, without trying to specify more nearly any of the respects in which the human being resembled its creator. When it comes, in the fourth *Meditation*, it has nothing to do with cognition, however well that would have fitted his epistemological stance at the outset of the work; the point of resemblance to God which Descartes singles out resides in the nature of the will and its freedom.

[7] Leibniz: *Discourse on Metaphysics* para. II.

Nor does he leave it at that. First he makes a gesture towards the doctrine of qualitative similarity combined with the infinite quantitative gap: God's will is incomparably greater than man's in efficacy and scope, but it is not greater 'considered precisely as will'—Galileo's distinction between the intensive and the extensive aspects could be used here without strain, one feels. And he goes on to explain this latter point by telling the reader what freedom of the will consists in: not in the absence of factors determining choice, and certainly not in the ability to choose between alternatives about which one is *indifferent*, but in the lack of determination by forces *external* to the mind. We sometimes are in such a condition, Descartes implies, that our choice is subject to no factors other than internal ones, and there is no way of being any *more* free than that, even for God, though he is of course free to this extent in everything he wills.

Now it might be objected that all this need not have anything to do with the Similarity Thesis. What Descartes is doing, so the objection would run, is making a claim about human freedom which will enable him to say that man, and not God, is the author of human error. And that this is so is even clearer from a passage in the *Principles of Philosophy* XXXVII, in which the words: 'It is a supreme perfection in man to act voluntarily or freely . . .' are immediately followed by: '. . . and thus to be in a special sense the author of his own actions, and to deserve praise for them'. Of course it is true that this is *one* of Descartes' aims. But to refuse to see anything more is to be insensitive to the details of the text, such as the effect of the words 'a supreme perfection' in the sentence just quoted from the *Principles*; on the hypothesis that he was only trying to secure human responsibility there was no need for him to awaken theological overtones by that choice of vocabulary. In the fourth *Meditation* it is not so much insensitivity to detail that is required—one would have to overlook entirely two whole sentences that are directed explicitly to the Image of God doctrine. That it is present, and obviously present, is undeniable. If the objection we are considering is to carry any weight at all it will have to be reformulated as the claim that the Similarity Thesis is merely instrumental to Descartes' thought on this question, and that

means that the objector will have to, first, convince us that
Descartes felt that he could not have the essential thesis about
the authorship of our own actions without going so far as to
say that human will, when 'considered precisely as will', is
just like the divine will; second, he must explain why, given
that Descartes believed this, he was happy to display the fact
as prominently as he did. And he must do all this without in
effect retracting his whole objection and admitting that
Descartes found the Similarity Thesis, and this particular
variant of it, attractive *per se*.

I remarked earlier that at the point at which Galileo comes
to argue for a likeness between man and God a gap becomes
apparent in his logic; and I slanderously implied, quite
without proof, that it might be the pull of the 'dominant
philosophy' which was helping him to jump it. Here in the
fourth *Meditation* another piece of circumstantial evidence
comes to light, for it has to be admitted that the way in which
Descartes presents his (very different) comparison of us with
the deity is, as an argument, extraordinarily weak. Let us
accept that the freedom of the will consists in the absence of
external determinants of choice; then we must further agree
that complete absence of such determining factors constitutes
the highest degree of freedom it is logically possible for there
to be. But what reason is there to think that *we* ever attain it?
Descartes says that under certain circumstances we 'feel
ourselves not to be determined by any external force'. Perhaps
we do, but might not this feeling be deceptive? Why should we
trust it? Plenty of feelings are untrustworthy, and nobody
knows this better than Descartes, but at this stage he appears
to have forgotten his heuristic scepticism, which otherwise so
characterises his philosophy. If we 'clearly and distinctly' saw
ourselves to be free of external determinants of choice, then
perhaps by this stage of the *Meditations* he might be allowed to
rely on it; but he does not say that, nor could he in all
conscience do so. As with Galileo, so even more blatantly with
Descartes: the final step leading to his preferred form of the
Similarity Thesis is fudged.

One should not underestimate the force of this point. Many
readers find Descartes' whole strategy of reliance on 'clear and
distinct' perception to claw his way back from universal doubt

to fully certified belief an objectionable one—the so-called 'Cartesian circle' is one of the issues notoriously involved. But at least that strategy is one which Descartes consistently operates, and there is therefore nothing unusual or surprising about his using it in any particular argument. It is therefore important to notice that the weakness of this paragraph about the will has nothing to do with its leaning too heavily on clarity and distinctness, or on any other general Cartesian principle. Just the opposite: it is due to Descartes' breach of one of his own rules in taking at face value just the kind of feeling or state of consciousness which, in the early *Meditations*, he has thoroughly trounced as unreliable guides to truth. Whether the appearance of this anomaly on the very brink of the Image of God doctrine is coincidence or not is a question which I can only leave to the judgement of the reader.

3. *Fixing the shape of the likeness*

Having taken a preliminary look at the Similarity Thesis in philosophical action, we should stand back a little and try to get a more systematic view of it and its likely ramifications. It turns out to be possible, drawing on a few well-entrenched features of the European tradition, to hazard a reasonable guess as to the directions in which the thesis would grow when philosophers began to transform the 'Image of God' motto into a theory and so embody it in their various systems. What makes this abstract exercise interesting is that the guess turns out to be amply confirmed by the historical evidence.

Two things, God and man, are to be compared with each other. We start, as we must, from a position in which we have a great deal of experience, however unsystematised, of one of the terms of the comparison, and a number of beliefs, however indefinite, about both. By the beginning of the century which we are now considering this body of material, I need hardly say, had long been worked into certain stable, if rather general, shapes; these form the outlines of our theology and anthropology, and may act as signposts to the areas where comparisons, or contrasts, between God and man are likely to be attempted. Thus man has understanding, a faculty of knowledge; he has passions, emotions, feelings; and he is an agent who brings about changes in himself and his environment. God is also represented as knowing the world and himself; as being benevolent, loving, and sometimes wrathful; and as the ultimate agent, the creator of the universe, or, more primitively, as the one who makes the crops grow if suitably propitiated.

Such parallelism need not be seen as the result of man's having created God in his own image, if that means that God is a mere phantasm of the human imagination. Perhaps he is; but I am not concerned to offer an opinion, and it is certainly no part of my argument to decide. Whether or not there is any truth of *principle* in the dictum that human beings can only understand that which is a construct from their own experience, it certainly carries great weight in the practical politics of understanding and communication (not to say popularisation), and so it should be no great surprise that God turns out to be, where not ineffable, to some degree anthropomorphic.

Let us begin with the understanding, with reason. Because it is what allows human beings to be their own authorities for the formation of belief, that faculty had to take pride of place in this epoch. Not only was it the favoured feature for drawing a comparison with the deity; its pre-eminence also militated against mysticism, the willingness to talk of ineffability and to regard the divine nature as sheerly incomprehensible to the human mind. Thus when it came to the articulation of the Similarity Thesis, the somewhat blank version which held that whilst there were indeed points of qualitative identity between God and man, they were in principle unspecifiable and essentially mysterious, did not find much support. Those who thought that there were such points of contact with God were generally also prepared to take up the challenge and say what they were—as we have seen in the cases of Galileo and Descartes.

In this endeavour they were restricted, or directed, by the dogma of God's perfection. We saw them arguing (somewhat spuriously, as inspection showed) that there was some property or other which human beings possessed *to the highest possible degree*; in one case it was the utmost objective certainty attainable, in the other total freedom from external determinants of choice. If a property was desirable, God would have it to the maximum; and so a good way to stake out our claim to a share in the divine nature was to show that something of that 'maximally perfect' kind held for humans too. The question arises, then: what would a perfect understanding be like? Its function, we may say at once, is to produce knowledge, so what does it know and how? The first of those questions is answerable in a single word: everything. The second has two aspects. It may be understood to mean: how does it attain this knowledge? Presumably it attains it instantly and effortlessly—speed and ease are valued, and these are their maxima. But the question may also be understood as asking after the manner of the knowing itself rather than the manner of its acquisition. We want our beliefs to be reliably true; so the ideal knower will be infallible, his relation to his subject matter will be such that he has complete certainty about it.

If a seventeenth-century philosopher wanted to compare human cognitive powers with those of God, this was the blueprint with which he had to work. Could he find features of human knowledge to match any of these? The extent, the quantity of knowledge would almost certainly strike him as hopeless targets.[8] So would speed and ease, though here he might think, as did Galileo, that the frequent rehearsal of simple trains of thought could eventually result in some kind of approximation to the ideal. If he is to spot a good chance anywhere, it will surely be in the region of infallibility and certainty. For there are two types of human knowledge which *prima facie* appear and have traditionally been taken to exhibit these characteristics. One of them we have already seen: our knowledge of mathematics and logic, especially of their most obvious and elementary propositions. One very readily gets the impression that it is impossible that we should be mistaken in thinking that, for instance, two plus two is four, or that *modus ponens* is a valid rule of inference. If it is a matter of the various physical objects which we take to surround us, we can form some idea of what the Cartesian demon might be doing in order to induce false beliefs: he is giving us the right perceptions by the wrong causal route. But we do not have

[8] 'Almost', because we are due for a surprise here—from Leibniz, see Chapter 1 Section 6.

any corresponding hypothesis about how he is to make us think that two twos are four when really they are nine. I do not say—emphatically not—that the impression of our infallibility in these matters just couldn't be an illusion, or that no philosophers have ever held it to be one. They certainly have, but it is significant that they are nearly all to be found in the twentieth century rather than the seventeenth. At least the impression exists, so that anyone attracted by the Image of God doctrine and interested in developing it in epistemological terms will be likely to seize on it—and no questions asked.

The other field which naturally suggests itself to the seeker after complete certainty is our knowledge of some of our own mental states. The demon may deceive us about what really is there, but not about how things *seem to us*:

These objects are unreal . . . but at least I seem to see, to hear, to be warmed. This cannot be unreal; and this is what is properly called my sensation . . .[9]

The thought is well known. Again, it *may* be deceptive, but it is only quite recently that the doctrine that we have incorrigible knowledge of our own mental states has been put under serious pressure. Again, it would be an obvious resource for a philosopher interested in giving detailed shape to the Similarity Thesis. It was indeed used for that purpose, first by Newton and his school, and a little later more explicitly and spectacularly by Berkeley. That it was so used is, of course, another heavy blow to the interpretation which makes a fascination with mathematics a basic fact about the seventeenth-century mentality. We have seen that the mathematical method was valued not just for being mathematical, nor just for offering hope of certainty, but because certainty meant support for the Similarity Thesis. We shall shortly see that this other candidate for certainty, our knowledge of our own perceptual states, also proved attractive, though without being thought of as having anything in common with mathematics except this supposed certainty.

In the writings of Newton, and of his disciple Samuel Clarke, we find an account of God's awareness of the universe.

---

[9] Descartes: 2nd *Meditation*.

It is couched in somewhat quaint terminology (and not, it seems, just to our ears—the use of the word 'sensorium' sent Leibniz chasing wild geese[10]), but the message is clear: God's awareness of physical things is of the same kind as, to be understood by analogy with, our awareness of 'the images of things', that is to say our perceptual states. Clarke, in the second letter of his controversial correspondence with Leibniz, formulated it like this:

a living substance can only there perceive, where it is present either to the things themselves, (as the omnipresent God is to the whole universe;) or to the image of things, (as the soul of man is in its proper sensory.)[11]

The meaning of the key word 'sensorium' emerges clearly from a passage from Newton's *Opticks* which Clarke may well have had in mind; equally clear is the intention of drawing a parallel between God's awareness and the perceptual process in the consciousness of human beings (and of animals as well):

Is not the Sensory of Animals that place to which the sensitive Substance is present, and into which the sensible Species of Things are carried through the Nerves and Brain, that there they may be perceived by their immediate presence to that Substance? And these things being rightly dispatched, does it not appear from Phaenomena that there is a being incorporeal, living, intelligent, omnipresent, who in infinite Space, as it were in his Sensory, sees the things themselves intimately, and thoroughly perceives them, and comprehends them wholly by their immediate presence to himself; of which things the Images only carried through the Organs of Sense into our little Sensoriums, are there seen and beheld by that which in us perceives and thinks.[12]

The sensorium, it seems, is where the brain meets the mind, where the physiological processes give rise to a representation of the world in consciousness. Manifestly, Newton is relying on the view that there is complete and incorrigible knowledge of what is thus immediately present to the mind, the unclouded transparency of our own perceptual states as one

[10] Leibniz: *The Leibniz–Clarke Correspondence*, ed. Alexander (Manchester University Press 1965), esp. Leibniz's first and second papers.
[11] Ibid. p. 21.
[12] Newton: *Opticks*, Bk. III Pt. I Query 20—in 2nd Edn. Query 28.

might call it—they are 'immediately seen, thoroughly perceived, wholly comprehended'. And this is to be our model for understanding God's awareness of things themselves. His cognitive relation to the universe is like our relation to our own mental states; in our knowledge of these, in our 'little Sensoriums', we have an image of God's knowledge of the universe.

Two points may be noted. Firstly, we see here another variation on the theme which we found in Galileo and Descartes: quantitative difference but qualitative identity. God 'intimately sees' everything, we see only our own perceptual states; but the seeing is equally intimate, equally thorough; it is the same kind of act. Secondly, Newton is not unique to this period in matching our relation to our thoughts with God's relation to everything.[13] We shall find Leibniz enlarging on this topic, though not so much with an eye to cognition as to activity or creation. Here is a foretaste:

created substances depend on God who conserves them and also produces them continually by a kind of emanation, as we produce our thoughts.[14]

This approach naturally leads to a variant of the Image of God doctrine, in which man is not expected to show his likeness to the deity in his commerce with the external world, but solely by his knowledge of and control over the thoughts and perceptions of his mind, a god in his little inner realm. As with so many of these auxiliary themes, we shall hear more of this one when we come to Leibniz. But there was one philosopher, Berkeley, who had the nerve to try for both: the status of knowing the real world just as God knows it, and the security of remaining within one's own perceptual consciousness.

An investigation of the way in which Berkeley's metaphysics served the Similarity Thesis should start on the title

[13] It is interesting to note that in his *Clavis Universalis* (1713) Arthur Collier tells us of certain 'Aristotelian philosophers' who say that 'God and the angels know external matter *per propriam speciem*, but we are supposed to know it only by consequence'. Here *speciem* alludes to the sensory nature of the knowledge, *propriam* presumably carries the contrast with 'by consequence', that is, by inference; on this view, the physical world has for God an immediate, non-inferential sensory presence—as our perceptual states do for us.

[14] Leibniz: *Discourse on Metaphysics* XIV.

page of his famous *Three Dialogues between Hylas and Philonous*;
there is more to be found there than is generally noticed, or
indeed always printed. It reads:

Three Dialogues between Hylas and Philonous, the design of which
is plainly to demonstrate the reality and perfection of human
knowledge . . .

It does not stop there, but we may do so. Berkeley proposes to
demonstrate 'the perfection of human knowledge'. We may be
quite sure that he of all people did not use the word 'perfection'
lightly; it was not for him merely a strong term of approval, but a
central concept of theology. Seeing it, we should at once expect
to meet with some epistemological version of the Similarity
Thesis. And although I am not aware that he ever explicitly said
or wrote that he had provided one, it is easy enough to locate
those features of his philosophical system which could have
made him feel that he had.

Before describing them, we should notice that Berkeley
manifestly had a philosophical stake in the Image of God
doctrine. I say a *philosophical* stake to distinguish him from
persons in whom I have no particular interest, namely those
who express the doctrine because it forms part of Christian belief
without thereafter going on to do anything with it, to expand it
or build it into a system of thought in any way that takes it
beyond the sphere of standard Christian teaching. Berkeley was
not one of them. When he wrote: '. . . I have . . . in myself some
sort of an active thinking image of the deity',[15] it was not a
gratuitous piece of piety—he needed some such point to secure
the compatibility of his claim that he could meaningfully think
about God with the charge that his opponents could not
meaningfully think about matter.

Let us now look at Berkeley's account of the physical world
and our knowledge of it. His stalking-horse was a theory of
perception according to which our perceptual states are caused
by the action of material objects on our sense-organs. Essential
to this theory was the view that material objects are things
located in space, non-mental things which have no consciousness, thought or perception; the mind's access to them is

---

[15] Berkeley: *Three Dialogues*, Vol. 2 p. 232 in *The Works of George Berkeley*, ed. Luce
and Jessop.

mediated by the 'ideas' (perceptual states) which they cause in us. Berkeley had three basic objections to such a material world; all three, or the principles behind them, will at some stage be of interest to us. He held, first, that this world of matter was unknowable—the mediacy it ascribed to the perceptual process allowed a scepticism against which no defence could be found. Second, it could not be used to explain what its proponents had invented it to explain, namely why we should have the perceptual experiences that we do have; this was because it could not be the cause of mental states, since it had none itself, and: '. . . how can . . . that which is unthinking be a cause of thought?'[16] Third, he held that the existence of matter was actually a self-contradictory hypothesis. I shall not here go into his grounds for that amazing claim—we are at the moment more interested in the conclusions he drew from all this than in the reasons he gave for it, though we shall return to some of them in another context. The conclusion was that there is no such thing as matter; there exist only spirits and their mental states, or 'ideas'.

What, then, are houses, mountains, rivers? Berkeley didn't hold back: they are collections of ideas. So perceiving them is not a matter of being causally or inferentially related to an external non-mental stuff; it is just to have such a collection of ideas, to be in a certain complex perceptual state. And with that step we are in the immediate neighbourhood of the perceptual model of the Similarity Thesis. Knowledge of one's own perceptual states, we recall, was one of the areas in which human knowledge can plausibly lay claim to the infallibility it needs if it is to be a likeness of the divine knowledge. By making physical objects a species of perception, Berkeley brought them into the fold of potential certainty.

The comparison lacks, as yet, its theological component. What, for Berkeley, was God's knowledge of the (so-called) physical world like? Infallibly certain, no doubt, but the similarity, in his metaphysics, between God's knowledge and the knowledge which he ascribes to humans goes much further than that. It has the same structure, as well as achieving the same indubitability. Relying on a version of the argument from

---

[16] Ibid. p. 216. See also p. 239: '. . . a thing that hath no ideas in itself cannot impart them to me'.

design, Berkeley concluded that our 'ideas' are produced in our minds by the will of God acting directly—somewhat as if Descartes' demon had turned benevolent. So God, whom we may safely assume to act (in Berkeley's estimation) in full knowledge of what he is doing, must himself have all the ideas which he generates in human minds, as well as those which he would generate, if the right human acts of will occurred to make them appropriate. And for Berkeley, this would amount to saying that God perceives the whole of physical reality, since physical reality simply *is* a certain infinitely complex constellation of ideas, and having them before one's consciousness *is* perceiving it. That would be, in itself, a welcome conclusion, and it has a corollary which fits the Similarity Thesis as if purpose-built: when we perceive the physical world, what we do is just the same as what God does when he perceives it; all that happens in either case is that a mind has certain perceptions, nothing more, and so the human mind can be just as sure of what it perceives as is the divine mind of what it perceives. The difference, as in Galileo's mathematical version, is one of quantity: God sees everything, we see only a tiny fragment of reality. But the manner of seeing, the mind's relation to what is seen, is the same in the two cases.

It is, I need hardly say, very much open to question whether this line of thought really can close the door against scepticism. How do we know, for instance, that the objects we perceive are public, in the sense that other percipients, if there are any, would have corresponding 'ideas'? For God, that is just a special case of knowing one's own intentions, but for us it is surely not something which we can know, if we can know it at all, with the certainty of immediate consciousness. If this, and similar questions, are pressed, Berkeley's position will collapse into the much less ambitious point which we have seen made by Newton to the effect that our cognitive powers are the same as those of God *so long* as we apply them only to our perceptual states. But this should not be taken to indicate that Berkeley wanted to make the Newtonian point and no more. For one thing, that would leave his claim to have demonstrated 'the reality and perfection of human knowledge' looking wildly exaggerated. He manifestly took himself to have rebutted scepticism (the title page goes on to say as much), and by scepticism he understood doubt about the reality of the ordinary objects of our environment. But the sight of a philosopher overreaching his arguments in the neighbourhood of the Image of God doctrine should by now have ceased to surprise.

We have now seen, though neither for the last time nor in all their forms, the two main lines of development of the Similarity Thesis in terms of the understanding, or epistemic capacity. But I would remind the reader that adherence to the Similarity Thesis is not to be equated with this kind of enthusiasm for the cognitive powers of man, and that for a number of reasons. As I have suggested, on the basis of general considerations one would anticipate that some philosophers would prefer to execute the thesis in terms of human powers of *action*; we saw Descartes taking this route, in spite of his seminal optimism about the potential of human reason. One philosopher who showed at least some degree of enthusiasm about reason, Thomas Hobbes, had no interest in the Similarity Thesis at all—his inclination was to regard the deity as incomprehensible and theology as beyond the reach of philosophical thought. In Pascal we find the converse: he maintained a deeply sceptical attitude towards the powers of reason (were it not for the enormous difference between the two philosophers in other respects, many of his utterances on this topic would instantly remind everyone of Hume). Nevertheless, we easily find in his *Pensées* the Image of God doctrine—tempered, it is true, by the opinion that since the Fall any similarity between man and God is the outcome of divine grace rather than a fact about human nature:

there are in faith two equally constant truths. One is that man in the state of his creation, or in the state of grace, is exalted above the whole of nature, made like unto God and sharing in his divinity. The other is that in the state of corruption and sin he has fallen from that first state and has become like the beasts. . . . it is clearly evident that man through grace is made like unto God and shares his divinity, and without grace he is treated like the beasts of the field.[17]

But Pascal does not, so far as I am aware, offer any account of the respects in which God's grace produces similarity to himself in his creatures. The anti-rational tendency of his religious thought—for all that he may have contributed to

[17] Pascal: *Pensées* para. 131 (end).

mathematics and physics—freed him from any need to achieve detail or clarity on the point.

4. *Intelligible causes*

When some metaphysical vision becomes the dominant philosophy of an epoch, as did the Image of God doctrine in the seventeenth century, it can easily happen that certain other views or principles acquire impetus by virtue of their connection with it. One such was the principle that there must be similarity between effects and their causes. It had almost axiomatic status for seventeenth-century thought, a circumstance which has turned many commentators either perplexed or dismissive, according to temperament. In fact, though it may at first sight seem to have little to do with it, it can be seen to be a close relative of the Similarity Thesis, and it should not surprise us in the slightest to find them flourishing, and later decaying, together.

If we find some proposition espoused by nearly all the philosophers of a period it is not a satisfactory explanation to point out that it was at that time already a traditional philosophical belief. Traditions do, after all, die out, or turn into minority opinions, so that when one is enthusiastically received and preserved it is no explanation merely to point out its traditional status. If it does not fit the spirit of the new age it will quickly begin to wither. But if the philosophical spirit of this particular age is well captured by the Similarity Thesis, and in particular by its elaboration in terms of understanding and reason, then the idea that common elements were needed between causes and effects would have been very much at home in it, as I shall now argue.

We are thinking about an epoch which deified reason, figuratively and almost literally. What reason can and cannot do is a matter of epistemology, but for various reasons such an epistemological theory was bound to generate a corresponding ontological belief: that reality was an appropriate object for man's cognitive powers, that the world, in other words, was a thoroughly intelligible place. To begin with, it had been created by God; the Similarity Thesis told us that God's reason resembled human reason, and the doctrine of the divine perfection insisted that he possessed it and used it to the logical maximum. So there would be no brute fact in the

world, nothing that God simply 'happened' to have done or
chosen without there being some reason why it should have
been *that* rather than any other of the logically possible
alternatives. The principal monuments to this thought are
Leibniz's use of the Principle of Sufficient Reason and
Spinoza's equation, with no exceptions admitted, of the actual
and the necessary. Furthermore, this highly optimistic view of
the potential of human reason was hardly likely to be
accompanied by so pessimistic a belief as that the world was
not a proper object for it; or, if theological backing was
needed, that God had equipped man with these powers and
then put him somewhere quite unsuitable for their exercise.
Nothing would be more natural, therefore, than to hope and
expect that the universe was in principle intellectually
transparent, even though quantitative considerations put
complete insight beyond human grasp.

All this at once destroys any apparent equality of status
between the two main branches of the Insight Ideal, as the
cognitive versions of the Similarity Thesis may be called. The
balance tips decisively against the 'perceptual states' model
and in favour of the logico-mathematical model. The reason is
that the former might be enough to give one a grasp, even an
infallible grasp, of the facts, but cannot serve to explain any
understanding of the reasons for them, or their inter-
connections. It is suited to giving complete knowledge of a
collection of brute facts, but not to giving knowledge of a
system. Consider, if the point is not already sufficiently clear,
the situation of a God like the one described by Newton in the
passage quoted from his *Opticks:*[18] he has an immediate,
infallible view of everything in the universe. Suppose now that
this is his *only* form of access to reality. Then he knows each
fact by virtue of its being, as an individual fact, immediately
present to his mind. He sees *that* it is the case; to see why it is
the case is a quite different intellectual operation calling for a
rather different mental capacity. As Inspector of the Universe,
he registers only a heap of brute facts; if he is also Creator of
the Universe, then he did what he did without having any
reasons for doing it thus rather than otherwise, or for doing it
at all. That thought being unacceptable, the perceptual model

[18] Above, Chapter 1 Section 3.

must be replaced or at least supplemented by the mathematical one, which by virtue of the intuitive evidence of
axioms and the deductive interconnection of theorems does
offer the required properties.

In the period we are considering there are therefore very
strong forces at work promoting the logico-mathematical
model as a normative ideal for man, occasionally attained to,
and as a descriptive ideal for God and the universe. But what
is involved in applying this model to the world? How must we
think of it if it is to be susceptible of being known in this way?
Presumably we shall see the series of successive states of which
it consists, the chain of causes and effects, as being the
embodiment of a deductive system and analogous to the
sequence of propositions that makes up a mathematical or
logical proof. I do not wish to say that this is positively the
only way in which it could be done. Hegel represented reality
as the embodiment of a logical system, at least that was what
he called it; but it is not at all clear that his view fits the
pattern described, and he himself would surely have denied it.
We have to remember, however, that one very important
accompaniment to the package of ideas we are discussing was
the startling advance of the physical sciences, providing
overwhelming evidence of the power of the understanding and
the extent to which it was in harmony with the object of its
investigation. It would have been an odd thing if men whose
belief in individual rationality and the rationality of the
universe was largely inspired by the progress of science, and
some of whom contributed to that progress in no small way,
had not felt that science pointed the way towards the
unveiling of that rational structure which surely underlay
God's world. But an essential part of the scientific enterprise
was to see how causes cause their effects, to find functional
relationships between earlier and later states of affairs and to
account for their existence. When they envisaged their ideal
cognitive goal, it would be very natural for them to take it for
granted that it was something like a complete science of reality
adorned with complete insight into the necessity of all its laws.

It is only a short step from there to the belief, so often
expressed in this period, that causal connections had to be
'intelligible'. There had to be something, in principle detect-

able by reason, which made *that* effect suited to *that*, *that* lawlike relationship between *those* two variables appropriate rather than any other. If it were not so, there would be facts about the course of events which were intrinsically inexplicable; and this thought, because of its position in the complex of ideas composing the epistemological version of the Image of God doctrine, was in the seventeenth century widely felt to be intolerable.

What conditions do two events have to satisfy, in order that a causal nexus between them may be 'intelligible' in the strong sense which that complex of ideas encouraged? As good a way of putting it as any is this: one has to be able to find the second event, or the relevant properties of the second event, within the first. 'Find it within' is the joker here, of course. It might just mean 'deduce it from', without any particular view about what sorts of pairs of events could allow such a deduction. But it is very easy to feel that deduction can only work by identity, overt or covert; the first argued denial of this principle came from Kant,[19] and I need hardly say that his opinion has not met with universal agreement, not even amongst those who have thought intensively about the nature of logic. The great logician of the seventeenth-century, Leibniz, held all necessary truth to be analytic; and the ontological correlate of that is that cause communicates to effect, or transfers to it, some part or property of its own. Thus it was that the scholastic doctrine that there must be as much reality in the cause as in the effect was able to survive for so long, if slightly transformed, at a time when much of the medieval tradition was being supplanted.

One of the most radical employments of the principle that cause/effect connections are necessary is found in the argument of Malebranche,[20] that the only cause is the will of God, since nothing else whatever is *necessarily* followed by its customary or intended effect—this argument is fundamental to the proof of his Occasionalism. But for examples of the use

[19] Locke denied it, though without argument. His claim that there are 'instructive' necessary truths is indistinguishable from Kant's claim that there are synthetic *a priori* judgements. But he did so quite casually—there follows no inquiry into the nature of these truths, or sign of puzzlement that there can be such things. (See *An Essay Concerning Human Understanding* Bk. IV Ch. VIII).

[20] E.g. Malebranche: *Recherche de la Vérité* 6.2.3.

of the more specific principle that there must be a likeness, or an identical element, between cause and effect, we may go to Locke and Berkeley. This fact ought in itself to be of interest, because the principle in question is generally thought of as part of the equipment of *rationalism*, whereas these two philosophers are widely taken to be paradigmatic *empiricists*. The truth is—here I add my voice to that of Loeb[21]—that this rather crude distinction, although it may have some value, has been grossly overworked as a tool for understanding the early modern period, and we would do well to try the effect of forgetting about it for a while.

Most readers will be familiar with this principle about causality as it occurs in Descartes:

Now it is already clear by the light of nature that the complete efficient cause must contain at least as much as the effect of that cause. For where, pray, could the effect get its reality if not from the cause? And how could the cause supply it, without possessing it itself?[22]

That Locke also appealed to it is less well known, partly no doubt because he did so in those theological contexts which professional philosophers of the last fifty years have tended to find rather embarrassing. In one of the founding fathers of the analytic movement, this? Never! But there it is—Locke's most Cartesian-sounding formulation of it goes like this:

Whatsoever is the first of all things must necessarily contain in it . . . all the perfections that can ever after exist, nor can it ever give to another any perfection that it hath not actually in itself . . .[23]

In the same paragraph it occurs in a more specific version, helping to show that the original being must have had a mind and an understanding, since some of its effects, namely human beings, have them:

[It is] as impossible to conceive that ever bare incogitative matter should produce a thinking being, as that nothing should of itself produce matter.

[21] I refer to L. E. Loeb: *From Descartes to Hume* (Cornell Univ. Press 1981).

[22] Descartes: 3rd *Meditation*. One can find the same thought in Spinoza, e.g. *Ethics* Part I, Proposition III, and Letter 4; also in Leibniz, e.g. Monadology para. 7.

[23] Locke: *An Essay Concerning Human Understanding*, Bk. IV Ch. 10 para. 10.

And also:

Next, it is evident, that what had its being and beginning from another, must have all that which is in and belongs to it from another too. All the powers it has must be owing to and received from the same source. This eternal source, then, of all being, must be the source and origin of all power; and so this eternal being must also be the most powerful.[24]

Berkeley also uses the principle; not, however, for proving God, but for destroying matter. Materialists want it for the cause of our ideas, but it cannot have that function, he says. Nothing could cause an idea unless the idea were already present in it; from which it follows that the cause of our ideas, far from being matter, can only be a mind. To think otherwise would be to fly in the face of the 'old known axiom', that 'nothing can give to another that which it hath not itself.'[25] To deny this, he implies, is actually inconsistent. *Prima facie* that is a very startling claim, and it is hard to see how Berkeley could make it unless he were reading 'give to' in the sense of 'hand over' rather than 'cause in'. But quite likely he is. It would after all be in full accord with the principle now under discussion, which precisely does equate causing with the making over of properties. A passage a few pages later lends further weight:

That a being endowed with knowledge and will should produce or exhibit ideas is easily understood. But that a being which is utterly destitute of these faculties should be able to produce ideas, or in any sort to affect an intelligence, this I can never understand.[26]

Berkeley's comfortable assumption that what he cannot understand cannot be requires a special belief about the harmony between one's mind and the universe, a belief of just the kind that the Image of God doctrine would support (and be supported by), for it tells us that the intelligence that designed it has close affinities with ours. But for his views about causality the decisive phrase is 'produce or exhibit', which seems to have just the ambiguity needed to make this passage seem to work as an argument. 'Produce an *X*' may

[24] Ibid. Bk. IV Ch.10 para. 4—see also para. 5.

[25] Berkeley: *Three Dialogues*, Vol. 2 p. 236 (note) in *The Works of George Berkeley*, ed. Luce and Jessop (Nelson 1949).

[26] Ibid. p. 242.

mean 'being without an X, manufacture one', or 'starting with a concealed X, display it'. To use the word 'produce', apparently as a synonym of 'cause', and then invite the reader to take it in the second sense by adding 'or exhibit' is the precise equivalent of using 'give' (in the quotation of footnote 25) in the sense of 'hand over'; and it is just some such conflation that Berkeley needs to get away with if his point is to look cogent. But to think that we are dealing with nothing else than a crass conflation would be superficial; we should first try the hypothesis that there is something more to it, and of course there is. For given Berkeley's requirement that causality be comprehensible, and his interpretation of that requirement, the two meanings of 'produce' will coincide in their application. For whatever properties A brings about in B must have been present in A before the interaction, so that production (=bringing about) will involve production (= displaying what was already there). Berkeley's God, we might say, not only produces ideas *in* us, he also produces *his* ideas *for* us, or 'exhibits' them to us; and that, according to Berkeley's conception of causality, is the only way in which it could be done.

Something similar may well underlie his double use of 'depend', to which Jonathan Bennett has drawn attention:[27] 'ideas depend on minds' means, in Berkeley's usage, both that ideas are *caused* by minds and that they are *owned* by minds. Again, this is not very surprising, given his understanding of causation. If an idea is caused by a mind then it, or at any rate an exactly corresponding idea, must be owned by that mind, otherwise the comprehensibility of causation would be lost. And the converse also holds, for Berkeley: if an idea is owned by a mind it must have been caused by one. For an idea cannot just be there, uncaused, since that would import a multitude of brute facts and destroy the much desired comprehensibility of the universe. What then can they be caused by? Not by other ideas—although that would not infringe the principle that there be likeness between cause and effect—because ideas themselves he takes to be passive. But 'an idea can be like nothing but an idea:'[28] so the causal agent

[27] J. F. Bennett: 'Berkeley and God', *Philosophy* Vol. XL (1965).
[28] Berkeley: *Principles of Human Knowledge*, Part I para. 8.

can only be a mind which has a like idea. We do not have to suppose, then, that Berkeley simply mixed up causation and ownership; that he found no need to distinguish sharply between them is explained by his view of causation, which is itself explicable by reference to deep features of the philosophical climate in which he grew up and operated: the attachment to the Image of God doctrine, especially (in this case) to its cognitive branch, the Insight Ideal.

5. *Spinoza: a part of the infinite intellect*

It would be quite natural to think that the Similarity Thesis, the doctrine of man in God's image, can flourish only in the context of Christian thought, and (this might seem obvious to the point of triviality) that in addition to Christianity it would require a strong anthropomorphic tendency. But that neither of these assumptions is correct is shown by the remarkable example of Spinoza. Nobody, I imagine, will want to describe his intellectual background as Christian, though they may wish to point that out the idea of our being made in God's image occurs in Judaism as well; but plenty of readers will find the suggestion that the Similarity Thesis can occur without anthropomorphism self-contradictory. Isn't anthropomorphism precisely the view that God is like man and man like God? So here I must explain my meaning at greater length.

In one sense the objection is undeniable. That there can be no Similarity Thesis which does not find points of resemblance between God and man is indeed a triviality, and that anyone claiming such resemblance thereby commits himself to a degree of anthropomorphism is, in one interpretation, equally trivial. But also to be considered is what one might call the *direction* of a philosopher's approach to the question. In the case of many writers one has the feeling that, whatever their avowed intentions may have been, they have been guided in the first instance by their view of man and the nature of human experience, and that their vision of the nature of God is an outcome of it. In their philosophy, the human being appears as an easily recognisable object, God as a fairly familiar figure verbally multiplied by infinity. Spinoza is most emphatically not one of these. He generates his concept of God (or nature) from the logic of the claim that God is an infinite being, and man's potential for being like God turns on his ability to achieve a state in which the personal, the individual, has been to a large extent left behind. It is this that I have in mind in saying that the Similarity Thesis, as found in Spinoza, is not at all strongly anthropomorphic; if we need a word for his cast of thought, then 'theomorphic' would capture it better.

Furthermore, Spinoza is in fact both explicit and forthright in his rejection of anthropomorphism. The divine conception of good and evil, or, what is for him the same thing, the purposes of nature, have nothing in common with human purposes or evaluations. Anthropomorphic styles of speech may have their place in theology (presumably because they are of help in one of theology's aims, that of making men better), but those who have a clear understanding eschew them:

> while we are speaking philosophically we must not use the modes of expression of theology. For theology has usually, and not without reason, represented God as a perfect man; therefore it is quite appropriate in theology that it should be said that God desires something, that God is affected with weariness at the deeds of the ungodly, and with pleasure at those of the pious. But in philosophy, where we clearly understand that to apply to God the attributes which make a man perfect, is as bad as to want to apply to a man those which make perfect an elephant or an ass, these and similar words have no place; and we cannot use them here without thoroughly confusing our conceptions. Therefore speaking philosophically we cannot say that God demands something from someone, or that something wearies or pleases Him, for all these are human attributes, which have no place in God.[29]

That sounds as strong an attack on the Similarity Thesis as anyone could wish to see mounted. God and man are of different kinds, like man and elephant; the term 'perfect' is species-relative, and perfection *qua* man has no more to do with the perfection of God than it does with perfection *qua* donkey. But in spite of this a striking version of the Similarity Thesis is at the very centre of Spinoza's metaphysics and his

---

[29] Spinoza: Letter 23 in *The Correspondence of Spinoza*, ed. Wolf (Allen and Unwin 1928) pp. 190-1.

conception of the good for man. It will be noticed that in the above passage it is primarily anthropomorphism with respect to desires and emotions which is under attack. There is one point, however—and the reader should by now have no difficulty in guessing which—where the human mind and the mind of God naturally coincide: the nature of their *Reason*. That what our best endeavours tell us is a valid inference might not be so in the sight of God is a thought that never seems to enter Spinoza's head. If it had, he would probably have dismissed it both instinctively and on grounds internal to his philosophy; as we shall see, his system tends to be self-supporting in this respect.

To see how the concept of reason thus acts as the fulcrum for Spinoza's version of the Similarity Thesis we need briefly to review his whole philosophy, metaphysical and ethical. In doing so we shall observe several features which can by now be recognised as characteristic of the basic seventeenth-century stance: not only the doctrine of similarity with the divine as an approachable, though for quantitative reasons unattainable goal for man, but also the moral conception of the good as being largely contemplative, consisting in the proper insightful use of reason and understanding, much as we saw hinted at in Galileo; and in addition to that the view of reality, the single substance which Spinoza identifies with both God and nature, as being in principle totally penetrable by reason.

God is an infinite substance, so runs the definition, and from this Spinoza concludes that everything there is must be identified with God, for otherwise he would have limits, something would lie outside him. And this the definition rules out, since Spinoza takes infinity not as endless repetition but as all-inclusiveness. So nothing exists but this one (divine) substance and its modifications.

What then of the twin substances of Descartes, matter and mind, extension and thought? They are not two substances, but rather two aspects of the same substance. And (here we come to a crux as far as Spinoza's variant of the Similarity Thesis is concerned) they are wholly parallel aspects: for every truth about nature seen as extension there is a truth about nature seen as a system of thought, every material fact has its

mental correlate and vice versa. The latter, in Spinoza's way
of putting it, is said to be the idea of the former.

The human mind, he holds, is the idea of the human body;
it is the system of thoughts corresponding to the system of
material facts which are our other way of seeing the
modification of reality that is a human being. Analogously,
the system of ideas which corresponds to the whole of nature is
the divine mind. With that we arrive at two theses, either of
which may be taken to rest on the other: nature is a rational
system, an infinite sequence of necessitating causes and their
effects. But causes run parallel to reasons; to every cause/
effect pair there corresponds, under the aspect of thought, a
premiss/conclusion pair. So the mind of God, which is the
idea of all nature, is a fully coherent system of thoughts
deductively interconnected; the mind of God is the 'proof' of
nature *ordine geometrico*.

What, then, can the human mind hope to become? It is, in
the first place, the idea of the human body. It has, to be sure,
some kind of ideas of other things, but only *passively*, in so far
as they affect the state of its own body, and even they are,
strictly speaking, ideas of those states rather than of outer
objects:

the ideas, which we have of external bodies, indicate rather the
constitution of our own body than the nature of external bodies.[30]

To have ideas that represent objects as they are it would have
to be *active*, that is generate the ideas deductively from within
its own intellect. This we can *sometimes* do, as in arithmetic and
geometry, so that even if '. . . the things which I have so far
been able to know by this kind of knowledge have been very
few . . .'[31] we nevertheless already do have *some* experience of
the top grade of insightful knowledge. We therefore have a
certain 'intensive' likeness to the deity (to borrow the concept
from Galileo once again), and we may seek to increase our
'extensive' likeness by seeking to increase our insightful
knowledge of nature. For the closer we come to a deductive
grasp of the deductive system which nature embodies, the

---

[30] Spinoza: *Ethics* Part II, Proposition XVI, Corollary 2.
[31] Spinoza: *The Emendation of the Intellect*, Works of Spinoza, trans. Curley
(Princeton University Press 1985) p. 14.

more nearly do our thoughts approach an identity with the
mind of God.

One might be inclined to interpret this ideal, though of
course for man ulimately unattainable, identity in the sense of
exact likeness, but there is good reason to think that Spinoza
intends it in the full-blooded numerical sense of *one and the
same*. My body is a part of the extended, material system of
nature. So if my mind is the idea of my body, as Spinoza
maintains, it becomes natural to infer that my mind is just as
literally a part of that system of thought, the extended aspect
of which is the whole of material nature, that is to say part of
the mind of God. And this is in fact Spinoza's explicitly stated
opinion:

the human mind is part of the infinite intellect of God . . .[32]

What we have here is the Image of God doctrine in a very
strong form indeed, that of the partial identity or union of the
human and the divine mind; a version of it is also found in the
writings of Malebranche, as we shall shortly see. And we are
also in a position to see what was meant when I said that had
the thought occurred to Spinoza that human reason might be
simply on the wrong track, out of tune with God and nature,
he would have been inclined to dismiss it on grounds internal
to his philosophy. Holding the mind to be the reflection of a
part of nature, and so a part of the total (and totally adequate)
reflection of nature in thought, the idea that it might be in
principle the wrong sort of instrument, having nothing in
common with the principles that nature embodies, would
have struck him as not seriously to be entertained. Though
plausible, this is admittedly speculative, but I mention it now
in order to introduce a theme that we shall hear again,
particularly in the discussion of Hegel but also in the
twentieth-century context: how it can happen that an assumption is made which then has more or less remote consequences, and how these consequences may then lend to the
proposition originally assumed a kind of psychological stability, with the result that it becomes very hard to recognise it
for what, as far as the *logic* of the matter is concerned, it really
is.

[32] Spinoza: *Ethics* Part II, Proposition XI, Corollary.

The question remains for Spinoza: if our minds are literally parts of the divine mind, whence comes human error? Is there error in God? Not at all—we are to take error to be the product of incompleteness, so that error in the isolated part does not necessarily imply error in the whole. Spinoza puts it like this:

But if it is . . . of the nature of a thinking being, to form true or adequate thoughts, it is certain that inadequate ideas arise in us only from the fact that we are a part of a thinking being, of which some thoughts wholly constitute our mind, while others do so only in part.[33]

It is presumably those thoughts which it is given to us to think in their entirety which provide us with our tantalising taste of Spinoza's third and most perfect type of knowledge, *scientia intuitiva*. And with the same move Spinoza can fend off another objection: if the human mind is the idea of the human body, a thing about which human beings do not in fact know a great deal, why should we suppose that the mind which is the idea of the whole of nature knows nature any more fully and adequately? Why should we think that it would pass any of the obvious tests for being the mind of *God*? The answer, I take it, is that it is only their partiality which prevents our thoughts from attaining adequacy or truth. The mind that corresponds to the whole of nature *ipso facto* thinks every thought in full; besides that, it also thinks every thought *actively*—none of its thoughts are reactions to any states of itself which have any *external origin*. In full, because for Spinoza to think something in full is to think it along with all its causes (or reasons), and this the mind of God inevitably does. For it corresponds to all nature, and nature, as *causa sui*, contains all its causes. Actively, because it is everything, and therefore there is no external cause to which any of its states could be a passive response.

It appears, then, that the attempt to formulate a deductive system of nature is equally the attempt to bring our minds as far as possible into congruence with the divine mind. In certain very limited areas, those where the mind has succeeded in grasping everything that is relevant to the truth

[33] Spinoza: *The Emendation of the Intellect*, Works of Spinoza, trans. Curley p. 33.

of what it knows, we have already done so, and we have the potential to extend it. So here we have the Similarity Thesis in its cognitive form, now elevated to a claim of identity: our understanding is partially, and can come to be less partially, identical with the mind of God. As we have already seen with other writers, and will see again, this cognitive enterprise has a moral dimension as well, and in the case of Spinoza this dimension is strikingly well developed. The desirability of insightful understanding does not arise, for him, just from the consideration that we must be more perfect the more closely we approximate to the divine state. It is connected, or rather identified, with the achievement of freedom and happiness.

To see how this identification comes about, recall that for Spinoza our freedom is not understood in terms of spontaneity, or acts of choice which initiate causal chains whilst being themselves uncaused. On the contrary, Spinoza is as strict a determinist as anyone, and regards the ideas of spontaneous action and uncaused choice as illusions which only flourish because of our ignorance of the true causes of human behaviour. Freedom consists rather in *how we view* the necessary sequence of events: if I fully understand why something happens, then the reasons for its happening are present to my mind. And then, Spinoza thought, *I have reasons* for its happening, since nobody can coherently wish for not-X whilst having a clear intellectual perception of the necessity of X:

For, in so far as we are intelligent beings, we cannot desire anything save that which is necessary . . . wherefore, in so far as we have a right understanding of these things, the endeavour of the better part of ourselves is in harmony with the order of nature as a whole.[34]

So, if I have full understanding, *the* reasons for X become *my* reasons for X, and this is what it is for me to do X freely or freely to acquiesce in its coming about—another of those suspicious fudges, incidentally, since the passage from 'I cannot desire not-X' to 'I do desire X' is not to be made as quickly as this, even if it can be made at all. The result, however reached, is closely related to some 'compatibilist' theories of free will that are widely held today.

Finally: not only freedom, but also happiness, is dependent

---

[34] Spinoza: *Ethics* Part IV, Appendix XXXII.

on the depth of our understanding of reality. For happiness, in
Spinoza's view, is the awareness of our own activity, the
feeling that what we do and shall do is in accordance with our
rationally formed wishes and therefore proceeds from us in the
sense in which he allows that to be possible. This occurs, as we
have seen, when and in so far as we achieve clarity about the
reasons for what happens; then, as we read in the passage last
quoted, our 'endeavour' joins in with the natural order of
causes. Thus, for Spinoza, everything that is worthwhile for
us, our freedom, our happiness and the realisation of what is
godlike in us, turns on the attainment of true understanding.
The Similarity Thesis and the Insight Ideal with their
associated moral message are here triumphantly inscribed.
Nowhere more so, although one writer, Leibniz, was more
explicit about it.

6. *Leibniz: children of God's house*

From the *Discourse on Metaphysics* and the ensuing correspondence with Arnauld, to the *Monadology* and the *Principles of
Nature and Grace* at the end of his life some thirty years later,
Leibniz's texts bear constant witness to his adherence to the
doctrine that man is made in the image of God, and to his
determination to place it at the heart of his philosophical
system. For obvious reasons, I shall only cite a few passages,
ones that seem especially apt for illustrating the structure of
his thought on the topic; but to get a feeling for the
significance it had for him the reader must experience at first
hand their frequency in Leibniz's writings.

We may begin with an example from the correspondence
with Arnauld, a blank statement of the Similarity Thesis
without any indication of the respects in which the similarity
is supposed to hold. But, whilst being in this sense 'blank', it
could hardly be more explicit, and the form of the thesis stated
could hardly be stronger: not only are we here compared with
God, we are actually described as gods:

It is this society or commonwealth of minds under this sovereign
monarch which is the noblest part of the universe, composed of many
little Gods under this great God. For it can be said that created minds
differ from God only as lesser from greater, as finite from infintie.[35].

[35] Leibniz: letter to Arnauld, 9 October 1687.

Prima vista not even Spinoza's version of the doctrine is stronger than this. He appeared to be thinking of the identification or union with God, but only as an unattainable ideal to which we have the potential to approximate to some extent, whereas Leibniz seems to be describing the position as he takes it actually to be: we *are* gods, if only little ones, distinguished from the 'great God' by (a return of the now familiar theme) a matter of quantity rather than quality, differing 'only as lesser from greater'.

Leibniz, of course, does not leave the Similarity Thesis anything like so indeterminate. In the first place, he divides it into its two main branches, one concerned with man as a cognitive being, the other with man as an agent:

spirits alone are made in his image and as it were are of his race or like children of the house, since they alone can serve him freely and act with knowledge in imitation of the divine nature; one spirit alone is worth a whole world since it not merely expresses the world but also knows it and conducts itself in it after the fashion of God.[36]

We not only know the world, but also *conduct ourselves* in it after the fashion of God. Up to now we have concentrated almost exclusively (the one exception was a brief consideration of Descartes' comparison of God and man in point of freedom) on the Insight Ideal, the articulation of the Similarity Thesis that focuses on human powers of *knowledge*. Now we come to look at an attempt to execute it by focusing on the fact that human beings *do* things. How is the attempt likely to go? What, in general terms, might we expect the relevant points of comparison to be?

I do not wish to give the impression that there is an *a priori* answer to that question. There are indeed answers which are a very natural and unsurprising outcome of our own tradition as it stood in the century of Leibniz (and some way beyond), but it should not be forgotten that these are cultural facts and not facts of logic. To illustrate the point: if my meagre knowledge of anthropology does not play me false, it is perfectly possible to think of the reproductive faculty as the link between the human agent and the gods, and to select one's iconography, forms of worship and conception of the principal ends of life accordingly. I shall not insult the reader by trying to explain

---

[36] Leibniz: *Discourse on Metaphysics* XXXVI.

why this particular variation on the Similarity Thesis would have been ill suited to storming the minds of seventeenth-century Europe.

When looking at the cognitive interpretation of the doctrine, the Insight Ideal, we started from the orthodox dogma of God's perfection[37] and asked how perfection in knowledge would most naturally be understood. In the same way, we may ask how Leibniz and his contemporaries would most naturally conceive the perfect agent, or perfect activity. Certain central features at once suggest themselves: the perfect agent would always choose the right goals; he would infallibly achieve them, because he would always choose the right plan and be able to execute it, and he would do so effortlessly. Furthermore, he would act freely—there would be no question that his actions were the results of other forces acting, so to speak, 'through' him. That, of course, provides only the framework. It does nothing, for instance, to say what the right goals are. It leaves open what enters into the judgement of whether the chosen means are the 'right' ones: should they be the most economical, and if so most economical of what? Or does the unlimited power of a perfect agent render the concept of economy superfluous, a miserly necessity for lesser beings only? Does a perfect agent always choose means that are in conformity with general laws, or may it act in a 'one-off' way on individual occasions? Such questions were the (sometimes implicit) subject of considerable debate. But that did not affect the framework of the discussion, to which, as we shall see, Leibniz's views about the human agent fit very precisely. Before we turn to that, however, we should notice that he at times draws comparisons between God and man as agents which need not be thought of as deriving from any particular idea of the divine *perfection*—though they do make use of what God is found, *de facto*, to have done. For example:

As regards the rational soul or mind . . . it is not only a mirror of the universe of created things, but also an image of the deity. The mind not only has a perception of the works of God, but is even capable of producing something like them, though on a small scale. For, not to mention the wonders of dreams, in which we invent without effort

[37] There can be no doubt of the prominence of this dogma in Leibniz's thought. See e.g. the opening sentence of the *Discourse on Metaphysics*.

(but also without will) things we could only discover after much thinking when awake, our soul is architectonic in its voluntary activities also, and, discovering the sciences in accordance with which God has regulated things, it imitates in its own sphere, and in the little world in which it is allowed to act, what God performs in the great world.[38]

We may recall seeing a hint of this earlier in the cognitive variant: Newton's doctrine that space is the sensorium of God. Within the sphere of our minds, so the thought went, we can know in much the same way as God does; now it is said that we can act much as he acts, namely create a world in thought as he creates the world in reality. The same idea is found in another passage which we glanced at in that context, where Leibniz said that God produces '. . . created substances . . . by a kind of emanation, *as we produce our thoughts.*'[39] None of this essentially involves any of the foregoing considerations about perfection *qua* agent, though the willing ear may hear an echo of them when Leibniz mentions the *effortlessness* with which we produce our dreams. God is not *found* to act effortlessly, but *assumed* to do so—no doubt that assumption makes an appearance by virtue of its connection with the concept of perfection. Be that as it may, however, this comparison of the creative control that we have over our minds with that which God has over the universe is very far from exhausting what Leibniz has to say in development of the 'agency' version of the Image of God doctrine.

A human mind, in Leibniz's philosophy, is a substance. As such it contains within itself—this is how he understands his principle that in a true proposition the notion of the predicate is contained in that of the subject—the sufficient ground of all that will ever be true of it. Everything that it ever does (since we are now thinking first and foremost of its activity) is thus a consequence of its own nature. That a substance having this nature exists at all is due to a decision of God, taken in accordance with the principle that the best logically consistent universe was to be brought into being. But once such a substance exists all truths about it follow from its nature. In view of this, any external influence on it would be redundant.

---

[38] Leibniz: *Principles of Nature and Grace*, para. 14.
[39] Leibniz: *Discourse on Metaphysics* XIV (italics mine).

But external influence is in any case impossible; every substance is causally isolated from its fellows.

We are now interested in the consequences that this theory has for the nature of human action, but first it is worth taking a parenthetical look at the grounds for it in Leibniz's system, since they link up with what was earlier said about Locke and Berkeley and the widespread tendency at this time to require that causation be 'intelligible'. Leibniz imposed the same requirement, and understood it so strongly that causation between two substances would call for the *transfer* of an element from one to the other, a metaphysical 'influx'. This he held to be impossible, since it meant that an accident would have to cross over from one substance to another, absurdly implying that it could (briefly?) have an existence independent of any substance which it characterised. Besides, a second consideration supported the same conclusion. For Leibniz, a substance is a simple entity, in the sense of having no distinguishable parts; and this rules out, he says, the only way in which one substance can conceivably act on another, that is, by causing movement of its parts.[40] Some commentators have clearly felt that prehistoric metaphysics has come to the surface here; perhaps it has, but at least it will help to explain why Leibniz was so keen to put the fossil on show if we remember the demand for 'intelligibility' and the shape and force which the dominant philosophy of his era gave to it.

We were concerned, however, with the consequences of the doctrine of the causal isolation of substances for Leibniz's theory of action. To be able to act freely, as he sees it, is not to have the power to choose between alternatives when one has no determining grounds either way: to think that would be to confuse freedom with indifference. It is rather to be in a position, from one's own nature to choose what appears to one to be the best. And this a rational soul or mind, being a Leibnizian substance and consequently subject to no external causes but only to the dictates of its own nature, can do. Therefore it is free and 'imitates in miniature the nature of God', whose actions are of course also dependent solely on himself.

[40] For both these points see *Monadology* para. 7.

That argument went a little too quickly for comfort. It may be, given Leibniz's premises, that the human agent resembles God in respect of being free from external interference; but not, surely, in respect of choosing the best ends and the best means to them. We frequently do not choose either, and as for ends, we often do not choose even what *seems* to us to be the best—we suffer from weakness of will as well as moral blindness.

Leibniz, as one might expect, had had this thought, and it is interesting that his response to it preserves the 'activity' version of the Similarity Thesis to the maximum that is possible without falling into obvious falsehood. In the first place, it is to be remembered that we are created substances, and finite in our powers; an exponent of the Image of God doctrine can happily work within any restrictions which these facts impose. One such restriction is that human knowledge is bound to be 'extensively'—again Galileo's term comes in useful—limited; however well we know what we do know, there will always be a great deal that we do not know. How will that affect our capacity to act? There are two points at which knowledge will arguably be needed: in recognising the right *ends* of action, and in deciding upon the *means* to them; since our limitations make us liable to error on both counts, the most that can fairly be expected of the proponent of the Similarity Thesis is that he make us resemble God in that we at least pursue goals that *seem* to us to be the best by the method that *appears* to us to be the most suitable. He does not have to assert that we also resemble the deity in always, or even very often, getting it right.

That still leaves the problem of *akrasia*: isn't it common for us to choose a course of action that doesn't even seem to us to be the best? Leibniz takes a firm line: he simply denies it. To think that it is true is to take too narrow a view of the grounds on which our 'corrupt taste' can find something to be the best. In the following passage, the opening sentence of which clearly advertises a comparison between God and man, he makes both of the above points:

When God makes a choice, it is through his knowledge of the best; when man does so, he will choose the alternative that seems to be the best. If, nevertheless, he chooses what appears less useful or pleasant, it will probably have come to seem the most attractive because of a whim, a spirit of contradiction or similar reasons of his corrupt taste—reasons that still determine his choice, even though they would not otherwise be valid. There are no exceptions to this rule.[41]

Thus Leibniz secures for the human mind, in respect of its ability to set itself ends and select means, and of its freedom from external influence in the execution of its plans, the most godlike profile compatible with its status as a created, finite substance. The modern reader may find the manoeuvre just quoted too glib and easy, and the last sentence somewhat over-confident. So do I; but I can only repeat that, as a fact of the history of thought, such considerations do not carry much weight when the central conception of a philosophical system is only one step away.

It would be surprising if Leibniz, one of the greatest of logicians, had let his articulation of the Image of God doctrine rest there, without paying at least equal attention to the cognitive side of human nature. We have seen that there are two forms of human knowledge which are pre-eminently employable in this connection, one being our knowledge of logic and mathematics, the other our knowledge of our own conscious states. Leibniz made extensive use of the former, logico-mathematical model in his elaboration of the Similarity Thesis; he had a well-developed theory of God's knowledge of the world, patterned on his theory of our knowledge of necessary truths. Whether he used the second model or not is a nice question; on the whole I would prefer to say that he did not, but that he invented a third possibility bearing a close relation to it—the reader will shortly have the chance to decide this (possibly only verbal) issue for himself.

At the end of the *Discourse on Metaphysics* IX there occurs a passage which is noteworthy for at least two reasons. One is Leibniz's amazing attempt to conjure out of his metaphysics an analogy, to be found not just in the human mind but in every substance, to the divine omnipotence. The other is that it might *prima facie* be taken for an appearance of the perceptual or 'states of consciousness' model for the Similarity Thesis. It runs as follows:

[41] Leibniz: letter to Coste, December 1707.

One can even say that every substance bears in some sort the character of God's infinite wisdom and omnipotence, and imitates him as far as it is capable. For it expresses, albeit confusedly, all that happens in the universe, past, present or future, and this has some resemblance to an infinite perception or knowledge; and as all other substances express this one in their turn and accommodate themselves to it, one can say that it extends its power over all the others in imitation of the omnipotence of the Creator.[42]

Leibniz's contention that each substance expresses every fact—a near relative, incidentally, of his view that every substance contains within itself something corresponding to every truth about it[43]—has of course nothing to do with a belief in any reciprocal causal influence; if anything, it is for him this fact that creates the *illusion* of such influence. So he is riding his luck very hard in speaking of omnipotence at this point and on these grounds; the Image of God doctrine has grabbed the reins, one suspects. But that criticism does not apply with the same force to his claim to have found here an analogy for the infinite *perception* of God. For though the states of a substance have no causal contact with the corresponding states of any other substance, they may still quite plausibly be said to represent them.

It is easy to see, however, that what is going on here is rather different from the 'perceptual states' version of the Insight Ideal as we have encountered it so far. Indeed, in one respect it is quite different from *anything* we have encountered so far. In nearly all writers, including Leibniz himself, we meet the suggestion that as regards quantity (extension) of knowledge and power God is infinitely superior to man; but that qualitatively (intensively) man can occasionally rise to the same level. This way of preserving the image of God whilst reserving a well-defined place for the speck of dust has been common to everything we have looked at up to now. In this passage we find just the reverse: the resemblance to God lies precisely in the *infinite number* of the mind's perceptions and the fact of its perceiving *everything*, precisely not in their *quality* or the level of insight that they permit, for they are said to be to a

---

[42]. Leibniz: *Discourse on Metaphysics* IX.

[43] See e.g. 'Primary Truths' in Leibniz: *Philosophical Writings*, ed. Parkinson (Dent 1973) p. 90.

greater or lesser degree 'confused', that is, to offer us only *distorted* representations of their objects. Besides, the standard use of the perceptual model, as we have seen it in Newton and Berkeley, was to say that our knowledge *of our own perceptual states* was like God's knowledge of all reality. But that is not Leibniz's point here at all: he is talking about the knowledge we have *through* our perceptual states, not *of* them. That this is the Similarity Thesis again there can be no doubt whatever, but it is certainly an original variation on it.

In another, related way this thought of Leibniz contrasts sharply with the perceptual states model as used so spectacularly by Berkeley. We introduced this model as being particularly suitable to the epoch because of its promise of certainty and infallibility. Whether that promise can ultimately be fulfilled or not, it definitely cannot be fulfilled unless the perceptual states in question are adequate representations of whatever it is they are to represent; and however adequate they may be, it still cannot be fulfilled if their possessors can be ignorant of their nature. In Leibniz's scheme neither condition is satisfied. In the first place the perceptions are, as we have just seen, confused. In the second, of the vast majority of them their possessors are not conscious, so that even if all we are interested in is our knowledge *of* our perceptions rather than our knowledge *through* them, there is no path here to infallibility. In higher substances like human minds, for Leibniz, *some* of the states which express all other facts about the universe do reach the conscious level of apperception, but only some of them; and Leibniz is speaking here not just of the higher but of all substances, most of which cannot be said to *know* anything.

Even if all these states were both adequate and fully conscious, Leibniz would still be as far as ever from the goal for which Berkeley wanted this equipment, the defeat of scepticism. So long as the sceptic is at large, it must be said, the cognitive version of the Similarity Thesis must be subject to serious limitations; but the rebuttal of scepticism does not appear to be one of Leibniz's interests. He tells us on more than one occasion[44] that God could have placed a single substance all alone in the universe, and since everything about

---

[44] See e.g. *A Specimen of Discoveries*, ibid. p. 79.

it and *a fortiori* which perceptions it has follows from its own nature, from its point of view things would have appeared exactly the same as they do now. And he seems to leave it as a matter of faith that God has not turned Cartesian demon and actually done so. Whatever animal we have here, it is not the one which Berkeley tried to domesticate. For Leibniz, our perceptions reflect the infinity of God; but in connection with infallibility he has no use for them.

When it comes to the logico-mathematical model and the appreciation of necessities we are on more familiar ground:

It can also be said that minds are . . . the closest likenesses of the first Being, for they distinctly perceive necessary truths, that is, the reasons which moved the first Being, and must have formed the universe.[45]

That sentence may serve as a declaration of intent. Leibniz has, as I have remarked, a detailed theory of necessity and our recognition of it; how he turns this theory to account in filling in the outlines of the Similarity Thesis is a story best approached via his famous distinction between truths of reason and truths of fact.

The basic doctrine, that some truths can be established *a priori*, or without recourse to anything known only from experience, whereas others essentially require experience for their justification, has become firmly embedded in logical theory, and remained virtually intact until well into the twentieth century. I shall assume familiarity with it, and also with the view, which Leibniz advocated, that all truths of the former kind are analytic. This he understood to mean not just that they are true by virtue of the meanings of the terms involved, but in the more precise sense that they are strictly speaking *identities*. A concept may be resolved into a list of properties (not necessarily a finite list), and an analytic statement is one which picks out a subject using a certain concept, and then predicates of it some property from the list. A trivial example would be 'vixens are female', for the concept of a vixen can be analysed into just two properties, that of being female and that of being a fox. So this proposition is an identity: whatever is female (and a fox) is female. The same is

---

[45] Leibniz: *A Résumé of Metaphysics* para. 22, ibid. p. 147.

true (Leibniz holds), though less obviously so, of an arithmetical proposition like '$7^3 = 343$', or 'multiples of twelve are multiples of four'.[46]

The application to arithmetic is of course controversial, but nobody with a smattering of philosophical logic will find anything unusual about the doctrine of analyticity itself. Leibniz, however, gives this familiar doctrine an unfamiliar twist, by relativising the distinction between truths of reason and truths of fact to the powers of the mind that apprehends them. For human minds there is indeed a difference. We can analyse completely only such concepts as have a finite analysis, those, that is to say, which resolve into finitely many other concepts. Where concepts are involved which have an infinitely long analysis, we can have no a priori knowledge—these are for us truths of fact. But for the divine mind, which can conduct an infinite analysis, there is no such barrier; for it our truths of fact become truths of reason, since it can analyse them and so perceive them to be identities.[47]

That the ability to grasp an infinite analysis should turn truths of fact into truths of reason is far from obvious, but, as so often with Leibniz, surprisingly good reasons can be given for it. Consider one of his favourite examples of what is, for us, a truth of fact: that Judas betrayed Christ. Significantly, it is a fact about *individuals*, whereas our examples of truths of reason were not— it was no particular vixen, no particular grouping of seven by seven by seven objects, but all and any such. So if it is possible to grasp this truth by the analytic method it has to be done by first grasping the analysis of the concept of the individual Judas. Whether that will be sufficient or not is of course a further question. But it is a question which Leibniz answers affirmatively, because he thinks it can be demonstrated that the concept of an individual must contain absolutely everything that is true of it. Consequently, for him who grasps the concept fully every truth about the individual may be derived from it; but on the other hand, grasping that analysis is work for an infinite intelligence, since the concept of an individual, in containing every truth about it, must be infinitely complex.

[46] See e.g. *Necessary and Contingent Truths*, ibid. p. 96.
[47] I here neglect one exception which Leibniz makes: existential propositions (apart from 'God exists') are not analytic, even to God.

How is this to be shown? The individual concept of Judas has
to be such that only one individual, Judas himself, could
possibly fall under it. And that condition could not be satisfied
by a concept which was analysable into finitely many properties.
Allowing ourselves, as did Leibniz, the assumption that an
individual has infinitely many (independent) true descriptions
or properties, such a concept could always have several
instances, objects which possessed all the properties contained in
the concept but differed from each other in respect of the other
properties not so contained. There could then be two—or
several—Judases, and the concept would after all not be an
individual concept but the concept of a kind. It follows that a
truly individual concept must contain an infinity of properties—
it must in fact stipulate for *every* property, and so for infinitely
many, whether or not the individual possesses it.[48] The mind,
therefore, that can analyse this concept sees all truths about
Judas *a priori*, in other words in the way in which we discern our
finite analytic truths of mathematics and logic:

> In the case of a contingent truth, even though the predicate really is
> in the subject, yet one never arrives at a demonstration or an
> identity, even though the resolution of each term is continued
> indefinitely. In such cases it is only God, who comprehends the
> infinite at once, who can see how the one is in the other, and can
> understand *a priori* the perfect reason for contingency.[49]

We are back with the Similarity Thesis in a familiar form.
God, it appears, can see all truths in the way in which we see
our truths of reason. To put it the other way round: in the way
we know our *a priori* truths we have the image of the divine
knowledge in general. The act of intellect by which God
recognised that Judas would betray Christ is *qualitatively* like
that by which we recognise that two and two make four. The
difference between the two acts is *quantitative*: in the one case
an infinite, in the other only a finite analysis has been
performed. Created minds, we may recall, '. . . differ from
God only as lesser from greater, as finite from infinite'.[50]

---

[48] Compare Leibniz: letter to Arnauld, July 1986, in *The Leibniz–Arnauld
Correspondence*, ed. Mason (Manchester University Press 1967) p. 61.

[49] Leibniz: 'Necessary and Contingent Truths' in Leibniz: *Philosophical Writings, ed.
Parkinson p. 97.

[50] *See above, this section, and footnote 35.*

It is interesting to note that the argument leading to this conclusion is valid only if a considerable input of characteristically Leibnizian premisses be allowed. I mentioned only one, the infinity of independent real properties in any individual, but there are others. A second is that spatio-temporal position is not a real property of individuals. A third, from the point of view of this chapter perhaps the most interesting, is that there *are* individual concepts in the sense that the argument requires, that is, concepts which could not possibly have more than one instance. Isn't our concept of a given individual in good enough shape if there is just *as a matter of fact* only one thing in our corner of the universe that satisfies it?

Why Leibniz consistently allows himself this very strong premiss is a matter for speculation. The fact that he sometimes speaks of individual concepts as the concept of the individual as it is 'in the mind of God' rather suggests that it has to do with the commitment to the ultimate intelligibility of the universe. But whilst it is easy to see how that would motivate the assumption that there must be, in God's mind, concepts from which every truth, and *a fortiori* every truth about Judas, follows, something more is needed to produce the conviction that the concept of *Judas*, by itself, must be capable of doing that much work. That Leibniz should go so far as to make that claim, equivalent to the doctrine that there are individual concepts in the sense he requires, may be more comprehensible when we remember the thesis that individual substances are causally isolated from the influence of all others. That might make one think that if there are concepts from which all truths about Judas follow, it must be the concept of Judas itself, since no other object has any real influence on truths about him. Then the belief in the complete intelligibility of the universe, which demands that there be some such concept, can do the rest. I hasten to repeat, however, that if this is to be taken as an account of Leibniz's thought-process it is no more than speculative.

Be all that as it may, there can be no doubt of the centrality for Leibniz of the Image of God doctrine, nor of the intensity with which he set about the work of providing it with philosophical foundations. Knowing this, we should not be surprised to find him also a proponent of the contemplative ideal, convinced of the value of insightful knowledge for its own sake. The increase of that kind of knowledge is, after all, what brings our minds closer to the condition of God:

Now since what perfects our mind (the light of grace apart) is the demonstrative knowledge of the greatest truths by means of their causes or reasons . . .[51]

Notice the use of the word 'perfect', which Leibniz was not likely to have used carelessly. Notice also 'demonstrative'; it is not any old kind of knowledge that works the magic, and indeed Leibniz could be quite condescending about unsystematic, non-theoretical knowledge, whatever practical advantages it might offer its possessor:

But in order to discriminate more clearly between what enlightens the mind and what merely leads it on blindly, here are some examples drawn from the crafts: if a certain workman knows from experience or from tradition that since the diameter is 7 feet long the circumference of the circle is a little less than 22 feet; or if a gunner knows by hearsay or from often having measured it that bodies are thrown farthest at an angle of 45 degrees, it is the confused knowledge of a working-man who will make very good use of it in earning his living and doing service to others; but the items of knowledge which enlighten the mind are those which are distinct, that is to say which contain causes or reasons, as when Archimedes gave the proof of the first rule and Galileo of the second; and in a word, it is only the knowledge of reasons in themselves or of necessary and eternal truths, particularly of those which are the most comprehensive and have the most connexion with the sovereign being, which can perfect us. Only this knowledge is good in itself . . .[52]

God, it appears, is a scientist, not just an engineer. Technology is not beatific, mathematics is. By a completely different route, the twentieth century has rediscovered at least the negative part of that message.

7. Malebranche—and many more

At much the same time that Leibniz wrote that letter,

[51] Leibniz: letter to the Landgraf: Ernst von Hessen-Rheinfels, in The Leibnitz-Arnauld Correspondence, ed. Mason p. 104.
[52] Ibid. p. 103.

Malebranche was composing his *Entretiens sur la Métaphysique*, in which he also gave expression to the contemplative ideal. The good for man lies not so much in action as in the insightful contemplation of truth, especially of theological truth:

Man is made for the adoration of God in the wisdom of His conduct; let us try to lose ourselves in the contemplation of His depths. The human spirit can be in no better state, than when adoring in silence the divine perfections.[53]

Taken by itself, that sentence may sound merely monkish and withdrawn; but one should remember that, for Malebranche, the 'divine perfections' are most clearly expressed in the order of nature, and especially in the laws which govern its workings. Then the tone begins to sound much more like that of Leibniz, or to be reminiscent of Galileo's statement that '... turning over the great book of nature ... is the way to elevate one's gaze'.[54] And indeed Malebranche's reasons seem to have been much the same as those of Leibniz: insightful knowledge was to bring our minds closer to the mind of God. At first sight the cognitive version of the Image of God doctrine may seem better suited to the individualistic pro-testantism which Leibniz represented than to Malebranche's devout catholicism with its submissiveness to the authority of the church. We should remember, however, that there is more than one dimension involved. How closely man, in his most rational, most insightful moments, can approach the divine state is one question; how far he is self-reliant in the attempt is another, and two philosophers who are not far apart on the first point may differ sharply on the second: we have already seen Pascal combine the assertion that man can be like God with the view that this does not come from human nature but is solely the effect of grace. We find a certain, though weaker kind of denial of self-reliance in Descartes, when he feels that our cognitive instrument can only be guaranteed via a guarantee of the goodness of God, a proof that he is no deceiver. Malebranche's denial of self-reliance takes a rather different form: the best of human thinking is participation in

---

[53] Malebranche: *Entretiens sur la Métaphysique* X (closing speech of Theodore).
[54] Galileo: *Dialogue Concerning the Two Chief World Systems*, Author's Dedication.

the divine thought, God as it were thinking in us. Leibniz went to the trouble of an explicit denial:

> Yet I am not of the sentiment of certain able philosophers who seem to maintain that our ideas themselves are in God and not in us at all. In my opinion this comes from not having yet considered enough what we have just explained concerning substances . . .[55]

He is referring, of course, to his highly individualistic doctrine of the isolation of the monad: once it has been created nothing comes to it from outside; all its states, its actions, its perceptions, flow entirely from its own nature. Its quasi-divinity is a matter of similarity, not of union or partial identity. For Malebranche, on the other hand, it does take the form of a union with God's mind, and not just a similarity. Sometimes, it is true, he speaks in terms which imply no more than similarity, as when he says that the natural procedure for a human investigation of the universe has something in common with the principles according to which God's mind worked in creating it—which is why we have a reasonable hope of success:

> To consider in order the properties of extension, one ought to begin with their most simple relationship, as did Descartes, and advance from the simpler to the more complex, not just because this is natural and helps the operation of the mind, but also because, God always acting in an orderly manner and taking the simplest route, this way of examining our ideas and their relationships is best suited to bring us to knowledge of His works.[56]

But as well as contending for the similarity of mental structure between God and man, Malebranche also claims a much more intimate relationship, as for instance when he writes of how:

> The spirit of man is united with God, with the eternal wisdom, with the universal reason which illuminates all intelligences. And it is united by general laws, of whose operation our attention is the occasional cause.[57]

Students of the 'self-reliance' theme may note the last phrase.

---

[55] Leibniz: *Discourse on Metaphysics* XXIX.

[56] Malebranche: *De la Recherche de la Vérité*, Bk. 6 Pt. 2 Ch. 4.

[57] Malebranche: *Entretiens sur la Métaphysique* XII Sect. IX: 'L'esprit de l'homme est aussi uni . . .'

We are only an 'occasional' cause of the union; it is God who brings it about, as indeed it is only God who really brings anything about within Malebranche's philosophy.

I hope that enough has now been said to give the reader an idea of the main way in which the doctrine of the Image of God animated the philosophical thought of the seventeenth century and the beginning of the next. I have tried to outline its various ramifications, and especially those of its epistemological variant, the Insight Ideal. It is clear that many commentators have felt the presence of the Insight Ideal, though they have used different terminology, some of it, like the over-divisive 'rationalism', as confusing as enlightening. I suggest that our understanding of this period of intellectual history will benefit if we learn to see it in the wider context which has formed the core of this chapter.

I have, of course, left a good deal of relevant material untouched; a rich source to which attention should at least be drawn is the work of the Cambridge Platonists, where the approximation of human reason to the reason of God is a recurrent theme, and where we even find the near-mystical, Malebranchian and Spinozistic suggestion that under favourable circumstances they may actually merge. Rather than an unwelcome deluge of quotation from the Platonists themselves I offer just one remark made about their most eminent representative, Ralph Cudworth, by Richard Price, writing in the middle of the eighteenth century:

According to Dr. Cudworth, abstract ideas are implied in the *cognoscitive power of the mind*; which, he says, contains in itself virtually . . . general notions of things, which are exerted by it, or unfold and discover themselves as occasions invite and proper circumstances occur. This, no doubt, many will freely condemn as whimsical and extravagant. I have, I own, a different opinion of it; but yet, I should not care to be obliged to defend it. It is what he thought, Plato meant by making all *knowledge* to be *Reminiscence*; and in this, as well as other respects, he makes the human mind to resemble the Divine; to which the ideas and comprehension of all things are essential, and not to be derived from any foreign source.[58]

The Insight Ideal promotes a certain programme in the

[58] Richard Price: *A Review of the Principle Questions of Morals*, ed. Raphael, pp. 30–1 note.

theory of knowledge; it suggests that a certain type of deeply insightful and secure knowledge is attainable by human beings. But is it? If not, was there then no knowledge, and the triumph of the sceptic; or was it rather that the programme was misconceived along with the dominant philosophy that gave rise to the ideal of godlike knowledge in the first place? A word in conclusion of this chapter, but also in introduction of the next, goes to Thomas Reid. Are the words 'and to be as gods' merely a routine biblical reference, or do they indicate Reid's perception of what was really at stake?

But if . . . we resolve to go deeper, and not to trust our faculties, without a reason to show that they cannot be fallacious; I am afraid, that seeking to become wise, and to be as gods, we shall become foolish, and being unsatisfied with the lot of humanity, we shall throw off common sense.[59]

[59] Thomas Reid: *Essays on the Intellectual Powers of Man* Essay VI, Ch. VI.

2

ONE WAY TO READ HUME

1. *Hume's target*

We have now taken a sighting of some of the manifestations of the conception of man as made in the image of God. Some were fully explicit; others took the form of doctrines which can be seen, on reflection, to fit that conception particularly well. I now want to take the argument a stage further: knowledge of the 'dominant philosophy' can sometimes serve as a clue leading to revisions of interpretation—it reaches down, as it were, to make itself felt in matters of fine textual detail. And the reader who approaches the text with awareness of the dominant philosophy sometimes finds his reading fruitfully assisted. To illustrate this, I shall now make a much closer investigation of a particular philosopher than any that would have fitted the scheme of the first chapter. Hume is a good instance of Hegel's dictum that something is not necessarily known just because it is well known; we shall find that this treatment modifies, even reverses, some aspects of the 'standard' view of him. Some of these changes, though not all, have already been proposed by the deeper commentators; this treatment reinforces them and incorporates them into a larger view of his concerns. It also introduces another point: a philosopher's antagonism to the dominant philosophy of his time can be just as formative as support of it.

David Hume was born in 1711, at the end of the period spanned by the last chapter. He was exposed to many intellectual influences, amongst them Cartesianism, the triumph of Newtonian physics and the apparent success of the corpuscular theory, the rising tide of enthusiasm for Locke's philosophy, the chill breath of a stern northerly mutant of Christianity. Inspired by some of them and repelled by others, he fashioned a philosophical system of the most revolutionary stamp. 'Revolutionary', though, needs to be rightly understood. The content of Hume's thought is in many ways strongly conservative in tone. He counsels resignation to the dictates of human nature, which he sees as a historical constant, and the greatest caution in any departure from traditional values and institutions. His work was a revolution within philosophy, so to speak: he sought to destroy man's favoured picture of man and replace it; though the picture he sought to replace it with was in a sense as conservative in its essence as the one it was to depose. The philosophy was far from revolutionary, as that is normally understood; but it was a revolution. It aimed at no less than the destruction of the doctrine of the image of God, and substituted for it an anthropology which looked not to the divine but to the natural world for its comparisons, and to the sciences for its methods. Man was a natural object; not, as for Leibniz, a little god beside the great God, but a great animal amongst the lesser animals.

In the negative, or critical, part of this programme Hume was perhaps as successful as is possible. It may be that the *Weltbilder* that underpin philosophical thought are not themselves capable of being established by argument starting from neutral territory. It may even be that they are not definitively refutable either, if only because they are protected from refutation by the flexibility (or vagueness) of their least-developed forms. No amount of epistemological fire, for instance, could bring down the Image of God doctrine *in general*, since it does not have to be articulated in terms of human knowledge. But in fact, as we have seen, the cultural situation of the seventeenth century constrained and channelled it into a fairly precise shape, precise enough for Hume to take very damaging aim.

The central contention of this chapter is that this gives us a legitimate and illuminating perspective from which to read Hume. On the one hand there are in his writings certain explicit indications of a concern with the Similarity Thesis. On the other hand there are many more indirect signs, by which I mean that his basic methods, concepts and emphases are to a remarkable degree those which one would have reason to expect, if the Similarity Thesis were his primary target. A number of major features of his texts fit that hypothesis, and

ONE WAY TO READ HUME

certain well-known interpretative trouble-spots can be clar-
ified by pursuing it. The hypothesis, I should add, has nothing
to do with the existence of secret, or unconscious, intentions
on Hume's part. Although, understandably, he did not
announce them as front-page headlines, he made no very
strenuous attempt to keep them secret; *a fortiori* there is no
suggestion that they were unconscious. The predominance of
the Similarity Thesis shaped his questions, and his antipathy
to it shaped his answers; both of which facts, I suggest, he
knew perfectly well.

Of the two types of evidence for this, it is what I have called
the 'indirect signs' which are perhaps the more interesting,
since it is here that one's reading of Hume may be most
significantly altered by thinking of the Image of God doctrine
as setting the scene. But before passing to them we should take
a brief look at some instances of the other type, cases in which
Hume is openly talking about either the Similarity Thesis
itself or something extremely close to it.

Norman Kemp Smith taught that it was the basic ideas of
his moral philosophy which Hume conceived first. That
would place the material of Book III of the *Treatise of Human
Nature* quite early in his thought. We do not have to get very
far into it to find this statement of the target position:

virtue is nothing but a conformity to reason; that there are eternal
fitnesses and unfitnesses of things, which are the same to every
rational being that considers them; and that the immutable
measures of right and wrong impose an obligation, not only on
human creatures, but also on the Deity himself . . .[1]

God and man are alike in point of their reason, and
consequently also in point of their morality. Hume then goes
on, admittedly, to shelve the theological aspect of the question
and simply argue that human reason will not by itself generate
human morality. But before doing so he makes clear his
opinion that that conclusion will be sufficient to demolish all
such theologically connected ways of thinking of ethics. The
passage continues:

All these systems concur in the opinion, that morality, like truth, is

[1] *A Treatise of Human Nature*, ed. L. A. Selby-Bigge, 2nd edn. revised by P. H.
Nidditch (Oxford 1978) (hereafter THN) Bk. III Pt. I Sect. I (p. 456).

discerned merely by ideas, and by their juxta-position and comparison. In order, therefore, to judge of these systems, we need only consider, whether it be possible, from reason alone, to distinguish between moral good and evil, or whether there must concur some other principles to enable us to make that distinction.[2]

Knowing the undoubted status of the Image of God doctrine, one will be less inclined to read straight over the first half of that paragraph. It is an early sign that the young Hume knew well the nature of the beast.

The same concern is visible in Hume's organisation of the material of the *Dialogues Concerning Natural Religion*. One could not, I believe, summarise their content better (if one had to do it so briefly) than by saying that they ask the question whether there is any reason, independent of revelation, to accept the Similarity Thesis; and that they answer, though with just a shadow of a concession to the affirmative view, that there is not. I do not propose to rehearse the whole argument of the *Dialogues*, but just to draw attention to some facts about their structure which will be obvious enough to anyone who reads them with the Similarity Thesis firmly in mind.

The question before the company, Demea tells them, 'is not concerning the being but the nature of God';[3] and Philo agrees, for 'the original cause of this universe (whatever it be) we call God'.[4] But, he goes on almost at once:

we ought never to imagine, that we comprehend the attributes of this divine Being, or to suppose, that his perfections have an analogy or likeness to the perfections of a human creature.[5]

Thus Demea and Philo jointly throw down the gauntlet. Cleanthes picks it up, states the argument from design, and concludes with all possible explicitness:

By this argument . . . we do prove at once the existence of a Deity, and his similarity to human mind and intelligence.[6]

Whereupon Hume has Demea say, just in case any reader is

[2] Ibid. pp. 456–7.
[3] *Dialogues Concerning Natural Religion*, ed.Norman Kemp Smith (Nelson 1947, now publ. Bobbs–Merrill) (hereafter DCNR) p. 141.
[4] Ibid. p. 142 (Part II).
[5] Ibid. p. 142 (Part II).
[6] Ibid. p. 143 (Part II).

still unclear as to what is being made the central issue:

I shall be so free ... as to tell you, that from the beginning, I could not approve of your conclusion concerning the similarity of the Deity to men . . .[7]

Here, just where the main debate of the *Dialogues* is getting under way, Hume could hardly be more insistent. But he still allows Philo to hammer it in once more by remarking, when a few pages later he is squaring up for his first attempt to refute the teleological argument, that he was 'scandalised' by Cleanthes' anthropomorphism.

The disputants very properly divide the Similarity Thesis into two components. First, in Parts II to VIII, they discuss the reasons for thinking that the cause of the universe has a theoretical intelligence like that found in man. After a break spent trouncing the cosmological argument (Part IX), they return to consider the second question, that of a likeness between God and man in respect of moral preferences. Demea, who holds no brief for the intellectual comparison, is pleased to treat Philo as an ally in the first half of the debate, but finds himself betrayed in the second half, when Philo turns his sceptical armoury on the moral comparison, and declares the conclusion best supported by experience to be that '. . . the original source of all things . . . has no more regard to good above ill than to heat above cold . . .,'[8] and that:

we have no more reason to infer, that the rectitude of the supreme Being resembles human rectitude than that his benevolence resembles the human. Nay, it will be thought, that we have still greater cause to exclude from him moral sentiments, such as we feel them . . .[9]

This, Demea finds, is too much, and he takes 'occasion soon after, on some pretence or other, to leave the company'.[10]

In Part XII Philo and Cleanthes, predominantly the former, sum up; the operation is conducted in terms of the very same question: how great an analogy are we justified in postulating between the cause of the universe and human

---

[7] Ibid. p. 143 (Part II).
[8] Ibid. p. 212 (Part XI).
[9] Ibid. p. 212 (Part XI).
[10] Ibid. p. 213 (Part XI).

thought? That there is much analogy is unfounded; that there
is *some* is undeniable, though just how weakly Hume is
prepared to understand this claim emerges from a sentence in
which Philo says that 'the rotting of a turnip, the generation of
an animal, and the structure of human thought' are 'energies
that probably bear some remote analogy to each other',[11] for
these may be taken, one would at least hope, to span quite a
wide range of phenomena. His final statement of the position
is couched in very similar terms: reason allows us to say no
more than that

*the cause or causes of order in the universe probably bear some remote analogy to
human intelligence . . .*[12]

As regards the intellectual version of the Similarity Thesis,
reason offers only cautious ('probably') support to it, and then
in an extremely weak form ('some remote analogy'); as
regards the moral version, Hume's view seems to be that it
offers it no support whatever. One of the philosophers' main
instruments for establishing the Image of God doctrine is
gone.

That doctrine was a serious obstacle, not just to particular
Humean views, but to the whole enterprise as he conceived it.
There was to be a science of the mind on the Newtonian
model; those were the terms in which he consistently
presented his work. But then his audience had to be willing to
see the human mind as a part of nature, to accept, at least as
discussible possibilities, such claims as the one which Hume
made loudly in Section IX of the *Enquiry Concerning Human
Understanding*: that reason is a faculty essentially similar in
humans and animals. If man was as much a supernatural as a
natural object, as much a denizen of heaven as of Earth, and if
(as was widely held) it was primarily his reason which made
him so, then to want to bring the workings of that faculty
under natural laws was at best futile and at worst blasphemous: it carried the implication that God's mind (to which the
human mind was assumed similar) was a causal device,
reliant on the operations of some kind of mechanism for
arriving at the truth.

[11] Ibid. p. 218 (Part XII).
[12] Ibid. p. 227 (Part XII).

I spoke also of *indirect* signs that Hume's philosophy was conceived against the background of the Similarity Thesis. What sort of signs are these? Consider the Insight Ideal, the cognitive version of the Thesis. It has as its centre an epistemology, a view about the type of knowledge possible to man; and the epistemology, we noted, tends to bring certain ontological claims, beliefs about the way reality is, along with it. Besides those two general areas of philosophical concern we should bear in mind a third, one with which Anglo-Saxon philosophers of the twentieth century have been much preoccupied. It may be called the conceptual or analytical: the investigation of the content of our thought, or the meanings of the expressions of our language.

If we conjecture, therefore, that Hume's principal destructive intention was to expose the emptiness of the Insight Ideal, we would have to expect indications that his primary interest was in the epistemological area, in questions about the ways in which human beings can and do come by their beliefs, and that his discussion of ontological and analytic matters was subservient or secondary to it. In saying 'subservient or secondary' I have a certain distinction in mind, which may be illustrated by considering the relation between Hume's theory of ideas and their origin in impressions—this is the analytic component of his theory—and his scepticism about the scope of reason, followed by the associationist theory of the generation of belief—the epistemological component. By saying that the former was subservient to the latter I would mean that Hume made use of it when, and in so far as, the theory of ideas was needed to establish scepticism and the Humean theory of the formation of belief. Saying that it was secondary would imply that although Hume developed it and made use of it in ways not strictly necessary for grounding his epistemological contentions, these have the nature of excursions which could be excised without great damage to the whole structure; and we might expect that the details of such passages would suggest a slightly lower intellectual intensity in their composition. Possibly there will also be times when the author forgets his 'secondary' thesis entirely, and allows himself to make remarks not even compatible with it. Our conjecture would suggest just such a relationship between the epistemological and analytical aspects of Hume's thought.

What would it suggest about his likely attitude towards ontological questions? We must remember that he has a detailed positive theory about the origins of our ideas, beliefs, emotions and evaluations, and this theory will clearly need an ontology of some sort—an obvious minimum is that of impressions, plus whatever else is needed, if anything, for the principles of association to exist and do their work. But the beliefs that he is concerned to investigate go beyond this minimum: we believe in 'power or necessary connexion', independent physical objects, mental continuants, values, for instance, and with regard to this sort of item Hume is altogether free of a pressure which weighs heavily on his opponents. The friends of the Insight Ideal could hardly avoid postulating a universe which was a proper object for the cognitive capacities they took man to have—the God who gave us throats would not have failed to provide us with beer. And besides, since his intellect was supposed similar to ours, that was precisely the sort of universe he would have designed in any case. Someone whose chief contention, however, is that certain things *cannot* be known in a certain way can afford to be agnostic about the question, whether they *really are* as they are believed to be or not; to make dogmatic negative claims about 'what there isn't' would usually be to give unnecessary hostages. So we might expect from Hume a good measure of ontological agnosticism.

I shall argue that there are, in Hume's writings, quite enough features of these sorts to compel us to take very seriously the view that he is first and foremost concentrating on epistemological issues, the foundation and genesis of our beliefs. His interest in conceptual or analytic considerations— the theory of ideas as an instrument for discovering the content of our thoughts—is subordinate to this purpose. The same is true of his ontological claims: he makes them only when they are required for his epistemology. Both these issues are to some extent obscured; the status of the theory of ideas by his presentation and that of his ontology by the nature of his epistemology itself; but the underlying position turns out to be as I have described. Because of this the gap between Hume and the logical positivists of the 1930s is *far* greater than many, especially the positivists themselves, have thought; we shall return to their understanding of Hume when we have looked at the evidence.

2. *How not to criticise Hume*

One way of beginning will enable us at the same time to deal with two points very commonly made in criticism of Hume. First, he is supposed to have stipulated that 'Reason' meant deduction, and hence that reasons had to be deductive or not be real reasons at all. Secondly, he is held to have confused logical considerations with psychological, the justification of belief with the causal explanation of its occurrence. On the former subject, here is a passage from a well-known book on Hume:

> What is at issue is whether rationality and likelihood are notions which Hume (in this respect a high rationalist) is correct in restricting to deductive demonstrations . . . Hume's stance on this fundamental question is a wholly dogmatic one.[13]

This sort of comment is frequently accompanied by remarks to the effect that Hume's sceptical arguments are easily overcome: just deny the dogma and sit back. Hume specifies an arbitrarily strong condition that a train of thought has to satisfy if it is to count as the work of reason, shows that outside geometry amd arithmetic hardly anything satisfies it, and then tells us that we have no reason for this, that or the other central and universally held belief.

After what we have seen so far, one thing, at least, ought to be immediately clear: there may be dogma here, but if there is it is not *Hume's* dogma; *he* hasn't stipulated anything, whether arbitrary or not. What he has done is to take a historically existent conception of reason and show that it has practically no application to human thought. Secondly, the (then) existent conception of reason has nothing arbitrary about it either; it embodies a requirement of the dominant philosophy of the age, the Image of God doctrine taken in its cognitive version. Reason was the divine element in man, and so it had to be thought of in whatever terms might plausibly yield infallibility. Deduction might be held to do this, or at any rate

[13] T. Penelhum: *Hume* (Macmillan 1975) p. 53.

to be theoretically capable of doing it, whereas probabilistic considerations certainly won't, not even in the mind of the perfect statistician - the improbable *can* happen. So, thirdly, whether or not this treatment of reason is indicative of 'high rationalism', Hume is not being a high rationalist in adopting it; he is simply addressing himself sensitively and accurately to the philosophical problems and attitudes of his times. Just now we saw, in a passage from his ethical writings, how he distilled from a moral variant of the Similarity Thesis a claim about the capacity of reason in practical thought, and then undertook to refute it - and all relevant versions of the Similarity Thesis along with it. He is doing just the same in the sceptical parts of his theoretical philosophy.

It is not at all difficult to find, in the works of Hume's immediate predecessors, a certain lack of interest in a phenomenon which has much fascinated many twentieth-century thinkers: strong but inconclusive argument, confirmation as opposed to proof. The fact is not surprising, on my hypothesis. Consider, for example, the following passage from Berkeley:

Suppose—what no one can deny possible—an intelligence, without the help of external bodies, to be affected with the same train of sensations or ideas that you are, imprinted in the same order and with like vividness in his mind. I ask whether that intelligence hath not all the reason to believe the existence of Corporeal Substances, represented by his ideas, and exciting them in his mind, that you can possibly have for believing the same thing? Of this there can be no question. Which one consideration were enough to make any reasonable person suspect the strength of whatever arguments he may think himself to have, for the existence of bodies without the mind.[14]

To contemporary thought this paragraph, taken by itself— and that is how the words 'Which one consideration . . .' invite us to take it—is not very impressive. It overlooks what is to us an important possibility, namely that our 'sensations or ideas' might be such as to give us strong grounds for belief in an independent material world; all it shows is that these grounds cannot be deductively conclusive. There is nothing to make the 'reasonable person suspect the strength of whatever

---

[14] Berkeley: *Principles of Human Knowledge* para. 20.

arguments he may think himself to have', if he takes these arguments to be confirmatory rather than deductive. Perhaps there are other lines of attack which ought, even in that case, to raise his suspicions, but not this 'one consideration' which Berkeley adduces.

I have already expressed and explained my view that those who pass this sort of thing by with the remark that it was just how these men 'happened to think' are making a historical mistake of some consequence. But I would also suggest that they may be making another mistake, perhaps ultimately more serious, of a methodological kind. We are speaking here of a technical thesis, 'Real reasons are deductive reasons', which surely has no intrinsic obviousness. How could such a thesis be nothing more than what a number of people, spanning a period of some hundred years, 'just happened to think'? One can imagine that within a somewhat closed and introverted academic tradition, composed of cautious and defensive minds, some such doctrines might simply persist of their own momentum (which might feel like a satisfactory explanation provided we were not worried about how they built up momentum in the first place). But Galileo, Descartes, Spinoza, Leibniz, Malebranche, Newton and Berkeley did not form such a community, and they were not timid thinkers unwilling to clash with entrenched opinion. If they all show a strong inclination towards a certain belief, there are *prima facie* grounds to think that it must have had something to recommend it, either to reason, or to the emotions, or both. It is hard to believe, as I have said, that 'Real reasons are deductive' (to take one example; another might be: 'Causes and effects have an element in common') is intrinsically obvious, even harder to believe that it has *in itself* an emotional appeal. The presumption is, then, that it must have been connected to something which did, and that therefore something of the kind which I am proposing must lie behind the texts, even if my particular proposal be rejected. To ignore or deny this, which is what the 'arbitrary dogma' or 'what they just happened to think' type of approach implicitly does, encourages a split between philosophy as practised and its psychological foundations and *raison d'être* in human nature. And this must in due course tend to make a mystery out of the fact that philosophy has ever been pursued at all.

Our point of departure for that excursion was Berkeley's lack of concern about probabilistic reasoning; we reached that from Hume's exclusion of that kind of reasoning from his sceptical investigation of what can and cannot be achieved by 'reason'. But was Hume then uninterested in probability? By no means; he was even at pains to advertise his interest in the *Abstract of a Treatise of Human Nature*:

The celebrated Monsieur Leibnitz has observed it to be a defect in the common systems of logic, that they are very copious when they explain the operations of the understanding in the forming of demonstrations, but are too concise when they treat of probabilities, and those other measures of evidence on which life and action entirely depend, and which are our guides even in most of our philosophical speculations. In this censure, he comprehends the *essay on human understanding, la recherche de la vérité*, and *l'art de penser*. The author of the *treatise of human nature* seems to have been sensible of this defect in these philosophers, and has endeavoured, as much as he can, to supply it.[15]

Neither Leibniz's criticism nor Hume's reaction to it should surprise us. There were, of course, enough thinkers of this period who were interested in probability, Pascal, Leibniz himself and Bernoulli, to name three of the best-known. They came to the subject, however, from the direction of mathematics; the approach route from the side of philosophy was obstructed by the doctrine of the Image of God and its implications for epistemology, so it is understandable that Leibniz should have found it more or less untrodden. Nor is it surprising that Hume had no such inhibitions: the Image of God doctrine was not in his luggage. So nothing was pushing him towards the relatively rare phenomenon of quasi-divine certainty in human knowledge, and he could concentrate on those types of inference by which most human belief is in fact generated. To do so was in accordance with, or rather required by, his intention of founding an experiential science of man; here we see another kind of reason why such a science could only flourish where the Similarity Thesis had lost all importance. That intention, of course, has the further effect

[15] Hume: *An Abstract of a Treatise of Human Nature* ed.Keynes and Sraffa (Cambridge 1938) pp. 7–8.

that the way in which he deals with these types of inference is thoroughly naturalistic.

The first thing anyone hears of Hume is that he was a sceptic. Can we say, briefly but accurately, what this much-vaunted, oft-refuted scepticism comes to? It has two components; stating it and assessing it both require that they be kept distinct. First there is the thesis that reason, understood as the pivotal concept of the Insight Ideal with the resulting web of connotations of demonstration, incorrigibility and the like, is of *very* limited scope; hardly any of our beliefs have, even potentially, that degree of transparency. (The thesis fragments, of course, into scepticism about this and that particular subject-matter, but those details need not now bother us.) This form of scepticism has suffered the ironic fate that it has to many come to seem so obvious that they feel it to have been scarcely worth saying. That attitude is a natural companion of the one that holds Hume's conception of 'reason' to have been arbitrary, for once one sees why it was not arbitrary at all one has also seen the very deep philosophical point of saying it—and hence that its 'obvious-ness' must be a later historical development. But obvious or not, this sceptical thesis is nowadays held to be true by most philosophers; and I think they are right.

Hume's scepticism then has a second layer, nowhere to my knowledge stated, but very clearly implied. It can be put like this: when we have subtracted the concept of reason as demanded by the Insight Ideal, there is a still a weaker (or, to avoid evaluations, *another*) concept of being reasonable or rational left over. Here Hume's scepticism consists in believ-ing that the only thing that can be done with *this* concept of reason is to naturalise it: to give an account of it in terms of the normal healthy functioning of the human belief-producing mechanism, and to provide a theory of the way in which that mechanism works. Whether this second layer of scepticism is true or not is to this day controversial, and one of the crucial questions that confront the widely prevailing naturalism.

Hume, unfortunately, didn't make any very incisive con-tribution to this controversy, and it is instructive to think why not. But first the assertion that he didn't has to be argued for. In one of his most famous passages, after all, he apparently asks the question whether there can be any justification for 'our conclusions from experience', and decides that there cannot, whereupon he passes to naturalistic explanation of our propensity to draw inductive inferences. So here we might expect to find the grounds for the second layer of his scepticism. It is hard to be sure, however, whether what we find is grounds or just the begging of the question. I shall not make the attempt to comb all the relevant pages; I shall just illustrate my reasons for suspicion by discussing two of the strategies which Hume employs.

He starts from the case of someone in whose experience two 'objects', call them A and B, have always been found together—this is the first premiss of the inductive inference. Our observer then concludes that future occurrences of A will also be attended by B—this is the 'conclusion from experience'. Hume asks:

> whether experience produces the idea by means of the understanding or of the imagination; whether we are determin'd by reason to make the transition, or by a certain association and relation of perceptions.[16]

If it be reason, he then says, it 'wou'd proceed upon the principle' of the uniformity of nature. Let us overlook the point that the principle of the uniformity of nature, as Hume here states it, is altogether too vague a thing to help reason to proceed anywhere, and concentrate instead on another question. Is it Hume's thought that reason would need entitlement to take this principle as a *second premiss*? It seems so, for he then goes on with the famous argument that it cannot be known *a priori*, and that any attempt to argue for it from experience 'must evidently be going in a circle'.[17]

But what does this really show? We began with an argument consisting of one premiss and a conclusion:

(P) Every observed A has been a B.
(C) The next A will be a B.

Now the most Hume has shown is surely this: that if the

[16] THN pp. 88–9.
[17] Hume: *An Enquiry Concerning Human Understanding*, ed. L. A. Selby-Bigge, 3rd edn. revised by P. H. Nidditch (Oxford 1975) (hereafter ECHU) p. 36.

passage from (P) to (C) is not 'founded on reasoning'[18] *just as it stands*, then it will not help to add a further premiss:

(P') Nature is uniform.

But on the substantial question, whether the inference from (P) to (C) needs outside help of any kind in order to be a matter of reason, this argument says nothing. It does draw attention to the fact that it is not *deductive*, and that to get a deduction some further premiss is needed; but that is all, and the fact that Hume thinks it enough to do his work and leave naturalistic explanation of our inference patterns in sole possession of the field testifies to the way in which the prevalence of the Insight Ideal pushed 'reason' in the direction of deduction and obscured what is to us at the very least a *prima facie* possibility: that there is room for a position which is neither deductivist nor naturalist. Hume, in other words, tended to think of the first component of his scepticism as a sufficient condition for the truth of the second. To regard this fact as a mere oversight is to let ourselves off rather lightly; I hope to have shown that a deeper explanation is at hand.

A second strategy that Hume uses looks, at first sight, to offer something different. Consider this:

all inferences from experience suppose . . . that the future will resemble the past. . . . If there be any suspicion that the course of nature may change, and that the past may be no rule for the future, all experience becomes useless, and can give rise to no inference or conclusion.[19]

This does not speak of using the uniformity assumption as an extra premiss, exactly; rather the idea is that there must be no positive suspicion that it is false. I shall not ask the reader to spend time and energy on the question whether that difference really is a difference—the crux lies elsewhere. What is the nature of the suspicion that Hume speaks of? If it merely consists in the awareness that a change in the course of nature is a logical possibility, not to be excluded *a priori*, then we have not gone beyond the point that these inferences are not

---

[18] Ibid. p. 32.
[19] Ibid. pp. 37–8.

demonstrative. To get beyond it Hume needs to maintain that a suspicion backed by *no reason of any kind* can render experience rationally useless as a guide to the future. But this he makes no attempt to show, nor does he even show awareness of it. We do not really have anything more here than the first strategy offered; and that is really no more than the point that inductive inference does not and will not be made to conform to the demands of the Insight Ideal.

At the beginning of the section I spoke of two frequently heard criticisms of Hume. We have now considered the first; the second was the allegation that he confounded logical with psychological questions, the justification of belief with its genesis, the normative with causal fact. Now there are, from the twentieth-century point of view, certain oddities about Hume's conception of the relationship between logic and psychology. But in the first place they are not at all well expressed by saying that he confounded the one with the other, or that he confounded anything with anything; and in the second place they appear a good deal less odd when seen against the background of the role allocated to logic, or to reason, in the service of the Image of God doctrine.

Whatever the truth may be here, it cannot conceivably be anything so crude as that Hume could not tell logic from psychology. He wrote, after all, two books on the subject of religious belief, one of them accurately focused on its logic, the other on its psychology. He also told his readers plainly that that was what he was doing:

As every enquiry, which regards religion, is of the utmost importance, there are two questions in particular, which challenge our attention, to wit, that concerning its foundation in reason, and that concerning its origin in human nature.[20]

There is another version of the complaint which we should note, if only in order to be clear that it is negligible. It works by drawing attention to a habit of Hume's: first to argue that something cannot be supplied by logic (or reason), then that it *can* be supplied by psychology (the imagination), and in so doing to speak (as I have done in this sentence) as if what psychology had to offer were exactly the same thing as that

[20] Hume: *The Natural History of Religion*, Introduction.

which logic had failed to deliver. Thus two successive chapters of the *Enquiry Concerning Human Understanding* are entitled 'Sceptical Doubts Concerning the Operations of the Understanding' and 'Sceptical Solution of These Doubts'. The former chapter argues that reason cannot supply absolute certainty as to the trustworthiness of inductive inference; but the latter chapter, in spite of its title, does not suggest that the imagination can do that; rather it explains why the lack of absolute certainty does not, in humans, result in the weakening of the relevant belief. Again, there is the notorious passage from Hume's treatment of causality:

The necessary connexion between causes and effects is the foundation of our inference from one to the other. The foundation of our inference is the transition arising from the accustom'd union. These are, therefore, the same.[21]

Hasn't Hume pulled a fast one? Has he not used 'the foundation' in the first sentence to suggest 'what justifies the inference' and in the second sentence to mean 'what causes us to make the inference'? The contention that they are the same appears to be quite spurious.

But this feature of Hume's writing, whatever mistakes it may ultimately involve, is not the outcome of any inability to distinguish between the logical and the psychological. On the contrary, it would be better described as a way, perhaps not entirely happy, of making one of the most basic points of his philosophy: that where philosophers thought they saw the operations of reason, the divine spark at work in man, they were watching nothing more than a mundane mechanism and its natural effects in the mind. He didn't want to deny that they would have to adjust their conception of what was being done, along with their conception of what was doing it.

There is, however, another version of the criticism which is rather more subtle and interesting. It does not deny that Hume could tell the difference between a question of psychology and a question of logic. Instead, it says that when he addressed himself to psychological questions he seems to have been subconsciously influenced by the thought of corresponding questions of a logical kind, with the result that

[21] THN p. 165.

although his psychology is not very good psychology, it can yield excellent analytical points when 'translated' into the logical mode. What this comes to is best shown by considering an example of a case about which the claim has been made.

In the famous chapter 'Of Scepticism with regard to the Senses'[22] Hume sets out to investigate 'the *causes* which induce us to believe in the existence of body'. The answer, as might be expected, turns out to be complex, but only one aspect of it concerns us here: the nature of the input to the mind needed to trigger off the process leading to the formation of a belief in an external world which is causally and spatially distinct from us and which continues to exist when not perceived by us. The input to the belief-forming mechanism Hume always conceives of as consisting in impressions, items of perceptual consciousness not too far removed from the 'sensory states' or 'sense data' of recent perceptual theory. The question then is: just what sort of impressions have this effect? And that question has a close parallel in the sort of account of the physical world given by logical positivists and those of similar inclination. They took it that the content of the concepts we use could be analysed in terms of the type of sensory experience needed to justify their application. So if asked, not to explain causally the belief in an independent external world (a problem which they passed on to the natural scientist), but to *analyse* its content or meaning, they would take this as a question closely related to Hume's: what is the relevant type of sensory experience or impression?

What now struck commentators of the positivist and neo-positivist period was that the two questions tended to receive identical answers. When Hume told us what properties of impressions were apt to produce the belief in an independently existing object, they were the same (give or take a little imprecision and terminological change) as the ones which the positivist school would specify as giving the *content of the belief* that there exist such objects. This, it was felt, had to be more than coincidence, and the hypothesis arose that Hume was somehow really thinking of conceptual analysis when he took himself to be thinking of causal origins. This hypothesis is part of a general recent tendency to overestimate the importance of

[22] THN Bk. I Pt. IV Sect. II.

conceptual analysis in Hume's philosophy, no doubt partly the outcome of a tendency to overestimate his closeness to logical positivism. I shall return to it; what I want to say now is that the hypothesis is quite unnecessary to account for the textual facts. Hume is trying to find features of the input which, his theory about the workings of the mind being assumed, are necessary and sufficient to evoke the given belief. As we have seen, this input consists for him of impressions, which means that he will be seeking those characteristics which our impressions have when, and only when, we take them to be perceptions of an independent external world. The positivist is looking for necessary and sufficient conditions of the truth of the belief, and he holds that these must consist in the occurrence, actual or hypothetical, of certain types of impression. Now he only needs to think in addition—as most positivists did and nearly everyone does—that when we hold this belief it is in general true, to be faced with a question scarcely distinguishable from Hume's, namely: what distinctive features are possessed by just those groupings of impressions (sense data) which we take to be perceptions of independent physical things? So it would in fact have been quite surprising if their answers had not been pretty much alike, and the hypothesis that one party was somehow under the influence of the other party's question is completely redundant.

In spite of these failed attempts there is, I believe, a way in which Hume's vision of the relationship between the logical and the psychological really should make the twentieth-century reader pause for thought. If it is to be reduced to a formula, it would be this: that he thinks of reason as being in one respect much more like a psychological process than we are inclined to, in another way much less. Think of his standard procedure: given a certain type of belief, such as that in the conclusion of inductive arguments, or in causes, or 'body', or the continuity of the self, he will first show that it cannot be produced in us by reason; then he will go on to say how it is in fact produced, namely by the associative mechanism in accordance with his quasi-Newtonian theory of the workings of the mind, often given the general title of 'the imagination'. This way of thinking puts reason and the imagination, logic and psychology, very much on a par with each other. They are, admittedly, different things having different modes of operation; but both have the same kind of output: they both produce beliefs, and given any belief, one can sensibly ask whether it was reason, or the imagination, or something else again (the senses, perhaps) which produced it. They are competitors in the same market.

If nowadays we were asked to give the origins of a belief, we would not regard the answer 'It is produced by reason' as an alternative to an answer in causal, psycho-physiological terms. We would rather suppose that for every belief there is an answer of the latter kind, and that of some beliefs one can further show that they satisfy certain normative principles of logic and evidence. But for Hume, as we have seen, to say that it was produced by reason *is* an alternative answer to the genetic question; in this respect he regards it as rather more like a psychological answer than we would.

In other respects, however, he regards it as less like a psychological answer. For when he says that a belief is produced by reason (and for all his scepticism, there are a few beliefs which he holds to be produced by it), that is not the prelude to any more detailed explanation, whereas the claim that a belief is the product of the imagination is always followed by an exact account of the workings of the associative mechanism, the transfer of 'force and vivacity' from impressions to ideas, and suchlike. Reason just perceives 'relations of ideas', and there's an end to the story, as far as Hume is concerned.

One might be inclined to explain this by saying that Hume simply didn't get round to it—the trend of his investigation was away from the *a priori* and towards the formation of *a posteriori* beliefs. But not only would that be doubtful; there is another fact to be explained as well: Hume has a marked tendency to treat 'reason' as a normative concept, not just a genetic one. It is, after all, one of his favourite strategies to argue that since there can be no valid *a priori* argument for a given type of belief, therefore beliefs of that type are not produced in us by reason. But if reason is conceived of as a faculty of the mind, parallel to the imagination, such a strategy tacitly assumes that it is infallible and cannot malfunction. For if it could malfunction, why should it not be responsible for the existence of a certain belief, even though no *valid a priori* reasoning from known premisses could be given for it. Couldn't reason be in some way misshapen and hence productive of certain natural illusions? Kant was shortly to take that view, and Hume himself certainly took it with respect to the imagination.

So what Hume calls 'reason' appears as a part of the machine, but one that does not itself have any inner mechanism (in contrast to the imagination), and one that cannot go wrong—*prima facie* an odd collection of attributes. But if we think of reason as the concept which Hume, for his polemical purposes, has taken over from the ambience of the Similarity Thesis, the apparent anomaly becomes quite understandable. Within the tradition, the possession of reason is one of the main links between the human and the divine natures. Reason in human beings is to be that same faculty which is pre-eminently found in God. Its operation, in man, may be sluggish and limited in scope, but still it is the divine spark present in us, and as such it will *in itself* be perfect— such defects as it may seem to have must be due to the faulty performance of some other human capacity. This helps us to see how a philosopher of this period could think that reason, though an independent part of the human cognitive apparatus—and not merely a way of talking about the operations of other parts of the apparatus in so far as they meet certain standards—must always function properly when it functions at all, and hence that no belief for which there was no completely cogent argument could possibly be due to it. And at the same time it also helps us to see why he would not expect there to be any account of how the faculty worked, anything like a mechanism by means of which it acted. For he would think of reason in man as basically the same faculty as reason in God, differing through finitude of power and range only; and he would not think of God's reason as working by any 'mechanism' or intermediate steps, but rather as a direct comprehension of its objects. To suppose otherwise would come too close to holding that God's power of thought was dependent on certain laws of (divine) nature which he could therefore not in any way have designed or planned, so making him a subordinate part of a larger system rather than the origin of all systems and all things.

In building these seemingly anomalous features into his concept of reason, Hume is not creating a monster but displaying the accuracy of his deeper philosophical instincts. One must always remember, of course, that this is the doctrine of reason on which his scepticism focuses; he is quite happy to use the word 'reason' in his own positive attempt at a science of the mind—but there it is a different creature altogether.

3.   Thinking, believing and being: the hunt for causes

We now return to the subject of the relative importance of the epistemological, analytic and ontological strands in Hume's thinking. Our underlying hypothesis suggested that it will be the epistemological strand, that is to say the rejection of a particular theory of the origin and justification of our beliefs and its replacement by something more acceptable, which will take pride of place, and that analysis and ontology will have a subordinate role. It might be thought, however, that even should this prove to be the case, any attempt to connect it with his opposition to the Image of God doctrine is gratuitous, since the same order of priorities can be seen as the consequence of the fact that Hume had set himself to produce a science of man.

As a preliminary to this section I should like to point out, therefore, that this is at best only half true. The anthropological nature of Hume's project may, admittedly, explain his relative indifference towards ontological questions. If we are concerned to investigate the issue of why do human beings believe that X, or fear that X, or prefer X to Y, then whether or not X is *really the case* may well be of little interest, since it may have no work to do in the explanation of these mental phenomena. For Hume, that will in fact be the normal position: his explanation of our beliefs starts with the nature of our impressions, so that if a belief is not actually about our impressions but, for example, tomorrow's sunrise, or some necessary connection between the events perceived, then the truth or falsehood of the belief is no part of the history of its origin; if *those* impressions occur, so will the belief, even if it is false; if they don't, it won't, even if it would have been true.

But what can be said of ontology cannot with anything like the same plausibility be said of the analytical strand, represented in Hume's philosophy by the theory of ideas. Facts about the content of our thought, whether we believe them or not, about the nature of our concepts and how we come by them, are just as much facts about our mental life as are facts about what we believe and under what conditions. There is no reason why a science of man should have a preferential interest in either above the other; if a preference is found we need some further explanation of it.

This section will argue that a preference is indeed found, that Hume's interest in matters epistemological does take pride of place over questions of conceptual analysis, that his theory of belief is more important to him than his theory of ideas. It will do so by looking closely at his writings about causality. If the precedence of the epistemological over the analytical can be observed here the fact will be particularly telling, since *prima facie* one might well think just the opposite, as many commentators clearly have done. After all, what is undoubtedly the kernel of his thought on the subject begins with a search for the impression from which the *idea* of power is derived, and ends by *defining* a cause, activities which fall squarely in the analytic area; the search for the impression is supposed to allow us to apply Hume's 'mental microscope'[23] to the idea and so discern its exact content, whilst a definition is (is it not?) a statement of the content of the idea defined. Nevertheless, we shall see that the primacy of epistemology for Hume expresses itself here in two ways. One is the fact that, having approached his problem in terms of the theory of ideas and their related impressions, he soon stops taking the details of that theory at all seriously. The other is the way in which, whilst to all intents and purposes arguing about the origin of the idea of power, he employs as his main argument a point from the epistemological side of his thinking, the connection of which with the conceptual question (whence, if at all, do we obtain the idea of cause?) is mysterious and is allowed to

[23] ECHU p. 62.

remain so. The emphasis of Hume's concerns emerges clearly—more clearly than it emerged to Hume himself, it seems.

As is well known, Hume presents his investigation of causality as the search for a particular impression, that from which the idea of 'power or necessary connexion' is derived. The problem is to find the nature of the idea which corresponds to 'causes' when we think or say that *A* causes *B*. Given Hume's principles governing the origin and nature of ideas, this is equivalent to discovering the impression in which it originates, since it is simply a copy of this impression. Therefore:

To be fully acquainted . . . with the idea of power or necessary connexion, let us examine its impression; and in order to find the impression with greater certainty, let us search for it in all the sources, from which it may possibly be derived.[24]

His first move is just what this programme leads the reader to expect: it is to ask exactly what is perceived when we observe some causal interaction. When we see one billiard ball collide with another there is nothing, apart from the motion of the first ball and the subsequent motion of the second, that 'appears to the outward senses'. This overstates the case a little: there normally is a third impression, an auditory one. But the strength of Hume's point does not rest on the literal truth of the claim that there is no other impression, but rather on the fact that any others there might be would all be regarded as impressions of further events or objects, further members of the causal chain, *not* as the impression of the linking power or 'necessary connexion'.

So far there are no surprises. We are investigating the properties of a certain idea, so we look for the corresponding impression, the one from which it is copied. An impression is a perceptual state of a mind, so we ask what perceptual states occur when we perceive one event causing another. But with the next paragraph comes something unexpectedly different:

From the first appearance of an object, we never can conjecture what effect will result from it. But were the power or energy of any cause discoverable by the mind, we could foresee the effect, even

[24] Ibid. p. 63.

without experience; and might, at first, pronounce with certainty concerning it, by mere dint of thought and reasoning.[25]

Here epistemological considerations, questions about the circumstances under which we could know something, have suddenly come to the fore. But it is only reasonable to assume, from his silence on the subject, that Hume is still continuing on the same course, and giving another argument for the claim that there is no outward impression of power. If he is not, then he has abandoned the analytical question right at the beginning, and the thesis that analysis is less important to him than epistemology is already strongly confirmed. But to suppose that he has abandoned it would surely be premature: the thought appears to be that if there were an impression of power we could then tell by inspection of the cause what effect it would have, without waiting for, or drawing on, experience. Hume then calls up one of his most famous epistemological results, shown by the argument from the conceivability of the contrary, that the effects of a cause can never be known *a priori*. Therefore there is no impression of power.

What reason have we been given, however, to accept the first premiss, that if there were an impression of power we could predict the effect *a priori*? One can imagine the following response from the opposition: 'We admit your point that causal truths cannot be known *a priori*, but what we maintain does not conflict with it. All that it shows is that the idea of causing *B* isn't part of the idea of *A*, with which we fully agree. We simply hold that sometimes, when we perceive a causal interaction, we have an impression of "bringing about", or "causing", as well as the impressions of the two events involved; and that this is the impression from which we copy the idea you are looking for.'

Hume has, in theory, two lines of reply. One would be to say that such an impression, because of what it is supposed to be the impression of, *would* have to make *a priori* knowledge of causal truths possible. This line, as we shall see, leads into deep complications. The other would be to refer back to his first argument, that there just is no such impression. That would be to admit that the second argument does not work: if

[25] Ibid. p. 63.

the first argument succeeds, the matter is settled; if it doesn't, the second won't help.

If the second argument made just this one brief appearance, no doubt we could and probably should shrug it off. But in fact Hume now continues by presenting variants of it for several pages. Having considered the outward case, he now wants to show that the missing impression cannot be found by looking at mental causation, either when we move our body, or when 'we raise up a new idea'. There are a number of such arguments,[26] and all of them have the same form: if there were an impression of power we should know things which in fact we do not. Thus, if there were such an impression we should know how the mind is able to affect matter,[27] we should know *a priori* what we can in fact only know from experience, such as that the will can move the fingers but not the heart or liver. But why the impression of power, if it occurred, would necessarily bring all these benefits with it, we are not told. Consider this example, of the many available:

> Secondly, we are not able to move all the organs of the body with a like authority; though we cannot assign any reason besides experience, for so remarkable a difference between one and the other. Why has the will an influence over the tongue and fingers, not over the heart or liver? This question would never embarrass us, were we conscious of a power in the former case, not in the latter.[28]

But why not? The position would simply be that in some cases we could exert the will, then observe the impression of power and that of the required bodily movement, whereas in others we could exert the will without either of these further impressions making any appearance. The puzzle would remain: to know why they sometimes did and sometimes did not follow upon the act of willing, depending upon which organ one willed to move. So isn't Hume imposing a gratuitously strong condition on the impression, one that suggests that his real interest is in the epistemological questions, how we know or come to believe truths about causes, and only secondarily in the content of the concept as

---

[26] Ibid. pp. 63–69.
[27] Ibid. p. 65.
[28] Ibid. p. 65.

revealed by the dictum that every idea is a copy of an impression?

What might account for this apparent (and seemingly unconscious) drift towards the epistemological, apart from the hypothesis that knowledge and belief, rather than the nature of ideas, is Hume's real focus? One suggestion I have heard can be disposed of quickly. It says that the drift is only apparent: what happened in the first argument was that Hume denied that the idea of cause might have its origin in the senses, and he is now going on to ask whether it could have its origin in reason. Two major difficulties rule this interpretation out, however. In the first place, Hume tells us clearly in the opening sentences of each of the next two paragraphs that he is still pursuing the question of what is and what is not *perceived*. In the first he is speaking of outward impressions:

In reality, there is no part of matter, that does ever, *by its sensible qualities*, discover any power or energy . . .[29]

In the second it is inner perceptions, what Hume calls 'impressions of reflection', that are involved:

let us see, whether this idea be derived from reflection on the operations of our own minds, and be *copied from any internal impression.*[30]

This stress on what is not perceived would be irrelevant to the question of whether the idea of causality may not be arrived at by reasoning. And the hypothesis that it is that question which Hume is here addressing himself to faces a second difficulty at least as great. In the footnote to this passage,[31] where Hume really (and explicitly) is considering the possibility that the idea of power may be arrived at by reasoning, he dismisses it almost contemptuously in a couple of lines. It is not to be entertained that he was simultaneously engaged in producing, over several pages, strenuous and detailed arguments against the very same possibility.

But to go back a step: could it really be a necessary condition of an impression's being the impression of power

---

[29] Ibid. p. 63. (italics mine).
[30] Ibid. p. 64 (italics mine).
[31] Ibid. p. 64 note.

that its mere occurrence make possible this *a priori* knowledge of which Hume writes? Hardly: there is no impression the mere occurrence of which gives us knowledge, since any impression can be illusory; why should this putative impression be asked to pass a test which any impression must fail? But perhaps we ought to reformulate the test: the occurrence of the impression should at least make us *believe* in the existence of some *a priori* knowable connection between the cause and the effect. That would in a sense be very reasonable. For, given Hume's theory of belief, where there is an impression of an X there ought to be belief in an X: belief, on his view, is the occurrence of a particularly vivid idea, and nothing more vivid than an impression. Arguably, then, were there on some occasion an impression of 'power or necessary connection', there should be a belief that power was being exercised, or that some necessary connection obtained. But even then we would still be well short of what Hume demands: not just that we believe that there is power, or necessary connection, but that in addition we can see that it is the power of A to produce B; and in addition to *that*, that we could forecast its existence just on the basis of our idea of A—and this seems to be simply gratuitous.

Besides, this whole line is in confusing conflict with at least two features of Hume's thought. First, there is his somewhat underdeveloped epistemology of *a priori* knowledge, which consists, according to him, in the perception of relations between ideas, not of the two related ideas and a third. If in some cases we did know *a priori* that A and B were connected, we would know it by having perceived a relationship between the idea of A and the idea of B, not by having both of these accompanied by a further idea (or impression). Second, although there are *some* grounds for attributing to Hume the view that where there is an impression of an X there is *ipso facto* a belief in an X, equally there are grounds for not doing so. For the impression of a table, for Hume, appears to be a visual (?) image of a table. But to believe in a table is to believe in the presence of an independent and continuing object, and Hume of course spends a whole chapter explaining that such beliefs come about only when these images occur in an intricate context of consistency and coherence amongst our various perceptions. He does not, therefore, seem to hold the general principle just stated relating impressions to beliefs; so the question returns: why should he hold it in respect of *causality* in particular?

Another feature of Hume's approach is also puzzling. Why does he speak of the idea of 'power or necessary connexion'? Does he take it that the idea of power could only be an idea of necessary connection, where 'necessary' implies that it belongs to the kind of which *a priori* knowledge is possible? It seems that he does, since he never gives any indication that they might be different ideas, whilst the speed with which his thought passes to the topic of *a priori* knowledge strongly suggests that he understands 'necessary' in that sense. It looks as if he has just ignored what the modern reader will think of as an obvious *prima facie* possibility, that there is a necessity stronger than concomitance but weaker than the deductive, and it is of this that we are seeking the impression and idea.

It is noteworthy that this is just the direction in which a polemical concern with the Image of God doctrine would have led. We have seen[32] how that doctrine would promote a view of causal connections as being infallible[33] and open to the highest degree of rational insight. The wording of Hume's text leaves little room for doubt that he has that type of connection in mind; at one point its pedigree appears on the surface in full view:

Volition is surely an act of the mind, with which we are sufficiently acquainted. Reflect upon it. Consider it on all sides. Do you find anything in it like this creative power, by which it raises up a new idea, and with a kind of *Fiat*, imitates the omnipotence of its Maker . . .[34]

That last phrase could be copied from Leibniz.

All that is clear here is that there is a muddle, but enough can be seen for us to make a plausible guess at what is causing it: Hume is trying to force his analytic theory about ideas and their origin in impressions into a very uncomfortable and dubious relationship with his epistemological theory about the

---

[32] Above, Chapter 1 Section 4.
[33] A word which Hume sometimes uses: see e.g. ECHU p. 65, top.
[34] ECHU p. 69.

acquisition of knowledge and the formation of belief. Whether this is a misguided attempt to gain further evidence for his claim about the idea, or a manifestation of the tendency to slip away from the theory of ideas and impressions to the area where his interests really lie, is something on which it would be premature to be confident. But there is much more in Section VIII of the first *Enquiry* (and elsewhere) to favour the latter alternative—we have not yet seen anything like the full extent of the tangle between the conceptual and the epistemological in Hume's pages.

So far we have seen the tangle in Hume's choice of arguments. It is also visible in his choice of words. Such expressions as 'were we conscious of a power'[35] show just the right ambiguity: they can mean 'were we to have the impression of a power', but equally easily 'were we to have knowledge of a power'. Nor does the first entail the second, since presumably any impression can occur illusorily—and yet an illusory impression of power, one which occurred though no power had in fact been exercised, would do just as well as the original of someone's idea of power as would a veridical one. So one might have the idea of power by this route without any justifiable claim to knowledge. They are therefore not equivalent, and if Hume failed to notice this then *that* fact calls for explanation, all the more so since he uses one example which ought to bring the thought of a possible illusion clearly to mind:

A man, suddenly struck with a palsy in the leg or arm, or who had newly lost those members, frequently endeavours, at first, to move them, and employ them in their usual offices. Here he is as much conscious of a power to command such limbs, as a man in perfect health is conscious of a power to actuate any member which remains in its natural state and condition. But consciousness never deceives. Consequently, neither in the one case nor in the other, are we ever conscious of any power.[36]

The key phrase here is 'consciousness never deceives'. For the argument to go through, this has to imply that if there *is* no power, there is no *impression* of power. From that we could

---

[35] Ibid. p. 65.
[36] Ibid. p. 66.

indeed conclude, given that the palsied man and the healthy man have the same impressions, as Hume claims, that there was no impression of power in either case. But if that is what is meant by 'consciousness never deceives', it isn't true, and Hume cannot seriously have thought that it was, once he got the question into sharp focus. The example in fact shows nothing at all about the immediate contents of our consciousness as they are in themselves, and so does not connect with the theory of ideas and their origin in impressions. The point that it can legitimately be used to make is an epistemological one: it is impermissible to conclude from the feeling that we have the power to move our limbs (assuming that there is such a feeling) that we do indeed have the power. At least, the conclusion is not deductively drawn. Nor is it the strongest kind of induction, for Hume has just specified a factual counter-example. That we can (almost always) move our limbs is something we find not by deduction from the immediate presentations of consciousness, but from our (almost invariable) success in moving them. Which is exactly what Hume says in the very next sentence: 'We learn the influence of our will from experience alone.' Contrary to the author's professed intentions, this passage is not about the formation of the *concept of power*. It is about what we *know* and how we come to know it: not from reason operating on the deliverances of consciousness, but more mundanely from what experience tells us about the constant course of nature. Epistemology rules, and Hume's appeal to the slogan that 'consciousness never deceives' only indicates that he has not, at this stage, fully realised what he is up to.

The tendency to slough off the theory of impressions and ideas in favour of his epistemological aims emerges ever more clearly as the denouement approaches. We find ourselves facing a crisis of the analytic or conceptual kind; meaninglessness threatens, words without ideas:

the necessary conclusion *seems* to be that we have no idea of connexion or power at all, and that these words are absolutely without meaning . . .[37]

Hume is still hopeful, however. The belief in a causal

37 Ibid. p. 74.

connection arises only from the experience of multiple instances of the conjunction of cause and effect—here he comes close to the rather optimistic assumption that we only believe causal propositions when we are justified in doing so— so, since the belief presupposes the idea, there must be something about the multiple case which is capable of generating it. What special new impression arises, then, from 'a repetition of similar instances'? Answer:

> only, that . . . the mind is carried by habit, upon the appearance of one event, to expect its usual attendant, and to believe that it will exist. This connexion, therefore, which we *feel* in the mind, this customary transition of the imagination from one object to its usual attendant, is the sentiment or impression from which we form the idea of power or necessary connexion.[38]

This is extremely curious. Over the last ten pages Hume has argued repeatedly that there is no impression of power that is observed when we move our bodies or call up ideas in our minds. Now it turns out that after all there is some such feeling of connection (a 'sentiment or impression') when an idea arises involuntarily by virtue of its association with another idea (or impression) which is already present to consciousness. Nothing is said as to how this can be, how this case can differ from the ones previously dismissed. One would have thought that both types of argument used then could be used again with the same effect. Firstly, that there is no third impression of reflection, but just the impression of one idea followed by that of the other. Secondly, the 'feeling', if it occurs, does not allow us *a priori* insight into the necessity of this particular succession of ideas[39]—which was earlier deemed enough to show that no impression of power is found. So careless is he about the detail of the conceptual branch of his theory, and that at the very moment of climax when the elusive impression is (supposedly) finally being revealed.

That, however, is not the only startling feature of the passage. Hume does not just speak of the 'connexion . . . which we feel in the mind' as being the sought-after

---

[38] Ibid. p. 75.

[39] E.g. THN p. 169: 'The uniting principle among our internal perceptions is as unintelligible as that among external objects, and is not known to us any other way than by experience.'

impression; he also adds, in apposition, the phrase 'this customary transition of the imagination from one object to its usual attendant'. But a transition, customary or not, is not a further impression. 'Customary transition' is simply Hume's way of referring to the fact that the impression or idea of the causing event is followed regularly in the mind by the idea of the effect. So whatever one may think about the rest of the sentence taken by itself—as we have seen, it is quite mysterious enough—the words 'this customary transition of the imagination from one object to its usual attendant' do not fit into it at all. They belong, clearly, to the epistemological side of Hume's enterprise, not the conceptual; they do not go along with the theory of ideas and impressions, the hunt for an impression of which the idea of cause may be the copy, but with his associationist theory of the origin of belief. The repeated experience of a concomitance between A and B generates an association between their ideas, which results in a 'transition of the imagination' from the thought or perception of one to the thought of the other, and then in certain cases allows the first to enliven the idea of the second to the point at which it becomes a belief in the existence of its object. Thus the mind is brought '. . . upon the appearance of one event, to expect its usual attendant, and to believe that it will exist'.[40] Once again the epistemology, here in the form of the theory of belief, asserts itself, and in the very sentence in which Hume is trying, albeit somewhat half-heartedly, to make the decisive pronouncement about the theory of ideas and impressions in its application to the concept of causality.

There is, it is true, an ambiguity in the phrase 'the idea of a necessary connexion' which spans just the distinction that Hume here smudges over, that between thinking of something and believing in its existence. It matches very closely the ambiguity of 'consciousness of a power', upon which we have already dwelt. But to try to attribute the vacillations of Section VII of the *Enquiry Concerning Human Understanding* to a failure on Hume's part to perceive this ambiguity would be very shallow. When he writes on the nature of belief he shows unmistakably how well he understands the difference between merely entertaining an idea and believing in its content; his

[40] ECHU p. 75.

whole approach to the subject is precisely to pose the question, in what this difference may consist.[41] Besides, the alternative hypothesis, that the weight of Hume's interests lay in the epistemological sector and that he had made something of a false start by beginning with the theory of ideas and impressions, has at least two major advantages. In the first place, it is itself explicable in terms of the preoccupations of his immediate philosophical ancestors; the prevalence of the Insight Ideal accounts for the epistemological bias, and the contemporary prominence of Locke's *Essay* with its heavy emphasis on the nature and genesis of ideas accounts for the attractiveness of the false start. In the second place, it can help us to find our way through other parts of his text, where the ambiguity just mentioned cannot be part of the story. We should now look at one of these, closely related to the passage we have just been discussing: Hume's notoriously disparate 'two definitions of cause'.

4. *Thinking, believing and being: the two definitions*

The problem is well known. Towards the end of the relevant sections of both the first *Enquiry* and the *Treatise of Human Nature* we find two statements, each of which is said to be a definition of cause.[42] We are used to the idea that there may be two definitions of one concept if the alternatives are allowed to differ from each other only verbally whilst still counting as two, but Hume's two definitions are not like that. His *definienses* quite certainly differ in intension, and arguably in extension as well. I shall consider them as they appear in the *Treatise*, since one of the best-known discussions of the puzzle, J. A. Robinson's paper *Hume's Two Definitions of 'Cause'*, and the consequent exchange between him and Thomas J. Richards, takes the *Treatise* as its basis. Here, to refresh the reader's memory, are the two definitions:

(1) We may define a CAUSE to be 'An object precedent and contiguous to another, and where all the objects resembling the former are plac'd in like relations of

[41] Ibid. pp. 47–8.
[42] THN pp. 169–70, ECHU pp. 76–7.

precedency and contiguity to those objects, that resemble the latter'.

(2) 'A CAUSE is an object precedent and contiguous to
another, and so united with it, that the idea of the one
determines the mind to form the idea of the other, and
the impression of the one to form a more lively idea of
the other.'

Robinson and Richards take their cue from Hume's statement[43] that in the first definition cause is defined as a
'philosophical relation', in the second as a 'natural relation'.
Their understanding of this distinction is, I think, quite
correct: any many-placed predicate is a philosophical relation,
but only those relations are 'natural' which bring about an
association of the relevant ideas in the mind of an observer.
According to Robinson the first definition really is a
definition, in the modern sense of being an analysis of the
concept of cause. The second is not a definition at all, but ' . . .
simply a restatement of the proposition that the (already
defined) cause—effect relation is a *natural* relation, in a
somewhat elliptical formulation.'[44] Richards[45] finds the supposed ellipse too eccentric to be credible. One has to agree;
Hume's command of English would have needed to fail
completely for him to use the wording of (2) just to make that
point. So, whilst accepting Robinson's account of the first
definition, Richards provides an alternative reading of the
second: it is a statement of the conditions under which one
may properly believe, or assert, that one thing causes another;
the two definitions give us respectively truth conditions and
assertibility conditions for causal propositions.

Robinson's response to this contains several acceptable
points. He chides Richards for introducing a normative
element into his reading of the second definition, holding that
it is better regarded as a statement of the conditions under
which belief in a causal connection does *in fact* arise, rather

[43] THN pp. 169–70.

[44] J. A. Robinson: 'Hume's Two Definitions of "Cause"', in *The Philosophical
Quarterly* Vol. XII (1962) pp. 162–171, this quotation p. 167. Reprinted in *Hume*,
ed.V. C. Chappell (Macmillan 1968) pp. 129–147, this quotation p. 139.

[45] T. J. Richards: 'Hume's Two Definitions of "Cause"', *The Philosophical Quarterly*
Vol. XV (1965) pp. 247–253. Reprinted in ibid. pp. 148–161.

than those under which it is proper to hold a causal belief. He agrees that Richards' suggestion '. . . certainly makes sense of the fact that Hume does state that (1) and (2) are both definitions . . .', (which his own version did not), but claims on the other hand that '. . . it surely does not make sense of Hume's further claim, that (1) and (2) are both definitions *of the same notion* ("different views of the same object"),' (whereas his version did). He continues: 'However, any attempt tò sort out Hume's intentions in this matter is going to fail to make sense of *part* at least of what Hume said about (1) and (2) . . '.[46] Here we diverge; this pessimism is premature. It is forced upon him by an assumption which he and Richards apparently share, namely that Hume's term 'definition' must, if at all possible, be taken in its modern sense of the exhibiting of necessary and sufficient conditions for the defined concept, much the same as that of 'analysis'. It is an offshoot of a much more general assumption, to which I have already referred: the widespread tendency to think of Hume as a forerunner of the logical positivist movement, hence to emphasise the importance in his thought of conceptual and analytical considerations and to read in that light any remarks which look as if they might allow of it. The word 'definition', given its usage in twentieth-century philosophy, invites such a reading, so let us try to forget its connotations in the area of synonymy, analysis and intensional equivalence, and locate it instead in Hume's mechanics of belief, in accordance with the general policy of emphasising his epistemology.

We may then take a tip from Robinson's treatment of the second 'definition', and hypothesize that a definition of cause, for Hume, is a statement of the conditions under which belief in a cause—effect relationship does in fact come about. Can we not understand both definitions in this way, as two different descriptions of the conditions that generate belief? If we can, it will make sense both of Hume's assertion that they are 'different views of the same object' and of the fact that he calls them both 'definitions'.

There is, of course, a *prima facie* objection to this procedure, and it looks to be a serious one: at the beginning of his first

---

[46] J. A. Robinson: 'Hume's Two Definitions of "Cause" Reconsidered' in *Hume*, ed. V. C. Chappell p. 165. Preceding two quotations same reference.

paper Robinson contends that the two definitions are not even extensionally equivalent; put less technically, there are circumstances to which one applies and the other does not. My proposal could perfectly well survive their lack of *intensional* equivalence, the fact, in other words, that they are not synonymous. The point would be that they would always apply together if they applied at all, in virtue of the way in which Hume's laws of association operate. Thus if the condition stipulated in (1) held of a given pair of objects, that would produce the association of the ideas of those objects that is described by (2). And since there is, on Hume's account, no other way to produce that type of association, the truth of (2) would, conversely, require the truth of (1). But if, on the other hand, they are not even *extensionally* equivalent, then clearly there is a problem. If one can be true when the other is not, how can they be called 'views of the same object'?

It certainly looks as if they are not extensionally equivalent. In the first place, a pair of 'objects' could satisfy the first definition without ever having been observed to do so, or even without ever having been observed at all. Presumably there actually are many such pairs in the world, and Hume, who sometimes speaks of 'the operation of secret causes', is far from denying it. But if the relations between the objects have not been observed, nobody will associate the idea of one with that of the other, therefore they will not satisfy the second definition. Conversely, the second may be satisfied without the first. That will happen, for instance, in cases where we *wrongly* believe some pair of events to be respectively cause and effect of each other. The associations of ideas will exist, as specified in (2), but it will not be the case that all events like the first will be followed by events like the second, so that (1) will not hold of them.

All this has to be admitted, but the problem is not insoluble so long as we approach the passage with the general principle in mind that Hume is stating the conditions which give rise to a belief in causal connection. There is then no special difficulty about the second definition, at least: Hume is saying that, for any pair of events for which it holds, the observer in question will believe the first to be the cause of the second. He may later be disappointed in his expectations, the concomitance between events of these types may turn out to be less universal than he had thought, in which case he will revise his opinions. The first definition, however, looks more troublesome. It is clear that no belief will arise unless there is some mind that observes the regular concomitance. Definition (1) makes no mention of any observer, so it doesn't, on Hume's or anyone else's view of causality, state sufficient conditions for the formation of a causal belief.

But how much of a problem is this, really? If at this stage Hume's mind was firmly fixed on the mechanics of belief, might he not have felt the need for an observer to be so obvious that explicit mention of it would be superfluous and pedantic? All the more so since he has given a hint of it in the preceding sentence, where we were told that the two definitions differ by asking us to consider causality '. . . either as a philosophical or as a natural relation; either as a comparison of two ideas, or as an association between them'. To say that the first definition makes us consider causality as a comparison of *ideas* indicates that the thought of the observer is not too far away.

There is some tidying up still to be done before this reading can be accepted, but first I should like to point out that the suggestion, that what Hume calls a definition is not, in our technical sense, a definition at all, is no *ad hoc* measure designed to deal with this one passage, nor is it wholly innovatory. It is not *ad hoc* because, firstly, it fits well with the hypothesis that Hume's prime philosophical concern was the destruction and replacement of the Insight Ideal, a hypothesis which itself fits well with the fact of the Insight Ideal's prominence in the thought of nearly all his greatest predecessors. Secondly, it is needed to solve another textual problem, this time from his writing on ethics. And it is not wholly innovatory, because it actually has been used in this connection.

That last remark refers to Antony Flew's article 'On the Interpretation of Hume',[47] in which he discusses a paper by Geoffrey Hunter.[48] Hunter had held it absurd to attribute to

[47] A. G. N. Flew: 'On the Interpretation of Hume', in *Philosophy* Vol. XXXVIII (1963) pp. 178–182.

[48] G. Hunter: 'Hume on Is and Ought', *Philosophy* Vol. XXXVII (1962) pp. 148–152.

Hume (as is of course standard practice) the view that no *Is* can entail any *Ought*, since he '... thinks that Ought-propositions are logically equivalent to certain Is-propos-itions.[49] This Hunter asserts on the basis of the sentence: 'So that when you pronounce any action or character to be vicious, you mean nothing but that, from the constitution of your nature, you have a feeling or sentiment of blame from the contemplation of it.'[50] He evidently supposes that when Hume writes 'you mean nothing but that' he is announcing a synonymy claim or analysis, involving at least logical equiva-lence of *definiens* and *definiendum*. But it is at least as plausible to place this terminology, which would nowadays belong firmly to *semantic* inquiry, in the context of Hume's quasi-Newtonian science of man. After the comment, only a little less apposite in the 1980s than when he wrote it, that Hume is often read as if his works had been written for publication in *Analysis*, Flew points this out, and closes his article by saying:

Hume's choice of phrase is also, surely, significant ... 'You pronounce ...' but 'you mean nothing but that ...' When phrases of this sort are employed the point usually is: not that this is what your words actually mean; but rather that this is what, if you would only face the facts and be honest, you would have to admit.

Even more interesting from our present point of view is another passage, this time from the first appendix to the *Enquiry Concerning the Principles of Morals* (and also mentioned by Flew), since in it we find the very word, 'define', which was at the centre of the trouble over Hume's account of cause. It runs:

The hypothesis which we embrace is plain. It maintains that morality is determined by sentiment. It defines virtue to be *whatever mental action or quality gives to a spectator the pleasing sentiment of approbation*; and vice the contrary. We then proceed to examine a plain matter of fact, to wit, what actions have this influence.[51]

If we really are to take this for a definition, as the term is nowadays understood, then it becomes quite inescapable that,

---

[49] Ibid. p. 149.
[50] Quoted from THN p. 469.
[51] Hume: *An Enquiry Concerning the Principles of Morals*, Appendix I, ed.L. A. Selby-Bigge, 3rd edn. revised by P. H. Nidditch, (Oxford 1975) p. 289.

for Hume, whether a given action is virtuous or vicious is 'a plain matter of fact'. Given that last sentence, the point could hardly have escaped him. Yet only two pages earlier he has based his proof that morality cannot rest on reason on the premiss that 'reason judges either of *matter of fact* or of *relations*', and challenged the opposition to produce the matter of fact or relation in which they hold morality to consist. We have the option of charging Hume with the most glaring howler, or concluding that this is not, in modern philosophical usage, a definition at all.

It seems, then, that there is good reason to be wary of reading Hume too heavily in terms of the conceptual—analytical part of his theory. Because of recent concentration on semantic analysis, those who have written about the history of philosophy, being all too ready to find their embryonic selves in the past, have played up this aspect of his thought until the reader became prepared to find it doing all the central work, whereas in truth it belongs quite near the periphery. We shall see yet more evidence for that claim before the end of the present chapter.

There is a residual puzzle about the 'two definitions' passage. I have said that it is best understood as presenting two descriptions of the circumstances under which belief in a causal connection arises, one concentrating on the outward situation, the other on the state of the believer's mind that those outward facts induce. This steers clear of the problem with which Robinson and Richards were grappling, but it does leave an important fact about the text unexplained: nowhere in the paragraph in which the two definitions are stated does Hume say anything about belief or knowledge, but he does say a great deal about *what a cause is*. Is that not the language of someone who is making an ontological point, telling us something about the way reality is, rather than an epistemological one about the genesis of our opinions?

Hume's attitude to ontological issues is complex; like that of Kant, it has at least two levels. We have already remarked that the negative aspects of his programme would lead us to expect a degree of agnosticism about the nature of reality: the claim that the real cannot be known in a certain way does not commit one to any further claims about what it is or is not

like. We have also remarked, in effect, that the positive side of
his endeavours would do little or nothing to reverse this
tendency. They are only concerned with what is real in so far
as it is necessary to account for our beliefs, for which job
Hume needs no more equipment than minds and their
impressions, at most. And there are in fact plenty of signs of
such agnosticism. For instance:

I am, indeed, ready to allow, that there may be several qualities
both in material and immaterial objects, with which we are utterly
unacquainted; and if we please to call these *power* or *efficacy*, 'twill be
of little consequence to the world.[52]

There is a tradition which, spurred on in a way I shall later
describe by the disastrous assimilation of Hume's philosophy
to logical positivism, sees such passages as ironical expressions of the negative ontological thesis that there are no such
qualities; but that assimilation needs to look to its own
defences. In any case, it is much harder to see irony in a
sentence like the following, used by Philo (and seemingly
assented to by Cleanthes) in his refutation of the cosmological
argument in Part IX of the *Dialogues Concerning Natural
Religion*:

and may it not happen, that, could we penetrate into the intimate
nature of bodies, we should clearly see why it was absolutely
impossible, they could ever admit of any other disposition?[53]

Cleanthes has just made the very similar point, that if there is
a necessarily existent being, it may be matter—the contrary
cannot be proved:

It must be some unknown, inconceivable qualities, which can make
[the Deity's] non-existence appear impossible, or his attributes
unalterable: And no reason can be assigned, why these qualities may
not belong to matter. As they are altogether unknown and
inconceivable, they can never be proved incompatible with it.[54]

It is very hard to read these as anything other than sincere
expressions of Hume's mature opinion, nor, since that should
not now surprise us, is there any reason to try. But Hume has

[52] THN p. 168.
[53] DCNR p. 191 (Part IX).
[54] DCNR p. 190 (Part IX).

another way of using ontological language: *for us*, human beings in the natural state of mind, there *are* causes, bodies, minds that preserve an identity through time—this is a consequence of his doctrine that we cannot help having these beliefs and seeing the world accordingly. It is only to be expected, therefore, that he will sometimes speak as if he firmly took there to be causes (and the rest); and equally it is to be expected that when he sets himself to investigate the question of what a cause is he will talk about the *belief* that there are causes and the circumstances under which this belief is held. On his theory, after all, this is the only thing that can be investigated under that heading; the deep metaphysical question about what it is, ultimately, that shifts the universe from one state into the next he regards as being beyond the reach of human inquiry. In a very similar way Kant, speaking as an empirical realist, will say that there are spatio-temporal objects, causes, substances, but then investigate them by talking about the way in which our sensibility and under-standing do, and must, work. So when Hume asks what an X is, and embarks on an answer rather than counselling a resigned agnosticism, we will do well to remember that there is a vague tacit clause roughly along the lines of 'so far as X can concern, or be known to, or pointfully investigated by, the human mind'. In fact, the clause is not even always tacit:

And as the constant conjunction of objects constitutes the very essence of cause and effect, matter and motion may often be regarded as the causes of thought, *as far as we have any notion of that relation.*[55]

Hence the famous equation of the causal connection with the genesis of our belief in it—no conflation of the logical and the psychological this, but a concise and powerful statement of the heart of Hume's position:

The necessary connexion between causes and effects is the found-ation of our inference from one to the other. The foundation of our inference is the transition arising from the accustomed union. These are, therefore, the same.[56]

Hence, also, the less consciously provocative explanation of

[55] THN p. 250 (italics mine).
[56] Ibid. p. 165.

his procedure in the paragraph of the *Treatise* immediately preceding the 'two definitions':

This order would not have been excusable, of first examining our inference from the relation before we had explain'd the relation itself, had it been possible to proceed in a different method. But as the nature of the relation depends so much on that of the inference, we have been oblig'd to advance in this seemingly preposterous manner . . .[57]

It should not therefore be felt as an objection to my suggested reading of the 'two definitions' that it treats statements which, *prima facie*, are about causality as being in the first instance concerned with what is *believed* about causes, and why. On the contrary, it is almost an argument in its favour. For since the two themes are (at any rate for purposes of serious investigation) virtually identified with each other by Hume's philosophy, it is highly likely that when he uses the language of ontology it will sometimes be illuminating to read what he says in terms of his theory of belief. This point is not restricted to his writings on causality; it can also be used to give an improved reading of the famous chapter 'Of Personal Identity', and indeed of his whole philosophy of mind, as I shall now try to show.

5. Thinking, believing and being: the mind

There is a widespread understanding of Hume's view of the mind according to which he held it to be nothing more than a sequence of ideas and impressions. That is not to say that he thought that any such sequence would do—it had to be a sequence possessing a certain unifying property—but that he positively denied the existence of a further item, distinct from the ideas and impressions, in which they occurred or by which they were perceived. This interpretation doesn't lack textual support:

They are the successive perceptions only, that constitute the mind . . .[58]

It is also widely held that this simple fact about Hume's

---

[57] Ibid. p. 169.
[58] Ibid. p. 253.

theory is enough to undo it; whereas a phenomenalistic account of physical objects may be a possibility, there is no possibility of a corresponding account of the mind. I am not concerned to argue this point in general, but I do believe that it has force against Hume, given other things which he certainly holds about mental activity.

Hume describes a mechanism by which the belief in the unity of the mind is generated. In choosing that starting-point, I am of course opting for my own favoured perspective, the epistemological; but the reader should notice that it is quite inessential to the following reasoning, which would be unaffected if we took the ontological road and supposed that Hume's mechanism is to generate the unity of the mind, not just the belief in it. What activates the mechanism, he tells us, are similarities between perceptions (the hold-all word for ideas and impressions) and causal relations between them.[59] Again, it is not essential to this critical argument that Hume should have selected precisely those features, but they will do as well as anything else to illustrate the crucial point: they are both properties which, as well as holding between various pairs of *my* perceptions, also hold between many of the perceptions that I have and some of the perceptions that others have. Presumably, many of one's perceptions resemble those of one's close associates, in virtue of such facts as that one does similar things, hence remembers many similar things, is frequently in much the same place at the same time and so has similar perceptions, and so on. Presumably, also, one's mental states sometimes stand in causal connection with those of others, as when for instance one talks to them. All of which raises the question: why do I not then take some of your mental states for mine? Or, in the ontological formulation, how do we come to have *separate* minds?

The difficulty, I should say at once, is not whether these questions can be answered—in fact, there is hardly anything easier—but whether they can be answered without inconsistency by Hume. The answer, obviously, is that your perceptions are no part of the input to the device which produces my belief in the unity of my mind. It is not as if there were a mechanism which was allowed first to survey all the

[59] Ibid. pp. 260–1.

perceptions there are, and then parcelled them out; if there were, and if it worked on anything like Humean principles, it would parcel them out very differently from the way it is actually done. But this is not how things are, nor is it how Hume saw it: perceptions arrive already done up into bundles and the apparatus of laws of association and the rest goes to work in each case on a *given* bundle. That means that each bundle must be seen as possessing some sort of unity, distinguishing its contents from those of other bundles, for which the mechanism cannot be responsible; this has to be a property of the *raw materials* for the process which Hume describes, without which the end-product would be something quite unrecognisable. So, the objection concludes, his position falls. He cannot dispense with a further element in his ontology of the mind, as it were some string to tie up his bundles. Given that string, there is at least the theoretical possibility of explaining in Humean style how each bundle comes to contain, as one of its constituent perceptions, a belief in its own unity; but without the further element, that is to say given the sum total of all perceptions with the demand to sort them out into individual minds, a Humean device would either do the wrong thing, or nothing at all.

The attack devastates its target, but whether it has hit Hume or only a decoy is another question. There must be at least a suspicion that only a decoy has suffered: the criticism is aimed at a theory which dogmatically denies the existence of anything other than the perceptions, and we have seen reason to doubt whether such a decisively negative pronouncement on an ontological point is really in the spirit of Hume's philosophy. Firstly, the nature of his enterprise does not appear to require it; secondly, we found examples of an explicitly stated agnosticism about such issues; and thirdly, we saw that even when he speaks in terms which, taken at face value, are ontological, it has to be seriously considered whether they may not be better understood by reference to his theory of belief. If we look at the chapter 'Of Personal Identity' with these points, and especially the third, in mind, the suspicion quickly ripens.

It is immediately noticeable that many of Hume's remarks to the effect that the mind *is nothing more* than perceptions are closely paired with the claim that we *have no idea* of the mind beyond our idea of the perceptions. A good example is the unequivocally ontological utterance of the last quotation, which turns out to be followed by an overtly conceptual one in the self-same sentence, separated only by a semi-colon:

They are the successive perceptions only, that constitute the mind; nor have we the most distant notion of the place, where these scenes are represented, or of the materials, of which it is compos'd.[60]

Another is to be found in the appendix to the *Treatise*, where Hume first argues that our perceptions 'must be the same with self', as if he were showing that there is nothing else to the mind, and then follows it closely with the paragraph:

Philosophers begin to be reconcil'd to the principle, *that we have no idea of external substance, distinct from the ideas of particular qualities*. This must pave the way for a like principle with regard to the mind, *that we have no notion of it, distinct from the particular perceptions*.[61]

These two claims, that we have no notion of something, cannot form any conception of it, and that it does not exist, sit rather oddly together; the oddity is highlighted by a comparison with Hume's procedure elsewhere. If there is no conception, no idea, then there is no rational argument, one way or the other—recall the passage from the *Dialogues Concerning Natural Religion* in which Cleanthes argues that if there are properties which confer necessary existence on their possessor, they may just as well belong to matter as to God, since 'As they are altogether unknown and inconceivable, they can never be proved incompatible with it.'[62] In the first *Enquiry* Hume put the same point in more general terms. Some philosophers, he tells us, finding natural causation incomprehensible, have tried to make God the only true cause of anything. But the power by which the mind of God acts is equally incomprehensible; we no more have an idea of it than of any other form of causation. So:

Were our ignorance, therefore, a good reason for rejecting anything, we should be led into that principle of denying all energy in the

---

[60] Ibid. p. 253.
[61] Ibid. (appendix) p. 635.
[62] DCNR p. 190 (Part IX) See also above, Chapter 2 Section 4.

Supreme Being as much as in the grossest matter. . . . All we know is our profound ignorance of both.[63]

It may be said that the *Dialogues* and the first *Enquiry* represent a later and less radically sceptical stage in Hume's development. Perhaps they do, but before we take that to mean that we should read all Hume's negative ontological pronouncements in the *Treatise* at their face value we should remember that we have seen in the earlier work evidence both of his ontological agnosticism and of a tendency to modify superficially ontological statements by a clause such as 'in so far as we have any notion'. We have seen reason why his ontological and epistemological theses are likely, as a perfectly proper consequence of his underlying theory, to become entangled. And if they become entangled conceptually, what cause for surprise if they also become entangled verbally? We have also seen in detail how this hypothesis facilitates understanding of the otherwise mysterious two definitions of cause.

Must it not then be worth the attempt to apply these same interpretative principles to Hume's theory of the mind, so far as proves possible? Perhaps we should take seriously—neither read straight over nor dismiss as ironical—the sentence from the Introduction to the *Treatise* which runs:

For to me it seems evident, that the essence of mind being equally unknown to us with that of external bodies, it must be equally impossible to form any notion of its powers and qualities otherwise than from careful and exact experiments, and the observation of those particular effects, which result from its different circumstances and situations.[64]

No unprejudiced reader would hear in that a denial of the 'essence of the mind', only that it is *unknown*. Newton-like, we may discover the laws that govern the phenomena, but to anyone who thinks that we can grasp the deep reality behind those laws there follows the sharp warning:

any hypothesis, that pretends to discover the ultimate original qualities of human nature, ought at first to be rejected as presumptuous and chimerical.

---

[63] ECHU p. 72–3.
[64] THN (Introduction) p. xvii (also next quotation).

What then are we to expect? Not that there is no mind apart from perceptions, but that we cannot know anything of it. But also that, as in the case of causality, we can as it were change gear and add our tacit rider to give the question: what is the mind *in so far as it is investigatable by us?* There will then follow an inquiry into the types of perceptions we have and the way in which they give rise to the beliefs we hold about the nature of our minds. When we are told that it is 'the successive perceptions only, that constitute the mind', we should hear this in much the same way as we hear 'the constant conjunction of objects constitutes the very essence of cause and effect'.[65] For we hear that knowing, firstly, that Hume does not wish to assert that causality is *in reality* just the constant conjunction of objects, secondly, that he does not think that the belief in causality is just a belief in constant conjunction, though it is constant conjunction that produces it, and thirdly, that it is followed in the text by the crucial caveat: as far as we have any notion of that relation. At least we will not then find ourselves attributing to Hume a position which collapses immediately under the impact of the considerations of the beginning of this section, and we shall have avoided that pitfall without foisting upon him anything discordant with his general approach.

When, in the chapter 'Of Scepticism with regard to the Senses', Hume considers external objects and our belief in them, he does not raise a question about the idea of body and start a search for the corresponding impression. Instead, he pitches straight into the issue of the *belief*: 'The subject, then, of our present enquiry is concerning the *causes* which induce us to believe in the existence of body . . .',[66] so making a direct line for what I suggest to be his real interest. But in 'Of Personal Identity' he reverts to the procedure observable in his writing on causality, beginning, apparently, with a hunt for the relevant ideas and impressions: '. . . nor have we any idea of *self*, after the manner it is here explain'd. For from what impression could this be deriv'd?'[67] Just like the search for the idea of 'power or necessary connexion', so too this one

---

[65] Ibid. p. 250.
[66] Ibid. pp. 187–8.
[67] Ibid. p. 251.

turns out to be not quite the genuine article, but another awkward amalgam with the question about the origin of the belief. We have been warned, in fact, before the word 'idea' is ever mentioned: the first paragraph of the section introduces the view, not just that there is an impression of the self, but that there is in our immediate consciousness an *infallible* basis for all manner of claims to *knowledge* about it. Must the impression of the self satisfy that condition? One is reminded of the demands Hume appeared to make of the impression of power, that its mere occurrence should render causal truths transparent *a priori*. In fact, he seems to have no intention of forcing any candidate for the title 'impression of the self' to take quite so stringent a test, but the test he does impose is still strong enough to justify the raising of eyebrows. Scarcely has he asked the question 'from what impression could this idea be derived?' when he gives us this concisely argued answer:

If any impression gives rise to the idea of self, that impression must continue invariably the same, thro' the whole course of our lives; since self is suppos'd to exist after that manner. But there is no impression constant and invariable.[68]

The impression, it seems, has to have the properties we attribute to the self; it must itself exist in the manner in which 'self is suppos'd to exist'. Why so? Why should we not have intermittent views of a constant object, or varying views of an invariable object? Once again the reply suggests itself that Hume has at the front of his mind the question 'how does the belief in the self arise?', and that therefore what he really wants to know is whether there is any impression the occurrence of which is by itself enough to account for that belief. If so, what he says seems reasonable: given his account of what the belief in the self amounts to, there cannot be such an impression unless there is one which is constant and invariable—not to mention various other properties which it might need as well. Here too it looks as if Hume, after a quick bow towards the theory of ideas and impressions, is making straight for the topic of the genesis of belief.

There is an instructive comparison to be drawn between 'Of Personal Identity' and the earlier section 'Of Scepticism with

[68] Ibid. p. 251.

regard to the Senses', where the very title places us in the area
of epistemology, and the business of ideas and their corresponding impressions makes no appearance. Hume's tactic is
first of all to characterise the belief he is to investigate: it is the
belief in a 'continu'd' existence, one which persists whether or
not the object is being perceived; and a 'distinct' existence,
spatially external to and causally independent of the per-
ceiver. Comparable to this, though done with far less care, is
the account of the belief in the self as a simple, unchanging
object. Now Hume asks immediately 'the only questions, that
are intelligible on the present subject':

whether it be the *senses*, *reason*, or the *imagination*, that produces the
opinion of a *continu'd* or of a *distinct* existence.[69]

His first move is to show that the senses can produce neither
opinion. A number of reasons might be given for that
conclusion, some of which would show that the senses (by
themselves) cannot give rise to any opinion at all; but it is
interesting to see what reason Hume actually does give for it.
To think that the senses could be responsible for the belief that
objects continue to exist unperceived

is a contradiction in terms, and supposes that the senses continue to
operate, even after they have ceased all manner of operation.[70]

So only continuous perception can give the 'notion' (note that
Hume is prepared to make a passing use of this word,[71]
although he is quite certainly thinking of *beliefs* at this point,
not of *ideas*) of a continuous object. That, provided we
remember that these are to be the conditions which perception
will have to meet if it is to generate such a belief unaided, is at
least a comprehensible thought; and it bears a striking
resemblance to the *prima facie* much more mysterious claim
that only a continuous *impression* can be the impression of a
continuous thing—which was the fulcrum of Hume's demonstration that there is no impression of the self. One way to get
rid of the mystery is to assume that by this stage he is treating
the terminology of ideas (as he is clearly treating the word

---

[69] Ibid. p. 188.
[70] Ibid. p. 188.
[71] Ibid. p. 188 (line 6 from bottom).

'notion') as little more than an alternative way of talking about the theory of belief. As well as relieving the mystery over the course of his arguments about the self and causality, the assumption also brings the strategy of those chapters back into line with that of 'Of Scepticism with regard to the Senses'. And it does some more work besides: it helps us to understand what must otherwise seem a very surprising oversight on Hume's part, as I shall now explain.

The theory of ideas and impressions, as expounded at the beginning of the *Treatise* and the *Enquiry Concerning Human Understanding*, allows for ideas to be either simple or complex. To a simple idea there must indeed correspond an actual impression, but to a complex idea there need only correspond at most a possible impression. For a complex idea can be put together at will by the mind out of available simple ideas, and although these simple ideas must have had their related impressions, there is no need for the impressions to have occurred together in just the way in which their ideas are united in the complex.

That being so, some answer has to be found to the question why Hume spends no time on an issue that must surely be absolutely vital to his argument: whether the idea of the self might not be a complex idea. So long as that remains a possibility, the fact that there is no actual impression that is 'constant and invariable' does nothing to show that there is no such idea. Just a very bad blunder? Well, it cannot be said that philosophers have never been known to make them, but charity requires that we look further. Could it be that he takes the one remark from the very first sentence of the section, about the 'perfect identity and simplicity' of the self, to be enough, on the grounds that if the self is simple its idea must be a simple idea? Possibly, but it would be disappointing if that were the answer, since it leaves the whole argument looking restrictively *ad hominem*; Hume is only telling us what 'some philosophers' say, and if he wishes to write about the mind rather than just about their views on the mind he had better consider the possibility that it is a complex entity, something which seems on the face of it not wholly unlikely. But another explanation, of course, is the one we have been using in a number of contexts: what we see here is not really a serious attempt to use the theory of ideas and impressions at all; Hume is not genuinely looking for the origin of an idea, in the strict terms of that theory—he is inquiring into the origin of a *belief*. An idea, if it were complex, could originate in a number of scattered impressions, the ideas of which had been voluntarily united by the imagination. That process would not, however, lead to any belief in the object represented by the complex idea—otherwise we would find ourselves ascribing reality to everything we imagine, a point of which Hume was certainly aware. To produce a belief, the various impressions would have to occur together as a single, complex impression; and then the important point is that it must be an *actual* impression to generate a belief, and whether it is simple or complex is of no consequence. So this is a perfectly adequate explanation of Hume's lack of interest in the question. It is an offshoot of the more general truth that he has in fact little real interest in the theory of ideas and impressions.

6. *Hume's heirs?*

Not only are many of Hume's apparent references to the theory of ideas and impressions deceptive; he is also prepared to ignore it, or at least to weaken considerably his official formulation of it, at times when he really is on its home ground and speaking of meaningfulness and significance. At the beginning of the *Treatise*, and in Section II of the first *Enquiry*, he makes it sound as if he were offering a theory governing all thought: every thought is made up of ideas, and every idea is a copy of some at least possible impression. It is this doctrine that is closely related to the verification principle, and makes Hume look like an embryonic positivist of Viennese stamp. This somewhat 'hard-line' thesis could, admittedly, be held by a philosopher whose main interest lay not in the theory of meaning, but in the origin of belief—so the possibility is not excluded by what we now know about the focus of Hume's attention. Nevertheless, Hume does not hold it, or, as it might be more accurate to say, does not stick to it; he readily slips into a position very much like that of Kant,[72]

---

[72] For Kant the categories can be used *for thought* beyond the limits of possible experience, but they have no use for *acquiring knowledge* beyond those limits—see e.g.

in which he allows there to be thought, of a kind, where there are no possible impressions and hence no ideas, but denies that it has the necessary distinctness ever to be an object of knowledge or rational opinion.

Although persons brought up on the 'embryonic positivist' interpretation may find this surprising or implausible, it is not really so, given Hume's historical circumstances. On the contrary, what needs explanation is not that he took the theory of ideas and impressions to be incomplete as an account of the nature of thought, but that he took it to be as comprehensive as he did, in other words as a complete theory of the *rationally discussible part* of our thinking.

Hume's predecessors, admittedly, had a strong motive for thinking that the content of at least a great deal of our thought must be wholly transparent to us. The almost all-pervasive cognitive variant of the Image of God doctrine encouraged them to think of a high degree of insight into truth as potentially available to man, and this must have repercussions for one's views about thought and meaning. Put shortly, it requires that we have as much insight into the *content* of a thought as we claim for our knowledge of its truth. It isn't necessary to deny that there might be cases in which one could properly say that we knew some statement to be true but were not clear about what it meant; if so, I suppose the best candidates would be that of being told something by a reliable authority, or that in which the truth of a statement emerges as the end-product of a calculation which we have carried out purely formally, without bearing the interpretation of the symbols in mind. Be that as it may, the conception of knowledge involved is quite foreign to the Insight Ideal, which calls for the individual to have, for himself, a complete and wholly clear grasp of the grounds of truth. And that cannot occur without a correspondingly clear grasp of what it is that is known. So the desire for the transparency of the universe to reason very naturally brings with it the assumption of the transparency of thought to consciousness. It doesn't follow that the proponents of the Similarity Thesis had to adopt

Critique of Pure Reason B166 note, which also hints at the importance for Kant of avoiding the strict positivistic doctrine that where the possibility of experience stops , the possibility of thought stops as well.

precisely the theory of ideas and impressions; clearly they did not. But it does mean that there was work to be done for which that theory was well suited: it made thoughts constellations of ideas, ideas it made copies of actual or possible impressions. And impressions have, or so it was then generally supposed, the desired property of transparency: there is nothing to them but what their owner is conscious of, and consciousness can never be mistaken about them. To an adherent of the Similarity Thesis this must make it very welcome as a theory of thought, at any rate of that sector of thought on which he wants to base his claim that human knowledge could be the equal of God's. It would be worth looking for evidence that such considerations actually were an important factor in sustaining the theory of ideas in the minds of its supporters. It is not, after all, fully clear why a theory which now appears to us to be in flat contradiction with the facts of introspective experience (quite apart from any logical flaws it may have) should have found the audience that it did.

Hume, as an opponent of the Image of God doctrine, certainly did not have *this* motive for being friendly towards the theory, even as a partial account of thought (of that part, namely, which is accessible to rational inquiry). He could have had some other motive for it, for instance if he held it to be essential to the arguments he needed for carrying out his primary purpose, the refutation and replacement of the view of the foundations of belief associated with the Insight Ideal. Here the picture is blurred. At one level, Hume clearly took the theory of ideas and impressions to be important to him, otherwise he would not have placed it so prominently at the beginning of the *Treatise* and the first *Enquiry*, or at the outset of the material about causality. On the other hand, we have seen just how little work it actually does there; what does the work is the principle that we cannot tell *a priori* what type of event will follow what. Does *that* rest on the claim that all thought consists of ideas, and that all ideas are copies of impressions? And is there any good reason to suppose that Hume thought that it did?

To the first of these questions we may give a straight 'No'. Someone might hold that beliefs could have components other than ideas whilst still thinking that all knowledge of causal truths was *a posteriori*, if for instance he accepted that, firstly, our ideas of the events in question were insufficient to give us *a priori* knowledge of their connection, and secondly, that nothing but ideas is a possible source of *a priori* knowledge. But Hume surely held both of these, so that it remains obscure what motive he can have had for being hospitable, even to the extent that he was, to the theory of ideas and impressions, and I am driven to an explanation of the fact in terms of an early enthusiasm for Locke and the 'way of ideas'. Hume never got it out of his system, or realised how little, deep down, it actually meant to him.

The negative point remains: there is nothing on show, except perhaps twentieth-century prejudices, to tell us that Hume must have taken the theory of ideas and impressions seriously as a complete account of our thought-processes. There is, on the other hand, positive evidence that he allowed there to be a content to thought that did not consist of ideas. Whether it is strong enough to justify speaking of it as his opinion, or only as an option which he tried out and did not explicitly reject, is a subtlety I shall ignore; either would show a lack of regard for the theory as an attempt at a complete account of all thought. The fact is that Hume readily speaks of us as 'supposing', sometimes also as 'feigning', what we cannot 'conceive', or what is 'unintelligible' or 'incomprehensible'—the distinction runs parallel to that between having, and not having, an *idea* of the subject-matter. A rich source of information is the discussion of Spinoza in the section 'Of the Immateriality of the Soul'. There we find that we can 'suppose' what we cannot 'conceive': '. . . we may suppose, but never can conceive a specific difference betwixt an object and impression';[73] and that what is unintelligible (apparently because not expressible in ideas) may none the less be understood after a fashion:

I turn my attention to these hypotheses . . . and find that they have the same fault of being unintelligible; and that as far as we can understand them, they are so much alike, that 'tis impossible to discover any absurdity in one, which is not common to both of them.[74]

[73] THN p. 241.
[74] Ibid. p. 243.

What makes it possible to conceive something, or makes it intelligible, comprehensible, is the availability of ideas; without them, we can only 'suppose':

as every idea is deriv'd from a preceding impression, 'tis impossible our idea of a perception, and that of an object or external existence can ever represent what are specifically different from each other. Whatever difference we may suppose between them, 'tis still incomprehensible to us; and we are oblig'd either to conceive an external object merely as a relation without a relative, or to make it the very same with a perception or impression.[75]

Suppositions are not possible objects of knowledge; but notice that the following sentence does not sound like the writing of someone who held that they were literally senseless:

since we may suppose, but never can conceive a specific difference between an object and impression; any conclusion we reach concerning the connexion and repugnance of impressions, will not be known certainly to be applicable to objects . . .[76]

That is not about the meaningless, but the unknowable. So is this:

we can never . . . but by an irregular kind of reasoning from experience, discover a connexion or repugnance betwixt objects, which extends not to impressions; tho' the inverse proposition may not be equally true, that all the discoverable relations of impressions are common to objects.[77]

This is notable for two reasons. Firstly, Hume thinks that where 'irregular' kinds of reasoning are involved (here he gives a footnote referring back to 'Of Scepticism with regard to the Senses') we can at least come to have thoughts about objects which represent them as different in kind from impressions. Secondly, that if he held that all our thought about objects could be accounted for in terms of ideas he could not be expected to say that it 'may not be true' that all discoverable relations of impressions are common to objects. Either this would simply not be a thought, so that the remark would be quite incongruous, or, if we were to interpret talk

[75] Ibid. p. 241.
[76] Ibid. p. 241.
[77] Ibid. p. 242.

about objects in the only way in which, on this view, it would acquire any sense at all, thinking about objects could be nothing but thinking about impressions—and then Hume, far from saying that it 'may not be true', would surely have regarded it as a necessary truth. But not so—there is 'supposing' as well as 'conceiving'.

There are also 'fictions', which play a central role in Hume's account of our beliefs in the physical world and our own continued existence through time, as well as making an important appearance in the brief chapter 'Of the Antient Philosophy', where they have to do with beliefs in 'substances and substantial forms, and accidents, and occult qualities'. The interesting question for our purposes is: what, according to Hume, is the content of these fictions, what do we come to believe in when we 'feign' something?

It emerges that the question has two answers, because there are two vitally different sorts of belief covered by Hume's concept of a fiction. Some are 'unintelligible'; these are the cases in which we suppose or feign something different in kind from any possible perception, as for instance when the mind is caught in the dilemma posed by a gradually changing object. Then

the imagination is apt to feign something unknown and invisible, which it supposes to continue the same under all these variations; and this unintelligible something it calls a *substance*, or *original and first matter*.[78]

Other fictions, however, consist in the invention by the imagination of non-existent perceptions; these might be called 'intelligible' fictions, on the grounds that their content ought to be representable by ideas, if anything is—but Hume's tendency is to use the word 'unintelligible' of both types. Here we find them side by side in one sentence:

we feign the continu'd existence of the perceptions of our senses, to remove the interruption; and run into the notion of a *soul*, and *self*, and *substance*, to disguise the variation.[79]

The first of these fictions is a belief about perceptions. Its

[78] Ibid. p. 220.
[79] Ibid. p. 254.

defect is not lack of clarity, but demonstrable falsehood, in as much as it implies that perceptions can have an independent existence. The second is a belief about something different in kind from any possible perception, so that reason, which operates by spotting relationships between ideas, cannot pronounce on it either way. Its defect is to be incapable of clear formulation.

What should one expect Hume's attitude towards the second sort of fiction to be? If he takes the line that the theory of ideas is an account of *all* thought, he will have to say that they are not thoughts at all, just verbalisations in which a word fills a grammatically correct position but is backed by no mental content. If, on the other hand, the theory of ideas is now subservient to the epistemology and is only to cover that area of thought which is susceptible of reasoning, experiment, clarity, knowledge of truth and falsehood, then he will very likely speak disparagingly of 'fictions', but without the implication that they are utterly empty.

The second of these we have already seen in the distinction between 'conceiving' and 'supposing'.[80] But it is worthy of note that we do find something that sounds very like the first, and, despite the incompatibility, within a few pages of it. In 'Of the Antient Philosophy', speaking of the terms 'faculty' and 'occult quality', he says:

For it being usual, after the frequent use of terms, which are really significant and intelligible, to omit the idea, which we wou'd express by them, and to preserve only the custom, by which we recall the idea at pleasure; so it naturally happens, that after the frequent use of terms, which are wholly insignificant and unintelligible, we fancy them to be on the same footing with the precedent, and to have a secret meaning, which we might discover by reflection.[81]

But whether this really is the hard-line doctrine that without *ideas* there are no thoughts *at all*, only words, it is impossible to be sure. And why should it be possible? We have repeatedly seen Hume slurring the theory of ideas into his theory of belief. Why should he not also have started by looking on it as a theory of the thinkable and then found himself happy to

---

[80] 'Supposing' is closely related to 'feigning', as the last quotation but one shows.
[81] THN p. 224.

transform it into a theory of the knowable? His deep underlying interest (as I hold) in the downfall of the Insight Ideal, the cognitive branch of the Similarity Thesis, required a theory of knowability, since it was precisely certain claims about what was knowable and how that had to be refuted. But it gave him no particular reason to have, or not to have, a theory about the limits of the thinkable. On this hypothesis, he probably would not be too bothered about whether he had one or not. And that, if there were any need to do it so briefly, is probably the best way of summarising what we actually find.

The whole trend of this chapter poses a question that is still to be answered: if Hume's interest in the theory of ideas and impressions was in reality so lukewarm, why did he give it such a place of honour as Part I of Book I of the *Treatise*? And why is it still present ten years later in the *Enquiry Concerning the Human Understanding*? A credible reply is not too hard to find, if one remembers certain well-known facts about the composition of these works. There is always a tendency for an author to find out what he is most interested in, or for it to emerge, while he works. For Hume, in his early twenties, expounding his system for the first time, thinking and writing fast enough to have a work of the size and scope of the *Treatise* drafted, and two-thirds of it ready for the printer, when he was twenty-seven, that tendency would come close to a certainty, and what is surprising is that we do not find even more, and even more obvious, signs of it. That a young philosopher of his period, bent on approaching philosophical problems via a science of the human mind, should have quarried Locke's *Essay* for his basic apparatus needs no special explanation, any more than does the fact that he looked to Newton for his model of scientific method and the form of a scientific theory. Hume, feeling that the theory of ideas was at least moving in his direction, simply took it over. And the manner in which he took it over, to which other commentators have also drawn attention,[82] does not suggest any great intellectual intensity. The part of the *Treatise* which presents the theory may be placed first, but only Part I of Book III is shorter, and then only very slightly. As regards content, there are precious few

[82] See for instance Barry Stroud: *Hume* (Routledge 1977) p. 17.

deviations from Locke. First the fledgling researcher flexes his muscles by introducing a terminological innovation, then mentions the difficulty of the missing shade of blue,[83] a potentially very damaging example which he is tactful enough not to press. He treats this material as if it were just the obvious starting-point, which is how it would probably (and quite understandably) have looked to him; the fact that it was not ideal for his purposes, as they turned out, should not make it surprising that he chose it.

Nor is it very hard to conjecture an answer to the second part of our question, why the same structure should be found in the first *Enquiry*. The *Treatise* was widely ignored, and where it was not ignored it was mostly misunderstood. Hume, fortunately having enough self-confidence not to drop the whole business, naturally felt that what was needed was a more readable presentation of the same material; he encountered no critic of anything like his own stature who might have caused him to rethink the matter as well as the manner. Besides, much of the time between the publication of the two works was taken up with the attempt to find a congenial way of earning a living. First conceptions have a habit of sticking; and nothing about Hume's circumstances at the time was specially suited to dislodging them.

Something which I hope will be dislodged by these considerations, and for good, is the logical positivist's encampment on Humean territory. Their claim to be Hume's twentieth-century heirs is not only misleading; in a certain very important respect it is the exact reverse of the truth. They were aware, of course, of psychological elements in his work quite foreign to any intentions or aspirations of theirs. But they nevertheless believed that there was an analytic core, based on a thesis not at all far removed from the verification principle, that represented Hume's true contribution to philosophy. I overlook here the implied restriction on the scope of philosophy, which is a defect of positivism, not of positivism's understanding of Hume; there is still quite enough left to object to. They saw an embryonic version of the verification principle in the text because they took the theory of ideas and impressions to be a theory not only of the

---

[83] THN pp. 5–6.

knowable, but of the meaningful or the thinkable, a reading which we have seen to be highly controversial, at best. And then they thought that Hume's use of the principle was like theirs: he used it (did he not?) to enforce *analyses* of key concepts in terms of impressions and their properties. No, he did not. It was only the positivists themselves who did that, and it was one of the factors that led some of them into the most unHumean assertions imaginable. I close with my favourite example.

The passage I have in mind comes from Moritz Schlick's paper 'Meaning and Verification'. Schlick, having established the verification principle to his satisfaction, asks whether there could be matters of which we are in principle ignorant, questions to which we could not possibly find the answer. His response is characteristic of the tough-minded positivist:

it is easy to see from what has been said before that this calamity could only happen if the question itself had no meaning. . . . We must say that a question is meaningful, if we can *understand* it, i.e. if we are able to decide for any given proposition whether, if true, it would be an answer to our question. And if this is so, the actual decision could only be prevented by empirical circumstances, which means that it would not be *logically impossible*. Hence no meaningful problem can be insoluble in *principle*. . . . This is one of the most characteristic results of our empiricism. It means that in principle there are no limits to our knowledge. The boundaries which must be acknowledged are of an empirical nature and, therefore, never ultimate . . . there is no unfathomable mystery in the world.[84]

This is an amazing paragraph. The verification principle tells us that what we cannot know, we cannot understand either—the second inability follows upon the first. The way in which Schlick, by adding one *inability* to another, with such massive self-confidence conjures our potential omniscience into being is a show-piece of human self-deception. His triumphantly leaping logic has nothing at all in common with Hume's sceptical caution in this area ('Were our ignorance . . . a good

---

[84] M. Schlick: 'Meaning and Verification', in *The Philosophical Review* 1936 (also in Schlick: *Gesammelte Aufsätze* (Gerold, Vienna 1938) pp. 337–367, this quotation pp. 350–1; and *Readings in Philosophical Analysis*, ed.Feigl and Sellars (Appleton–Century–Crofts 1949) pp. 146–170, this quotation p. 156.

reason for rejecting anything . . .'[85]). And Schlick's conclusion, 'in principle, there are no limits to our knowledge', no very distant relative of the Image of God doctrine, is not so much Hume's teaching as his target. Hume's heirs indeed!

[85] ECHU pp. 72–3 See above, Chapter 2 Section 5 and Footnote 63.

3

THE METAPHYSIC OF THE ROMANTIC ERA

1. *Philosophy in different dress*

In Chapter 1 we surveyed a period of approximately one hundred years running from the early seventeenth to the early eighteenth century and looked closely at one of its most prominent philosophical features, the vision of man in the image of God; in Chapter 2 we then set Hume down in this landscape and hoped for illumination. In this chapter and the next I shall attempt something similar, first delineating a certain metaphysic or *Weltbild* that shaped the intellectual climate of the years shortly before and shortly after the beginning of the nineteenth century, and then bringing the findings to the study of Hegel, where we will notice two effects. First, it will give a different significance to most of his central doctrines, which turn out to emerge directly from that climate. Secondly, by redirecting our expectations, it will alter our reading of certain particular passages. This way of putting it may make it sound like a rerun, transposed by some hundred or so years, of the machinery and results of the earlier chapters. But whilst there are indeed considerable, and of course wholly intended, parallels, the change involved is not just a change of detail; on the contrary, the new subject-matter seems to me to require a radical change of approach, and the way in which an appreciation of the cultural background eases the way through a text of Hegel is quite different to that in which it can deepen our understanding of Hume.

That remark touches a subsidiary, though important, theme of this second pair of chapters. It can be succinctly formulated: Hegel is a good deal less like us, and a good deal less continuous with those parts of the history of modern European philosophy which we in the Anglo-Saxon tradition know best, than we tend to think. The theme is important because of the recent revival of interest in Hegel in English-speaking philosophical circles; sadly, we shall find certain influential commentators holding up a mirror to themselves in the belief that they are holding up a telescope to the past. Those who undertook the work of returning Hegel to our consciousness often did so in the hope of furnishing new perspectives which would enable us to broaden the bounds of a subject grown overnarrow, and that praiseworthy aim makes any tendency to cram the past unwillingly into the mould of the present doubly regrettable.

The men whose thought was the concern of Chapter 1 were, with the minor exceptions of Galileo and Newton, people whom current fashion would unhesitatingly classify as philo-sophers. I speak of 'minor exceptions' not, of course, absurdly to suggest that Galileo and Newton were minor figures, but because that same philosophical fashion admits close relation-ships between the natural sciences and what it takes to be philosophy properly so called; also because it would regard Galileo and Newton as having stepped outside their scientific concerns in just the sort of passage on which Chapter 1 focused attention. So they are scarcely exceptions at all. Nevertheless, their presence in the discussion may help to serve notice of a point which will now emerge with much greater obviousness and force: there is no reason in principle why the 'dominant philosophy' of an epoch should not be carried by persons who do not count as philosophers at all in contemporary and recent university practice. The underlying metaphysical convictions of the romantic period can in fact best, or at the lowest estimate perfectly well, be studied in works nearly all of which belong fairly and squarely to literature.

That this can be so should not occasion any great surprise if we recall what sort of thing the dominant philosophy of any period actually is. What, to make a start, is 'a philosophy'? The usage of the word is very wide: sometimes a philosophy is scarcely any more than an attitude which, because of the breadth of its application, makes a deep difference to the way in which life is lived. Thus one who is calm and resilient in adversity is said to react philosophically, and if this is a general characteristic of his behaviour he might just be said to have a philosophy, even if this attitude is unconnected with any theory or set of beliefs as to how reality is or ought to be. But very often there *are* beliefs underlying such general attitudes and behavioural patterns. They can display a very wide range of degree of detail and precision, but once they are there, even in a vague or largely unarticulated form, we have arrived at what I would like to call a philosophy. Such a set of beliefs is a 'dominant' philosophy if it is sufficiently widespread and firmly held to be a major force in the intellectual climate of a society, rather than just in the thought and life of a few scattered individuals.

A philosophy, in this sense, however dominant it may be, is far removed from what we normally understand by a *philosophical system*. The creator of such a system will characteristically attempt to give the underlying ideas a precise form, to weld them into an intellectually coherent and hence satisfying structure, and to provide them with rational foundations; a philosophy may be an altogether more primitive, shapeless affair that makes its appeal purely to feeling. The dominance of a philosophy, it is true, may well be a spur to systematisation, and systematisation may sometimes be an aid to dominance, but they are not by any means the same thing. Thus, to use an example which we have already looked at in some detail, the work of Leibniz forms a philosophical system of great coherence and sophistication, but the dominant philosophy which it embodies is simply the half-formed thought that we are, as thinkers and agents, the same kind of thing as the author of the universe.

It is only to be expected, then, that a philosophy, being in itself yet undeveloped, will be capable of many different developments and many different forms of expression. If a philosopher can embody and articulate in his work some statement about the nature of reality, man and human life, so can the novelist and the poet; they will give that statement force and content by filling it out with narrative, or imagery, but it could still be a very similar statement to the one which the philosopher fills out with what we may, speaking very broadly, call logic. Whether the nonverbal artforms have the capacity to express beliefs, and to what degree, is controversial; but without trying to adjudicate the controversy we may say that in so far as they can they are also possible vehicles for a philosophy. And should there be, associated with the beliefs that constitute the philosophy, any sufficiently distinctive set of feelings or attitudes, then some generous spirits might be prepared to regard them as possible vehicles if it could be shown that they were particularly suitable to awakening those feelings or attitudes; I know no reason to object. However, we need not venture into these deep waters. We shall only be concerned with the literary case, where the ability of the medium to convey beliefs is relatively un-problematic.

One thing we should notice before moving on is that this approach lets us see a relationship between areas, philosophy and literature, which recent philosophical tradition has tended to think of as quite sharply distinct. Each may, in its own way, incorporate a philosophy—though that is not to say that every philosophy will lend itself equally well to both types of treatment. Secondly, it suggests that it may even be wrong to speak of *two* types, with the implication that although both may be doing to some extent the same thing, they are nevertheless separate and unmixable ways of doing it. A novelist or poet can, and sometimes does, find ways of introducing direct and literal statements of philosophical beliefs into his writing, as well as illustrative evidence or even logical argument for them. And on the other hand the recognised philosophers do not always deal in coldly literal language and rational argument; it does happen that literary devices, the allusive metaphor, the emotionally resonant phrase, the neatness of a well-turned aphorism, are important, one might sometimes say essential, ingredients in a philo-sopher's brew. It is no accident, and it certainly does not involve an equivocation on the word 'philosophy', that we speak of philosophical literature and literary philosophy. As so often happens, our two types turn out to be just salient cases on a continuum with two extremes; resistance to that view can only come, I believe, from restricted experience of the types of writing that exist or from highly selective attention to their features.

This chapter, therefore, though similar to Chapter 1 in

being the attempt to exhibit a metaphysic informing a certain period of intellectual history, will differ from it sharply in point of style of immediate subject-matter. And it may be said at this early stage that the next chapter, whilst it closely resembles Chapter 2 in trying to elucidate the work of a particular philosopher by making use of our knowledge of that underlying metaphysic, nevertheless differs by making use of it in an altogether different way. Whereas we saw Hume as the opponent of the dominant philosophy of the preceding hundred years, Hegel is the great philosophical champion of the *Weltbild* of his literary contemporaries, the man who took it over and spent his life in giving it precision and proof (as he claimed) and in illustrating in concrete detail its application to a wide range of cultural phenomena. In starkest contrast to Hume, Hegel preached to the converted—a readymade audience with readymade enthusiasm for his ideas. As a result, Hume's message was heard by a handful of contemporaries, Hegel's by thousands. The outlines of his philosophy were virtually common property at the time when his philosophical systematisation of them appeared.

2. *Spirits of stream and woodland—and the root of all bad dancing*

The title of this chapter speaks of the metaphysic of the romantic era, but I have to confess that the description is not ideal. The intended reference is, roughly speaking, the twenty years before and after the beginning of the nineteenth century; and I have the suspicion that many historians of European thought will find this period a little too early for the name. Secondly, it might make a reader with knowledge of German literature and criticism think of the Romantic School, *die romantische Schule* of Heine's sparkling essay,[1] the Schlegels, Tieck, von Arnim, Uhland and such writers; whereas the intellectual movement I have in mind is far less specific, and includes figures who would not, as far as I know, have thought of themselves as romantics, nor probably as having anything of much significance in common. My hope is that with these caveats entered, the label 'romantic era' will not serve my purposes too badly; and I know of nothing better.

[1] Heinrich Heine: *Die Romantische Schule* (1832–3) *Sämtliche Schriften* Vol. 3 (Hanser 1971).

The dominant philosophy of the romantic era, as I shall present it, is composed of a number of theses, but all of them are aspects of, or contributions to, the one great metaphysical theme with which the minds of this time were obsessed: unity, its loss and its recovery. Wherever they looked they found division and conflict in men's minds and actions: the conception of God as creator of and external to nature, the finite opposed to the infinite; conscious, feeling man surrounded by inanimate, unfeeling objects; moral freedom against physical necessity; the battle between reason and sentiment; the desires of the individual versus the requirements of society; the tension between church and state; the friction between I and Thou; the split between the knowing subject and the object known; the chasm between truth and appearance, the undistorted Kantian thing-in-itself and the humanly processed phenomena of empirical reality. They saw a picture of the universe as riven by strife, all its principles at odds with each other, fractured in every direction. And that this was the ultimate truth of things they could not or would not believe.

In a way which echoed (and in some cases explicitly involved) the Christian doctrines of the Fall and the Redemption, it was popular to suppose that this so-desirable wholeness of life and thought was not just an ideal but had once been possessed and thereafter lost; also that it could be regained, though not necessarily in quite its original form. Here two broad types of thought were current. On the one hand, it was possible to think in social or in long-range historical terms; on the other, one could operate on the much smaller scale of the individual and the individual life. Both the race and the individual had to find their way back home, and a similar model was applied to the two rather different journeys. In the case of the individual the favoured starting-point, the original state of wholeness and innocence, was that of childhood—an obvious choice, but not, it should be realised, the only one, since the more Platonic notion of a state before any physical embodiment was also in theory available. In the larger scale view it was—so ran the enthusiasm most fashionable at the time—ancient Greek civilisation that represented the peak from which later generations had slipped back.

A restrained, resigned lament for the lost felicity of the Greek relationship with nature is Schiller's poem 'Die Götter Griechenlands' (The Gods of Greece).[2] The ancient world was peopled with gods and spirits, living things with which the human being could feel empathy:

Through creation flowed the fullness of life, what will never feel, had feeling.

Everywhere, he goes on, the initiated eye detected the presence of a deity:

Oreads filled these heights, a dryad lived in yonder tree; the silver foam of the streams flowed from the urns of gentle naiads.

And since the gods, often for all too human purposes (such was the similarity between us and them), were frequently to be found on Earth in human shape:

To the tribe of Deukalion then the gods still descended. To conquer Pyrrha's lovely daughters Leto's son took the shepherd's staff.

There was, instead of a great gulf, the closest of bonds between men and the gods:

Between men, gods and heroes Amor fashioned a beautiful bond.

But now things are changed. The cold sense of fact has vanquished the imagination, with which it held in the Greek mind so well-adjusted and fruitful a balance:

Then the magic cloak of poetry wrapped itself lovingly around the truth.

And we are left with—what? An empty, lonely world in which the human being vainly seeks its own likeness:

Through the forests I cry, through the waves. Empty they echo back!

It is time to introduce the villain of the piece, the first target of the boos and hisses of the romantic era. Responsible for

---

[2] F. Schiller: *Werke in 3 Bänden* (Hanser 1966) Vol. II pp. 673–6

Schiller's *entgötterte Natur* is—the natural scientist. This does not, of course, mean any student of nature, regardless of aims and methods; it means the Newtonian scientist, the mechanist, he it is who has driven the gods out of the world and transformed a thing that was alive and free into a dead slave of the laws of motion:

Like the dead stroke of a pendulum clock, slavishly it serves the law of gravity.

Nature has turned clockwork. Schiller tells us again:

On an eternally unchanging spindle, moons wind themselves up and down.

and as he does so he takes the opportunity to emphasise the stupefying dullness of this new world. Life is all development and change, but this world of the Newtonian scientist just repeats, and repeats . . . and repeats, hypnotically, the very antithesis of mind, *ewig gleich*.

One of the great pillars of the romantic metaphysic, the thought of the return to the lost paradise, is absent from 'Die Götter Griechenlands'. It is true that Schiller does call upon the god-filled world of the ancients to return. But he finds nothing more forceful than the banal line:

Beautiful world, where are you? Come again . . .

This colourlessness may well be intentional, for he soon makes it very clear that he has no such hope or expectation. The simultaneously divine and natural world of the Greeks has departed, he says, into the 'fairyland of song', and that is very much where it is left at the end of the poem:

What is to live immortally in song must die in life.

Indeed, he goes so far as to imply that they never had any other existence in the first place. They were never factual, never of the inner essence of things; what produced them was 'the magic cloak of fiction'. Now they have gone home, and 'home' means, evidently, the realm of the fanciful:

Idle, the gods returned home to the land of the imagination . . . .

The feeling of oneness with nature was generated by a fiction;

perhaps a healthy fiction, but a fiction all the same. Elsewhere in Schiller, and in the work of others, the metaphysic of the romantic era was to make much stronger, and more optimistic, claims about the ultimate wholeness of the real and our chances of repossessing it.

Yearning for empathy with nature is one of the chords touched by Goethe's brief and well-known ballad 'Der Fischer'.[3] This apparently artless little poem can hardly be thought of as a serious philosophical statement, especially as Goethe himself is known sometimes to have rejected attempts to impose 'deep' readings on it. But his was a mind open to the widest range of influences and susceptible of the widest range of moods, able to take any of the ideas of his time and play with them, or take them seriously, at his pleasure. Most likely many interpretations and perspectives passed through his mind and helped to shape 'Der Fischer', without there being any one which he definitely, let alone exclusively, intended. Even if there were we would not need to know of it to read the text and notice the images and figures of thought that occur in it; still less do we need to know how seriously we are intended to take them as guides to metaphysical truth.

A fisherman sits by a stream, placidly watching his line. Instead of a fish, a water-sprite rises to the surface and addresses him in half-scolding, half-enticing tones. Why should he lure her fish up to their deaths in the bright light of day? If only he knew the pleasures of the fishes' life on the riverbed he would prefer instead to come down to them. The sun and the moon do so, she tells him; they dip themselves in the sea, and is their beauty not doubled in reflection? Does he not feel the pull of the blue sky, transfigured in its appearance in the water? And then comes the decisive blow—the appeal to the vision of self reflected in nature:

Does not your own face tempt you down into the eternal waters?

That thrust finds the mark: half of himself, half pulled by the sprite, the fisherman sinks into the water and is gone.

Here we see highlighted the force of, and the desire for, the discovery of our own likeness in nature—a nature into which, at the beginning, we dip not ourselves but only our fishing

---

[3] Goethe: *Werke*, ed. Trunz (Hamburg edn. 10th impression) Vol.I p.153.

line, hoping to snare and extract a few useful bits of it whilst preserving distinctions and keeping our distance. But there are plenty of other opportunities here to find, or think one has found, elements of the romantic *Weltbild* as we saw them in Schiller's 'Gods of Greece'. Is there not a suggestion that the fisherman, in his state of separation from the nature of which he is an almost completely passive observer, is somehow not quite whole? 'Cool right to the heart' is what Goethe calls him; the line suggests not just temporary quiescence, but a lack of capacity for emotion. The water-sprite leaves us in no doubt that therapy is called for. If the fisherman knew the delights of the depths,

You would climb down here, just as you are, and only then be healed.

The diagnosis is much less clear. But there are signs that it could be that same overdose of knowledge which produced the natural scientist and effected the banishment of the Greek gods. Could it be too much of the 'Human guile and human cunning' which the sprite finds in the fisherman? If so, then it is only a short step to seeing the 'deadly brightness' into which he seeks to draw the fish as the burning light of self-consciousness and the river as the place of oblivion, sensation without thought, where that light no longer shines. Can the cure be simply to drop back into it? So the fisherman is brought to think, but does he thereby achieve wholeness? Goethe makes it sound much more like extinction:

And he was seen no more.

It would be foolish to pretend that the later stages of this reading are obligatory, but at least they do not bounce back off the text as plainly incompatible with it, and they enable us to see it as a playful offshoot (if not forerunner) of the intellectual movement the existence and importance of which over the next fifty years is not open to question. Let us for our next illustration skip thirty-five of them[4] to look at a far more explicit piece of writing.[5]

[4] Goethe's 'Der Fischer' was written in 1778.
[5] Heinrich von Kleist: *Werke in 1 Band* (Hanser 1966) pp. 802–7.

This is a short narrative prose piece by Heinrich von Kleist, written for the *Berliner Abendblätter*, a paper which he founded and edited during the early 'teens of the nineteenth century. Called 'Über das Marionettentheater', it is presented as the record of a conversation between the author and an eminent dancer, who has (surprisingly, as the author feels) been taking an intense interest in a puppet theatre now showing in the market place. His interest, explains the dancer, is professional: how can a puppet be made to dance so gracefully? Not as difficult as you might think, he replies to his own question. The puppeteer cannot possibly control all the puppet's limbs, but every movement has a centre of gravity, and if this is appropriately controlled, rhythmic and graceful motions of the other parts of the figure follow immediately. The problem is to find the correct path for this centre of gravity, which might also be called the path of the dancer's centre of motive force, or of the soul, he tells the author. This reflection leads the dancer's theorising off in a new direction: it should be possible to make a puppet that would outdance even the greatest contemporaries. What advantages, asks the author, would it have that would enable it to do that? In the first place, replies the dancer, it would be incapable of affectation or artificiality. These occur, he says, when the soul or motive force is not at the centre of gravity of the movement. Since the puppeteer has no other point under his control, the puppet must be free of them, but not so a human dancer—and he mentions some examples. The trouble, it seems, is that a human dancer can, and to some extent always does, *think* about what he is doing; this ability to plan and assess the performance robs it of the natural harmony and grace which it would otherwise have. As with Schiller, it is *knowledge* which has done the damage; Kleist's dancer now has direct recourse to the Christian image of the fall:

Such errors . . . are inevitable, since we ate of the tree of knowledge.

In one day's work the old serpent has given us, apparently, not merely sin but bad dancers as well.

The author now enthusiastically takes up the dancer's point, even accepting the invitation to attach it, if only allusively, to the third book of Genesis:

I said that I knew perfectly well what damage consciousness can do to a human being's natural grace. A young man of my acquaintance had lost his innocence before my eyes, almost, as the result of a mere remark, and, in spite of every conceivable effort, never again found his way back to that paradise.

In the incident of which he now tells we see the romantic thesis of the loss of unity and harmony with nature through knowledge applied not, as in Schiller's 'Die Götter Griechenlands', to mankind as a race, but to the individual human being. A certain youth of the author's acquaintance was of outstanding natural physical grace. One day, having quite by chance taken up a posture like that represented in a famous piece of sculpture which he had recently seen, he happened to catch a glimpse of himself in a mirror. Noticing the resemblance, he remarked on it to the author; but when the author, who had in fact already noticed it himself, pretended not to know what he meant, the boy's efforts to reproduce the position were a complete and almost laughable failure. From that very moment a deep change gradually came over his life:

He began to stand in front of the mirror all day long; and his charms left him one by one.

Within a year the transformation was complete—all elegance of stance and gesture had disappeared without trace.

The dancer's concluding tale about the fencing bear, with which 'Über das Marionettentheater' ends, I leave as a pleasing exercise for the reader. Charming in itself, it adds little to the philosophical content, and if anything tends to upset the unity of subject-matter which Kleist has up to then preserved. Given the nature of our present interest, an altogether different point takes priority. In the poems of Schiller and Goethe we found the idea of a loss of unity and harmony between man and the natural world; of its *return* Schiller made no mention, other than to imply that it was impossible; and whether Goethe's fisherman found the health that the sprite promised him, or rather annihilation, was left at best ambiguous. But the dancer of Kleist's conversation unmistakably has something far more positive to say: the golden age, the childhood paradise are in a certain sense recoverable.

His favourite way of expressing this idea is by means of a topological metaphor. Here is its first occurrence, immediately following the sentence quoted above about the effects of our having eaten of the tree of knowledge:

But paradise is bolted and barred and the cherub behind us; we must make a journey round the world and see whether it may not be open from the back.

What this thought amounts to is for the moment obscure, however easily the mind may take in the image—but help is on the way. Let him argue the case for his paradoxical claims as he may, says the author, the dancer will never bring him to believe that a mechanical puppet could be more graceful than a human body. Certainly it can, replies the dancer, it would be quite impossible for a human being to match a really well-made puppet in this respect. And with an unmistakable gesture towards his previous metaphor, he adds that:

Only a god could rival matter in this arena; and this is the point at which the two ends of the ring-shaped world come together.

The route that brings us full circle back to our starting-point would make him who could traverse it into a god. What route is it, and why would it have that effect? It is, as we find out in the closing lines, the path of ever-broadening consciousness, ever-increasing knowledge. At the unconscious beginning of it we have seen nothing and know nothing; at the end, we know everything. Then true grace can be found again. The puppet's thought cannot be out of tune with its body because it does not think; the god's cannot, because it is completely and absolutely right. In between the two cases come the bad dancers:

so that [grace] appears at its purest in that human form which either has no consciousness at all, or an infinite one, that is to say, either in the puppet, or in the god.

Perhaps Goethe's fisherman was seduced into opting for an illusory option. Once we have acquired a little knowledge there is no way back except the extinction of consciousness, perhaps also of the self (behind us stands the cherub); the goal lies not back but further down the same path, if at infinity. Is it then, asks the author, that we must revisit the tree of knowledge if we are ever to recover the lost state of innocence? Precisely, replies the dancer, suddenly giving the impression that he is not just prescribing a strategy but describing a real process, and 'that is the last chapter of the history of the world'.

The two thoughts, that the only way for man lies in the increase of knowledge and the development of consciousness, and that the apotheosis of this process involves the merging of the human with the divine mind, are of course strongly Hegelian. But that is for later; at present we should notice that they are at least as strongly reminiscent of Spinoza, whose philosophy begins in this period to find a receptive audience, in the first place largely due to the interest and sympathy it aroused in Goethe and Lessing. The two thoughts also connect very smoothly with the tradition that had its centre in the Image of God doctrine. In locating God at the end of an infinite path and then, with every appearance of optimism, inviting us to follow it, they very easily suggest the old formula of qualitative likeness and quantitative difference. It is not even clear that Kleist does, in 'Über das Marionettentheater', represent the goal as being in principle unattainable. It would seem to amount to that when he says that it is *simply impossible* for a human being to match his imaginary puppet—but perhaps he says this only because a human being that could do so would perforce have left the human condition behind. Against this, in any case, one has to set the remark about the last chapter of history (though it is not, I suppose, obligatory to take this as a description of something which, in his view, will actually happen) and his recommendation that we should take a trip 'round the world' to see whether the back gate into paradise may not be open. And what are we meant to make of the words 'in that human form' from the passage last quoted? That a god, having the infinite consciousness, could also have human shape, is clearly implied; but whether a human being could reach that state is left vague. Why this indeterminacy over a point which Kleist makes central to the structure of his piece? It is as if he could not quite bring himself to believe, or at least to write, what he felt—whichever of the alternatives that may have been.

3. *The aesthetic education of man*

In 'Die Götter Griechenlands' we saw Schiller taking a purely nostalgic look at the past. But that was not the only mood in which he ever contemplated the topic of unity and division. At other times he made the most strenuous efforts to show society the way back from the state of opposition into which he believed that it had fallen, as for instance in the more overtly philosophical *Letters on the Aesthetic Education of Man*, written in 1795.[6] Schiller had high hopes of the arts. Not only did he think that artistic experience involved the reconciliation of opposing tendencies which had come into conflict in contemporary man, and so could contribute decisively to the task of making him whole again; he also believed that a true understanding of the arts was the only reliable route to political wholeness—if achieved, it would lead on to the adoption of constitutions capable of reconciling interests that were now seemingly in a perpetual state of strain, if not of open war.

Still it is ancient Greek culture which represents the highest point that humanity has so far attained:

The Greeks put us to shame not just by a simplicity which is quite foreign to our age; they are often our rivals, nay our paradigms, in the very advantages with which we try to console ourselves for the unnaturalness of our *mores*.[7]

In particular, this was true of their political institutions, in which they had found a happy solution to the problem of the relationship between the individual and the state:

Those polyp-like Greek states, in which every individual had an independent life and yet, when necessary, could merge into the whole, now gave way to an artificial clockwork, in which from the grouping of parts infinite in number, but lifeless, there results a mechanical life of the whole.[8]

A pattern is now beginning to emerge in Schiller's thought, a

---

[6] F. Schiller: *Werke in 3 Bänden* (Hanser 1966) Vol. II pp. 445–520.

[7] F. Schiller: ibid. 6th letter.

[8] Ibid. 6th letter. It is interesting to observe the recurrence of the image of the clockwork machine, also found in 'Die Götter Griechenlands'. Not just the physical world, but the state as well has turned clockwork under the influence of the mechanistic *Zeitgeist*.

crucial development of an idea we have now encountered several times. For Kleist, we may remember, what caused the trouble was the power to reflect on ourselves and our actions; the trouble it caused was an obscurely described dislocation of the centre of movement, obscurely connected to the existence of self-consciousness. In Schiller's thought all this assumes a shape that is, if not clearer, at any rate rather more familiar to students of philosophy, especially Hegel's: the disease manifests itself as a pressure to make the world consist, or see it as consisting, of opposed forces whose conflict is pulling life and experience apart, and what causes it are the unrestrained or uncompensated operations of a faculty called *Verstand*, translatable, though none too adequately, as 'the understanding'. We shall shortly return to the ill-translatable *Verstand*; first let us look at the mess of which it stands accused. Schiller sees a world littered with divisive dichotomies, some of them requiring us to heed this rather than that:

Now were church and state, law and morals torn apart . . .[9]

some obliging us to spend long hours doing what we otherwise would not, were there not something *else* to follow which depended on it:

the enjoyment was separated from the task, the means from the end, the labour from the reward.

Caught in some fenced-off corner of life, some fragment of the whole, the individual turns into a fenced-off fragment of a human being:

instead of expressing humanity in his nature, he becomes a mere imprint of his occupation, or of his branch of knowledge.

This picture, as Schiller presents it, has no very great argumentative cohesion: it is itself somewhat fragmented. If that final point about human narrowness is true, as to some extent it undoubtedly is, then that has far more to do with the time and energy given to work than with the fact that work is sundered from enjoyment—after all, it is arguably worst in those who enjoy their work most. But hush, we are in the presence of a *Weltbild*, and Schiller enforces its central

---

[9] Ibid. 6th letter—also next two quotations.

concepts of fragmentation, dispersal and possible subsequent reunification with all the means at his disposal. The means at his disposal are, in general terms, literary rather than logical devices—where he does try some abstract argument *à la* Kant the result is pale and derivative[10]—and he wields these literary devices with enormous skill. In a manner impossible to illustrate within a small space he saturates the text with conceptually antithetic pairs: dissolution, connection; whole, part; individual, species; unity, multiplicity; form, content; reason, nature; physical, moral; objective, subjective; change, permanence. It is not, of course, just that all these concepts occur, nor just that they occur prominently, which could equally well be said of the *Critique of Pure Reason*, and no doubt of many other works. It is their exact placing in the text, the way Schiller positions them so as to give rhythm and balance to his sentences. This is something that can be illustrated, in its manner if not its extent. To start with a minor instance: see how he chooses a construction which, by bringing the antithetical pair *Auflösung* (dissolution) and *Verbindung* (connection) as close together as possible, maximises the impact of their contrast (I hasten to add, for any reader with no German, that a variety of other constructions were open to him—there is no question but that the effect is consciously intended):

so findet der Philosoph nur durch Auflösung die Verbindung.[11]

Or here, where he does the same with *Mannigfaltigkeit* (multiplicity) and *Einheit* (unity):

eine Staatsverfassung wird noch sehr unvollendet sein, die nur durch Aufhebung der Mannigfaltigkeit Einheit zu bewirken imstande ist.[12]

But these are very simple examples compared with the following pair of sentences, in which Schiller operates simultaneously with the three contrasting pairs *Vernunft/Natur*, *physisch/moralisch*, *Mannigfaltigkeit/Einheit*, placing them with a

[10] Ibid. 11th letter—e.g. para. beginning 'Die Person, die sich . . .'

[11] Ibid. 1st letter: thus only through dissolving does the philosopher find the connection.

[12] Ibid. 4th letter: a constitution will be very imperfect, that can only produce unity by removing multiplicity.

studied symmetry fit to satisfy the taste of any eighteenth-century architect:

Wenn also die Vernunft in die physische Gesellschaft ihre moralische Einheit bringt, so darf sie die Mannigfaltigkeit der Natur nicht verletzen. Wenn die Natur in dem moralischen Bau der Gesellschaft ihre Mannigfaltigkeit zu behaupten strebt, so darf der moralischen Einheit dadurch kein Abbruch geschehen . . .[13]

There is a certain irony in the way in which this style, so suited to the expression of a balanced and harmonious state of mind, is here used (and most effectively, be it said) in the service of a metaphysic of a very different kind, one for which the actuality is strain and opposition, and balance and harmony only the ideal.

We were to devote a paragraph to the concept of *Verstand*, and a final example of Schiller's favourite stylistic device can take us there. The antitheses are *Natur/Verstand* and *vereinend/trennend* (uniting/separating):

Warum qualifizierte sich der einzelne Grieche zu Representanten seiner Zeit, und warum darf dies der einzelne Neuere nicht wagen? Weil jenem die alles vereinende Natur, diesem der alles trennende Verstand seine Formen erteilten.[14]

Schiller has, so far as I am aware, no independent specification of the workings of *Verstand*, independent, that is, of the idea that it is whatever type of thinking is responsible for the catastrophic product, the fragmentation of life and thought. He does not, it should be said, stick consistently to this derogatory sense, but sometimes falls back into the neutral and colloquial usage in which the meaning of *Verstand* can quite well be captured by 'understanding'. In its more specialised use it is opposed to *Vernunft*, the faculty which, properly applied, can lead us back to the lost unity of nature.[15] Both the distinction and the terminology are, of course, highly characteristic of Hegel. It is, I hope, gradually beginning to emerge just how many of the central theses round which his philosophy is woven were ready and waiting

[13] Ibid. 4th letter.
[14] Ibid. 6th letter.
[15] See for instance the use of this word in the last quotation but one, or the end of the first paragraph of the sixth letter.

for him as well-developed elements of the intellectual world in which he grew up. We shall come back to that story; in any case, it still has a long way to unfold.

It is clear enough that, as Schiller conceived things, there was abundant work for the healing *Vernunft* to do. How, in outline, was it to do it? Was it, for instance, to wipe the slate clean of all those destructively dichotomous pairs and, with a wholly fresh start, generate from within itself a new, and unifying, way of looking at reality? No, or at any rate not exactly; the answer Schiller gives is altogether more Hegelian than that. The opposed tendencies are in themselves perfectly legitimate, even inescapable; they are therefore not to be erased, but combined, and our problem is to find some way of bringing that combination about. To see in a little more detail what he has in mind, let us look at what is, in the *Aesthetic Education of Man*, his principal concern: the nature of beauty and aesthetic experience.

A person, viewed from the highest level of abstraction, comprises a permanent, and a permanently changing factor— the former is the self, the latter its states. The highest development of these two factors would thus involve bringing the widest range of states under the most stable set of principles. In man, where the two factors appear pre-eminently as the faculty of sense on the one hand and the faculty of reason on the other, this means the greatest sensory variety combined with the greatest unity of outlook. That readily makes one think of the natural sciences, aiming to bring a multiplicity of phenomena under a minimum of laws; but where art might fit in is less obvious. Critical for Schiller is the point, drawn like so much of his equipment from the conceptual tools provided by Kant, that the senses are receptive, passive, and the reason spontaneous, active. The senses portray what is given to them from somewhere else, reason imposes upon the sensory material forms and structures it has generated from within itself. This, however, is just another dichotomy, something to be overcome. When we try to unify these two aspects of human nature our search is therefore for an activity which is creative, in which the creative reason imposes on some material a shape or form (hence Schiller now refers to it as the *Formtrieb*) satisfying to itself; and which simultaneously has the effect that the senses receive what is satisfying to them. And so the *Spieltrieb* (which is Schiller's name for the union of the two *prima facie* opposed tendencies):

> will therefore strive to perceive what it has itself produced, and to produce what its senses strive to perceive.[16]

This creative activity in a sensory medium is that of the artist. A beautiful object is something which through its form harmonises with our reason and through its concrete detail satisfies the senses. So that Schiller can now say:

> We have seen the beautiful emerge from the interaction of two opposed drives and the union of two opposed principles. Its highest ideal will therefore be the most perfect possible bond and balance between reality and form.[17]

One need hardly comment that, for all its conceptual euphony, this is in important respects very obscure. We are told of the demand to satisfy the senses, to create something that they can perceive *wie der Sinn zu empfinden trachtet*. But exactly how do the senses 'try to perceive'? That is something we are only given one clue to: apparently they try to perceive with the greatest possible variety, which raises a picture of the greatest works of art as being things of enormous complexity and comprehensiveness. And whilst this might be thought to have some contact with certain tastes, perhaps that for a profusion of baroque detail, for Wagner's *Gesamtkunstwerk*, or for music composed with an eye to Mahler's alleged remark that 'A symphony should contain everything, like the world', it is hardly likely that Schiller himself, with his intense admiration for the attainments of the ancient Greeks, really wanted to recommend this sort of thing as the great artistic ideal. Apart from that, how shall we recognise the 'most perfect possible bond' between form and content, what scales are there to tell us whether they are 'in balance' or not? But such problems should not be unexpected. They are all concepts from the immediate neighbourhood of the great ideal of unity and harmony, the dominant metaphysical concept of

---

[16] F. Schiller: *Äthetische Erziehung des Menschen*, 14th letter.
[17] Ibid. 16th letter.

the era; and we have seen before that such notions usually carry, so long as their time lasts, too many unrecognised hopes and fears to be subjected to clinical examination.

Let it be noticed meanwhile that we are also very much in the neighbourhood of something else: the great cosmic waltz, the metaphysical three-in-a-bar of Hegel's dialectic. There is no systematisation of the dialectic here, it is true; no idea of it as progressive and self-repeating. But the basic idea of the single dialectical triad is open to view: from the clash of two opposed concepts comes a higher concept in which they are fruitfully combined, from the conflict of two opposing forces comes a new and more advanced state. We were asked, after all, 'But how can art combine in itself two contradictory properties?'[18] And now we have been told. Beauty is the synthesis that results from the simultaneous satisfaction of the two opposing drives, the sensuous and the formal. It is not that art, and artistic experience, enables us to dispense with them. On the contrary, it is essential that both be operative; the change is that in the aesthetic life they operate in unison. So we have here a very close parallel, perhaps too close to be called a parallel at all, to one of Hegel's dialectic configurations, with the contradictory thesis and antithesis being *aufgehoben* in their synthesis.

The attentive reader of the *Letters on the Aesthetic Education of Man* will notice much else that is strongly reminiscent of Hegel's central doctrines. One of the most striking I shall postpone until the next chapter, since its appreciation calls for a knowledge of Hegel a little deeper than anything I would wish to presuppose at this stage of the exposition. But three points may appropriately be mentioned here. First, it is widely known that Hegel believed the historical process of the development of consciousness to be both compulsive and self-moving; compulsive because it took its course of necessity, self-moving because he represented the necessity as an *inner* necessity, one that arose from its own nature rather than being imposed from outside, so that within any state of culture there were to be found the materials which would inevitably in due course bring about its decay. The germ of both of these ideas can be found in Schiller's *Letters*, though not, admittedly, in

18 Ibid. 10th letter.

anything like the generality which Hegel was later to give them. Schiller applied it, it will be no surprise to hear, to the modern decline from the cultural excellence of ancient Greece:

The development of humanity in the Greeks was indubitably a maximum, that could neither remain at this point nor climb any higher. It could not remain there, because the understanding was necessarily forced, by the store that it had already acquired, to separate itself from sensation and perception and strive for clarity of knowledge; it could not climb higher, because only a certain degree of clarity is compatible with a given level of variety and warmth. The Greeks had reached this state, and if they wished to go forward to higher developments then, like us, they had to give up the unity of their being and pursue truth by separate paths.[19]

So the bloom of Greek culture had to wither, and it was its own content, the 'Vorrat, den er schon hatte', which made it inevitable. And a third feature should not be overlooked: although Schiller represents the inevitable change as negative, the falling away from what was 'indubitably a maximum', he also allows it a positive aspect. It is decay, but it is also development, or at least it prepares the way for a development leading to a higher plane, in which a sharpening of the clarity of knowledge may be one of the essential ingredients. The course of the dialectic is progress, advance, even though the individual steps may look like, and to those caught up in it feel like, a retreat, the descent from a peak. All this, I need hardly say, is familiar to anyone who knows a little of Hegel.

The second point is this: Hegel was to hold that the state, its laws and institutions, were at any time an embodiment of the current condition of consciousness. Now Schiller, as one might anticipate, needed some such doctrine with which to prosecute his aims as stated in the *Aesthetic Education of Man*. For he there represents the aesthetic as an instrument for the improvement of political circumstances. But what aesthetic experience does, on his account of the matter, is to help us achieve an improved state of consciousness, one in which a better balance is struck between those two essential features in our make-up, sense and reason. If a change of that kind is to have political change as a consequence, political conditions

---

[19] Ibid. 6th letter.

must be taken to depend in some intimate way on the type of consciousness most typical of the citizens; so a doctrine of a Hegelian kind would clearly be welcome to Schiller. And in fact one does find a strong hint of some such thing in a paragraph early in the fourth Letter which, though fogged by some unclarity over when the author is speaking of the state as it is and when of the state as it would ideally be, nevertheless conveys the idea that the state represents, or is 'the objective form' of, whatever is common to the minds of the individuals that compose it:

This pure human being, who can be recognised more or less clearly in every subject, is represented by the state, the objective and as it were canonical form in which the multiplicity of subjects strives to become one.[20]

Third, we can find an anticipation of Hegel's famous doctrine of 'the cunning of reason'. The progress of history is rational; reason drives the world. But it can only do so through the actions of particular individuals, and it hides itself behind them, as it were, so that its ends are realised while they pursue theirs. Schiller's *Vernunft* does something very similar:

Reason will not herself do battle . . . and descend into this dark theatre to act in her own person. But from the midst of the combatants she picks the most worthy, arms him, as Zeus armed his grandchild, with the weapons of the gods, and through his victorious power decides the day.[21]

Missing here is the idea, prominent in Hegel's exposition, that the human instruments of reason do not normally realise whom they are serving. They pursue their own ends—hence the cunning with which reason is said to work. But we do have the picture of reason as agent, operating through the 'world-historical individual' whilst keeping herself in the background. Hegel, less literary and more philosophical in temperament than Schiller, gave this metaphor, and especially the idea of reason as keeping in the background, a rather more literal content.

---

[20] Ibid. 4th letter.
[21] Ibid. 8th letter.

4.   Pantheism, dialectic—and again the image of God

Of the greatest importance in the *Weltbild* of the romantic era
was something of which we have as yet seen only the slightest
trace: a strong leaning towards pantheism and panpsychism.
The trace was in Schiller's 'The Gods of Greece', his depiction
of 'nature according to the ancients', a place flooded with
deities, major and minor. But that was no statement *in propria
persona*, only a sympathetic and somewhat regretful look at the
way things were once thought to be. If we want to find signs of
a belief in panpsychism we must look elsewhere; there are,
however, plenty of places to look. One such place—to head off
any impression that all this was a purely German phenomenon—would be Wordsworth's 'Lines Composed a Few
Miles above Tintern Abbey' of 1798, with its

> . . . sense sublime
> Of something far more deeply interfused,
> Whose dwelling is the light of setting suns
> And the round ocean and the living air,
> And the blue sky, and in the mind of man;
> A motion and a spirit that impels
> All thinking things, all objects of all thought,
> And rolls through all things . . .[22]

Nearly a quarter of a century later the same theme is just as
strong in 'Adonais', Shelley's lament for Keats; here the
emphasis on the formative activity of the spirit invites even
closer comparison with Hegel:

> he doth bear
> His part, while the one Spirit's plastic stress
> Sweeps through the dull dense world, compelling there,
> All new successions to the forms they wear;[23]

a comparison which is made closer still by 'all new suc-
cessions' and its suggestion of a continual process of change
which the spirit fuels and guides. In this verse we have the
elegiac variation on the same theme as was heard three years
earlier in the famous 'Ode to the West Wind', a poem also
much concerned with change and the power that produces it,

[22] Wordsworth: 'Lines composed a Few Miles above Tintern Abbey', 1.95–102.
[23] Shelley: 'Adonais', Stanza XLIII lines 2–5.

the ubiquitous spirit of decay and renewal carrying that dialectical polarity in its own nature:

> Wild spirit, which art moving everywhere;
> Destroyer and preserver . . .[24]

Not only nature, but also 'the mind of man' is its province: Shelley, as we find in the last stanza, can call upon it to reanimate his thoughts as well as to turn winter into spring; its quickening force can act in and through us:

> Make me thy lyre, even as the forest is . . .[25]

For German expressions of panpsychism, such as would have fed directly into Hegel's intellectual world, one thinks immediately of Goethe. But although the next piece to which I shall draw attention has been attributed to him, all that modern scholarship will allow it to claim for certain is a very close connection. It is a short sequence of aphorisms, headed *Die Natur*, which originated in the early 1780s. In his old age Goethe commented that he could not remember writing it, but that it was in good agreement with the state of his thinking as it had been then. There is in some minds a strong suspicion that it was the work of an acquaintance, probably written after discussion with Goethe. I am in no position to referee the dispute, nor is it necessary: it will do that someone was penning such thoughts at the time. Certain is that from his viewpoint of 1828 Goethe wrote of it:

[These remarks] are in close agreement with the conceptions which I had reached at the time. . . . One sees an inclination towards a sort of pantheism, whereby an unfathomable, unconditioned, humorous and self-contradictory being is thought of as the basis of the world of phenomena . . .[26]

Whether it is exactly pantheism which pervades *Die Natur* may involve subtle considerations, though the closing remarks about his attitude to nature do suggest that he thinks of it much as one might think of a god:

---

[24] Shelley: 'Ode to the West Wind', stanza I l.13–14.

[25] Ibid. stanza V l.1.

[26] Goethe: *Erläuterung zu dem aphoristischen Aufsatz 'Die Natur'*, *Werke* (Hamburg edn.) Vol. VIII pp. 48–9.

She has put me here, she will lead me out. I entrust myself to her. Let her play with me. She will not hate her own work.[27]

Be that as it may, one could reasonably claim to find here more than an 'inclination' to panpsychism, for the personification of nature is certainly more than a superficial stylistic device. Nature both feels and speaks, and she does so, apparently, in us—as by Shelley in the 'West Wind', we are cast as vehicles of nature's consciousness. Not only does this mean that nature is being personified in quite a strong and literal sense, it also raises another point: this is not just any brand of panpsychism. It has specific features which make it far more like the system of Hegel than of, for instance, Leibniz, though Leibniz is certainly panpsychist. In such a sentence as: 'She [nature] makes tongues and hearts, with which she feels and speaks' we see a prototype, which in respect of the basic doctrine is not so very different from the finished model, of Hegel's view that the *Idea* rises to consciousness in finite minds.

'A self-contradictory being': so Goethe also described the nature which *Die Natur* portrays, and one can easily see what he meant, for many of the aphorisms make their point and effect precisely by their air of paradox. Of the many possible, one example is this:

She seems to set great store by individuality, and yet not to care for the individual.

Of the myriads of individuals, all are distinguishable from all others in some way, however microscopic (this is the value that nature sets on individuality), but at the same time the natural order treats particular individuals as thoroughly expendable, sometimes in enormous numbers. This raises the temptation to think that we here also see the dialectic anticipated, but it is a temptation that should probably be resisted. The *surface* of nature, it is true, is described in ways which might loosely be called self-contradictory (though the looseness, it must be said, is no looser than in many of Hegel's uses of the word), but there is no clear statement that these effects are the result of any *inner* tension. Looking back from

---

[27] Goethe(?): *Die Natur*, ibid. Vol. VIII pp. 45–7—also next two quotations.

1828, this was one of the things which Goethe noticed; moreover, it then struck him not as a neutral fact but as grounds for criticism. What was missing in *Die Natur*, he then wrote, was: '. . . the vision of the two great springs of all of nature: the concept of polarity and progression . . .'[28] This begins to sound much more Hegelian, though some may find that unsurprising in a piece written when Hegel's mature philosophy had been on public display for some twenty years. But Goethe, it should be said, does not appear to have had a very high opinion of Hegel's mature philosophy,[29] so it is very doubtful whether he could have held this distinctly Hegelian view of nature because of it. Besides, one can find in some lecture notes written down in 1805 a position which, in its description of the ways in which the polar opposites can combine, is if anything even more reminiscent of Hegel. Combination goes with elevation:

What appears must put itself asunder, just in order to appear. That which is asunder searches for itself, and it can find itself again and unite; in a lower sense, by merely mingling with its opposite . . . whereupon the result is zero or at any rate indifferent. But the unification can also take place in a higher sense, in which what has been separated first intensifies itself and by the combination of the two intensified sides brings forth a third thing, new, higher, unexpected.[30]

We were speaking, before this excursus into the subject of contradiction and the dialectic, of the form of pantheism expressed in *Die Natur*, in particular the implication that the divine mind comes to consciousness in man. This view, which might be thought to be a near relative of Spinoza's philosophy, is certainly a near relative of the Image of God doctrine, or rather, it is a further variant of it. Put like that, it is just a fact about the logic of the ideas that were widespread and popular in the romantic period; it does not mean that the thinkers of this period were interested in the Image of God

[28] Goethe: *Erläuterung zu dem aphoristischen Aufsatz 'Die Natur'*, ibid. Vol. VIII pp. 48–9.

[29] See J. P. Eckermann: *Gespräche mit Goethe*, especially the entries for 28 March and 18 October 1827, in *Gedenkausgabe der Werke*, ed. Beutler (Artemis Verlag, 3rd impression 1976) Vol. 24 pp. 602, 669–70.

[30] Goethe: 'Polarität', *Goethes Werke* (Böhlau, Weimar 1893) Section II Volume 11 p. 166.

doctrine, or that they welcomed its close relationship with their other beliefs. But the truth is that they did so, for they were a long way from having pulled up all their seventeenth-century roots; and in the two examples I shall give it is even noticeable that they used it with the same kind of exhortatory overtones which, in Chapter 1, we saw in Galileo and Leibniz.

The first example comes from a work of Goethe's old age, *Wilhelm Meisters Wanderjahre*. It relates—as one might easily have guessed—to an epistemological question, the nature of discovery and invention, and runs as follows:

Everything which we call invention, discovery in the higher sense, is the conscious exercise, the activation of an original feeling for truth which, long since developed in secret, suddenly with lightning speed leads to a fruitful insight. It is a revelation that develops upon the Outer from the Inner, and gives human beings a presentiment of their likeness with God. It is a synthesis of world and mind, that gives the most blissful assurance of the eternal harmony of existence.[31]

What we have here is clearly a new version of the old doctrine, so central to the philosophical thought of the preceding century. What is old about it is the way it postulates a divine state of mind in eternal harmony with the world, and sees our cognitive achievements as momentary participations in this harmony, and so as sure indications of a close similarity between the mind of God and the mind of man. Less common in the seventeenth century (Found only, to the best of my knowledge, in Spinoza) is Goethe's belief in the immanence of the divine mind in the world. That is a development fully in accord with the romantic era's craving for unity, and it makes a veiled appearance in the above passage when we hear of a 'synthesis' of world and mind in the act of discovery or invention—rather than a correspondence or congruence between them.

For the second example we return to Schiller's *Letters on the Aesthetic Education of Man*. It is easy enough to quote a decisive sentence; to explain the thought that lies behind it will take a little longer.

---

[31] Goethe: *Wilhelm Meisters Wanderjahre*, *Werke* Vol. VIII (Hamburg edn.) p. 302.

Man incontrovertibly carries the tendency to divinity in his personality; the route to divinity, if something can be called a route which never reaches its goal, is revealed to his senses.[32]

The path is an infinite one, that is why it never arrives at the goal. But *what* is it which man 'carries in his personality' that can be called a tendency or disposition to divinity?

To begin with, it should be said that 'carries in his personality' is not the happiest of translations. What Schiller is talking about are those properties which a human being has simply by virtue of being a person. This, at the most abstract level, consists in the existence of a permanent component, called the person, and changing components, called its states. (We are thus back in the region of Schiller's account of aesthetic experience.) Both are equally necessary, for: 'Only by changing does he *exist*; only by remaining unchanged, does *he* exist.'[33] The changing component, as Schiller conceives of it, is the world of temporal experiences, the world of the senses (in the broadest meaning of the term). The unchanging component is the reason, or the urge to Form, as he sometimes Platonically calls it. The former stands for multiplicity, the latter for unity. The demand that man realise his full potential is thus the demand that he simultaneously maximise the performances of these two capacities:

From this flow two opposed demands on man, the two fundamental laws of sensory–rational nature. The first calls for absolute reality: all that is just form shall be made world ... the second calls for absolute formality: all that is just world, it wants to swallow up, and bring harmony into all its variety.[34]

He is required, therefore, to set out on an infinite road. The ideal is that everything that is possible for him should become actual, he should experience all the reality that it is possible for him to experience; and simultaneously that all his experience should be grasped as a unity, as flowing of necessity from a single central principle of his rational nature. And to be subject to such a requirement is a mark of divinity, since to be able to meet it is the most distinctive mark of

[32] Schiller: *Ästhetische Erziehung*, 11th letter.
[33] Ibid. 11th letter.
[34] Ibid. 11th letter.

divinity: the full realisation of one's potential on the one hand, coupled on the other with the fact that this realisation is no mere accident felicitously imposed from outside, but the necessary outcome of one's own inner nature.

This, then, is Schiller's version of the Similarity Thesis. It has some interesting features, first amongst which is the essential and integral part played by the notion of agency, the activity of reason in 'forming' reality. That the nature of their active powers should be one of the respects in which human beings are comparable with God is of course nothing very new—we saw earlier how it was developed by Leibniz, for instance. What has changed is the *role* of agency in the treatment of the thesis. Think of Leibniz again: in his philosophy man was compared to God in two principle ways, as a cognitive being (both rational and perceptual) and as an active being. There was, however, no organic interplay between the two; for all that Leibniz said to the contrary, the cognitive comparison might have held even if the agency-based comparison had not, or vice versa. But for Schiller no such separation is possible; the whole basis for the comparison, as he presents it, resides in the way in which the two capacities combine—the sensory, which he sees as passively receptive, and the rational, which he sees as active and formative. As we have just seen him say, man's very existence is tied to both, and when he comes to tell us what man would be like without the rational *Formtrieb* he scarcely paints a picture of a creature on the road to divine status:

So long as he merely feels, merely desires, and acts from mere desire, he is nothing more than world, if by this word one understands merely the formless content of time.[35]

There is indeed action here, but it is the wrong sort of action; only the activity of imposing form on matter, which is supposedly the special province of reason, will do. Leibniz, we recall, was prepared to draw a comparison between man and God on the grounds of *quantity* of perception alone,[36] whereas perception alone does not impress Schiller in the slightest.

What makes this worthy of special notice is the way it

---

[35] Ibid. 11th letter.
[36] Leibniz: *Discours de Metaphysique* IX; see above, Chapter 1 Section 6.

relates to the largest of this book's historical themes. Schiller's doctrine looks both ways. Explicitly, it looks back to the Image of God doctrine; implicitly, it also looks forward to the epoch in which the concept of agency, of doing and creating, would take over the centre of the philosophical stage and in so doing change the tenor of European thought entirely, a phenomenon we shall be more or less exclusively concerned with in Chapters 5 and 6, and to a considerable extent in Chapter 4. In the period we are now thinking about, this new movement was just beginning to gather momentum, set on its way on the one hand by Kant,[37] , on the other by the forces of the romantic metaphysic. In Schiller, manifestly, both are at work—the knowledgeable reader will long since have noticed how much of Kant there is in his view of human nature as the interaction of sense and reason.

In passing, it is instructive to notice how Schiller adapts Kant to his own purposes, which features of the Kantian philosophy he chooses to emphasise. No stress here on the split between the phenomenal and the noumenal, the knowable and the unknowable. For the romantics, this was the dark side of Kant, another of the fateful dichotomies, a cleft in the intellectual landscape which he in no way helped them to bridge—quite the contrary. The bright side, on which Schiller seizes, was the one that had to do with wholeness: the doctrine of the essential co-operation of perception and thought, sense and reason, and, here of special relevance, Kant's doctrine of our experience of the beautiful as the feeling of pleasure arising from the *harmony* of our cognitive faculties in a perceptual experience.

Notable also is a fact about the way in which Schiller, in the *Aesthetic Education of Man*, achieves his own position: by means of an enormous and undiscussed input of idealism. He seems to take it as read that reason in human nature *forms* the reality of sense, rather than makes discoveries about a reality already there; and once one does that one has already placed the notion of agency, creativity, unquestioningly at the heart of one's metaphysic and theory of knowledge. No doubt this is in large measure due to the proximity of Kant, but it can still be asked why Schiller found Kant's basic idea of the active role of

[37] On this point much more in Chapter 5.

the mind in the formation of (empirical) reality so smoothly acceptable. Was it perhaps the attraction of being able to regard the human mind as creative, emancipated, autonomously generating its own world? That is not the only possible answer: one might point out that it also satisfied the romantic wish to find one's own image in nature. So it did, but this is a wish which can be satisfied in other ways, and in a sense previously had been, by other means not involving Kantianism; it can be satisfied, for instance, by supposing an affinity between the human mind and the mind that was responsible for the design of nature, and so understanding our discoveries as a matching up between our thoughts and the principles embodied in nature by the creator. It can hardly be said that such a philosophy was unavailable at the end of the eighteenth century—it had recently been standard doctrine for well over a hundred and fifty years. So an explanation in terms of the narcissistic wish exemplified by Goethe's fisherman cannot be the whole of the story, and it still looks as if the wish to make the human mind itself a creator, and no mere spectator (however divinely equipped), is exerting a direct influence.

5. *Hyperion*

Let us now recapitulate the principal features, as it were the bare bones, of this material. What we have seen is the occurrence, in the writings of several prominent figures of the period, of a number of interconnectable beliefs. The figures were selected with an eye to the documentation of the claim that what we think of as philosophy proper is not the only medium that should attract the historian of philosophy; and the beliefs were selected with a view to the discussion of Hegel which is shortly to follow. The intention was to give an impression of the extent to which the skeleton of his philosophy was already independently in existence at the time when his thought was forming, and of the types of writing in which it was to be found.

The first theme we met was that of alienation, the loss of unity with one's surroundings; this was then connected with the current state of the sciences, and more generally with the ill effects of the faculty of *Verstand*, which created conceptual division and was powerless to heal it. There followed material concerned with the recovery of unity, especially with the unity of the trio of nature, man and God. Pantheism united God and nature; doctrines such as those we have seen in Schiller and Kleist gave man a certain share in the divine, and, granted such human participation in the divine, the romantics' echo of the Similarity Thesis, pantheism makes a link between man and nature—the principles that man embodies are declared also to animate the world. This latter connection could also be made, as by Schiller, by appeal to the transcendental idealism of Kant. We have also seen that there is a progression, in some sense a necessary progression, both in the natural world and in the realm of thought, both in the development of the race and in the life of the individual. Finally, there were some hints about the nature of the progression and the forces that fuel it: the conflict of opposites and the resolution of the conflict in a way that affords full recognition of the rights of each, a way that elevates both and does not require the liquidation of either.

These thoughts we have found scattered amongst various works and authors of the period. But there is one author, and indeed one single work, where all of this is found at once: Hölderlin's novel *Hyperion*. We need not enter into bio-graphical detail any further than to remark that Hölderlin and Hegel were friends as students, and that they were very close to each other for much of the period[38] during which *Hyperion* was composed. Nothing in the early (and mostly theological) writings of Hegel from these years is half so 'Hegelian' as this novel; no more thorough attempt to incorporate what were to become the main principles of Hegel's mature philosophy into the fabric of a work in a literary genre can readily be imagined.

Hyperion consists of a series of letter-like chapters, none very long, nearly all of them written by the hero Hyperion to one Bellarmin, a figure who stands aloof, completely external to the events and thoughts of the narrative—this might just as well be soliloquy. Certainly it is *of* himself that Hyperion

[38] 1792–7. See D. Henrich: 'Hegel und Hölderlin' in *Hegel im Kontext* (Suhrkamp 1971) pp. 9–40, and H. S. Harris: *Hegel's Development: Toward the Sunlight* (Oxford 1972), esp. p. 253.

writes, if not actually *to* himself; almost all the text is directly
autobiographical, as well as being heavily introspective. We
have already seen that the then favoured picture of the
journeyings of man had two variants, one in which the subject
was the pattern of the individual life, one in which the interest
centred rather on the history of the race. The weight of the
autobiographical element in *Hyperion* ensures that the emphasis falls squarely on the former. But it is only a matter of
emphasis. Hyperion is a latter-day Greek, and so feels with
the special sharpness of a compatriot the pain of the
deterioration from the golden age of Greek antiquity which
was such a favourite theme with German writers of the
romantic era. He tells of a visit, in the company of Adamas his
boyhood mentor, to the island of Delos. More than a distant
echo of Schiller's 'Die Götter Griechenlands' is to be heard as
he describes the ancient festivals of Mount Cynthus and their
inspirational effects upon his ancestors:

Here lived the sun-god once... here Greek youths threw
themselves, like Achilles into the Styx, into floods of joy and
enthusiasm—and emerged, like the demi-god, invincible.[39]

But now:

why speak of it?... Under the curse which lies heavy on us not even
a beautiful dream can flourish.[40]

One source of this state is the political circumstance of
Greece's domination by a foreign power, against which
Hyperion later takes arms (to 'drive the Sultan back to the
Euphrates'). But the real trouble is something different,
something internal to the spirit: that pervasive obsession of
the period, division, alienation, the loss of unity with nature
and God. '... a divine, undivided life'[41] is the ideal for man:
'To be one with everything, that is the life of the deity, that is
heaven for men'.[42] The curse of which Hölderlin writes is not

[39] Hölderlin: *Werke und Briefe*, ed. Beissner and Schmidt (Insel Verlag, Frankfurt
1969) Vol. I p. 303. Page numbers in all following footnotes are to this edition, and
refer to Vol. I unless otherwise stated. English translations given in the text are mine.
There does exist an English version of *Hyperion*, trans. Willard R. Trask, published by
New American Library inc.1965.
[40] Ibid. pp. 303–4.
[41] Ibid. p. 416.
[42] Ibid. p. 297.

so much that of the Ottoman empire as the loss of the right relationship with the rest of reality. It is (though this time Hyperion says it with explicit reference to the Germans): '. . . the curse of an unnatural nature abandoned by God . . .'.[43] That unity, which Schiller also lamented, is gone. Hyperion 'stands before nature like a stranger, and does not understand her'. If we have heard this before, we have also heard Hyperion's opinion as to what is responsible for it: the old enemy, knowledge, the sciences, the understanding and its art of making distinctions:

Alas, if only I had never gone to your schools. The knowledge which I followed down into the pit, from which in youthful foolishness I expected the confirmation of my joy—that is what has spoilt everything for me. I have myself become so very rational, I have learned sharply to distinguish myself from what surrounds me; I am now isolated in this beautiful world, thrown out of the garden of nature where I grew and blossomed, and I parch in the midday sun.[44]

This image of Eden at once draws his mind back to his childhood, that time of wholeness:

Yes! A child is a divine thing. It is wholly what it is, and that is why it is so beautiful . . . it is not yet inwardly at variance with itself.[45]

And what is true of the individual can also be said of peoples: 'From childlike harmony the nations once set out . . .'.[46] For Hölderlin, this childlike wholeness is something which only a god can share. Like the natural grace of the adolescent boy in Kleist's 'Über das Marionettentheater', it is a state to be found only at either end of the infinite road: '. . . only gods and children are not touched by fate.'[47] But infinite though the road may be, man is well enough equipped to travel on it; there is nothing tentative about Hölderlin's belief in a divine element in humanity:

Is the god in us, before whom infinite paths open up, to stand and wait until the worm gets out of his way?[48]
But man is a god, as soon as he is human.[49]

[43] Ibid. p. 434.
[44] Ibid. p. 298.
[45] Ibid. pp. 298–9.
[46] Ibid. p. 349.
[47] Ibid. p. 419.
[48] Ibid. p. 316.
[49] Ibid. p. 365.

Here we have reached an old friend: the Image of God doctrine in its new romantic dress. And if we find God in self, we also find self in nature:

as the sun in the sky saw itself in the thousandfold play of light which the Earth reflected, so my spirit recognised itself in the abundance of life which surrounded it and fell upon it from all sides.[50]

This thought we also know, having met it in two rather different treatments by Goethe and Schiller. (Incidentally, we have also met the imagery: in Goethe's 'Der Fischer' the thoughts of the reflection of the sun and that of the fisherman himself were similarly juxtaposed.) These two, the vision of self in nature and the closeness of man and God, are several times during the novel found in each other's company:

Lost in the broad blue, I often look up at the sky and into the sea of heaven, and it feels as if a kindred spirit were opening its arms to me, as if the pain of loneliness were dissolving into the life of God.[51]

Sometimes this point is couched in language which is more directly reminiscent of Hegel's way of speaking: mind and nature are not so much related, they are rather to be thought of as *identical*:

Blessed nature! You are the same within me and without. It cannot be so difficult, to unite what is outside with the divine within me.[52]

And the goal which Hyperion confidently looks forward to:

There will be but one Beauty; and man and nature will combine in an all-embracing deity.[53]

The great triangle of oppositions, man/nature, nature/God, God/Man, will collapse into a single point.

We should notice in passing one particular detail of Hölderlin's treatment of this theme of the potential divinity of man, or, as he sometimes sees it, the actual divinity of man which shows itself in brief and infrequent moments of ecstasy. It concerns the way in which the process of releasing the divine in human nature may be advanced by contact between

[50] Ibid. p. 309.   [52] Ibid. p. 374.
[51] Ibid. p. 297.   [53] Ibid. p. 375.

persons, the way in which a more advanced traveller may draw another after him. There is, for Hölderlin, a tendency to become (to speak now with Hegel) like one's 'other', to find one's consciousness heightened by contact with another mind in which that heightened consciousness is already present. Its interest for our investigation is the similarity it bears to certain remarks Hegel made about the relationship between master and slave in the famous chapter from the *Phenomenology of Spirit*. Hyperion describes his response to the company of the older Adamas:

And I, was I not the echo of his quiet enthusiasm? Did not the melodies of his being repeat themselves in me? What I saw, I became, and what I saw was divine.[54]

One final point before leaving the topic of Hölderlin's portrayal of the unity between man and nature: it is not something which he carries on only in direct and explicit statement. He also crowds the text with natural descriptions used as images for his characters' states of mind. Again one can illustrate the kind, but not the quantity. Here is an example, drawn from the hero's description of the companionship of Diotima, shortly after the first flowering of their love for one another:

Our conversations slipped away, like a sky-blue stream from which the sand occasionally flashes golden, and our silence was like the silence of mountain peaks, where in lordly, lonely height, far above the storms, only the divine air rustles the hair of the bold climber.[55]

Not only the nearness of man and nature, but the way in which this nearness brings man near to God, is the subject here. That is explicit at the end; but it is implicitly present from the beginning of the quotation. In the lovers' conversation was a reflection of heaven—*himmelblau* is not just a longer word for blue, nor is it there by accident; the reflection of the blue sky was a symbol of a beckoning heaven on Earth. Recall how Goethe's water-sprite tempted the fisherman:

> Does the deep sky not entice you,
> The transfigured watery blue?

[54] Ibid. p. 302.
[55] Ibid. p. 360.

Hölderlin, incidentally, was evidently well equipped for his climbing expeditions; without the right metaphysic in the rucksack mountain-tops often seem rather more inhospitable places than this.

Hyperion is, as I have said, broadly autobiographical in form; hence it is, when seen from a little distance, narrational. But the primary function of the narrative is to provide a series of situations on and around which the autobiographer-hero can weave his web of philosophico-poetic comment; they have little depth of their own beyond what is needed for that purpose, and if one could free the narrative elements from the rest they would appear utterly commonplace and banal. Neither they nor the *dramatis personae* of *Hyperion* can be said genuinely to illustrate, and so in any measure to justify, the theses which the author pins to them; they are not so much the portrait as the nail on which a portrait is hung, and they share a nail's approximation to one-dimensionality. Because there is so great a gap between scenes and persons as described and the philosophical reflections which they are supposed to generate and support, *Hyperion* will doubtless strike many modern readers, as it often strikes this one, as an appallingly sentimental work. One can well understand how Hegel's imagination may have been fired by its metaphysic and by its author's sheer unashamed enthusiasm for it; but at the same time it is not surprising if he felt that some strictness had to be reintroduced into thought, that contact had to be renewed between philosophical theorising and the facts of logic and cultural history. Whether his response to that feeling, to try to achieve the rigour whilst preserving the metaphysical picture, was the right, or even an admissible one, is another question.

One thing, however, must be said in mitigation of these remarks, for there is at least one respect in which the plot of *Hyperion*, even if it were stripped of its heroics and taken unembellished, would still do something to Hölderlin's purpose. It would still to some degree serve as an illustration of two themes that are of great importance, both to him and to the philosophical system of Hegel. One is that of the repeated succession, in nature and in human life, of the positive and the negative, the rhythm of joy and distress, progress and (apparent) regress. The second is the doctrine of commerce with the 'other' followed by the return to self, a self now modified by its experience of that 'other'. Hyperion is made to say:

Does not life consist in the motley of opening and closing, in going forth and returning to oneself—why not then the heart of man?[56]

Why not indeed? The novel is certainly structured with the idea of this movement, this ebb and flow of reality, very prominently in mind. Thus upon the angry, disillusioned parting from Alabanda there follows a period of withdrawn emotional inaction, mental convalescence, during which Hyperion, having (significantly) returned to his home island of Tina, inwardly and unconsciously prepares himself for his next great encounter with life and love, the meeting with Diotima: 'Now I lived very quietly and modestly in Tina. I let the sights of the world flow past me, like autumn mists . . .'[57] 'Like autumn mists', external things are become insubstantial, out of focus; they no longer impinge upon him: 'Now neither the distant nor the near forced its way into my senses; if people did not compel me to see them, I did not notice them.'[58] But then comes the reawakening, the spring of the spirit (for in Hölderlin's great hymn to nature every movement of the psyche has to have its natural parallel), and the mind awakens changed, and not just changed but improved and ready to occupy a higher plane of being:

Now my eyes really opened once again. Not, admittedly, as before, armed and full of their own strength. They had become more pleading, begging for life; but deep in me it felt as if my life could once again become what it had been, and better.[59]

Which indeed it does. Once more he begins to find contact with his companions and his surroundings, and soon an apparently chance invitation from a friend leads him out into the world again, away from Tina to new territory, where he finds Diotima. Thus in the psychological patterns of Hölderlin's narrative is seen a principle which Hegel was to set at the centre of his metaphysics: the return to self from the *other*, and

---

[56] Ibid. p. 325.
[57] Ibid. pp. 327–8.
[58] Ibid. p. 330.
[59] Ibid. p. 331.

the going forth again both altered and elevated by the encounter.

That is not, of course, the only example; we may briefly mention another. Hyperion, close to death from wounds received in battle with the Turks, is in convalescence in the care of Alabanda. For six days he lies 'in deathly sleep', intermittently conscious of pain and of nothing else whatever. Gradually recovery begins, and once again we see the same pattern of withdrawal into self followed by an out-going, a return to the world: 'I returned to life with senses more tranquil, and my soul had become more attentive.'[60] Those 'more tranquil' states signal another step towards the peace of mind that he has been seeking since his story began, and which he appears to have achieved in its closing pages.

The other rhythmic figure that pervades the plot of *Hyperion* is that of the alternation of the positive and the negative, joy and pain, success and frustration: '. . . I . . . reflect on my life, its rise and fall, its bliss and its sadness . . .'[61] So Hyperion experiences the inspiration of his relationship with Adamas, and the pain of parting from him; the joy of his friendship with Alabanda, and the anguish of their quarrel; the delight of his love for Diotima, and the misery of leaving her; the enthusiasm for the cause of Greek independence, and the despair over his military failure. Always it is the agony and the ecstasy, and the agony again, for Hyperion has a talent for experiencing both to the full, and a deep scorn for those who do not:

Do not envy those who do not suffer, those wooden idols. They want for nothing, because their souls are so poor; they do not ask for rain and sunshine, because they have nothing that needs to be nurtured.[62]

Only he who feels what Hegel came to call 'the pain of the negative' can be a leader in the life of the spirit. Progress consists of death and rebirth, and therefore the negative, through which the road to salvation must therefore inevitably pass, is not to be shunned but welcomed:

---

[60] Ibid. p. 407.
[61] Ibid. p. 334.
[62] Ibid. p. 327.

Let what passes pass, I cried to the enraptured crowd. It passes that it may come again, it grows old that it may rejuvenate itself, it divides that it may unite more intimately, it dies that it may be more alive.[63]

We can find, in Hölderlin's writings, not just the broad outline of Hegel's dialectical movement; if we look more closely we begin to see some of its finer detail as well. Crucial to the theory of the dialectic is the doctrine of *Aufhebung*, according to which the earlier members of the dialectic progression, though superseded, nevertheless continue to be present in their successors, which are what they are only because they have precisely that ancestry. In Hölderlin's essay 'Das Werden im Vergehen', written a little later than *Hyperion*, we find a very similar thought unmistakably expressed:

But the possible which becomes real when reality dissolves, this is active, and it produces not just the sensation of dissolution but also the memory of what was dissolved.[64]

Two of the Hegelian senses of *Aufheben* are here catered for: there is dissolution, the old reality disappears, but with the pain of that dissolution there goes the memory of what was, a trace that persists and will colour the future. The third sense, that of raising something to a higher level, we have already seen in *Hyperion* itself.

Such are the main pillars of Hölderlin's philosophy. Individually, we have seen them all elsewhere, but only in his work, and particularly in *Hyperion*, are they brought together to form a single vision of life and reality. It is in its essentials the same vision as that purveyed by Hegel,[65] though the dress in which it appears is wholly different in the two men. Hölderlin's is a poetic mind, full of flamboyant imagery and extrovert enthusiasm; these, and the insistence on psychological observations which the willing reader can easily apply to his own experience, are the instruments with which he attempts to generate support for his beliefs. Hegel's stylistic exterior is cold and contorted, though it hides more repressed

---

[63] Ibid. p. 456—this passage is from the *Fragment von Hyperion*.

[64] Hölderlin: *Das Werden im Vergehen* ibid. Vol. II p. 642.

[65] H. S. Harris (in *Hegel's Development: Toward the Sunlight* p. 253) toyed with the idea that Hölderlin is the true originator of German idealism—I would not have dismissed it quite so quickly.

poetry than is generally imagined, poetry which occasionally breaks out on the surface in some of his more pregnant and memorable utterances. What he added to the metaphysical vision of his student friend was an amazing intellectual systematisation of the vision and the application of it to an amazingly wide range of empirical fact. In doing so, he made the additional claim to have *proved* its truth. And although this claim, soberly considered, was amongst the most spurious ever to have attained a position of honour in the history of human thought, the mere existence of this systematisation clearly had enormous power to carry the conviction of his audiences. Whether the breadth and structure of a conception are by themselves an argument for it is a deep question in the theory of truth; but there can be little doubt that they are important factors in its propagation.

To the student of Hegel I recommend a reading of Hölderlin's *Hyperion* in the strongest possible terms. It is a short book, so that no great investment of time is involved; and I would go so far as to say that there is no understanding Hegel without it.

4

ONE WAY TO READ HEGEL

1. *A child of his time*

Knowledge of Hegel in the English-speaking world has been
on the increase for some years, but things are not yet so
advanced as to permit the assumption that every reader will
effortlessly and instantly follow the connections between the
materials of Chapter 3 and the grand philosophical system
which he left us. So at this juncture I shall sketch that system
in its essential outline with a view to making these connections
clearer, and ask the growing bunch of the informed to bear
with me while I do so. In the preceding chapter there was
more than a hint that the dozen or so theses we looked at, as
they made their appearance in the literature of Hegel's time,
form the skeleton of his philosophy. But it should not be
supposed that he simply accepted and repeated them; rather
he transformed them by incorporation into a whole in
which all the various oppositions and disunities, the bane of
the romantic intellectual's world, were resolved or resolvable,
every hope and expectation fulfilled.

Besides attaching Hegel to Chapter 3, the present chapter
has another matter on its agenda, that of locating Hegel in the
wider scheme of this book as a whole, which means relating
his philosophy to the two major themes of the title. First, it is
to be shown how he picked up the idea of the divinity of man;
that, as we have seen, is a prominent feature of the romantic
Weltbild, so that this part of the task fits smoothly into the
business of displaying his affinities with that movement. But
we shall also see that he did it in such a way as to keep contact
with the Similarity Thesis as it had existed in the period that
was the subject of Chapter 1: it is the possession of reason
which makes the link. Hegel did not simply mouth that by
now hackneyed slogan; he provided a genuine articulation of
it in the form of a detailed and far from hackneyed theory of

what reason, and the possession of reason, amounts to. That theory, what was more, was highly appropriate to the romantic metaphysic of his contemporaries, so that he was able in a sense to achieve a synthesis of the traditional Image of God philosophy and the quite particular and relatively short-lived intellectual climate of his own generation. Second, we are to see how Hegel added impetus and theoretical weight to a style of thought then near the beginning of its subsequently all-conquering career: that which, by stressing human autonomy and creativity, turns the philosophical spotlight away from the divine mind and the knowledge of its works and on to *the works of man*. It is what, I suppose, Nietzsche had in mind when he wrote of Hegel: '. . . a symptom . . . of a new strength: the "spirit" itself is the "self-revealing and self-realising ideal" . . .'.[1] From section 4 of this chapter onward the rest of the book is devoted to this theme—so I shall not here try to anticipate.

Two other general themes will also appear: the idea that the underlying metaphysic can influence what an author regards as a sufficiently cogent argument, and the claim, earlier illustrated at length with reference to Hume, that a knowledge of it can affect one's reading of close details of the text (down to the meaning of individual words) and so make comprehensible reading out of passages that are otherwise baffling. Thus sections 2 and 3 are of the former type, section 5 of the latter.

Hegel's philosophy, in its most systematic statement in the *Encyclopedia of the Philosophical Sciences*, consists of three parts, corresponding to the three branches of his ontology. There is first the Logic, which he also refers to as the Science of the Idea; there is the Philosophy of Nature, and finally the Philosophy of Mind (or 'Spirit'—neither word is a wholly satisfactory translation of Hegel's *Geist*[2]). We shall not go far wrong in understanding these headings if we take 'nature' in its current sense, that is to designate the totality of the objects of the natural sciences. As another approximation, we may anticipate that the Philosophy of Mind will deal with the

---

[1] Nietzsche: *The Will to Power*, trans. Kaufmann and Hollingdale, para. 253.

[2] 'Mind' is not theological enough in its overtones, 'spirit' not intellectual enough—as will become apparent.

phenomena of consciousness, though we must notice that the word will have to be very broadly understood—it will turn out to include cultural phenomena such as religion, art and social institutions, all such as influence and are influenced by the way in which we think and the things that we value. But the fact that Hegel's Nature and Mind are concepts not too strange to the modern reader should not lead him to suppose that the second and third divisions of his system, the Philosophy of Nature and the Philosophy of *Geist*, are philosophy of science and philosophy of mind (with a little aesthetics, theology and social theory thrown in) as we now think of them. What Hegel understands by 'the philosophy of' is something highly individual, and to grasp it one needs prior acquaintance with the first division, the Logic or Science of the Idea.

We may approach Hegel's conception of logic in steps, starting from more familiar ground. Kant had proposed a set of categories, as he called them, twelve concepts of very wide applicability, having two especially salient properties. First, their use is obligatory if there is to be thought at all; second, in using them we give form to our experience and therefore also to the world-as-we-experience-it, Kant's 'empirical reality'. But he said very little in answer to the question why there should be just these categories and no more, apart from deriving them from a table of twelve judgement-forms, of which just the same question can be asked.[3] And apart from dividing them into four groups of three he said little about the internal structure of the set, with the notable exception of a solitary remark to the effect that the third category in each of his four trios 'arises from the combination of the second with the first'.[4] Hegel, who actually makes much use of this idea, nowhere to my knowledge allows that the beginnings of it are to be found in Kant; if anything, he implies the contrary, though he does give Kant credit for his emphasis on triadic conceptual structure.[5]

Hegel took over this conception of a category but supplemented it and modified it in certain decisive respects.

[3] See *Critique of Pure Reason* B145–6.

[4] Ibid. B110–1.

[5] See *The Phenomenology of Spirit*, trans. Miller (Oxford 1977) (hereafter PG), preface para. 50.

Briefly, he rendered it far more systematic, in that he claimed to discover and exhibit a far more closely knit structure than Kant had contemplated; it seems that in Hegel's scheme a clear view of any one of the categories would in principle enable the derivation of all of the others. He extended it, in that he believed that the discovery of the structure led to the discovery of far more categories than Kant had allowed. He also—and this is perhaps the main stumbling-block to modern understanding of his thought—*objectivised* it. Whereas Kant had regarded the categories as the basis of *our* experience and so formative only of the 'empirically real' or the world-as-it-appears-to-us, Hegel—no friend, as we shall see, of any such subjectivism—made them objective constituents of the *Ding-an-sich*, whilst retaining Kant's idea that they were formative, and hence determined the nature of reality—a reality that was no longer merely 'empirical'. The view that *concepts* can be thus embedded in reality and actively determinant of it is doubtless a difficult one. But Hegel did something, at least, to smooth the way by referring to these concepts as 'thoughts' and equating them with *universals*, a tactic which enabled him to call upon the Aristotelian tradition of *universalia in rebus* to give his doctrine a degree of familiarity.

This system of intimately connected thoughts, or universals, Hegel now calls 'The Idea'; the Logic undertakes the detailed investigation of it. Which thoughts constitute the *Idea*, and how are they related to each other? His answer reflects the romantic obsession with the clash of opposed forces, conflict and its resolution. If we start with any concept we shall find that the thought of it inexorably gives rise to the thought of its opposite, a concept which we would naturally regard as its contradictory. In a second step, these two opposed concepts are seen to be united in a third, which thus in a sense contains them both and resolves their conflict. This new concept is then the starting-point for a repetition of the triadic process, and so further concepts come to be formed. There are problems about this account of the matter, admittedly. For one thing, it is not at all clear (and never becomes clear) just what this 'giving rise' amounts to—that Hegel was able to insist on it, and its centrality, without being more explicit about its exact nature, is in itself a significant pointer to the intellectual mood for which he wrote, and its willingness to find opposition and conflict inherent in all things. And for another, I have allowed myself to smooth off a few corners, inasmuch as the simple formula of thesis, antithesis and synthesis, with the latter becoming the thesis for the next round of the dialectic, does not give a perfect fit with all details of the text. But as approximations go it is no bad one, and seems to have been favoured by Hegel whenever he stood back and described his own procedure.

To follow the development of this conceptual structure from its origin in the concept of being (Hegel favours this starting-point because, he says, it is the emptiest, most general concept available) is the work of the Logic. But the oppositions or 'contradictions' which occur repeatedly on the small scale within the Idea also characterise the mutual relationships of the larger elements of the Hegelian ontology. When we think of the system of interconnected universals which is the object of the Logic we are brought to think of nature, an extended system of particulars; for we cannot think of the universals as existent unless they are embodied in particulars—no more, for that matter, than we can think of the particulars as existing without instantiating universals. For Hegel this means, however, that out of the thought of either there arises the thought of its opposite; for thought and things, universals and particulars, the abstract and the concrete, are all opposed pairs. And yet we can also see that they are essentially united: neither has any being independently of the other.

That nature embodies the Idea means much more to Hegel than just the anodyne thought that objects have properties or are instances of universals. It means, much more excitingly, that in doing Logic, tracing out the structure of the Idea, we are at the same time uncovering the basic principles that actuate nature; what we acquire is not just a catalogue of properties of natural things, but an understanding deeper than that which natural science can give us of just why Nature is as it is. Hegel quotes with approval[6] an expression of Schelling, who had said that Nature was 'petrified intelligence'; and he himself wrote of the way in which '. . . the Idea

---

[6] *Encyclopedia of the Philosophical Sciences* (hereafter E) Part I para. 24 Zusatz.

interprets itself in space as Nature'.[7] Here, then, is the much-desired union of opposites. The romantic obsession finds its consummation, an event which Hegel celebrates in somewhat dramatised language, announcing Idea and nature to be each the other's *Other*, and at the same time to be *Identical*. In this vein, he describes the Philosophy of Nature as 'The Science of the Idea in its Otherness',[8] that branch of philosophy which lays bare the workings of the Idea in the physical world, its material manifestation.

The pervasive fact of dialectical progression, by which is understood the now-familiar pattern of emergence of conflict followed by the resolution of the conflicting tendencies, is equally important in the third section of Hegel's philosophy, in which he turns to the phenomena of consciousness and culture. This prominence is only what we should expect, since consciousness, on Hegel's conception of things, has a deep metaphysical purpose: in it, the Idea is to rise to self-knowledge, an awareness of its own nature. Consciousness (which means human consciousness) is to achieve this on its behalf by gradually discerning the principles which govern its own thinking; these are the same as those we encountered in abstract form when, in doing Logic, we studied the Idea as it is in itself, that is to say in abstraction from its intimate connections with nature and mind. These principles are the same because mind is the conscious manifestation of the Idea. And it is only because it is a conscious manifestation of it that we are able to study the Idea—all that is required is for us to look in on our own essential thought-processes. In the contemplation of the Logic, the traditionally opposed terms of the thinker and the subject-matter of his thought melt into one—the basic formula again. Whether Hegel's arguments come anywhere near entitling him to this conclusion is a question we shall investigate later,[9] but there is no doubt

---

[7] *Lectures on the Philosophy of History*, Introduction C(c). (I have chosen a way of giving references which, whilst not the most convenient, since the sub-sections located are not always very short, at least gives the reader a chance of tracking down the passage in most editions—though it has to be said that there are editorial problems, and hence considerable variations in the text. Note that there are editions which denote the main sections by I, II, III, rather than A, B, and C.)

[8]. E Part I para. 18.

[9] See below, Chapter 4 Section 2.

either that he holds it or that he thereby met the wishes of his time.

The romantic vision called for the oneness of man and nature, the immanence of God in nature, and an element of divinity in man. We are already in a position to see how Hegel's system satisfied demand on the first of these points: since the same principles underlie both nature and human consciousness we can, given sufficient philosophy (the Hegelian kind, of course), find *ourselves*, or the reflection of our own operations, in the natural world. The same had been true for Kant, but with two differences: since there are many more such principles than the ones he proclaimed, the permeation of nature by *Geist* is accordingly very much more extensive; and whereas for Kant it had arisen out of the fact that nature is to a certain extent of our own making, for Hegel it exists because nature and the human mind have, in the Idea, a common ground.

If Hegel straightforwardly identified God with the Idea, the other two sides of the romantic triangle would follow immediately; but the matter is not quite so simple. God is infinite, and that means, for Hegel, that there is nothing which is not God. To be infinite is to have no limits, in the sense not of just (monotonously, as Hegel sees it) going on for ever, but in that of including everything. Now since everything is, in his terms, identical with the Idea, it would be permissible to identify the Idea with God, and he often does speak in this way. But we must remember Hegel's penchant for the notion of 'identity-in-difference', and the fact that nature is equally to be seen as the Idea's 'Other'—similarly, nature and mind are 'Others' too, as well as being identifiable. From this perspective it is therefore proper to say that God is not *one* out of Idea, nature and *Geist*, to the exclusion of the others, but that each is a part or aspect of him. (Hegel even went so far as to identify these aspects with the persons of the Trinity.) This surely makes the relation between God and nature intimate enough to satisfy any romantic pantheistic leanings. It also does the same, though here the issues are a little more complex, for man and God, and this in the particularly interesting way on which we have already briefly touched.

The Idea, as such, is not conscious. If it is to become

conscious of itself and its own nature it is only in minds, which in effect means human minds, that this can come about. So it is that for Hegel our consciousness is the vehicle of God's self-knowledge, and in our thought the *Weltgeist* gradually comes to know itself as it is. And so he attached himself to the Christian saying and the philosophical motto of the seventeenth and eighteenth centuries:

Philosophy is knowledge, and it is through knowledge that man first realises his original vocation, to be the image of God.[10]

In this passage he understates his real view, however, which is rather that, in a manner reminiscent of Spinoza and Malebranche, we participate in the divine thought. But even that is an understatement, for Hegel has a trump card to play which Spinoza and Malebranche lacked: we are not just some fragmentary part of the divine mind, a drop in an infinite ocean. In so far as it is consciousness that is in question, there is nothing to God's thought but what is in our minds—our conscious thought *is* the consciousness of the deity. The Image of God doctrine, the thesis of the divinity of man, reaches its climax. In much the same way, the author of *Die Natur*[11] had made us the vehicle of the feelings of nature, and our words the vehicle of her speech. It is worth noticing also that the idea of a human being acting as a vehicle for divine activity is found (once again!) in Hölderlin's *Hyperion*:

Man is a cloak, which often a god throws around himself, a chalice into which heaven pours its nectar that its children may be allowed to taste of the best.[12]

Two points should at once be noted. First, it is not necessarily all our conscious thought which has this status; second, as could be heard in the words 'the World-spirit *gradually* comes to know itself', there is a historical thesis in the offing. In Hegel's hands, we shall see, these two points are made to combine. What is crucial is the extent to which, at any one time, there is awareness of the nature of the Idea; the level of awareness he holds to be historically variable, and more specifically to be steadily rising. Such features of conscious-

[10] E Part I para. 24 Zusatz 3.
[11] See above, Chapter 3 Section 4.
[12] Hölderlin: *Hyperion*, in *Werke und Briefe* ed.Beissner and Schmidt Vol. 1 p. 359.

ness, if any, as have nothing to do with awareness of the Idea
are irrelevant to this process, and to the equation of human
thought and the mind of God in its conscious aspect. But the
reader should beware of the implication that, since it is
philosophy which increases our awareness of the Idea, it
follows that we are only speaking of philosophical consciousness and hence only of the history of philosophy. That would
be to concentrate exclusively on the most explicit type of
awareness of the Idea; on Hegel's view the less conceptually
explicit forms, particularly those of Art and Religion, also
belong to this story, so their history is also our subject-matter,
as is the history of social and political institutions, for all these
cultural phenomena manifest the contemporary level of
awareness and with Hegelian hindsight can be seen to have
done so. They are, after all, the works of man's mind, and will
therefore reflect its state. The history of philosophy, it is true,
does occupy the centre of the stage, firstly because philosophy
is the enterprise in which one tries to grasp the nature of the
Absolute in the appropriate, which is to say non-pictorial,
terms, and secondly because it is a philosophy (that of Hegel)
in which we finally attain the conscious knowledge that the
self-revelation of the Idea is indeed what the course of history
embodies and advances. No philosopher ever ascribed greater
importance to the activity of philosophising, or fashioned a
more prestigious pedestal for his own philosophy to occupy,
than did Hegel.

We have already taken one look at the unity of thought and
thing, Idea and nature, as it appears in Hegel; but there is
another aspect of their relationship which must not be missed,
especially since it again picks up a theme which we find in
Hegel's literary contemporaries. It is the idea that self-
consciousness is and can only be the outcome of encountering
one's own image in something external to oneself. The reader
will recall that what brought the boy in the second episode of
Kleist's 'Das Marionettentheater' to that destructive consciousness of his elegance was the sight of a statue in a posture
resembling one of his own. Hölderlin makes Hyperion say, as
he enthuses over the art of classical Athens, that art satisfies
the artist's wish for self-cognition by allowing him a view of
his own beauty: 'He wants to sense himself; and so he puts his

own beauty in front of himself.'[13] Hegel applied the same thought to a people and the culture that it creates:

Geist makes itself what it implicitly is, its deed, its works; in that way it has itself before its own eyes as object. So is the spirit of a people. . . . In these its works, its world, the spirit of a people finds enjoyment of itself and is satisfied.[14]

We come to self-awareness by finding ourself in our 'Other', that which is distinct from us, set over against us. So if the Idea is to rise to self-consciousness, as the ultimate purpose of things demands, there will have to be something set in opposition to it which is its 'Other', and yet which is at the same time a reflection of it. And so there is: nature, concrete where the Idea is abstract, particular where it is universal, thing where it is thought, but none the less its embodiment and manifestation, in Hegel's vocabulary 'identical' with it. Geist, the third element of the great triad, arises out of this opposition of intimately related items which provides the necessary basis for the emergence of self-consciousness. The better Geist's grasp of this 'identity' the closer has the Idea come to full consciousness of its own essence.

The dialectical progression which Hegel saw in cultural forms and social institutions, in short in the life of the human race, he also saw in the life of the individual; and this means that his philosophy comfortably accommodates certain romantic themes of personal psychology that we have had opportunity to observe in Hölderlin and Kleist, the fall from childhood happiness and its reattainment so hardly won, the suffering that goes with nobility of soul and the subsequent recovery of joy. He is also able to assimilate the story of the fall of man, treating it as mythical representation of aspects of the history of mankind which are then played out again in each human life. It tells of a fall from a state of unthinking, unknowing wholeness to one of separation and the pain that comes from consciousness of it. And in his diagnosis Hegel seizes another chance to link arms with a theme of romantic as well as religious literature: what brings this fall about is the increase of knowledge. 'Would I had never gone to your

[13] Ibid. p. 365.
[14] Lectures on the Philosophy of History, Introduction C(c).

schools!' is Hyperion's cry; and what so afflicted the graceful youth of Kleist's tale was knowledge as well, the realisation of his own beauty; for Schiller, writing 'Die Götter Griechenlands', it was the knowledge of the natural scientist which had banished spirit from the world and left it alien and hollow.

None of these three, however, recommended the abandonment of knowledge, and Kleist, with his metaphor of the infinite road that would eventually lead back to Eden, implied that if anything could heal the rift, it would be more knowledge, not less: the best dancers would be the puppet, that knew nothing, and the god, that knew everything. That was also Hegel's view: diremption, or the feeling of diremption, was the result of partial knowledge; fuller and fuller understanding would bring us back to the conscious realisation of the oneness from which we had originally, and unconsciously, set out. But it is not just a matter of the partial versus the complete; crucial also is the type of equipment which thought brings to the task. We have already seen in Schiller the hint of a distinction between two faculties, that of *Verstand* (the understanding), which divides and sets at odds, and that of *Vernunft* (reason), which offers a return to wholeness. Hegel develops this idea along lines indicated by his highly individual conception of logic and strongly encouraged by the communal romantic metaphysic. The understanding is the capacity for sharp conceptual division; it operates only with hard and fast distinctions, with what he calls the inflexible 'Either-Or': 'In such exclusions the said viewpoint shows itself to be a relapse into the metaphysical understanding, into its *either-or* . . .',[15] whereas what will heal the rifts and close the gaps caused by exclusive adherence to the partial knowledge of *Verstand* is completer knowledge, but knowledge that comes of *reason*, produced by its grasp of the true, which is to say dialectical, logic. Precisely because the dialectic works, in Hegel's view, with fluid boundaries, the connections it reveals to us are invisible to the understanding. Reason, by virtue of its appreciation of fluidity and its disdain for divisive conceptual barriers, in short by its acceptance of the romantic principle of Unity-in-Difference as a principle of

---

[15] E Part I para. 65.

logic, is to let us see the aspect of identity between items which *Verstand* had hitherto represented as unalterably different and opposed.

2.   *Hegel's response to scepticism*

Hegel, as we have now seen, had a ready-made metaphysical framework and an audience with ready-made enthusiasm for it. He still undertook, it is true, the *a priori* proof and the empirical confirmation of this metaphysic; but one cannot without naïvety expect that his efforts would have been so strenuous as those of a writer who felt himself to be in a climate basically hostile to his conception of reality, and so was driven to anticipate, so far as he was able, every likely objection and to secure himself against attack from every likely quarter. All writers, no doubt, are to some extent drawn on by their hoped-for conclusions, prone to jump gaps when the jump leads in a favoured direction; and Hegel was exposed to a powerful additional temptation, the temptation to tell his audience (including himself) what it wanted to hear. He was going to give full due to the Image of God doctrine and the romantic *Weltbild* by showing that they could be attained by the strictest application of reason.

There are a number of ways in which a writer might respond to this circumstance of an audience strongly pre-disposed to receive his message. If his medium was that of narrative fiction, for instance, there might be a tendency to leave a great deal to the reader, by way of importing his own experience and expectations, if he was to find the characters of the narrative convincing. Such, I would argue, is the case with Hölderlin's *Hyperion*. It is just about thinkable that there might be a person like the hero of that novel; but he could only be like that, the modern reader feels, if he were himself in the grip of an intense conviction of the truth of the very metaphysical vision which his autobiography is designed to illustrate, and only a reader who can easily imagine someone being thus convinced will be able seriously to entertain Hyperion as a possible character.

Hegel's medium is, of course, much more abstract; he advertises his road to truth as one that can be trodden by, and only by, reason, functioning as reason should. This means

that he is aiming at something akin to cogent argument—
something akin, because it should not be presumed that
Hegel's Logic proceeds by argument as generally understood
by logicians. That it is supposed to advance through the inter-
relations of concepts, this much is clear, but whether these are
translatable without loss of content into relationships between
propositional premises and conclusions is a delicate interpretative question, not to be begged. In any case, however, we are
presented with certain transitions of thought, which are to
convince by their accord with reason.

It is, I need hardly say, widely observed that persons who
are antecedently sympathetic to a certain opinion will accept
as satisfactory grounding for it trains of thought in which
another, driven by his very opposition to their conclusion to
examine them more minutely, will quickly detect fallacy.
Proving to the converted is almost as simple as preaching to
them, and those who are engaged in either activity often take
things fairly easily. The aspect of Hegel's writing to which I
shall draw attention is related to this. I shall not dwell on the
fact—though it is true enough—that the willingness of his
audience to believe his grand result allowed him to get away
with imperfections in the way in which he reached it; I have in
mind a somewhat more detailed point about the movement of
his thought.

In the course of Hegel's writings one frequently comes
across arguments (or passages, as it might be more prudent
neutrally to call them), which cannot be said to have as their
intended outcome anything so vast as the truth of the
Hegelian system—no more than every argument which one
encounters in the *Critique of Pure Reason* is an attempt to
establish Transcendental Idealism. They are directed to some
point of detail of the system, or perhaps to the refutation of an
earlier doctrine or of what Hegel considers to be an error of
philosophical method. What gives these passages buoyancy
cannot really be a general tendency to believe their conclusions—not, at any rate, if that is to be equated with a
willingness to believe the outlines of Hegel's finished system,
the dozen or so theses we have been looking at since the
beginning of Chapter 3. For that, the connection between the
conclusions of these arguments and the dozen theses is too

remote. But there is another possibility. We may find a passage which is, on the face of it, fallacious; perhaps it overlooks some seemingly obvious possibility, so that anyone who is comfortable with the argument may be presumed to be under some influence which helps him overlook, or discount, it. It turns out, as I shall seek to show by reference to examples, that in many cases a prior faith in the romantic metaphysic could easily have just this effect, that the relevant possibility would not be recognised, or if recognised would not be taken seriously. The *Weltbild* may provide, in other words, hidden premises; they may for one thinker stabilise an argument which for another, differently primed, totters at the gentlest push. A number of examples in which objections to Hegel's text, as it stands, may be fended off by the importation of material from the *Weltbild* can be found in his treatment of scepticism.

It is sometimes said that Hegel simply bypassed epistemology, sometimes that, in contrast to both Hume and Kant, he took ontology to be prior to epistemology. But it would be more accurate to say that he regarded them as being inextricably intertwined, and took neither more seriously than the other. At various points in his output he explicitly confronts the threat of scepticism, and it is true that he gives it pretty short shrift, far shorter than many think it deserves; it is also true that these brief confrontations come mostly in passages that are introductory to his main philosophical enterprise. This easily gives the impression that he just wasn't interested, that sceptical thoughts are something he only mentions for the bravado of then barging straight past them and on to the job. In this section I should like to tell the story in a little more detail, not just for its own sake, but with a particular end in view, that of showing that Hegel's thought on these matters is buoyed up by the attraction of the romantic thesis of oneness with the ultimate reality—without it, his argumentative cupboard is quickly seen to be bare. What he does, far from being a neutral refutation of the sceptic, or of subjectivist theories of knowledge, is more like the assumption of some such principle and the detailed elucidation of its consequences for epistemology. In other words, it is not, as Hegel himself would have us believe, a proof; it is an articulation of one aspect of the dominant philosophy of his time.

Hegel usually places his discussions of scepticism in the context of the 'Critical Philosophy', that is to say of Kant and his doctrine that theoretical knowledge could only be of appearances, or 'empirical reality', not of things in themselves, things as they are independently of our ways of experiencing or thinking about them. His favourite tactic is to ridicule, by appeal to the story of the sage who would not enter the water until he had learnt to swim, the idea that we should investigate our faculties before we investigate anything else.[16] If there is a general problem about the trustworthiness of our powers of investigation, it will not be solved by turning them first upon themselves. That is no doubt true, but leaves at least two responses open. First (on behalf of the Critical Philosophy), it is clear neither that Kant conceives his problem as being as general as that, nor that he can be forced to do so. Second (on behalf of scepticism), what this point establishes is that *if* there is such a general problem, one possible way of trying to deal with it will not work, so that if anything it is a (minor) weapon in the armoury of the sceptic, not his opponent—but on the substantial question as to whether there is such a problem, it says nothing.

Another line which Hegel takes is to say, in effect, that the sceptic—the one who argues for his scepticism rather than just blankly refusing to believe anything—needs to make assumptions. And being assumptions, these have no more claim on our acceptance than any other assumptions, in particular those made by whoever he is currently attacking.[17] But, once again, this is not particularly serious-minded stuff. For one thing, it can be said that the sceptic doesn't need any more: if both sets of assumptions have an equal claim to be heard, his point is taken. For another, we may doubt whether the assumption (if that is what it is) that all assumptions are thus on a level with each other, itself has much of a claim; at least, one might think, we should first look to see which assumptions are in question on both sides of the dispute. And again, how is anyone whose procedure even faintly resembles

---

[16] E.g. Ibid. para.41 Zusatz 1.
[17] E.g. PG para. 74.

argument to manage without assumptions? If he cannot, what gives his assumptions ascendancy over those of the sceptic? If there are properties which can give some assumptions precedence over others, how can we decide so summarily that the sceptic's assumptions don't possess them? The speed of Hegel's passage does indeed suggest that he has no real interest in the theory of knowledge, only in the theory of being. But it is not so. Hegel has at least a *prima facie* response to all these difficulties, and the way in which it coheres with the rest of his system shows quite sufficiently that there is nothing casual about his approach to the sceptical threat of subjectivism.

A good place to begin is paragraph 17 of the first book of the *Encyclopedia*, where Hegel confronts directly the obvious objection that philosophy, like anything else, will have to start somewhere, and so can no more avoid subjective assumptions than can any other intellectual undertaking. Here he makes two points. Firstly, that in the practice of philosophy thought is concerned with itself, it 'produces and gives itself its own object'. Secondly, what one takes as the starting-point for philosophical thought, in the course of philosophical inquiry 'becomes a result', which is as much as to say that it is proved; so that the philosophical system 'has the appearance of a circle', that is has no beginning in the logical sense but only in reference to the biography of particular inquirers.

In company with the first of these points one sometimes finds another, oddly contrasting with it, but curiously enough designed to have just the same effect. Hegel sometimes says that in genuinely philosophical thought the mind does nothing, but is simply a passive spectator,[18] thereby giving the impression that, since it does nothing, it can have introduced no distortion into its objects. Elsewhere he invokes both pictures in a single formulation, writing that the 'forms of thought', which he takes to be the principal object of philosophy, '. . . examine themselves, have to determine their own limits and exhibit their own defects'.[19] This gives the impression of thought as something which actively investigates itself, is itself its own object, and at the same time

[18] E.g. E Part I para. 238 Zusatz, where the two are ostentatiously juxtaposed.
[19] Ibid. para. 41 Zusatz.

implies that since it examines itself there is no need for *our* thought to do anything active, but merely to 'look on'.

There is a fourth point that we should be aware of before proceeding to critical discussion. Kantian scepticism consists in contrasting phenomena, empirical reality, with the *Ding-an-sich*, reality as it is independently of our ways of approaching it; the former is knowable, the latter not. Hegel had no objection to the thing-in-itself, but an *unknowable* thing-in-itself he rejected. This was not just as a corollary of the rejection of scepticism; he took himself to be in possession of an independent line of argument showing that what was in principle unknowable was a non-entity. And since that by itself, if successful, would banish any scepticism of Kantian stamp, it must take its place alongside his other anti-sceptical claims.

Hegel's figure of the circle invites the figurative response: may it not be due to a subjective property of our way of thought that we find ourselves on *this* circle at all? A circle may have neither beginning nor end, but it doesn't therefore include every point in the plane, or even intersect with every other possible circle. Certainly the fact that, having selected an assumed starting-point, we come at length to a proof of that same assumption, does not sound likely to provide any kind of guarantee. For if I have assumed something at the beginning it will not be very surprising if I am able to prove it at the end, and indeed whether I have proved it or merely begged the question in its favour will still stand to be decided, if decided it can be.

What of Hegel's suggestion that in philosophy, properly conducted, one does not think about something external but about thought itself? It raises two major questions, and unless both are to be answered in the affirmative no significant impression is made on the sceptic. We have to ask, first, whether the *Ding-an-sich* is to be equated with thought; if it isn't, then philosophy, conceived as the investigation of thought, does not promise us illumination of the real, as it is in itself, at all. Hegel, however, believes that thought and reality, though commonly regarded as an opposed pair of concepts, are one; so that he is at this point protected from our first question by a romantic identity-thesis of a characteristic kind.

Whether he has anything to say in support of this thesis is
something we may briefly postpone until we have looked at
the second question that we are obliged to put to him: is there
any guarantee that our thought can reveal the truth about
Thought, when the latter is, as it were, objectivised and taken
to be the moving force of reality, rather than just another
name for our style of intellectual process? Those theologians
who from time to time have wondered whether God's ways are
our ways have been asking much the same question, and it
is certainly not a negligible one. Hegel, however, is again
forearmed, and with another of his identity-theses. In
philosophy, provided we make 'the effort to keep it free from
our own fancies and private opinions', our thinking becomes
identical with thought:

philosophical thought . . . shows itself to be the action of the concept
itself.[20]

This comes about towards the end of the Logic, where it is
said that:

Up to now *we* had the Idea as our object; from now on the Idea is its
own object.[21]

But we had been clearly forewarned, when, much earlier,
Hegel was considering the threat of Kantian subjectivism:

The activity of the forms of thought and their criticism in cognition
must become one.[22]

The issue comes down, therefore, to this: what basis does
Hegel supply for these identity-theses? There is, perhaps, a
preliminary question; for even if they were accepted, it is not
clear just how we are to tell whether the effort to keep our
thought 'free from our own fancies and opinions' has
succeeded. Indeed the position may be a little worse. That
way of putting it ('die eigenen Einfälle und besonderen
Meinungen') strongly suggests that we are talking of individual idiosyncracies of thought, which could be detected by
the simple discovery that others held different views; whereas
the real Kantian threat is that we may be dealing with

[20] Ibid. para. 238 Zusatz.
[21] Ibid. para. 236 Zusatz.
[22] Ibid. para. 41 Zusatz 1.

subjective features of human thought in general, something which would not be nearly so easily uncovered. How are we to close off the possibility that even when our thinking achieves universal human consensus it is still infected by 'human, all too human' factors?

It is undoubtedly convenient for Hegel to overlook this point, since once it is perceived it threatens his claims to have established the identity-theses that his approach to scepticism requires, the identity of the *Idea* with what is the case *in itself*, and the identity (under optimal circumstances) of *our* thought with the *Idea*. They are established, if at all, in the progress of the Logic; so whether they can be used to immunise philosophy from scepticism turns into the question whether the method of the Logic is such as to make it itself immune from scepticism.

Now it is clear enough that one would have to be very optimistic (as optimistic as Hegel, in fact) to suppose that there is only one way in which the categories of the Logic can, without arbitrariness, develop; that there are not various sets and orderings of categories which could be made to feel equally satisfying to us. Not wishing to get lost in the detail of Hegel's Logic, however, I pass over this in favour of a much more general point: if the Logic convinces us, it does so in virtue of the fact that the transitions from category to category seem to us to meet certain standards. But whether these be *the* standards or only *our* standards it cannot itself tell us. Its incapacity in this regard may be obscured by the fact that it can certainly pronounce our standards to be the standards— according to Hegel it does indeed do so. But whether that identity has been shown to hold by a process which satisfies the standards, or only our standards, is still unresolved—the sceptical possibility is always one jump ahead.

Interestingly, all of this is really quite obvious—if the witness's credit is in doubt, there is no point in getting him to affirm his own credibility; if it is not, there is no need. Even on a fairly low estimate of Hegel's acumen it is hard to imagine that, unless other factors were at work, he would have missed it; he was after all quick enough to make the point, of very similar structure, that a global worry about our powers of knowledge can't be allayed by setting them to work to investigate themselves. Active here, surely, is his enthusiasm for the romantic *Weltbild* with its enthronement of unity and oneness and its rejection of separation; this is what helped him and his contemporary audience across the argumentative gap.

It might be said, and a Hegelian would I think say, that there is also empirical vindication for the Logic: we find its structures reflected in nature, just as it tells us to expect. Again I shall not go into the minutiae of the question, whether and to what extent those structures are uncontroversially present in nature, but rather make the general point that this fact, if such it be, can be made to go very well with a subjectivism of thoroughly Kantian pedigree. For if the Logic exhibits the categories with which the human mind works, and if nature really is, as Kant thought, a construction of the human understanding, then that is precisely what we should find: that the structure of the categories recurs in nature. Such a discovery might indeed vindicate the Logic, but not so as to secure the claim that it provides knowledge of the real as it is in itself, independently of our cognitive approach to it.

Had Hegel not been so keen on his claim to have proved his metaphysic, he could have offered a much more effective response to Kant. Kant, he could have said, believed that empirical reality was an appearance, and not a thing-in-itself, because he thought that only on this supposition could one account for the existence of synthetic *a priori* knowledge of it. Hegel might have replied that he could allow the possibility of such knowledge of things-in-themselves. For he could have supposed, like Kant, that synthetic *a priori* knowledge would have to be, ultimately, insight into the workings of our own minds, whilst making this none other than insight into the workings of the Idea, and hence into the independently real. The existence of this alternative explanation would then have held up Kant's attempt to prove transcendental idealism with its attendant subjectivism. But Hegel was not one to rest content with such a hypothetical stance; and his eagerness to overcome the subjectivist's dichotomy of known appearance versus unknown reality by proof led him to make claims for his arguments which they will not sustain, except perhaps in the eyes of those for whom their conclusion is already foregone.

3. *The thing-in-itself*

I said earlier that when Hegel confronts the Kantian form of scepticism or subjectivism one support he depends on is a certain view of the *Ding-an-sich* that lies, supposedly, out of cognitive reach. It is not, so he seems to think, that given our capacity for knowledge the thing-in-itself can be seen to fall inside its scope; it is rather that, given the concept of the *Ding-an-sich*, it can be seen that having knowledge of it calls for no very special capacities at all, 'nothing is easier'. Why he should have thought this is something it has not proved easy for commentators fully to explain. Here is the classic passage:

> The thing-in-itself is the object, when we abstract from everything that it is for consciousness, all its emotional connotations and all determinate thoughts of it. It is easy to see what is left—total abstraction, complete emptiness, just what is *Beyond*; the negative of every image, feeling, determinate thought. But it is just as easy to reflect that this *caput mortuum* is itself only a product of thought, thought carried to utter abstraction, a product of the empty Ego which makes its own empty identity into an object. The negative determination which this abstract identity acquires as an object is also listed amongst the Kantian categories and is just as familiar as that empty identity. It is amazing to read so often that we do not know what the Thing-in-itself is; nothing is easier than to know this.[23]

This is a very complex paragraph. A first, and approximate, thought about it is that Hegel is running together in the first place the distinction between what the object is and how we think of it, and in the second place that between the *Ding-an-sich* and the substantial substratum of all an object's properties. What he seems to have in mind is something of which it is definitely asserted that it is not *A*, not *B*, for every *A* and *B* we can think of. That is hardly the thing-in-itself, which is opposed not to its properties but to the way the thing appears to us—there is nothing inconsistent with its definition (though it may be epistemologically risky) in asserting that things in themselves have many properties, even the ones that they appear to us to have. But on the other hand it might be a description of the substratum, which is indeed contrasted with

[23] Ibid. para. 44. ;

all the properties that 'inhere' in it. Even so, there would still be a gap to be crossed before reaching the conclusion that the thing-in-itself was nothing—the gap between saying that something has no properties and saying that it has no properties that we can think of, no properties 'for consciousness'. What would carry Hegel over? That it was a dash of verificationism is not a likely hypothesis, but neither is it needed: his underlying metaphysic bridges the gap like a charm—the 'identity' between our mental processes and those which sustain reality guarantees the coincidence of the properties really instantiated with those available to our thought; the possibility that our minds are thus alienated from the real was not one that Hegel was tuned to.

None of that, however, says anything about the larger puzzle: was it by sheer carelessness that Hegel equated the thing-in-itself with the substratum of the thing's properties, or should we suspect a more deep-seated cause? At least one leading commentator, Michael Inwood, prefers the latter:

Hegel's equation of these apparently different notions is based on more than confusion. For it is supported by his belief that the properties of a thing derive from its relationships to other things and that the distinction between a thing and its properties therefore coincides with that between the thing as it is (or perhaps would be) in itself—apart from its relationships to other things—and those features of it which consist in or depend upon its relationships to other things. If this is so, a thing which was unrelated to any knowing subject would be indeterminate and propertyless. A thing as it is in itself, apart from our cognitive interactions with it, is thus equivalent to a mere bearer of properties, unknowable only because there is nothing to be known.[24]

That may be so, but if it is the further question arises, how Hegel ever came to feel that this line of thought supported the said 'equation'. For, even supposing that it is true that a thing's properties derive from its relation to other things, it is something else again to say that they derive from its relation to knowing subjects, and yet something else to say that they derive from those relationships to knowing subjects which count as cognitive interactions, that is to say acts of knowing. Once again we have a gap, and only someone with an

[24] M. J. Inwood: *Hegel* (Routledge 1983) pp. 121–2.

antecedent preference for cognition or consciousness, an antecedent belief in the creative power of thought, would hop across it so lightly. Whether Inwood's conjecture is ultimately acceptable or not, at least in this respect it carries a thoroughly Hegelian hallmark.

I began the discussion of *Encyclopedia* I para. 44 by saying that Hegel appeared to have run together the halves of two distinctions; we have so far spoken only of the second, but the first, the distinction between what a thing is and the terms in which we think of it, deserves equal attention—his treatment of it is if anything even more revealing. Hegel is aiming at the conclusion that the thing-in-itself is simply nothing, just the empty projection of an act of mind in which we abstract from every property that we can conceive of in an object; and *ipso facto* nothing that could systematically elude knowledge as the sceptic would have it. We may remember that he starts from the premiss:

The thing-in-itself is the object, when we abstract from everything that it is for consciousness, all its emotional connotations and every determinate thought of it.[25]

As we have seen, things-in-themselves don't have to be thought of in this way—plenty of philosophers have ascribed plenty of everyday properties to them, as did for instance Locke. But at least the Kantian sceptic takes the view that nothing is known about them, so that when he thinks of them it is in highly abstract terms, 'how the thing is, rather than how it appears to us', and not as having this, that and the other particular property—a position which is of course sharply to be distinguished from that of thinking of it as not having any of these properties. But this doesn't, of course, allow one to draw Hegel's conclusion, that the thing-in-itself is propertyless; the possibility remains that it has any number of properties, perhaps even properties that are thoroughly familiar to us, even though we lack justification for thinking of it in these terms, and this is just the possibility that the sceptic insists on. To ignore it, and suppose that the thing-in-itself must be as blank as is the mind of the sceptic when he asks himself what he knows about it, is to equate it with the

[25] E Part I para. 44.

intensional object of his thought and give it the identical intensional content, so that apart from being 'the way things are independently . . .' it can have no nature at all, somewhat as if an 'object which no conscious being will ever perceive' had no property but that one.

Is this a mere oversight? Has Hegel just unwittingly demonstrated the value of a basic course in philosophical logic? Possibly, but it has to be said that the oversight, if that is what it is, occurs in a predictably sensitive area; for the tendency to run together the object as it is with the object as it is thought of, the extension with the intension, is a close relative of the tendency to see the object as the product of thought, and made or modified by it. That tendency is certainly present in the paragraph under inspection: notice how blithely Hegel makes ('But it is just as easy to reflect . . .') the unargued assumption that that is exactly what the thing-in-itself is—a projection of something very like the Kantian unity of apperception.

But Hegel also has another and completely different line about the concept of the *Ding-an-sich*; far from saying that it is really nothing, he more or less says that it is everything that an object will ever become, and knowable because the object will, in due course, come to manifest it completely. In this mood, he fairly hijacks the Kantian concept and presses it into typically Hegelian service. The thing-in-itself is as it were the early, undeveloped form of the object, the thing *in potentia* out of which the mature object will grow and then display itself openly for what it has all along implicitly (*an sich*) been.

Thus the Man-in-himself is the child, whose task is not to stay in this abstract and undeveloped *Ansich*, but to become *for itself* what at first it is only *in itself*—a free and rational being. . . . In the same way one can think of the seed as the plant-in-itself.[26]

The thought of something which, in a process driven by inner necessity, gradually unfolds itself and becomes, for all to see, what it has always potentially and secretly been, is of course deeply characteristic of Hegel and more or less ubiquitously present in his philosophical system. Just such a process is that by which the Idea achieves, in the course of world history, a

[26] Ibid. para. 124 Zusatz.

conscious grasp of its own nature. The same is true, in Hegel's view, of the development of *Geist*, and of the self-realisation of everything organic:

Thus the organic individual produces itself; it makes itself what it is *an sich*. (In the same way *Geist* is what it makes itself, and it makes itself what it is *an sich*.)[27]

This picture of the real in terms of an active centre or essence is in full accord with the then new, and rising, emphasis in metaphysics on practice, agency and process. (It reminds one of Leibniz and the self-impelled development of the monad— as well as of the fact that he, of all seventeenth-century thinkers, was most concerned to give agency its due position in his metaphysics.) In presenting the process as directed towards self-knowledge, and knowledge which could be made to satisfy the strictest standards, Hegel also retained firm contact with the Insight Ideal that had dominated the two centuries before him. The picture calls for a concept of that inner reality which under its own motive force comes to outer manifestation; and for this purpose Hegel appropriates the thing-in-itself, which thus becomes the essence, originally unknown, but becoming knowable in the process of self-development. The existence of that process defeats, for Hegel, the Kantian sceptic's claims, though it does not do so, one need hardly add, in any way calculated to satisfy the Kantian sceptic himself. Within Hegel's system, it may be that it lies in the essential nature of the covert to make itself overt, but the Kantian is at liberty to read all that Hegel offers by way of examples as descriptions of processes in *empirical reality*, and to that extent subjective from start to finish.

It may look to the reader as if Hegel has simply changed the subject—that the *Ansich* as germ and the *Ansich* as the independently real are two quite distinct concepts, and that what we have here is no more than an ambiguity in Hegel's vocabulary. But it is evident that for him it was much more. In the section of the *Lesser Logic* from which I have quoted above[28] a train of thought which opens with explicit mention of Kant and proceeds with a reference to the very obviously

---

[27] *Lectures on the History of Philosophy*, Introduction C(a).
[28] E Part I para. 124 and Zusatz.

Kantian view that the *Ding-an-sich* is unknowable then deals with that view by invoking the developmental concept of the *Ansich*. The implied equation of things as they are independently of how they are experienced with things as they are embryonically, prior to their development, may result in an apparent *non sequitur*, but it is perfectly comprehensible when taken in company with Hegel's metaphysical vision. Hegel treats thought, the Idea of which his Logic is the science, both as what is objectively real and as the hidden developmental force behind all reality which this development will ultimately reveal to consciousness. In his vision experience, consciousness of things, rises with the self-impelled development of reality and arises from it; so that when asked to think of the *Ansich*, that which is prior to experience, he (quite understandably) thinks of the first state of a thing from which the development sets out—experience only comes about in the course of that development. What has the prestigious status of the 'In-itself' is then naturally seen as the original active core of the process through which reality grows to its full stature. We meet, in this further doctrine of the *Ding-an-sich*, another aspect of Hegel's philosophy: the emphasis on agency as a central metaphysical category. We should now examine it more closely.

4.   *The works of reason, and of man*

So far we have been looking at Hegel's relationship to his past, in the form of the doctrine of the Image of God and the ideal of rational insight which for his predecessors was its immediate offshoot; and at his relationship to his present, in the form of the romantic metaphysic of oneness lost and regained. There is another strand in his philosophy which leads directly into the future of European thought. It is that which is concerned not with intellectual insight as such, but with activity, creation, change and process, goals and purposes. These, or rather the philosophical systems that took them as central, are the theme of the remaining chapters of this book; if therefore Hegel is to be seen in his historical place, some anticipation will be necessary. But I shall keep it schematic, and promise the reader more in Chapter 5.

Only a little knowledge of Hume and Kant is needed to

appreciate that they made the activity of the human mind
essential to the understanding of the phenomena with which
they dealt. For Hume the crucial phenomenon was belief, and
he saw the key in the way in which the mind generates beliefs
out of data utterly insufficient to provide any rational
guarantee of their truth. Kant took the central problem to be
our knowledge of the natural world; his solution lay in the
mind's propensity to shape and structure its experience. This
notion of activity and its companion concepts of process and
purpose were to turn into the next great focus of philosophical
thought–our interest now is in the way in which Hegel picked
this incipient movement up and urged it forwards.

So pervasive is this tendency that it can be illustrated from
almost anywhere in his work, but perhaps the easiest
approach lies through the historical dimension of his philosophy, of which we have up to now said little. For all its
superficial appearance of random multiplicity, the course of
history is subject, according to Hegel, to rational principles; in
it, the Idea is hard at work:

For like Mercury, the guide of souls, is the Idea in truth the guide of
the nations and of the world; and it is the rational and necessary will
of *Geist* which has guided, and still guides, world-events.[29]

We are to approach history, then, in the firm confidence that:

'. . . Reason rules the world, and world-history has proceeded
rationally'.[30]

If reason rules, we may well want to know, what purpose
does it have for the world? Hegel asks us to take two steps–
which turn out to bring us to a place already familiar. The
essence of mind is to be free, freedom is 'the sole truth of
Geist'.[31] Freedom consists, for Hegel, in being what he calls *bei
sich selbst*, which might be rendered, aiming more at spirit than
letter, as 'sufficient to oneself'. In other words, being free is
being related only to oneself, the lack of freedom is dependence on something *else*, something which is not 'I'. Being
thus self-related is, in the case of *Geist*, being *self-conscious*, and
so it transpires that the purpose of the world is for *Geist* to
achieve full awareness of its own nature.

[29] *Lectures on the Philosophy of History*, Introduction A.
[30] Ibid. A.
[31] Ibid. B(a).

It may seem that this train of thought makes its way only with the help of a gross conflation, a failure to distinguish between self-relation and self-dependence. Surely the mind could be related to something else, in the sense of being conscious of it, without being dependent upon it in any sense that would impair freedom? Conversely, whilst being conscious only of itself, might it not be in heavy unconscious dependence on external things? Besides, isn't freedom, as understood by Hegel, a feeble if not downright undesirable thing, something like the turning away from everything else to concentrate entirely on the self? But once again we discern the influence of the submerged philosophical vision that is, nominally at least, the conclusion of Hegel's philosophy. For what he understands by full consciousness of self is the awareness that the mind is the conscious vehicle of the principles that inform all reality, hence the realisation that one's own forms of thought are equally at work in what for everyday purposes, or for non-speculative philosophy, are simply *other* things. Full self-consciousness, then, overarches this gap. It realises that in its 'other' it only meets itself; and that what it thought was dependence on the 'other' is in fact dependence upon self. So the mystery of the argument disappears: being truly 'self-related', or free, permits relation to 'other' things, since these are not, after all, opposed to self. And in recognising that this is so *Geist* becomes simultaneously conscious of its own character, and of its freedom. This is what the Idea, or reason as it is at work in the world, takes as its goal: 'World-history is the advance of consciousness of freedom.'[32] Hence the advance of self-consciousness, since the essence of *Geist* is to be free.

Earlier, whilst drawing comparisons between Hegel and Schiller, I deferred one point until some more detail about Hegel's system should be in view. Now, having seen something of his accounts of freedom and of the thing-in-itself, and having raised the matter of the growing stress on agency and development, we can return to it. It concerns the way in which they see the ideal for man, or (more or less equivalently) the way they see the life of God. If we think of Hegel's account of freedom, the 'essence of *Geist*', we can describe it like this:

[32] Ibid. B(a).

Geist is to manifest in its works everything that it has all along been in itself–through its action it is to realise its full potential in concrete form; Schiller told us that there was to be 'complete revelation of capacity'. But it is also, for Hegel, to realise (now in the sense of 'recognise') that what there then comes to be, what it produces, is the necessary outcome of its own inner nature; Schiller spoke of the 'necessity of all that is real'. Man, he said, was to 'externalise all that is in him' and in so doing 'shape all that is external'.[33] Hegel, with greater stress on *Geist*'s self-consciousness and the union between man and the impersonally described Idea, asks for much the same.

Given now that the purpose of reason is to advance self-consciousness and freedom, how does it work towards it? The answer must be: through the actions of various individuals–these are the only agents available. And here of course we confront the problem that none of these individuals (or at best very few of them) have any conception of the purpose which Hegel ascribes to history; they act in pursuit of their own individual goals at the behest of their own needs and desires. Nor is this true only of the masses; those outstanding individuals whose lives change the course of world history are likewise motivated in their own particular way and influenced by their own individual conception of how their goals are to be reached. But behind this scene the 'cunning of reason' can be detected; the formative Idea lies hidden in their minds, and their actions do therefore advance the ultimate aims of reason whilst they themselves take conscious aim at targets altogether different and, from the absolute perspective, altogether more trivial.

The picture, then, is one of the Idea, or reason (and in theologically inclined moments Hegel is quite prepared to call this impersonal mental force God), actively engaged in working its purpose out, coming to full conscious awareness of what lies embryonically within it. To speak with Hegel: it is to become *for itself* what it is *in itself*. Here is the age-old injunction 'Know thyself' writ as large as could be; the universe is portrayed as a process, activated by Hegel's highly intellectualised God (hence the shortcomings of 'spirit' as a

---

[33] Schiller: *Letters on the Aesthetic Education of Man*, 11th letter; other quotations in this paragraph ibid. See above, Chapter 3 Section 4, Chapter 5 Section 1.

translation of *Geist*) to the final end of his own self-understanding. Thus Hegel introduced a factor of great moment, though one which it is not easy to describe lucidly. Previous philosophies and theologies had, of course, thought of God as being active with respect to the world. Either he was conceived as having made it in a single act of creation, since when it had run on in accordance with the plan he then laid down; or his active concurrence was needed at all times to sustain the world he had created. In either case he could be thought of as making, from time to time, miraculous intervention to alter the natural course of events. Or, as by the occasionalists, he could be held to be perpetually in demand to fulfil the otherwise impotent will of his creatures, and to ensure that their perceptual states corresponded to the states of their environment. All these ways of thinking still portray the universe as external to the action and the agent; it is a *thing* upon which God operates. Conversely, they portray God as external to his material; an independent authority commands, and it is done. In Hegel's philosophy this externality is gone, and God needs the universe as much as the universe needs God. Essential to *Geist* in any of its forms is to put forth an embodiment of its own nature and so come to self-knowledge, and the universe, one might say, *is the action* by which God fulfils this purpose.

Thus Hegel centralised the categories of action, process and purpose in metaphysics; we are invited to see the real first and foremost in those terms. And that means making a corresponding adjustment in our cognitive approach to it. Knowing the truth is not the attainment of a particular state of mind which mirrors the object, a state to be attained by *any* method so long as it leaves us with a guarantee that the object is indeed truly reflected. On the contrary, because reality is not an object but a process, not a thing but an action, knowing it calls for a process of mind in which we perform, in our conscious life, a corresponding action—no mere state of mind could be knowledge unless it were the outcome of just that process. Hence Hegel's revaluation of traditional methodology: no longer is mathematics an ideal, for in mathematics the goal is the theorem, and how the theorem is proved is a matter of indifference, so long as *some* proof is offered: '. . . when the [result] is reached, the demonstration is over and has disappeared'.[34]

But we have still not seen the full extent or value of the role that Hegel ascribes to this activity. For it is not as if we were to think of *Geist* (or God, in the explicitly theological formulation) as fully formed and having need of the universe only if it is to do anything, or come to consciousness of its own nature. As well as coming to *know* itself, *Geist* is also *making* itself, through its activity, what it has implicitly always been. *Geist*, Hegel holds, is 'essentially the result of its own activity'; it belongs to its essence to make itself in actuality what it is *in potentia* or '*an sich*':

Geist is only what it makes itself, and it makes itself what it potentially is.[35]

As well as 'Know thyself', there is also the injunction to '*Be* thyself', not in the passive sense of resisting outside interference, but in the active sense of developing one's potential to the full. This, in its theological version, is Goethe's god, which '*produces itself* from all eternity'.[36] So the activity we are speaking of is represented by Hegel not just as the acquisition of self-knowledge, nor just of creation, but of the self-creation of the creator, and whoever participates in it has a share in the making of God.

That last thought points towards the question: do finite minds, or more specifically does man participate in this creative activity? Nothing we have said so far in this section suggests that these actions are *our* actions. On the contrary, it might be thought that we appear in the picture as no real agents at all but rather as the mere instruments of a higher power, used for its purposes and then discarded when our utility flags. Humans do indeed act in pursuit of their trivial little goals, but as regards the grand purpose, what Hegel calls the substance, they have no such status. And it cannot be denied that he sometimes speaks in terms which strongly reinforce that impression:

---

[34] PG para. 42.

[35] *Lectures on the Philosophy of History*, Introduction C(a).

[36] My italics. See below, Chapter 5 Section 1.

While such business of reality appears as the action and so as the work of *Individuals*, these are in respect of the substantial content of their work *tools* . . .[37]

But one must always remember that Hegel is the great master of the dual perspective. Nothing appeals to him more than to take two apparently conflicting stances, as here the views that individual human beings are on the one hand themselves agents, on the other mere instruments of some universal force, and exhibit each of them as a partial truth within an all-encompassing vision. Indeed, this might almost be said to be his method. And sure enough, we find him warning us that the instrumental view of human doings, taken by itself, is as false as it is true:

But if we accept . . . that we are to think of individuals as *means*, nonetheless there is a side of them which we hesitate just to think of only in these terms, even when measured against the highest standard, because it is simply not something inferior, but rather something in them which is in itself eternal, divine.[38]

Why not? One reason is that, instruments or not, those human beings who (if unwittingly) further the cause of the *Weltgeist* at the same time further their own particular ends. Another, less perspicuous but evidently of central importance to Hegel, is that they 'participate in that purpose of reason itself'.[39] They participate in that purpose by virtue of 'the divine element that is in [man]',[40] namely (there should by now be no difficulty in recognising this theme) his reason. The seed from which, in Hegel's eyes, the universe grows, and of which the Logic is the direct investigation, is likewise present in the human mind, even if at times quite unconsciously. Therefore we are rightly said to share in the ends of the *Weltgeist*, and not just to be means to them. God is working his purpose out with us, at least as much as through us, and the realisation of his purpose would simultaneously be the realisation of ours— though only in its realisation could we become clearly aware that this was what our true purpose had, all along, really

---

[37] E Part III para. 551.
[38] *Lectures on the Philosophy of History*, Introduction B(b).
[39] Ibid. B(b).
[40] Ibid. B(b).

been. Such is the enormous significance which Hegel ascribes to human action.

In conclusion of the section, two points may be noticed. One is that Hegel should not be thought of as assigning this status to human action *as opposed to* human thought. If the Idea is to rise to self-consciousness, he thinks, it is in *our minds* that this must occur; hence it is of at least as much consequence that we grapple with it in its pure form—which is to say, pursue the science of logic—as it is that our deeds should help bring about the sequence of historical conditions in which it gradually finds increasingly adequate embodiment.

The other point is this: Hegel has once again managed to fuse together the two halves of what would naturally be taken to be another of those notorious pairs of opposites, in this case that of knowing God on the one hand and carrying out his purposes on the other. For since God's purpose is fully to know himself, and since we are the consciousness that must carry that knowledge if it is to exist, the two tasks merge into one.

5. *Sense-Certainty and the active mind*

'Die Sinnliche Gewissheit', Hegel's famous chapter from the *Phenomenology of Spirit*, can serve us in two ways. First, it offers an example of the tendency of recent commentators to get into trouble, both exegetical and philosophical, by trying to make Hegel too modern, to see his views and methods as too closely related to our own. Charles Taylor, we shall find, by being over-hasty to find in this chapter arguments of twentieth-century flavour, has attributed to Hegel views which are almost certainly not his, and quite certainly indefensible. Second, it provides another and striking instance of the way in which reading a philosopher in the light of his own period and its concerns can illuminate details of his writing which are otherwise hopelessly obscure and so likely either to be passed over or put down to incompetence on his part. It will be seen that a crucial feature of Hegel's argument is to speak of wholes as if, merely by virtue of being composed of parts, they were universals, and of things as if they were likewise universals merely by virtue of being capable of various states; and that rather than write this off as a gross conflation we can see it as a commitment to the doctrine of the ubiquitous activity of the mind in consciousness, hence as both picking up a Kantian theme and as furthering the growing emphasis on activity, the creation rather than the passive reception of experience. By following this clue we can arrive at the most perspicuous reading of the Sense-Certainty chapter yet offered.

So long as we keep the outlines broad enough, we can say with some confidence what transpires in the Sense-Certainty chapter: we consider a certain state of mind in which someone might try to cognise an object, and we consider it in the light of the claim that it cognises the object as it is. It turns out that the state of mind in question cannot, as it stands, live up to this claim; if it is to do so, it has to be modified in a way which, Hegel indicates, emerges from the argument of the chapter, showing how it fails in its original form. So much is clear, but the slightest further question brings uncertainties.

I should say immediately that there is one famous uncertainty with which I do not propose to deal: by whom is this claim, that the object is cognised as it is, made, and by whom is it realised that sense-certainty fails the test? Is it in each case the state of sense-certainty itself, or is it some other consciousness, maybe that of a philosopher who makes claims about sense-certainty's epistemic powers, and then that of an opposing philosopher who denies them? The puzzle is not, I believe, resolvable. It arises because Hegel imposes two inconsistent requirements. First, that sense-certainty, as the first state of consciousness to be considered, should have only the most meagre conceptual resources, if any; second, that the conflict which causes the collapse of a state of consciousness and its transformation into the next member of the series should be 'immanent', that is to say something which grows, and is felt to grow, from within it, and not just a matter of someone else's external judgement upon it. But in consequence of the first requirement, sense-certainty is too impoverished a state to satisfy the second, which calls for sufficient conceptual apparatus to formulate such notions as that of 'the object of consciousness as it really is'. Or, to put it another way, the conflict is to arise between what sense-certainty delivers and what it claims to deliver—but to hold a view about its own products needs an intellectual complexity for which sense-certainty is far too primitive. Yet even if this problem proves intractable, the chapter poses others which, I shall try to show, are not.

Right at the beginning, in the first paragraph of the chapter, we encounter unclarity about exactly what state Hegel is inviting us to consider. He describes it as one in which

Our approach to the object [is] *immediate* or *receptive*; we must alter nothing in the object as it presents itself. In apprehending it, we must refrain from trying to comprehend it.

There are two ideas here, and we shall do well to keep them distinct in our minds. There is the idea of a state of mind which is wholly passive, one which simply receives the object; and there is also the idea of a state which is non-conceptual. One who approaches the text in innocence of the commentaries might easily think that the first of these ideas is much more strongly present than the second; it is, after all, hammered home by 'we must alter nothing in the object', whereas the second, if present at all, must be represented by the veto on 'trying to comprehend'. Must 'comprehend' bear that meaning? The German is *das Begreifen*, cognate of course with *Begriff*, which, as we all know, means *concept*. But must Hegel have meant that as we do? Some commentators are quick to suppose so—it is from them that I take the idea that Hegel is here speaking of a non-conceptual state of mind. But even the brief context that I have quoted is enough to raise a faint doubt, for the second sentence of it sounds like a reformulation of the first, rather than an additional point, which implies that *Begreifen* would alter the object—not something that we would expect to do by just applying a concept to it. This might, of course (in fact the thought is quite plausible) be the effect of some Hegelian doctrine about the use of concepts in our everyday sense; but even if so, there is still a suggestion that it may be the passivity, rather than the lack of conceptualisation, that Hegel is most interested in.

Taylor, however, fastens on to conceptualisation as the key, from which beginning he is led to say that the state of sense-certainty is condemned to emptiness, an 'unconscious, trancelike stare', whereas Hegel, as Ivan Soll has pointed out,[41] does ascribe a content to it, though a minimal one:

All that it says about what it knows is just that it *is*; and its truth contains nothing but the sheer *being* of the thing.[42]

Admittedly, even this minimum must appear too much to someone taken with the idea that in the condition of sense-certainty there is a ban on all concepts, for isn't *Being* a concept? Enough of one, at any rate, to form the starting-point of Hegel's Logic; it seems that it makes this solo appearance in the consciousness of sense-certainty not because it is not a concept, but because it is, for Hegel, the only concept that satisfies a certain condition.

There are plenty of pointers to what that condition is. Hegel takes it to be the only concept in the application of which the mind is wholly passive. The idea sounds strange, and I am not concerned to defend it, but it emerges quite unambiguously from the opening paragraph of the Sense-Certainty chapter that the passive reception of material constitutes a grasp of its *Being*, and of nothing more about it. For apart from what he says in plain German about our being merely receptive (and attaining to knowledge of 'what simply *is*'), there is also the specifically Hegelian terminology of *mediation* and *immediacy* to be taken into account. In the second sentence, for our approach to be immediate is the same as for it to be receptive, to make no alteration to the object; and this is in good accord with the concept of the immediate as Hegel uses it elsewhere. 'Pure Being', he tells us, 'is . . . immediacy itself',[43] and this is why it is the appropriate starting-point for the Logic; thought has not yet gone to work on it. It is still 'simple', whereas all the later categories will be at least to some degree complex, since they contain all that precedes them *aufgehoben* within themselves. Composition, for Hegel, calls for an act of mind,[44] the Kantian synthesis come again, and in the second

---

[41] Ivan Soll: 'Charles Taylor's Hegel', *The Journal of Philosophy* Vol. 73 (1976) pp. 97–710. Reprinted in *Hegel*, ed. M. J. Inwood (Oxford 1985) pp. 54–66 (this point p. 57).

[42] PG para. 91.

[43] E Part I para. 86.

[44] PG paras. 119 and 121: '. . . it is this unity which consciousness has to take upon itself . . .'

paragraph we find the point made in vocabulary only slightly transmuted from that of the *Critique of Pure Reason*. First, it is essential to the state of sense-certainty that there should have been no mental activity on my part:

I . . . am certain of *this* thing, not because I as a consciousness have developed myself or thought about it in manifold ways.

Neither is there any question of complexity on the part of the object:

Nor because the thing of which I am certain, having several distinct qualities, is in rich connection to itself or multiply related to other˙ things.

These thoughts are then attached, as one might anticipate, to the concept of mediation:

Neither I nor the thing has the significance of a manifold mediation.

and at once the thoroughly Kantian-sounding idea of a manifold of representations comes into view:

I do not have the significance of a manifold of representations or thoughts (eines mannigfaltigen Vorstellens oder Denkens), nor the thing that of a manifold of qualities.

Contrasted with such a complex is, of course, the immediate:

the thing *is* . . . merely because it *is* . . . and this pure *being*, or simple immediacy, constitutes its *truth*.[45]

What we have to take away from these opening paragraphs and carry into our reading of the rest of the chapter is Hegel's stress on the passivity of the mind in the state of sense-certainty, and its connection in his mind with the simplicity of its thoughts and their objects. Before we pass on there is one further feature of the second paragraph which has to be noticed: the emphasis it places on the idea of an individual, a particular, a 'single item'.

The significance of this point must not be missed. On the one hand, Hegel contrasts *das Einzelne* (the particular or individual) with *das Allgemeine* (the general or universal), so that he is here introducing a third contrast to go alongside

---

[45] All these: PG para. 91.

those of active/passive and simple/complex. But that he
introduces it here, running on in one breath, so to speak, from
the foregoing discussion, implies that he feels a strong
connection, to say the least, between particularity, simplicity
and passivity, hence also between the complementary trio of
concepts, universal, complex, and active. The play he makes
with the demonstrative 'this', the idea that sense-certainty is a
purely ostensive form of consciousness, underlines the fact,
and the reader who can hear his philosophy polyphonically
will find all three themes sounding at once here, especially in
the second half of the second paragraph, beginning with 'I,
this particular I . . .', in which the active/passive line is carried
by the references to 'imagining or thinking', mediation and
immediacy, and the simple/complex line by 'various ways',
'rich complex', 'host of qualities', 'simple immediacy'.

Hegel repeatedly says, throughout the chapter, that sense-
certainty turns out to grasp the universal, and he clearly sees
in this a refutation of the claims made for it: if it can only
grasp the universal, then it collapses, and passes over into the
next stage of consciousness. This strategy raises a question
which most commentators seem to have ignored: why cannot
it just be admitted that the universal is what sense-certainty
grasps? Whence the demand that it grasp the particular? But
as we see the question we also get a glimpse of an answer: if
sense-certainty is defined in terms of its passivity, and
cognising the universal calls for it to be active, then the
discovery that in spite of our best attempts its content remains
doggedly universal functions as a *reductio*. And the fact that we
do find the link between the passive and the particular in
Hegel's thought supports this answer. Conversely, the fact
that he uses this strategy supports the view that there is
indeed such a link.

One very obvious source for that link is the *Critique of Pure
Reason*. Kant, defining sensibility, the faculty of perception, in
opposition to understanding, the faculty of conceptual
thought, had had the idea that by means of the former we
represented to ourselves the individual object, whereas the
latter faculty enabled us to think not of individuals but rather
of kinds. He also associated understanding with the active,
sensibility with the receptive posture of mind:

Concepts are based on the spontaneity of thought, sensible intuitions on the receptivity of impressions.[46]

A general concept, a 'universal', is an act of synthesis, a 'function of unity':

concepts rest on functions. By 'function' I mean the unity of the act of bringing various representations under one common representation.[47]

These thoughts connect the passive and the particular, the active and the general. Hegel, as we have seen, also connects activity with the complex, passivity with the simple. Again, there is a similar precedent: Kant also held that to experience a complex object called for the performance of a synthesis, the active judgement that a number of distinct qualities had a common centre. In this respect, at least, representing a universal and representing a complex particular do not differ. So if there can be a state of consciousness without activity, where the receptive sensibility operates alone, it is stuck with both particularity and simplicity. Just this is Hegel's position as well. His concern, in the chapter on sense-certainty, is to probe the limitations of a wholly receptive consciousness. Once this consciousness is forced to take cognisance either of universals or of complex particulars, those limits have been passed, and it can no longer exist; in this matter the distinction between the universal and the complex is of little interest, and so we must not expect that Hegel's writing will necessarily be tuned to it, or his vocabulary even allow him explicitly to draw it. If we fail to appreciate this fact we shall not arrive at anything like a satisfactory reading of the chapter. Evidently it is easily done; even Ivan Soll appears to have missed it, for he wrote (of arguments from the end of the chapter, which we shall scrutinise later):

But unless one conflates the notions of the instances of a universal and the parts of a whole (as Hegel seems to have done), all the arguments would show, if they work at all, is that *here* and *now* are divisible *wholes*, not that they are *universals*.[48]

---

[46] *Critique of Pure Reason* A68/B93.
[47] Ibid. A68/B93.
[48] Ivan Soll: 'Charles Taylor's Hegel'—see above, note 41.

Briefly put, the reason why without this awareness we shall get no satisfaction from the Sense-Certainty chapter is this: Hegel's first move is to argue that the indexicals, as they are now sometimes called, 'here', 'now' and 'I', are universals rather than pure denotations of particulars. The natural response is to incorporate into consciousness the act of showing, as it were a demonstrative state, and Hegel counters by arguing that what is shown is always a complex item. As such he holds it to be *vermittelt*, a product of the activity of thought, and consequently something that lies beyond the scope of sense-certainty as originally defined. But Hegel announces his point that what is shown is complex by saying that it is a universal, thus giving the impression (see the quotation from Soll, above) that he has clumsily conflated universals—as we most commonly understand the term—with complex individuals. Without the realisation that his true concern is with mental activity, and that consciousness of a complex object as such requires mental activity just as does consciousness of a universal—in the sense familiar to us—the commentator comes to a dead stop.

With the basic idea in mind, let us now go back over the argument in somewhat greater detail. Hegel begins by asking what the objects of this wholly demonstrative consciousness are: What is the 'this'?[49] It is what is here, now, so we may deal with these two terms instead. What, then, is 'now'? The answer is obscured by Hegel's treatment of 'now' as a noun (*das Jetzt*), and on top of that as one term of what seems to be an identity statement: *das Jetzt ist die Nacht*, something lying as far from normal German as its word-by-word translation would be from normal English. (Why sense-certainty should be made to give birth to this linguistic monster, and what state of mind it conveys by doing so, may well baffle the careful reader—no doubt but that it calls for more explanation than Hegel offers.) But in spite of this the general drift is clear enough, and not out of line with what we have seen reason to expect: 'now' is applicable to many different circumstances, and this is the characteristic of a universal. The same thing happens to 'here' (*das Hier ist der Baum*[50]), with the same

---

[49] PG para. 95.
[50] Ibid. para. 98.

outcome. Sense-certainty has failed, so far, to do anything which would allow it to grasp a particular; it can operate only with demonstratives, and they are universals.

Thus foiled, sense-certainty tries again, this time by importing the subject of consciousness, trying to fix the 'now' and the 'here' by appeal to the fact that they are mine—here and now for me. But just as there is another now and another here, so also there is another I, or many such. What is expressed by the first-person pronoun is, again, a universal.

This thought is, I think, fairly easily grasped, even if there is a tendency to dismiss it with the suggestion that it all rests on a misunderstanding of demonstratives, which neither name nor describe, and indeed do nothing at all unless taken together with a particular context of utterance.[51] It is no wonder, so the criticism might go, that Hegel will not allow sense-certainty to grasp particulars, when he will not allow it recourse to any particular situation in which its possessor might find himself. But more important for us, since we are trying to understand Hegel rather than undermine him, is to notice another feature of this passage which, through its unfamiliarity, can easily escape the analytical eye of the twentieth century. At the beginning of the next paragraph, Hegel writes:

What does not disappear in all this is the 'I' as *universal*, whose seeing is neither a seeing of the tree nor of this house, but is a simple seeing which, though mediated by the negation of this house, etc., is all the same simple and indifferent to whatever happens in it . . .[52]

There is no mention here of more than one subject of consciousness; on the contrary, it is as if Hegel reckoned 'I' amongst the universals precisely by virtue of its capacity to stay the same subject through different experiences, to be now this, now that, whilst retaining its identity;[53] and when one sees this one also sees that the previous paragraph does not demand to be read as speaking of more than one person either. If so, then we have to reckon with something for which the

[51] See J. N. Findlay's *Analysis of the Text* appended to Miller's translation, PG p. 510
[52] PG para. 102.
[53] see also E Part I para. 24 Zusatz 1: 'Every man is a whole world of representations. . . . "I" is the universal, in which we abstract from everything particular . . .'

earlier discussion has prepared us—a sense of 'universal' quite different from the one now most familiar. For in this sense any particular will be a universal, provided that it is a continuant, something which persists whilst passing through a variety of states. There is, it is clear, a link with the familiar sense, in which a universal is something that can be manifested in a variety of particulars, but just as clearly there is a radical extension of it.

Put like that, the point may sound merely speculative, for it is possible to read the text as referring to a number of different subjects, rather than different states of the one subject. But one finds elsewhere abundant evidence that the latter reading would have been (at least) perfectly acceptable to Hegel. In the following chapter ('Perception') we find him calling something a 'universal medium' (*allgemeines Medium*) on the grounds that it has various properties:

It is in truth, then, the Thing itself that is white, and *also* cubical, *also* tart, and so on. In other words, the Thing is the *Also*, or the *universal medium* in which the many properties subsist . . .[54]

If the object counts as universal in virtue of the synchronous possession of several properties, no doubt it will count as universal if it possesses several properties consecutively. When this is appreciated, the passage from 'Sense-Certainty' about the universality of 'I' falls into place.

Equally clear from this part of the text is that the thing's being universal is at least very closely associated, for Hegel, with the existence of a certain act of the mind, something much like a Kantian synthesis. For instance:

Through the fact, then, that we regard the characteristic of being a universal medium as our reflection, we preserve the self-identity and truth of the Thing, its being a One,[55]

—from which it also emerges, as suspected, that we are 'universal media', and for very much the same reason. Another example:

it is this unity which consciousness has to take upon itself; for the

[54] PG para. 120.
[55] Ibid. para. 119.

Thing itself is the *subsistence of the many diverse and independent properties*.[56]

A passive consciousness, then, cannot perceive things, which preserve their identity through different states. If sense-certainty can only claim for its objects things having that property, it gives itself away—from its very definition it follows that it could not have that kind of object.

From these same passages we also gather that consciousness of the composite depends on mental activity: grasp of unity, of whatever kind, calls for a unifying act, in Hegel as in Kant. It follows that sense-certainty likewise betrays itself if its alleged objects turn out to be complex, or 'pluralities'. As a purely receptive consciousness, it cannot have any such objects.

In general, it may be said that Hegel everywhere associates the universal with the activity of thought. We have now seen a number of particular examples; here is the point put in its full generality:

Its [Thought's] *product*, the nature or form of thought, is the *universal*, or the abstract. Thought, as *activity*, is therefore the *active*, indeed the self-activating, universal, since the act, what is produced, is precisely the universal.[57]

What Hegel is trying to show, then, is that sense-certainty cannot after all capture its objects by mere passive reception, but must, contrary to its first definition, be active. It is perfectly natural that he should express this by saying that sense-certainty turns out to be aware of the universal, when it was hoping to stay passive and so grasp the individual. What we must do is read him with the thought of mental activity at the front of our minds, rather than latch on to the word 'universal' and then take it in the sense to which we are accustomed. Something of that sort appears to have betrayed Taylor, as we shall shortly see.

The attempt to fix the object by the use of 'now' and 'here', and then of 'I', having collapsed, Hegel allows sense-certainty the further device of pointing, thereby pre-empting the

[56] Ibid. para. 121.
[57] E Part I para. 20.

criticism, which certain commentators have made neverthe-less, that he abuses the indexicals by asking them to function whilst allowing them no connection to a specific context of utterance. (See the remarks about Findlay, above.) But what we discover is that the attempt to point the object out results, once again, in the consciousness of the wrong kind of thing, not a ready-made individual which can just be received, but something which is a product or 'universal'. As usual, there is some obscurity as to exactly how this comes about. But I believe that two strands can be detected in the text, and certainly some things about what Hegel did not mean can be said with complete confidence.

Sense-certainty tries, then, to 'point to the now', ostensively to indicate the instant in question.[58] But as it does so, the instant vanishes; it is, in Hegel's terminology, *negated*. The hope was that whilst remaining purely receptive we might manage to capture what simply is, but at once it *is not*, and if it is to be recaptured in any way, active thought will be needed—we must now 'negate the negation'. This might mean that we must think, as it were, 'No, not *this* now, but *that* one that we originally picked out'; on the other hand, and more probably, it might mean that we must realise that the now is neither this one nor that one, but rather whatever is, at the time. Hegel likes to describe the universal as 'remaining self-identical in its Other', and he makes this formula fit universals normally so called, substances possessing several distinct properties, and continuants that successively pass through distinct states. For these experiences change (are negated, go over into their Other), whilst remaining them-selves—they are not to be identified with the particulars they characterise, or with the states they possess or pass through. Thus redness may be manifested in this piece of cloth, and also in something that is not this piece of cloth; and so, 'negating the negation', we observe that redness is not identical with either individual, and so 'return' to the universal redness. There is a similar movement of thought in the experience that I have this (present) state, but also a state which is not this one, but yesterday's; and so we 'return' to the self in the realisation that it is not the same as its states. The

[58] PG paras. 106–7.

reader may find the jargon clumsy, or worse; it is not my purpose to convert him. The point is that this is how Hegel speaks and thinks, and it is in the light of this that we are to understand his endeavours to show that sense-certainty only grasps the universal, in other words the product of active thinking.

A second line of thought leads him to the same place. The now that is grasped, the now that will hold still long enough to be pointed to, is a day, an hour, or a minute.[59] It is an individual day, hour or minute, and in that sense no universal. But it is complex, a plurality, and compression into the superficially simple concept *now* calls for 'negation' and the 'energy of thought'. And so we find that it is a universal, in Hegel's broad meaning of the word.

Taylor took his cue for the interpretation of this passage not from Kant, Hegel's close neighbour, but (rather implausibly, one might think) from Wittgenstein.[60] We can reconstruct his likely train of thought. Concentrating on Hegel's insistence that the object of sense-certainty is the 'universal', and reading this in our familiar sense rather than as a reference to mental activity, he supposed that the point to be made was that sense-certainty cannot achieve anything without making use of general concepts, in which he would be confirmed by his reading of the definition of sense-certainty as a non-conceptual state of consciousness. If it could then be shown that demonstratives like 'here' and 'now' rely on the secret help of such concepts and can do nothing without it, then it would follow that the supposition of a purely demonstrative state of consciousness was mythical—such a state would have no content. And this does indeed suggest comparison with Wittgenstein's discussion of ostensive definition:[61] the mere act of pointing fixes nothing, we need to know what kind of thing is being indicated, and this involves the use, implicit or otherwise, of a general term. So pointing is empty unless backed up by the sort of conceptual equipment that sense-certainty was stipulated not to have. However, there are two aspects of the text to which this does no justice. First, it fails to

[59] Ibid. para. 107.
[60] Charles Taylor: *Hegel* (Cambridge 1975) pp. 143–4.
[61] Wittgenstein: *Philosophical Investigations* (Blackwell 1953) para. 28 *et seq.*

explain Hegel's tendency to say that what sense-certainty is conscious of is really universal; on this account sense-certainty could certainly be conscious of individuals: the point would be that it needs the use of universal concepts in order to do so. Secondly, it leaves Hegel's emphasis on the fact that a day, an hour, a minute, are all pluralities, and indeed 'pluralities of nows', utterly mysterious, because totally redundant; all he need have said, on Taylor's interpretation, is that today is a day, and tomorrow is another day, so 'day' is a universal— and that hence without the aid of an implicit universal 'now' cannot operate.

If this reading is correct, we can see that the Sense-Certainty chapter is not to be understood without a massive input of material drawn from Hegel's wider metaphysical vision. In furtherance of the growing interest in constructive activity which was now well on the way to becoming the dominant philosophical idea, he is arguing that consciousness cannot avoid the activity of thought. The universal, in his vocabulary, is precisely the outcome of that activity, and the presence of the universal (as for instance general properties, substances, continuants) in reality is the manifestation of the activity of the Idea embodied in the concrete.

A final word to stave off a possible misunderstanding. I may in this section inadvertently have given the impression that Hegel held the unity of the object to be the work of consciousness, somewhat as if he had accepted unchanged Kant's doctrine of empirical reality and its dependence upon the mode of operation of the human mind. That was no more than a device to avoid confronting all the complexities of Hegel's real view simultaneously—though it is a device actually employed by Hegel himself. He did not allow of the Kantian distinction between the empirically real and the thing-in-itself. Nor did he think that the world that we encounter owes its nature to human nature or to that of human thought. Rather he hypostatises 'the Idea', which he views as a system of 'pure thoughts'; and it is their activity which is in question, and which results in an objective, and objectively unified, reality.

Now, however, comes a further finesse. We can if we wish consider the Idea objectively (as Hegel claims to do in the

Logic), that is to say as it is. We can also consider it as its activity manifests itself in our consciousness—this is the business of the *Phenomenology of Spirit*. Hegel thinks of our consciousness as the vehicle of the Idea in its progress towards self-knowledge, so that the facts about consciousness mirror the nature of the Idea. If the objective side of the story tells of the foundations of objective reality, there will be a subjective side which tells how the mind comes to be conscious of its (intensional) objects, and what those objects are like. And because of what Hegel thinks about the activity of thought in the objective sphere, we may expect that there will be, in his view of things, a corresponding activity of the mind, somewhat akin to Kantian synthesis, in the subjective sphere. When he is concentrating on the subjective aspect alone, therefore, as in the chapter of Sense-Certainty (and in general throughout the *Phenomenology*), he will sound highly Kantian. That does not mean that he simply is Kantian. It means that this feature of Kant's philosophy has been subsumed into Hegel's and to some extent transformed by it. It is now seen to have been a partial truth with a rightful place in the more adequate philosophical system which succeeds it—an excellent illustration of Hegel's general thesis about the way in which philosophy makes historical progress.

6.   *Why all the fuss?*

The last twenty years, as I have said, have seen a sharp increase in the amount of attention paid to Hegel in the English-speaking countries, and a corresponding increase in understanding. But in this understanding there is a gap which the new crop of secondary literature has not closed—it may even have widened it: we are as far as ever from understanding the obvious historical fact of Hegel's enormous success. This, it seems, is something about which philosophers schooled primarily in analytic styles of thought were not best equipped to enlighten us. What their work has on the whole revealed, to those who had not already guessed, is that Hegel was no great hand at constructing a cogent argument, or at giving unmistakable expression to whatever he had constructed; his logic is at best badly presented and at worst beneath criticism, whilst the details of his Logic have resisted, or repulsed, all the attempts of several generations to impose a coherent interpretation fit to carry conviction either as exegesis or as philosophy—they remain what they have always been, dimly and elusively suggestive of the accomplishment of his overall purpose. One frequently hears, and not least from his own compatriots, the complaint that for all the shelves filled with writing about Hegel, there exists very little detailed commentary on particular passages or close analytical work on his texts. Here is just one example:

the literature on Hegel is poor in detailed interpretation of text in which the interpreter follows his thought sentence by sentence and word by word. All too often people cling mindlessly to Hegel's well known saying, that Truth lies in the Whole.[62]

The entry of the analytic school into the Hegelian arena has done a little to remedy this situation, but it has not, to put it mildly, increased confidence that there is a reliable chain of argument buried in the texts, such as ought to convince the rational and impartial reader. So we are left with something of a hiatus. Why, we may ask, did a man spend so much of his life, so much intellectual and emotional energy, on the invention of so much bad argument? And given that, why these bad arguments rather than another set? Why was thought of such *prima facie* obscurity so enthusiastically received, and how did it come to its incalculable historical influence? One may talk here of Hegel's breadth of vision, his encyclopedic command of empirical fact. But many of these 'facts' were of somewhat defective factuality; and as for breadth of vision, surely being prepared to talk about almost everything ought to be of little weight, compared with the content of what one says about it?

Such irreverent thoughts may drive us towards a Popperian view of Hegel as a charlatan wind bag propelled into the status of a great philosopher by the chance play of social and political forces, aided perhaps by the human desire to be mystified, factors at any rate which had little to do with the content of his work, if content there be. His position in history,

[62] Wolfgang Wieland: 'Hegels Dialektik der sinnlichen Gewissheit' in *Materialien zu Hegels Phänomenologie des Geistes*, ed. Fulda and Henrich (Suhrkamp 1973) pp. 67–82. See also Fulda: ibid. p. 391 and Henrich: 'Anfang und Methode der Logik', in *Hegel im Kontext* (Suhrkamp 1971) p. 73.

for this type of understanding, has no doubt some explanation, but not one that lies within the history of philosophy. It is not difficult to detect the smell of prejudice here, but apparently it is not so easy to put one's finger on the exact features which the prejudice encourages us to overlook, so that the problem to which it is a manifestly prejudiced answer remains; the feeling, be it never so strong, that of course there is more to the matter of Hegel than this, will not drive it away, but only out of sight.

One of my hopes for this chapter is that, together with Chapter 3, it has provided materials for filling this lacuna in our understanding. With them at hand we can see why Hegel's philosophy proved, and in some quarters still proves, to be such a potent mixture. From the old and comfortingly familiar it picked up one of the most important threads, the idea of rational insight into the real, and so worked it as to keep the thesis of man's divine nature, our similarity to God, well to the fore. At the same time, and in fact as part of the same doctrine, it offered a taste of the new and exciting, linking arms with the up-and-coming stress on practice and creativity by making man the major participant in an active process that unfolded his, and the world's, destiny, and even the destiny of God. It was a spark perfectly suited to ignite the optimistic self-confidence which was such a marked and widespread feature of the nineteenth century. Besides, and to some extent as a consequence of the fact that he looked out over history in both directions, Hegel could be read in a number of ways: the conservative, quietistic temperament could find solace in his doctrine of the necessity and intrinsic rightness of all history; but equally the revolutionary could find an ally in him by concentrating on his treatment of process, the clash of opposing forces, the inevitable dialectical ascent of consciousness and the social order. Engels, for one, saw these two aspects of Hegel very clearly.[63]

These factors would by themselves have guaranteed him a front position in the intellectual life of the nineteenth century and doubtless, by virtue of the momentum gained, well beyond it. But there was more. His philosophy, when looked at from a suitable distance—and his style prevents almost

---

[63] See Engels: *Ludwig Feuerbach and the End of Classical German Philosophy*.

everyone from coming any closer—presents a most aesthetic and satisfying appearance: it is wonderfully comprehensive, yet at the same time wonderfully ordered and systematic. More still, it shows a capacity to incorporate the core of the Christian tradition, and thus makes itself welcome to two groups of people: on the one hand it makes Christianity a more comfortable stance for those whose upbringing has inclined them towards it, but whose education has made them feel that only what can be seen as intellectually rigorous is wholly respectable; on the other it makes Hegel's philosophy attractive to those whose approach to belief is more emotional, for whom Christian faith is the priority. To cap it all, Hegel also took a structure of much greater detail, the whole romantic metaphysic, his generation's favoured self-image, and claimed to prove its truth by the strictest standards. No doubt other factors played a part, but with all this on the table there is no need to wonder at the phenomenon of Hegel's contemporary reception, or of his subsequent influence. Rarely in philosophy has supply been so well tuned to demand, rarely has a philosophy served so well the three masters of past, present and future.

One further point may be mentioned. If we believe that there is some truth in the recommendation that one who wishes to be taken for a great man should be prepared to affirm his own greatness, and that it is human to crave great figures to whom to attach one's hopes and beliefs, the question of Hegel's effect on his audiences, contemporary and otherwise, becomes still more transparent. The course of world history consists, according to his doctrine, in the story of the world-spirit's struggle for consciousness of its own nature. Such self-conscious awareness arises for the first time in Hegel's own philosophy, in Hegel's own person. He never, to my knowledge, explicitly drew the consequence, indeed it is not to be wondered at if he shrank from formulating it clearly even to himself; but once the premisses are before their minds an audience could be expected to have at least some dim apprehension of it: the ultimate purpose of everything that has ever existed is to enable the emergence of Hegel's philosophy. To call the claim messianic would be an understatement, for not even of Christ is it alleged that his life and work was the final purpose of the universe.

5

THE WORKS OF MAN

1. *A change of focus: doing*

Twice now we have taken long-range views of certain stages in the career of European thought. Each time the hope was twofold. First, that we should get to see a wood where we might otherwise have seen only trees, begin in other words to discern philosophies where we might have been in danger of noticing nothing but philosophy. And second, that we might then descend from these vistas to the detail of particular writers and particular texts, and find ourselves equipped with a new and enlightening approach to them. This closing pair of chapters will attempt to bring the story more or less up to date; it will apply the same formula, though modified in certain respects to suit the somewhat different nature of the material and our very different, because participatory, relationship to it. For various reasons, and not just that one, this threatens to be a much more precarious task. Not only is there such a vast quantity of familiar material which time has not yet had the chance to sort out for us (though I hope and trust that it is hard at work); there is also the fact that the Anglo-Saxon tradition has recently been extremely coy about the relationship between its philosophising and any possible *Weltbild*, so that anything so explicit as what we have found in Leibniz or Hölderlin (to take two of the most explicit cases) is unavailable, and the work must proceed by trying to pick up indirect clues and implications.

Even this might be thought to understate the difficulty. Is it just that recent English-speaking philosophy has been reluctant to engage in discussion of the grand vision of reality? Hasn't it rather said a firm 'No' to any such engagement? I think we must agree that it has, on the whole; but the possibility nevertheless remains that this betokens only a lack of self-knowledge, or even self-deceit; and I shall make bold to proceed on that hypothesis. There is cause for some initial optimism. In the first place, this reluctance towards, or rejection of, the consideration of *Weltbilder* is both recent and parochial. Recent, because we do not have to look back at all far to find thinkers who, whilst obviously numbering amongst our closest philosophical ancestors, were not in the least shy when it came to the public exposure of their favoured metaphysic; and parochial, because it has evidently not been felt in anything like the same strength on the European mainland. And whilst it is not impossible that there should be such sudden discontinuities, either historical or geographical, neither does it seem very likely. We should not forget that the present century opened in Britain with a blaze of neo-Hegelianism, that its most influential 'British' philosopher, Ludwig Wittgenstein, was an Austrian, and that one of its most important orientations, logical positivism, came from Vienna. And besides just not forgetting this (we are hardly likely to, most readers will feel), we should ask whether there is anything to be learnt from it for our understanding of ourselves. In the second place, the popularity of doctrines popular in our own times frequently seems to me to pose a historical problem of just the same magnitude and kind as that posed by the popularity of much that has been popular in the past. Thus I do not believe, to take an example to which we shall return in Chapter 6, that recent thinkers about rationality and explanation 'just happen' to find the notion of a brute fact acceptable, any more than that all those philosophers of the seventeenth century 'just happened' not to. And I have too much scepticism to suppose that our own philosophical predilections are as they are because we have seen them to be the inevitable result of cogent argument beginning from undeniable, philosophically neutral and un-controversial premises.

In Chapter 1 we dwelt at length on what I called the Image of God doctrine and its ramifications. The philosophy that was produced under its aegis laid heavy stress on a conception of man as first and foremost a spectator, an onlooker who could, and should, acquire insight into the order of reality as God had disposed it and so realise to some degree his potential for affinity with the divine mind. There were, it is true, some cases to be found in which a comparison was drawn between man and God as agents;[1] but they were a small minority, and not such as to threaten the broad judgement that man's powers of action were not something which this epoch prized very highly— some of its most illustrious representatives held views according to which human action could hardly be said to exist. That is true of Spinoza, for whom freedom became merely a species of onlooking: that which is accompanied by acquiescence born of the mind's insight into the necessity of what it sees. Hume was moved, and understandably, to say of the occasionalists that 'They rob nature, and all created beings, of every power . . .'.[2]

Of Malebranche at least that can justifiably be said, for he would count nothing as a cause which was not necessarily connected with its effect, and denied that condition to be satisfied by anything except the will of God. Berkeley allows the spirit a certain limited control over its own states; but one's arm moves only by the intervention of God on the occasion of one's willing its movement.

Another factor reinforces the impression that man is best thought of as spectator. When, as in the Insight Ideal, the then most popular variant of the Image of God doctrine, the cognitive powers of the human being are represented as quasi-divine and so made the link between him and the creator, the feeling is encouraged that the business of coming to know the world is conducted from an Olympian position outside the ·natural order; this in spite of the fact that the potentially Olympian consciousness is temporarily and mysteriously lodged in a body which is very much a part of that order. A hint of remoteness is generated which does not easily lend itself to combination with any doctrine that gives the concept of human activity a philosophically central position. But all this was shortly to undergo a radical change.

We have seen that the Image of God doctrine persisted, or rather raised itself to a new intensity, in the thought of the romantic era. But it was now changed in two related ways of great historical import. The god with whom man strove to identify was an immanent god, the god of pantheism of nature

---

[1] See Chapter 1 Section 2 on Descartes, and Section 6 on Leibniz.
[2] ECHU p. 71.

instead of a supernatural, transcendent being; so that being divine, an image of the deity, no longer implied that degree of aloofness that previously had weighted down the scales in favour of the 'spectator theory' of the ideal for man. Furthermore, the identification of god with nature encouraged the conception of deity as mobile, actively engaged in endless self-transformation. The mind of a god who stood over nature could well be thought of as static, its consciousness the eternal contemplation of the eternal truths of which nature was the slavish embodiment; but a god who *was* nature would share nature's everchanging face as well as her everlasting laws:

She is for ever creating new forms; what is now, has not yet been, what has been, will never come again—all is new, and yet always the old.[3]

Goethe chose his god accordingly:

I should like to imagine a god that produces itself from all eternity . . .[4]

Here, it is clear, the concepts of activity, creation, change and process have gained a foothold in the very centre of metaphysics. Schiller was on the same path, we may recall,[5] when he explained man's 'tendency to divinity' in terms of the active power of the human mind to impose form on the given materials of sensation. The challenge to man is to make of his life and world an object as aesthetically satisfying (in Schiller's terms) as possible; he is to create a work of art:

all that is in him he must externalise, all that is external he must shape. Both tasks, when thought of as carried out to the highest degree, lead back to the concept of the deity . . .[6]

The extent of his success is the measure of his divinity.

Had European philosophy come to an end with Hegel (somewhat as Hegel was inclined to think that it had), this phase of its development would look like the final version of the Similarity Thesis. But it also turned out to be the transition to a very different philosophical era, one in which

---

[3] From *Die Natur*—see above, Chapter 3 Secton 4.
[4] Goethe: *Dichtung und Wahrheit*, Werke Vol. IX (Hamburg edn.) p. 351.
[5] See above, Chapter 3 Section 4.
[6] Schiller: *Aesthetic Education of Man*, 11th letter.

the view of man as the spectator of events in the natural world and out of it rapidly lost ground in favour of a more active conception that placed him firmly within it and saw his salvation in his power to change it. It was a period in which activity, practice and a closely related group of concepts came increasingly to be the tools that the philosopher first and instinctively grasped for to help solve his problems. It was also a period in which the purely contemplative values, the idea of the intrinsic desirability of knowledge, found it more and more difficult to make their way unaided by at least the arguable prospect of some beneficial connection with practice.

That the contemplative values should suffer this reverse is no very surprising fact if seen against the background I have proposed. They derived from the thought that contemplation could bring the human mind into a godlike relationship with reality and so allow it to make an approach to the divine perfection. But this was the century in which, whatever may have happened to God himself, at least his death certificate was issued over the signature of Nietzsche. Dead or not, God did largely disappear from philosophy at this time, and where he was allowed to remain it was often as the merest shadow of his former self, as a creation of the human mind which had once been his creation, and charged to prove beneficial to human life or be extinguished along with many another discarded fiction. Feuerbach had lead the way here, with Marx and Engels in enthusiastic pursuit. Later, from another tradition, William James wrote at the beginning of a chapter entitled 'Pragmatism and Religion': 'On pragmatic principles we cannot reject any hypothesis if consequences useful to life flow from it.'[7] The God of Leibniz, if not dead at the time, was presumably grateful to him. But a god like that of James, dependent on human utilities for his very permit to exist, could scarcely provide the metaphysical background needed to make the attainment of wholly disinterested intellectual insight into truth one of the highest of moral values, as Leibniz's God had done in his day.

[7] William James: *Pragmatism*, Lecture VIII. References to the works of James are either to individual lectures or papers, and so should not be too hard to find in any edition. But for what I hope is the reader's convenience, I give page numbers for *Pragmatism and The Meaning of Truth* (Harvard University Press 1975), which contains both the lectures on *Pragmatism* and the collection of papers published as *The Meaning of Truth*. (I refer to this volume as 'Harvard'.) This quotation p. 131.

This revision of priorities, this withdrawal of honorific status from pure contemplation, is, however, only a part, and not an especially central part, of the change which now came over European philosophy. To say that is not to deny its importance as an intellectual phenomenon—the extent to which the 'purer' subjects are expected to show 'applied' credentials (or the promise of them) is obviously a most significant factor in cultural life with all manner of social and economic repercussions. But it is not this aspect that I wish to concentrate on. Rather I shall focus attention on the way in which philosophers began increasingly to turn to the concept of practice for a solution to metaphysical and epistemological problems. Practice had, of course, always been a focus for philosophical questions: which forms of it were permissible, which obligatory, how it should be regulated, what was its relation to reason and the emotions, could it in any meaningful sense be free? And so on. Now, however, it began to be an essential ingredient in the answers. That is a promotion only granted to concepts of which philosophers have acquired the confidence that their audience—and if they are sincere, they are their own first audience—will find there a more comfortable resting-place for thought, will not feel that they have been offered a greater problem in solution of a lesser.

In that respect the concept of practice gives no great difficulty. From certain perspectives, such as for instance that generated by exclusive concentration on the Insight Ideal, it may come to appear problematic; but there is a strong natural tendency to take it for transparent: aren't we doing things all the time? How could anything be more familiar? A concept needs something more than this, however, if it is to join the élite of those on which philosophical solutions are allowed to be built: it needs what we may call philosophical prestige, which is not just the feeling (even if veridical) that we understand it. We have the feeling that we know what matter is, but many who have that feeling still feel that materialism is a doctrine which trivialises reality and human life. We need not fear, though, that the concepts of practice, agency and so forth will prove unfit for philosophical society. Their pedigree shows theological connections, after all; and these very

connections enable them to figure in the version of the Image
of God doctrine which makes comparison between the activity
of man and the creative fiat of God, as we saw in Leibniz and
again in the romantics. Nobody could accuse these ideas of
having no breeding.

Those who now began to philosophise on the assumption
that God was dead, or with the intention that he should
shortly be so, found that these focal concepts were quite
capable of a life of their own, independent of the theological
environment that had been their first home. That was not just
a consequence of their own momentum, if it was that at all;
other social factors were perfectly suited to encouraging them.
Both the groups primarily responsible, the socialist thinkers
led by Marx and Engels in Europe and the pragmatists in
America, consisted of people who found themselves in what
were effectively new societies, full of rapid change and
activity, living displays of man's ability to create his own
world, for good or ill. It would have been surprising if such
climates had not sustained philosophies which made practice,
and its associated family of concepts, their fulcrum.

But whatever may have been its cause or causes, this
change did occur; philosophers came more and more to allow
the concept of practice to dictate the terms on which argument
was to be conducted, and hence also the shape of the resultant
theories. In so doing it either stated or insinuated a new
picture of man and man's relation to reality: no longer a
spectator, but a being that actively creates, or shapes, its own
world. It did not, one cannot over emphasise, manifest itself
only or even primarily in moral or practical philosophy; the
striking thing about it was precisely the way in which what
might be called the practical concepts invaded the areas
previously thought of as purely theoretical, those areas where
'spectator' theories had been paramount, and whose connections with the practical had been thought of as a welcome but
wholly inessential extra.

I shall call the very general idea that underlies this
orientation the 'Agency Theory' or sometimes the 'Practice
Ideal'; but certain reservations about the appropriateness of
these labels must be mentioned if they are not to be
misleading. 'Practice Ideal' is a verbal parallel to 'Insight

Ideal', but whereas the exponents of the latter were indeed people who took insight as an ideal, one of the principal goals to strive for, it should not be thought that an adherent of the Practice Ideal in the comparable way regards practice as his ideal. Then one could not help asking how there could possibly be a sincere philosophy connected with it, since it would look as if its proponents ought to stop thinking altogether and go and push the world about instead. I wouldn't deny that, especially at the political end of the philosophical spectrum, this is occasionally in the air; it lurks, for instance, behind the socialist writers' sneering use of the word *gelehrt* (learned) to call down anti-intellectual prejudice on their opponents—without, of course, being clearly seen to do so. The Practice Ideal, as I understand the words, is something quite different, indeed incompatible: it is the attempt to develop philosophical theories in which the concept of practice, the idea of doing or making something, bears the main load. The other label, 'Agency Theory', has the different defect that what I am thinking of is not really itself to be called a theory; it is the tendency to select theories which stress a certain group of concepts.

One further caveat is to be entered. The two labels I shall use might give the impression that we are concerned with one, or at most two, concepts, whose content is antecedently clear. I have already hinted at the former point, by speaking of 'a closely related group of concepts' and 'an associated family of concepts'. The notion of acting, doing something, is surrounded by a bunch of connected ideas (whether the connection is a logical one or an association based on very general facts about human action is not important here), and an increase in its frequency and centrality of employment is very likely to go along with a similar increase in theirs. The main examples are the teleological ones of the agent's interest in the outcome of the action, his purpose in acting, and the dynamic ones of the change that the action brings about and the process by means of which it does so. All these, we shall see, are important outrunners of a theory rooted in the concept of practice. Sometimes, if I may be allowed a switch of metaphor, they come close to wagging the dog.

There is also the question of the antecedent clarity of the

central concepts. It has to be admitted that they are fairly elastic, for even if there are obvious examples of acting, doing something, with which no one would quarrel, it is much less definite how far the extension of these concepts can be stretched. At full stretch they can be applied to anything that can be captured by a verb, so that even pure contemplation of the most theoretical kind can be admitted to the class of actions, things that we do. Sometimes the reader may be given the impression that a writer, whilst making prominent and enthusiastic use of notions like 'interest' and 'conduct', then allows their content to be determined by extraneous considerations which slip in unawares; or allows nearly all their content to drain away whilst still insisting on their vital importance—we shall soon meet examples.

Whether all that makes the phenomenon we are concerned with too diffuse to be regarded as a single item is a subjective question that can only be left to the judgement of the individual reader in the light of the detailed evidence. It does not, I would agree at once, have quite the same kind of unity as that which the Image of God doctrine conferred on the period from Galileo to Berkeley, for the unity of that period was created by adherence to a common thesis (even if it was imprecise, and so capable of several different articulations), whereas the Agency Theory is characterised rather more loosely in terms of the unity of common emphasis on a certain bunch of concepts. But two points should be borne in mind in assessing the matter. First, the Image of God doctrine, in its classical form, lasted for just over one hundred years, and even so there was scope within it for a number of quite distinctive philosophical systems to be constructed. If we extend its reign to include the romantics and German idealism—which one legitimately can, since the notion of man's participation in the divine nature was manifestly still one of the forces giving philosophy its emotional impetus—the range becomes a good deal wider. Its life is then extended to a little more than two hundred years, much the same as the time-span in which the Practice Ideal has been effective, which I shall put (with various provisos to be mentioned later) at roughly 1780 to the present. It is only fair, therefore, that the latter should be allowed to exhibit some inner diversity without being held to have disintegrated. After all, the thesis that there exist such unifying themes can only be of interest if it is meant to cover material showing a marked variety, and the more variety the greater the interest. The question is rather whether the concepts that form the allegedly unifying thread maintain a sufficient identity in point of both meaning and centrality throughout the range of different philosophical systems that are found to occur. The danger is that they will not, or that they will do so only by virtue of being so generously interpreted that they could be discovered in almost any philosophical material whatever.

My claims do run this risk. But I think it will in the end be felt that they avoid it, especially if a second point is taken into account. In saying that the Agency Theory differed from the Image of God doctrine in being constituted by the emphasis on a particular cluster of concepts rather than on any specific thesis, I may have conceded too much and made the disparity sound greater than it actually is. For given the nature of the concepts in question, and the sort of use which is made of them by so many philosophers of the last two hundred years, the Practice Ideal does almost amount to the invitation to accept a certain thesis, namely that we are the creators of our own environment, that the realities which we meet with are *the works of man*.

2. *Good odds on God—and making the world yourself*

It is time to leave these abstract and anticipatory remarks and look at some of the real philosophy which is their concrete subject-matter. Let us warm up with an example which, whilst peripheral to the Practice Ideal, has the advantage of illustrating two important points about it, and the further advantage of being well known: the famous wager of Pascal.[8] Coming as it does from the middle of the seventeenth century, it reminds us not to think, as the outward form of this book might unhappily suggest, that the history of philosophy falls into chronological sections more neatly than is in fact the case. When we divide it into periods, as I am doing, we should not be thinking of the distinction between an idea's occurring and not occurring, but rather between its merely occurring and its

[8] Pascal: *Pensées* para. 418.

being prominent and (more or less) ubiquitous; we are to think of changing emphasis rather than the switching on and off of various conceptual illuminations. But as well as helping us to keep this general point in view the use of the wager as an example highlights an essential feature of the Practice Ideal as I would have it understood: it is not to be thought of as just the emergence of an interest in practice—philosophers had always been interested in that from some perspective or other—but rather as a tendency for the concepts of practice and agency (and their retinue) to invade all areas of philosophy. In Pascal's wager we see them at work on the colonisation of epistemology and the justification of belief.

The argument of the wager is well known in its outline, and an outline is all that we need for our present purposes. Does God exist or not? Which alternative should we believe? Pascal invites us to think of this as equivalent to the question of whether we should place a bet on the proposition that God exists, or alternatively on its negation. If we bet that he exists, and win the bet, the pay-off is enormous: infinite and eternal bliss. If we do so and lose, we have not staked very much: only that excess happiness, if any, which the unbeliever can enjoy over the believer during this earthly life. Suppose we place the opposite bet, and win—God does not exist; then we have gained just that questionable excess of happiness. Should we lose, we have missed the infinite bliss of heaven, and may also reap the eternal torments of hell. What to do? The answer is obvious: place the bet which obviates the possibility of the catastrophic loss, and which risks only at worst a minor loss whilst giving a chance of infinite gain. That is, bet on the existence of God.

This is not just the suggestion that we should do one thing rather than another because game—theoretic considerations recommend it. Although Pascal talks in terms of placing bets, what is meant here by 'placing a bet' is starting a train of events which will eventually lead to a belief in God. In this particular case, Pascal can ignore any difference between betting on p and believing that p—although there surely is a difference in general, since one might (and very sensibly) bet on an outcome one considered very unlikely if very favourable odds were on offer, or if a negligible stake gave a chance of

huge gains.[9] But beliefs, which are what we are really talking
about here, can necessarily be assessed as true or false, as well
as in or against our interests to hold. And there is a view that
the former is paramount, so that there is something disreputable about believing, or trying to believe, anything for
reasons which are not even taken to constitute evidence for its
truth. The legitimate function of belief, on this view, is to
mirror reality, and trying to bring oneself to hold a belief when
one has no reason to think that it does so is intentional self-
deceit.

This view Pascal evidently does not share. Or if he does, he
must regard the self-deception involved as too venial a sin to
be worried by the possibility that the gambler, if he wins his
bet, may find the winnings not to be quite what he had
expected—perhaps God does not award the jackpot to those
who have come to believe in him by that method and with that
motivation. He clearly does not think that the only legitimate
intention with which one may form a belief is that of correctly
representing reality—one may also form it with the intention
of maximising the chances of falling on one's feet. The reasons
with which he hopes to persuade us to adopt the belief in
God's existence have nothing to do with its truth; they
concern the results of our holding the belief, and its effects on
our expectation of happiness.

Compare this with the role of belief within the philosophy of
the Insight Ideal. Belief is what we accord to those propositions of which we have become certain; then, so far as our
beliefs reach, we see the universe insightfully and truly, after
the manner of God. There is no question of imitating the mind
of God in Pascal's argument; it is not a matter of believing
what God believes, in the way God believes it, but of believing
what it is good for us to believe. What one ought to believe has
ceased to be independent of what one wants; whereas for the
Similarity Thesis the achievement of a certain kind of belief
was the attainment of an end, here it is treated as an
instrument to an end. Furthermore, it is treated as something
which we do, in the sense of *intentionally bring about*, an action of
ours as well as an instrument that we make use of. Of course,
there is nothing unusual about intentionally seeking to believe

---

[9] In fact very much the circumstances of Pascal's bet, as he conceives them.

whichever is true of p and *not-p*; but here we are to seek to believe that p, for the instrumental value to us of believing it; the matter of truth, so crucial to the Image of God doctrine, has receded.

Though much of the conceptual apparatus of the Practice Ideal is at work in the argument of the wager, we should be careful not to make too much of it. For one thing, Pascal applies this apparatus only to the justification of one belief, and no ordinary belief at that; no general theory of this type is discernible in his writings. And for another, there is little sign in the wager of man as a creative force—apart from the thought that he might consciously generate his own beliefs, it is no more that one would be certain to find in any other writer. For anything significant of that kind, one has to wait until well into the next century.

At that stage it was given a considerable push by the work of Hume, though whether the impulse ever communicated itself to any of his successors is a moot point. Our experience of the world, for Hume, is decisively affected by the operations of the faculty of imagination. Of the three faculties that are involved in the production of human belief, imagination is the most active, the least spectator-like. The senses record impressions, reason perceives existing relationships between ideas, but the imagination generates belief in states of affairs which are not in any sense given to the mind. Unlike the process suggested by Pascal, this one is quite involuntary, being the quasi-mechanical outcome of Hume's principles of association and the laws governing the transformation of ideas into beliefs. But even more unlike Pascal's process, it is virtually ubiquitous: without it, there would be no belief in an independent physical world, no belief in causal connections, no belief in anything beyond the range of the observed (and that means 'observed by the individual in question'), no belief even in a continuing self. Without these beliefs, there would be no world for us, indeed there would be no *us* for us; Hume's famous remark that these principles are 'to us, the cement of the universe' is either an understatement or an underestimate of his own position. For us, everything is owing to the imagination, and since Hume sees it as much more active than recipient it could almost be said that in his philosophy we create (though involuntarily and unconsciously) our world; what surrounds us is no longer God's creation but the work of man's mind.

Almost—but, in fairness to history, perhaps not quite. Such views are indeed implicit in Hume's philosophy, or only one short step away from it; but I know of no firm indication that this was a step which Hume was at all interested to take. If anything, there are signs to the contrary; when he considers what would happen if the principles governing the imagination were to cease to operate, it is human nature he fears for—he does not take the opportunity to fear for the world as well:

[These principles] are the foundation of all our thoughts and actions, so that upon their removal human nature must immediately perish and go to ruin.[10]

The fact is that Hume does not command the right set of concepts for formulating the claim that we experience a man-made world. To do that one needs a notion of the world-as-we-experience-it, which can then be declared a mental construct, depending on the mode of operation of our minds. What he has is the world-as-it-is (the object of his agnosticism), our impressions, and our beliefs, which are beliefs about the world-as-it-is. He does not have a term for the subtle compound of belief and impression which I have called the world-as-we-experience-it, nor is it at all clear that he would accept that such a compound is coherent.

This line of thought now brings us, as will have become obvious, to Kant. He believed in the compound, called it 'empirical reality', and contrasted it with things-in-themselves in point of dependence on the human mind and its own peculiar workings. For Kant there is a world of which man is in a large measure the creator. There is no question of having to extrapolate that fact from the text; it is something which Kant constantly advertises throughout the *Critique of Pure Reason* as his decisive innovation, the application of Copernicus's hypothesis to metaphysics. Copernicus had the idea of explaining the apparent motions of astronomical bodies by making the observer active, that is supposing him to move and

---

[10] THN p. 225.

his motion to be partly responsible for the nature of his observations. The philosopher may also try the experiment of making the mind active and partially responsible for the nature of what it perceives:

A similar experiment can be tried in metaphysics, as regards the *intuition* of objects. If intuition must conform to the constitution of objects, I do not see how we could know anything of the latter *a priori*; but if the object (as object of the senses) must conform to the constitution of our faculty of intuition, I have no difficulty in conceiving such a possibility.[11]

The familiar outcome is Kant's view of the world of the senses as the joint product of the faculties of *Sinnlichkeit* and *Verstand*; all-pervasive features of it such as space and time are supplied by the mind and are 'nothing apart from the conditions of human sensibility'.

All of that is well-trodden ground; but what deserves consideration at some length is the question as to what Kant thought could be achieved by this 'Copernican Revolution' in philosophy, and whether his optimism was justified. What he claims for it is clear enough: a solution—indeed he regards it as the only possible solution[12]—to the problem posed by the existence of *a priori* knowledge of synthetic truths. So we have the idea of human agency being mobilised in the field of the theory of knowledge and effecting a deep change in metaphysics. And Kant has reasons for his implicit claim that a 'spectator theory' of the intellect could not cope with synthetic *a priori* knowledge: the inspection of the objects of the senses yields only contingent truths and the inspection of concepts only analytic. Along with his advocacy of mental activity goes a sharp challenge to his predecessors: to explain the phenomena without departing radically from their understanding of the function of human reason.

There seems little room for doubt, however, that Kant's enthusiasm for this new picture of man and his relationship with the empirical world betrayed him; the concept of the actively formative mind, so applied, will not do the job he asks of it, that of accounting for the possibility of the synthetic *a*

---

[11] Kant: *Critique of Pure Reason* Bxvii.
[12] Ibid. B41: 'Our explanation is thus the only explanation . . .'

priori. Let us put the problem in simple, non-technical terms—any slight loss of accuracy resulting from this will not affect my argument, which is itself simple and non-technical. Kant's problem is: how is it possible to know something contentful about the world in advance of taking a look at it and seeing what it is like? And his answer: it is possible just if it is you who fixes things so that they will be like that. He holds, to use an analogy, that someone who knows a synthetic truth *a priori* is in very much the position of an architect who knows what a building looks like without yet having been to see it, because it was built from his plans. But that only strikes us as acceptable because we make an assumption about this case which is, I believe, commonly true of architects: that when a building is being built in accordance with their plans they know that it is being built in accordance with their plans; they know where their buildings are going up. It is quite clear that to explain the architect's advance knowledge the additional assumption is indispensably needed. Imagine our architect standing on a site where in fact his building is in progress, mistakenly thinking that this one is someone else's, or that some people are just knocking up an improvised house from no plan at all: he won't have, or claim, any knowledge about how the finished thing is going to look.

Kant, however, is offering an explanation of the fact (as he takes it) that we both claim and have such contentful knowledge that is independent of observation, *a priori* knowledge of synthetic truths. And his explanation works only if we are allowed to make the parallel assumption: that not only is it true that empirical reality is constructed by our minds, but further that we are aware that that is how it is constructed. If we were not aware of it, no amount of knowledge of how our minds worked would give us any knowledge at all about the nature of the world, just as in the architect's case no amount of knowledge of his plans would give him any knowledge of what would appear on that site, if he did not know that it was his building.

But it is surely clear that the addition of this indispensable assumption, however satisfactory it may be for architects, is sudden death to Kant's attempted explanation of the synthetic *a priori*. It will explain such knowledge only when the knowing subject knows that, and to what extent, the empirical world is a creation of his own mind. On Kant's account of the matter, in other words, synthetic *a priori* knowledge could only exist when people had already recognised the truth of his philosophy. This is manifestly not what he believes, and it would anyway make pragmatic nonsense of his procedure when he argues for his transcendental idealism by saying, in effect: there is synthetic *a priori* knowledge, but that can only be the case if transcendental idealism is true. For this argument is not just at some risk of being circular in what I take to be the normal sense, namely that anybody who does not already accept the conclusion ought not to accept the premiss; it is circular in the stronger sense that until people accept the conclusion the premiss cannot even be true. One can evade this criticism only by adopting an explanation of the possibility of synthetic *a priori* knowledge quite different from that of Kant; but then its existence will no longer even look as if it might be sufficient grounds for affirming transcendental idealism.

So the attempt, starting from an alleged problem in the theory of knowledge, to enforce an ontological conception having the idea of human mental activity at its core turns out, if cogent logic is our first requirement, to be in a sad mess. Kant has overestimated his Copernican revolution, the thesis of the creative observer, in asking it to solve epistemological problems by itself, without support from the observer's knowledge that, and what, he is creating. But we have already seen several cases of logic being overtaken by enthusiasm in the neighbourhood of an attractive *Weltbild*, and this one does indeed seem to have proved attractive. When Kant's immediate successors criticised him, it was not for using weak arguments to establish the creativity of his observer, nor even for making the observer creative, but for not allowing his creativity a wider range, for leaving the *Ding-an-sich* outside its scope, untouched by human hand. Pretty soon Fichte had disposed of the thing-in-itself and announced a pure ego that created or 'posited' the world as a place in which it could, through its activity, fulfil its moral potential, a doctrine in which it will be seen that activity-based concepts are made doubly central.

Transcendental idealism is not Kant's only claim to being one of the founder-members of the school of the Practice Ideal. Another, relatively unspectacular at first, but in our own time at least as influential, is the notion of a *regulative principle*. There are two interpretations of this idea, both of them having some textual support; but we need make no decision between them, since both are conspicuous from our present viewpoint. One is the thought that what appears to be a statement of fact (usually, transempirical fact) may really be a disguised imperative, an injunction as to how to proceed; the other is that a belief in what is not logically or empirically verifiable may nevertheless be justified as a psychological aid to a desirable form of conduct. There are in fact, Kant thinks, certain beliefs or quasi-beliefs which need to be understood in this way if metaphysical error is to be avoided.

When the point is so put it may sound as if there were a close affinity between it and the conclusion of Pascal's wager; but on closer inspection the similarity is seen to be more remote. Pascal recommended the belief in God's existence to us on the grounds that it was a good bet: our holding it would prompt God, if there was one, to take actions very much in our interest. In the case of Kant's regulative principles the connection with action is more direct: our holding the belief enables *us* to act more effectively, and doesn't just improve our chances of ending up happy. So in a way there is more stress on practice here than in the case of the wager. Another considerable difference should also be noted: what Pascal recommends is quite certainly a belief, but when one reads Kant carefully it becomes at best very doubtful whether it is belief that he is recommending.

To see the problem we should retreat to Kant's own starting-point. Regulative principles make their appearance in his theory of dialectical error, those mistakes in metaphysics whose pervasiveness suggests that they arise out of the nature of reason itself. They consist in the belief that we have (or can attain) knowledge about certain transempirical objects of which we can in fact know nothing—Kant regards this as an illusion of a very natural and hence persistent kind, one that will keep on returning upon us even after we have seen through it. It is clear that he doesn't wish to recommend the belief that we can know such objects, but he might still wish to recommend belief in the objects themselves, once the further idea that we can know these beliefs to be true has been disposed of. Now there is no doubt that Kant does sometimes recommend belief in transempirical objects whose existence he asserts to be theoretically unverifiable; he thinks that such belief is justified by his 'practical proofs', that is to say proofs involving ethical premisses—this is the faith for which he has made room by banishing knowledge from the realm of the in-itself. But that is a different issue that should not cloud our view of the theory of regulative principles. Here, in some of Kant's clearest utterances,[13] it sounds as if all that he holds to be desirable is the *thought* of a certain object, and that misapprehension has occurred as soon as this thought is raised to the status of a belief or assertion. These thoughts, or 'Ideas of Reason' as Kant technically calls them, are to be understood as being regulative: we have them because (shaky though this may sound, it does appear to be his view) without them we should be unable to think of the world as a suitable object or arena for certain projects which it is in the nature of reason to pursue. Thus the ideal of a unified science requires the thought of a unified nature; and this unity we cannot think other than by hypostatising it in an object; hence the idea of a single being in whom the world originated.

But whichever of these readings may best fit Kant's intentions, the difference between them is from our present point of view not very significant. In either case some item, be it a belief or only an idea, has as its *raison d'être* the furtherance of the process of scientific investigation. Whether belief or idea, that involves a considerable change in its traditional role. The philosophy of the preceding epoch saw ideas as representations of possible states of affairs or objects and so as implicit challenges to the mind to know whether these possibilities were realised or not. In propounding a theory of knowledge which put them epistemically out of bounds Kant was 'curbing the pretensions' of the Insight Ideal; and he then took another, positive step by allocating them an essential role in human investigative practice.

Kant's attempts to show that human claims to knowledge

---

[13] Ibid. A681/B709: 'This object, as thus entertained . . .'

in certain areas fail, and must in principle do so, are of course much gentler than those of Hume; indeed he seems to have understood himself as replying to Hume's scepticism and reinstating the claims of reason. The direct clash between the two systems that this perception of them implies does not exist, however. If we forget his 'practical proofs' and remain on the level which was the only one that Hume took into account, Kant is just as much of a sceptic as regards the thing-in-itself and reason's power to reach it. The difference is that Kant then constructs another world, empirical reality, which he hopes to have insulated against scepticism. On that issue Hume makes no definite pronouncement, and cannot, since his ontology does not contain anything that clearly corresponds to the empirical reality of Kant's system. But I think that there is one thing which we can speculatively say with some confidence, so long as we remember that it is an extrapolation from the facts. Had Hume admitted such a thing as empirical reality in the Kantian sense (perhaps by regarding his system of natural beliefs as defining how the world is 'for us', and then allowing himself to speak of the 'world-as-it-is-for-us') he would not have taken its formation rules to be transparent to reason in anything like the degree which we find in Kant, who is of course at considerable pains (which he freely passes on to his reader) to show that it is not just that we do create the empirical world according to those very principles, but that we necessarily have to if there is to be any experience of a world at all. Even though he confesses[14] that the argument rests on the inexplicable brute fact that we operate with precisely the forms of judgement and intuition that we do, he gives the confession no prominence. The reader is left with a strong feeling, strengthened of course by Kant's claim to have licensed *a priori* knowledge of synthetic truth, that within the limits of the empirically real reason is restored to its former glories and confirmed therein. And it might occur to him to find in Kant's thought about empirical reality and our relation to it a twofold echo of the Image of God doctrine: God-like, our minds partially create it; and to the extent that they create it, is is also cognitively transparent to them.

I know of no explicit evidence that Kant ever thought in

[14] Ibid. B145–6: 'This peculiarity . . . a possible intuition'.

terms of the Image of God doctrine, however, and I would be a little surprised to find any. Asserting that doctrine, unless one is prepared to leave it totally unspecific, involves making determinate assertions about the nature of the deity, and this Kant's epistemology must make him reluctant to do. It is true that he recommends certain beliefs according to which the human and the divine minds resemble each other, as for instance when he says that we should think of the world as having been created by an intelligence like ours, though vastly more powerful, in order to encourage the aims of the natural sciences; but since he quite openly says that we should do this to help *satisfy the requirements of our reason*, it would make a curious basis for the claim that man is like God, as Kant seems very much aware. Perhaps the most that we should firmly assert is that he sought to reinstate the human capacity for knowledge of the world and of necessary truths about it, and in this respect looked back to the ideals of the seventeenth-century. But in the way he did it, assigning the bulk of the work to human agency, he looked forward to the nineteenth, whilst in throwing a cordon round the area of the thing-in-itself and neither permitting knowledge nor advocating scepticism there, but rather counselling something akin to faith, he made room in his philosophy for yet another major strand of European thought. There are very few philosophers who cannot find in Kant any echo or anticipation of some deep aspect of their own philosophical temperament.

3. *Engels: practice and change*

The shift to a metaphysical picture in which the human mind creates its realities, whether that be taken to mean the Kantian empirically real or just the real *tout court*, brings with it a bunch of awkward questions which have to be faced by anyone not prepared to dive down the burrow of solipsism. How come we all create the same thing? What if we didn't? How certain is it that we do?, and so on. Kant had some protection against this, in the form of a theory sufficiently blank to allow critics few handholds: there is one reality, things-in-themselves, to which we are all reacting when we compose the empirical world, and we all operate with the same equipment, the same forms of intuition, the same categories. That is why the products are uniform. But when the human creator expands his ambitions and dispenses with the thing-in-itself, the problem becomes acute. It is little comfort now to talk of common forms of intuition and pure concepts shared by all: that might account for the fact that we all construct worlds in the same style, but it leaves the question of congruence of empirical detail untouched; why do we all put just that kind of tree exactly there precisely now? One, somewhat fantastic, expedient would be to declare every single fact to be deducible by a faculty—this epoch would no doubt have called it reason—which all human minds share; but not even Hegel wanted to go that far.[15] Another way would be to disown the thesis that it is the individual mind that does the creating, and cast a single supra-personal mind in that role. This was the position which Fichte occupied in his later years, claiming as he did so—with what justification is controversial—to have meant it all along. And it is obviously very like that adopted by Hegel. Once we take it seriously we have removed the creativity from man, both the individual and the race collectively, and reinvested it in a power that is clearly a close relative of the traditional God. Like the philosophy of Spinoza, this metaphysic is destructive of all human agency. Individuals now appear as tools, instruments of *Geist*. Recall: 'While such business of reality appears as the action and so as the work of *individuals*, these are in respect of the substantial content of their work *tools* . . .'[16] The attempt to make human activity all-pervasive seems to have collapsed.

We have seen, in Chapter 4, Hegel's way of taking the sting out of that natural progress of thought, in effect by inviting us to take it as a single perspective that needs a counterpoise. There were others. For the problem as just formulated arises distinctively out of idealism, a philosophy which requires a constituting subject, and can then easily become embarrassed in the face of the question which subject it is to be. But that it is possible to put practice and its allied concepts at the focal point of one's thought, without having any truck with an idealism according to which the real depends upon the mind,

---

[15] Hegel: *Encyclopedia of the Philosophical Sciences*, para. 16.
[16] Ibid. para. 551.

is shown by the obvious example of Marx and Engels, who now appeared on the scene. They, whilst counting themselves deeply indebted to Hegel, had altogether different ideas about the efficacy of human action, and its centrality to a proper philosophy, than those that appealed to him. Their point was to change the world, not only to interpret it, nor to watch it with a slightly smug resignation born of knowing that it had to change, and had to change exactly like that. Nor did they wish to see themselves (even from one perspective) as the instruments with which another power worked its will for man, and they were delighted, so Engels reports,[17] when Feuerbach disposed of him as yet another creation of the human mind, made now by us in our image.

Their view of man was very much a product of this basic attitude. Whereas for Descartes we had been animals plus the faculty of reason,[18] for Engels the crucial extra was being able to use a flint. For that gave us power:

the generation of fire by friction gave man for the first time control over one of the forces of nature, and thereby separated him for ever from the animal kingdom.[19]

And in accord also was their ideal for man: he was to be the architect and builder of his own social world, by virtue of his grasp of the laws governing society and the processes of social change. The subject of this picture is no onlooker, however insightful and approving, but a constructive force:

The whole sphere of the conditions of life which environ man, and which have hitherto ruled man, now comes under the dominion and control of man, who for the first time becomes the real, conscious lord of nature, because he has now become master of his own social organisation. The laws of his social action, hitherto standing face to face with man as laws of nature foreign to, and dominating him, will then be used with full understanding, and so mastered by him. Only from that time will man himself, with full consciousness, make his own history—only from that time will the social causes set in movement by him have . . . in constantly growing measure, the

[17] Engels: *Ludwig Feuerbach and the End of Classical German Philosophy* (hereafter LF) in *Marx and Engels: Selected Works in One Volume* (Lawrence and Wishart, London 1970) p. 592.

[18] Descartes: *Rules for the Direction of the Mind*, Rule XII.

[19] Engels: *Anti-Dühring*, Part I Ch. XII (Moscow, Foreign Languages Publishing House 2nd edn.1959) p. 158.

results intended by him. It is the ascent of man from the kingdom of necessity to the kingdom of freedom.[20]

Nevertheless, the relation between human agency and these laws on which it was to base itself was sometimes the subject of some confusion, which the triumphal tone disguises only thinly. For instance:

Hegel was the first to state correctly the relation between freedom and necessity. To him freedom is the appreciation of necessity. 'Necessity is blind only in so far as it is not understood'. Freedom does not consist in the dream of independence of natural laws, but in the knowledge of these laws, and in the possibility this gives of systematically making them work towards definite ends.[21]

Now it is just when Hegel is in that Spinozistic mood that he can only dubiously think of the human being as an agent at all in any important sense. Rather than a distinction between being active and being passive, he then employs a distinction between merely being an instrument, and being a knowing and willing instrument—we are back again in the region of *Encyclopedia* para. 551. There is something awry here, for it would have been difficult for Engels to have chosen a less apposite way of introducing his favoured view of man. He appears to have conflated two very different things: falling in with the necessity of nature, and making use of the necessities of nature for one's own purposes. Nor is it simply a matter of having picked the wrong bit of Hegel, or having mentioned Hegel when he shouldn't have done; the problem lies deeper. The Spinozistic view of freedom which Engels here attributes to Hegel is a response to the belief that the necessities encompass the mind as well as the rest of nature: therefore freedom, if it exists at all, can only consist in the awareness and acceptance of that necessity. Engels holds a similar belief; he cannot restrict the necessities to inanimate nature, so as to allow the mind to stand back and make use of them, and that for two reasons, both at the heart of his philosophy. One is that for him the mind, even if not itself a material object, is totally dependent on the brain, which is a material object, and as such part of nature. The other is that the natural necessities

---

[20] Ibid. Pt. III Ch. II pp. 390–1.
[21] Ibid. Pt. I Ch. XI p. 157.

he is talking about are laws of social development, hence laws governing human behaviour; which makes it hard to see how we can 'make use of them' without allowing that they are not laws at all but at best *de facto* generalisations which may be broken—if we decide not to 'use them', for instance. Would they then just use us, regardless? If not, they are not laws, but if so, what could our using them consist in, beyond mere willing acquiescence? Perhaps these questions are answerable, but at least there is a tricky problem lurking around the concept of the human agent, and here Engels shows a marked disinclination to take notice of it. But then the philosophers of the seventeenth-century were no more inclined to notice the problems surrounding their concept of an idea and the part they wanted it to play in thought. Nor did they subject their fundamental view that there exist absolute and incorrigible insights to any very searching examination.

Such, nevertheless, is Marx and Engels' ideal for man: a being in control of his environment and the conscious author of his social forms. As one might expect, the concepts central to the ideal are also central to the corresponding theory of knowledge. One can see them at work in the section entitled 'The Criterion of Practice in the Theory of Knowledge' from Lenin's book *Materialism and Empirio-Criticism*,[22] but it is more instructive to go straight to the passage from Engels to which he immediately refers. In both of them Engels is dealing with the agnostics:

a set of philosophers ... who question the possibility of any cognition, or at least of an exhaustive cognition, of the world. ... The most telling refutation of this, as of all other philosophical crotchets, is practice, namely, experiment and industry.[23]

There is a point to that closing 'experiment and industry'; Engels does have at least two *prima facie* different things in mind: the ability to make predictions which prove successful in the light of subsequent observation, and the capacity to manufacture things and—arguably a third idea—make them 'serve our own purposes into the bargain'.

[22] V. I. Lenin: *Materialism and Empirio-Criticism* (Moscow, Foreign Languages Publishing House 1947) pp. 136–142.
[23] Engels: LF p. 595.

Let us start with experiment. What proved the Copernican hypothesis, says Engels, was the verification by observation of a prediction made on the basis of it, Leverrier's computation of the position of the then unknown planet Neptune. For the three hundred years before that Copernicus' theory had been only a hypothesis, even if it did have 'a hundred, a thousand, ten thousand chances to one in its favour'; but when Galle found the planet it was proved. Presumably then, although Engels is not quite explicit about it, there is in his opinion a qualitative difference between agreement with known facts and the fulfilment of a prediction. One can only speculate as to what lies behind this view, but it is surely significant that for someone for whom theory exists for the sake of practice there is indeed a vital difference between a theory's correctly systematising past and present, which are of course now beyond the influence of our action, and its being a reliable guide to the future. It is true that, if this is what underlies Engels' position, he has chosen an unhappy example—there isn't a great deal we can do about, or because of, the existence of Neptune, and in his day there was even less. This might give the impression that when he speaks of a theory proving itself in practice he has no more in mind than that it is confirmed when its consequences are found to agree with observation. But the textual evidence of a discontinuity (in his view) between the predictive consequences of a theory and the rest, those which relate to evidence already in, is strongly suggestive of the other, action-orientated line of thought.

There is, admittedly, another argument which might bring someone to think that one successful prediction had a force which the fact of agreement with a large number of observational results that were known at the time when the theory was formulated does not. Given any data, so the thought would run, there must be various hypotheses which fit them all, so the discovery of one such may just indicate human ingenuity. But when the one that has been found turns out to cover a new case which the designer of the hypothesis did not have before him when he sought an equation to fit the curve (or whatever), when the crucial experiment turns out positive—then one is forced to think that more than human ingenuity is in play. We needn't now try to assess that argument; the question is rather whether some such line of thought might have motivated Engels' views about what established the Copernican hypothesis. I know of no independent evidence, and one thing certainly speaks against it: it does nothing whatever to explain why Engels wrote of 'practice, namely experiment'[24] as being decisive; what is decisive, on this account, is the arrival of new and predicted data—there is no reason to mention *practice* or even *experiment* unless the concept be stretched so thin as to include any purposeful act of observation. The earlier idea is still the best, that is that Engels sees prediction as conclusive because he sees the success of action as special, and a correct prediction lies behind every successful action.

The suggestion is confirmed when we see what Engels has to say about putting things to use, making them serve our purposes. This he goes so far as to call 'an infallible test':

From the moment we turn to our own use these objects, according to the qualities we perceive in them, we put to an infallible test the correctness or otherwise of our sense perceptions. If these perceptions have been wrong, then our estimate of the use to which an object can be turned must also be wrong, and our attempt must fail. But if we succeed in accomplishing our aim, if we find that the object does agree with our idea of it, and does answer the purpose we intended it for, then that is positive proof that our perceptions of it and of its qualities, *so far*, agree with reality outside ourselves.[25]

I shall concentrate on just one feature of this passage. It makes great play with various activity-related concepts, 'turning to use', 'accomplishing aims', 'answering purposes'; later in the same paragraph we also hear of 'perceptions upon which we acted', and 'the result of our action' which is said to prove their conformity with reality. Nevertheless it is quite unclear what these concepts are really doing, and whether they need to be mentioned at all. I shall try to explain.

Engels' thought seems to be this: we perceive an object to have certain properties, let us say those appropriate to its being a heavy stone. We want to keep the door from blowing open, so we pick up the object and put it against the door. If it

---

[24] See previous quotation.
[25] Engels: Introduction to *Socialism, Utopian and Scientific*, in *Marx and Engels: Selected Works in One Volume* p. 381.

now stays shut, although the wind continues to blow, our action was successful, and this is 'positive proof', an 'infallible test', of our perception that the object was heavy. The example is of course crudely described for the sake of brevity, but adding refinements would not alter the aspect on which I want to focus: why all this talk about action, aims and utility? What difference would it make to this test of our perceptions, *qua* test, if we just sat there, inactive spectators, and someone else put the stone against the door; or if it rolled against the door as the result of an earth tremor; or if it just was against the door, and we first of all thought that it looked heavy, then noticed that it was the only thing holding the door against the wind? Would it matter to the test, *qua* test, whether we wanted the door open or shut, or if we were totally indifferent? 'Im Anfang war die Tat', Engels has just told us, and 'the proof of the pudding is in the eating'. But he gives us no clue as to why these notions are doing any real work, or what it is, which raises the suspicion that it was not accidentally, though it may have been inadvertently, that he chose that example from the history of astronomy which has so little to do with possible action.

A very similar observation applies to his point that the ability to make something is a special guarantee, beyond the ravages of scepticism, of having grasped its true nature:

If we are able to prove the correctness of our conception of a natural process by making it ourselves, bringing it into being out of its conditions . . . then there is an end to the Kantian ungraspable 'thing-in-itself'.[26]

Again, for all one can see to the contrary, the reference to what we do, though prominently advertised, is substantively inessential. Suppose that from our conception of some natural process we could predict that it would follow once such-and-such conditions held, and this turned out to be corroborated by observation. Why should the cogency of the fact as a test of our conception of the process depend on who brought those conditions about, or whether instead they just came to obtain in the natural course of events? How our activity is to make a vital difference here is left altogether mysterious and unex-

[26] Engels: LF p. 595.

plained. Engels, we know very well, had more pressing interests than getting his epistemology perfectly straight. But to be critical of him as an epistemologist is not the point here. The point is to see how practice, and its related group of concepts, doing, using, bringing about, eating puddings, aiming, intending and such, having acquired ideological status (like diplomats, they are exempted from inquiry, and brought in to grace every notable occasion) are as it were externally attached to material their real connection with which, if any, is allowed to remain completely obscure.

Over-enthusiasm about agency shows itself in other ways as well. We have seen Engels saying that successful action certifies the beliefs on which it is based. But does it? Consider someone whose beliefs about chairs are just those that a materialist would hold, and grant, for the sake of the argument, that he can be said to act on these beliefs whenever he sits down. Does his success in sitting down confirm his beliefs? Perhaps it does, but there is a problem: wouldn't a sincere Berkeleian, if there were one, sit down just as well? The materialist is poorly placed to deny it—one of his favourite jibes is that the idealist, or the sceptic, behaves just like everyone else. In any case, he shouldn't deny it, for the idealist will indeed behave just as his philosophical opponents would—the difference comes when he is asked to say what, at the deepest level, is really going on. And when he does so it will be clear that, described in his own terms, his action has been every bit as successful as that of the materialist; the change in his perceptions is exactly the one that he wanted to bring about. Now a dilemma arises: either we allow the Berkeleian to rely on the principle that success in action justifies the underlying belief and so claim confirmation (or even proof—for was this not said to be an 'infallible test'?) of the idealist view of chairs; or we draw the conclusion that the success of the action cannot, in either case, be due to the specific (materialist or immaterialist) beliefs of the agent; and then it would seem strange to think that either belief could derive confirmation from it.

There is the third possibility of denying that there is any such animal as a sincere immaterialist. But the relevance of this is unclear. It wouldn't alter the fact that, if there were one, he could rightfully claim whatever justification practical success has been deemed to confer, since both from his own and from another's point of view his actions would appear as successful as anyone else's. It begins to look as if the point comes at most to this: that we are all materialists really. If true, that is a serious blow to immaterialism; but it does nothing whatever to show a connection between truth in belief and success in action. It is in fact a close neighbour of the position taken by Hume about belief in an independent external world.[27]

That being so, it is interesting to find that Engels does sometimes sound rather like Hume. It happens, for instance, when he says that 'agnosticism' is not demonstrably wrong, but that the difference between it and the acceptance of materialism is of no real account. The agnostic, he says, simply makes certain 'formal mental reservations' and then goes on to talk and act as a materialist.[28] Ironically, Hume is one of the philosophers Engels here takes himself to be attacking; for him, Hume is just such an agnostic. To understand him as such, Engels has had to make two far-reaching mistakes. The first is to neglect the positive part of Hume's thought, the theory of natural belief. The second (particularly interesting in the light of the first two chapters of this book) is to miss the force of the negative part. Hume's sceptical claim that neither reason nor the senses can give us the various types of belief of which he writes, far from being a mere 'formal reservation', is in fact the rejection of the Insight Ideal and ultimately of the Image of God doctrine, and so an achievement of which Engels could only have approved. Probably a number of factors conspired to allow him to miss it. Current understanding of Hume would be one; another would have been his own attitude to the doctrine, one of hostile disinterest. That would have been a barrier to the comprehension of a writer for whom it was a live and unwelcome reality, to be opposed by all available powers of mind.

A final point before moving on. From what I have said up to now it might appear that the dialectical materialists had no

[27] See THN Bk. I Part IV Sect. II.
[28] Engels: Introduction fo *Socialism, Utopian and Scientific* p. 382.

legitimate claim at all to be descended from Hegel, but were simply caught up at an impressionable age in an intellectual climate which required that anything that was any good had to derive in some measure from him. I don't wish to encourage that mistake, especially as one of the main respects in which they really were related to Hegel is central to the general tendency in philosophy that we are now looking at, and continues to be of the first importance in our own time.

What the dialectical materialists so respected in Hegel was his systematisation of social and intellectual change. By creating a conceptual apparatus in terms of which they could be understood, he had raised the philosophical status of change, process and revolution. They recognised that his thought also had a conservative side, one to which he himself had a considerable leaning and which it was in certain persons' interests to promote, but it was the revolutionary aspect, the idea of change brought about by implicit internal conflict, which seized their imagination. So much so that for their own philosophy they were prepared to jettison the conservative part altogether, forget the suggestion that the 'Absolute Idea', the complete and adequate conception of reality, was waiting at the end of the road, and assert that this change was the only thing that was permanent. Engels disposes of Hegel's Absolute Idea with a good joke:

the Absolute Idea—which is absolute only in so far as he has absolutely nothing to say about it . . .[29]

and a mediocre argument:

if all contradictions are once for all disposed of, we shall have arrived at so-called absolute truth—world history will be at an end. And yet it has to continue, though there is nothing left for it to do —hence a new, insoluble contradiction.[30]

Though mediocre, the argument is not negligible. Notice that by 'history' Engels at first presumably means the process of historical change. That at any rate is the sense in which it can be said that history will come to an end when the Absolute Idea is attained; there will be no further change of scientific

---

[29] Engels: LF p. 589.
[30] Ibid. p. 590.

and philosophical knowledge, social forms or cultural styles. But it is not at all clear that history, so understood, has to go on for ever; what reason has been given to think that there could not be a state which was just inherently stable? There could not, of course, be life without change, if by that we mean the sort of change which occurs when Farmer Giles sells a pound of his potatoes to Fred Smith, who eats them and grows fatter for it. But that is not historical change, in the sense indicated; and that there has to be historical change so long as there is life is something which Engels here assumes without even appearing to notice the assumption.

How can he do that? I hope we are by now becoming immunised against such suggestions as that he has merely conflated two senses of 'history', the 'fat' sense needed for his premiss that history will stop when Hegel's Absolute Idea is reached, and the 'thin' one needed for his conclusion that history cannot stop so long as there is life. I offer a (loaded) alternative: someone who sees man as essentially agent will not be keen to recognise a state of affairs in which nothing substantial (as Hegel would have said), but only the trivial, remains for man to accomplish, one in which history, in the prestigious sense, is finished. If that is the goal of all the activity, then either man has lost his essential self in reaching it, or it is the end-state which is essential—man's activity is only a means to the achievement of this quintessence, in which his historical creativity shall have been left behind. Hegel, perhaps, could actively welcome this idea because for him so much still remained of the aims of the earlier epoch, the striving for a state of complete insight beyond which there was no advance, not even for God. For his materialist successors that ideal had faded; for them there was no joy, but only discomfort, in the thought of the final goal of history.

In any case, Engels, having disposed of the Absolute Idea, can tell us 'the true significance and the revolutionary character of the Hegelian philosophy', namely:

this dialectical philosophy dissolves all conceptions of final, absolute truth and absolute states of humanity corresponding to it . . . It reveals the transitory character of everything and in everything.[31]

---

[31] Ibid. p. 588.

Science now

mounts from lower to higher levels of knowledge without ever reaching . . . a point at which it can proceed no further.[32]

We have arrived at a doctrine of the fallibility of all theory, and the permanent revision of social forms and institutions. The former at least can be found in the American pragmatist movement, and is of course also at the heart of the thought of Sir Karl Popper and his followers. (Since neither group is known for its enthusiasm for Communism, this point may serve notice of the way in which the ramifications of the agency theory extend across ideological divisions.) It is how you will want things to be, if you are committed to a view of man as an essentially active being—unless you are pessimist enough to think of us as forging towards that state of rest in which we shall have done ourselves out of our own humanity.

4. *American pragmatism: creation, autonomy and the void*

The history of the Similarity Thesis, as told in Chapter 1, has a strong claim to be thought of as the history of one philosophical movement, as a succession of thinkers closely aware of each other's work and concerns. But it must appear doubtful whether the subject of the present chapter has any such unity. We have spoken of Kant, and of the dialectical materialists, and even if a certain continuity of influence between them can be traced through Hegel, there is not much that is common to them, either of mood or of doctrine. Both Kantians and dialectical materialists believe, in a sense, that this world is man's and not God's, but as soon as one thinks of the different emphases that have to be put on this formula, and the different qualifications that have to be added to it to make it fit the two schools it begins to feel as if it covers too much to be spoken of as a parallel to the situation of the seventeenth and early eighteenth centuries. Both stress human creativity, it is true, but whereas for Kant this is a static and involuntary fact about our relationship with empirical reality, for Marx and Engels it is an exhortation to seize hold of the world as it is in itself and bend it to our requirements.

[32] Ibid. p. 588.

This crack is best left unpapered. The practice ideal is a more diffuse phenomenon than the Image of God doctrine, because the latter was bounded by the demands of orthodox theology and the limited number of respects in which, within the European tradition, man could plausibly be held to be godlike. Far fewer restraints oppress the tendency to place heavy emphasis on human activity. It is equally at home, for instance, in contexts religious or secular, idealist or materialist; and because a philosopher has the freedom to apply it to any of a range of phenomena to the exclusion of others (to ethical but not to scientific reality, for example, or to necessary but not to contingent truths) it can easily appear in the discussion of a wide variety of subject-matter.

If the reader feels that continuity of theme and motivation has grown thin in the passage from Kant to the dialectical materialists, he may be sure that the next figure I shall discuss can thicken it again. Peirce, nominally the founder of American pragmatism, was a confessed and obvious Kantian. But here, just where one might suppose that the centrality of agency was going to find its apotheosis—isn't that, after all, pretty much what 'pragmatism' means?—we encounter a sharp shock: Peirce puts a large proportion of his philosophical effort into the justification of the *wholly disinterested* pursuit of truth. That might sound like an enthusiastic reversion to the Insight Ideal.

Here we need to draw certain distinctions. The question whether man should pursue knowledge is one thing; whether he should pursue it because it will be in his interests to do so is another. And one can hold that it is the creativity of the mind which makes the pursuit of knowledge possible, without supposing that this creativity has to be exercised in the knower's interest. One might think, as did Kant, that the pursuit was 'set us as a task' by certain deep features of human nature, a natural outcome of the constitution of reason, and so only secondarily concerned with the satisfaction of desires and the furtherance of our interests. Such is, if I understand him (he is not the most unmistakable of writers), also very much the position of Peirce; and though it sets him off sharply from some other pragmatist writers, it is in no way incompatible with a creativist theory of knowledge. Nor is it incompatible with a version of the Similarity Thesis, namely one which sees the creative activity involved in the acquisition of knowledge as a quasi-divine feature of the scientist. In fact, both of these are to be found in Peirce's philosophy.

At least in his earlier period[33] Peirce defined truth, and its correlative, reality, as the outcome of a certain kind of activity, scientific investigation: the truth was that opinion on which the scientific community would eventually come to agree and would not thereafter deviate from; and reality was whatever it then believed there to be:

The real, then, is that which, sooner or later, information and reasoning would finally result in, and which is therefore independent of the vagaries of you and me.[34]

This, be it noted, was a definition or analysis, not the expression of a belief that human cognitive powers would in the end succeed in disclosing the nature of an independent reality; thus Peirce did away with the Kantian thing-in-itself. It was, however, as he well knew, the expression of a certain hope: that there was such a thing as the 'final opinion' in this sense, and that the scientific method was the road that would lead to it. This, and others like it, he called '*regulative* hopes', in conscious imitation of Kant: we are to put our trust in them in order inwardly to arm ourselves for the practice of science.

Consideration of these regulative hopes leads into the metaphysical position which Peirce developed during the 1890s. The task of the metaphysician, he came to think, is to tell us what reality must be like, if these hopes are to turn out well founded. This he proceeds to do, with results strongly reminiscent of certain aspects of Hegel. The universe is evolving in the direction of increase of a property which Peirce calls 'concrete reasonableness'. The exact nature of this property is nowhere, to the best of my knowledge, clearly explained; but what is clear is that it has to do with being increasingly the embodiment of rational principles. Further (here Peirce allies himself to a nineteenth-century tendency

---

[33] Approximately 1870–90.

[34] C. S. Peirce: *Collected Papers* ed. Hartshorne and Weiss (Harvard University Press 1931) 5.311—I adopt the convention that has now become standard: the number before the point indicates the volume, those after it the numbered paragraph within the volume.

which we have just seen in Engels[35]), this process is eternal: reason can never find completely adequate embodiment but must always be in a state of activity, forever manifesting more and more of what it is *an sich*—the static picture is rejected:

[Reason] always must be in a state of incipiency, of growth.[36]

This growth of reasonableness—for Peirce's thought has a strongly religious turn—exhibits the gradual fulfilment of the purposes of God. And now comes the twist: it seems that an advance of knowledge, growth of accord between the mind of the scientist and the natural order he investigates, is part of what Peirce meant by the increase of 'concrete reasonableness'. So the scientist, in the disinterested search for truth, advances God's will, and:

the ideal of conduct will be to execute our little function in the operation of the creation by giving a hand towards rendering the world more reasonable . . . [37]

With this idea two chords are touched. In the first place, man is allowed to be, in his small way, like God, since he could not execute that function unless his reasonableness and that of God coincided. In the second, the comparison is also drawn in point of his activity: he is to help in the continuing process of creation, the furtherance of the divine aims. The Similarity Thesis, in both cognitive and active forms, unites with the Practice Ideal.

Whether this metaphysical position is really compatible with the empiricist doctrine of meaning which Peirce also advocated is something I shall not discuss. Nor shall I discuss whether a thinker to whom disinterested inquiry meant so much should really be thought of as the launcher of pragmatism, or whether this is not one of the factors leading to the distorted view of his *oeuvre* which undoubtedly exists. The truth is that these thoughts are clearly a prominent part of his philosophical make-up, no matter how we label it, no matter whether it forms a coherent whole or not.

The leaning towards the concept of action can also be seen in Peirce's formulation of this same doctrine about meaning,

[35] See above, Chapter 5 Section 3.
[36] Peirce: *Collected Papers* 1.615
[37] Ibid. 1.615.

the famous 'Pragmatic Maxim'. He begins his argument by considering the nature of thought. For the Insight Ideal a part, and the most important part, of its function would be to mirror reality, to provide a picture the agreement or disagreement of which which the real could be the subject of insight. But for Peirce: '. . . the whole function of thought is to produce habits of action',[38] and 'To develop a thought's meaning we have, therefore, simply to determine what habits it produces, for what a thing means is simply what habits it involves.'[39] One of the factors which eased the passage of this idea into Peirce's philosophy was surely Darwinism. This theory, though it makes no evaluatory claims, could all too easily give rise to evaluatory thoughts or unconscious evaluatory tendencies, or serve as a rallying-point for such tendencies already existing. And one with which it obviously has a close relationship is the exaltation of action and what is essentially connected with action at the expense of what is not. Only what makes a difference, actual or potential, to the organism's behaviour can make a difference to its capacity for survival and reproduction. And while the theory says nothing at all about features which have no effect, for better or for worse, on that capacity, it very easily comes to be assumed that there are none, or that if there are they are not worthy of notice. That evolutionary considerations weighed with Peirce is clear:

Logicality in regard to practical matters . . . is the most useful quality an animal can possess, and might, therefore, result from the action of natural selection; but outside of these it is probably of more advantage to the animal to have his mind filled with pleasing and encouraging visions, independently of their truth; and thus, upon unpractical subjects, natural selection might occasion a fallacious tendency of thought.[40]

Even for 'unpractical' thought it is the effect on practice that is decisive. The point is put yet more strongly by the Oxford pragmatist, F. C. S. Schiller:

For how can there be such a thing as 'pure' reason? How, that is, can we so separate our intellectual function from the whole complex of

[38] Ibid. 5.400.
[39] Ibid. 5.400.
[40] Ibid. 5.400.

our activities, that it can operate in real independence of practical considerations? I cannot but conceive the reason as being, like the rest of our equipment, a weapon in the struggle for existence and a means of achieving adaptation. It must follow that the practical use, which has developed it, must have stamped itself upon its inmost structure, even if it has not moulded it out of pre-rational instincts. In short, a reason which has not practical value for the purposes of life is a monstrosity, a morbid aberration or failure of adaptation, which natural selection must sooner or later wipe away.[41]

Returning to Peirce: there is nothing essentially empiricist about defining meaning in terms of habits of action. A habit, in general and very roughly, is the tendency to do X when Y obtains, and everything will turn on the ways in which we are allowed to specify the relevant Xs and Ys. But it very soon transpires that he does have an empirical criterion of meaning in view; by the end of the next paragraph we reach:

Our idea of anything *is* our idea of its sensory effects.[42]

Empiricism has been added to the habit theory, and, interestingly, something has been subtracted: the notion of action, or at any rate of our action, has gone. Elsewhere, too, the definition can be found in a formulation that makes no reference to action:

the whole meaning of an intellectual predicate is that certain kinds of event would happen . . . in the course of experience, under certain sorts of existential conditions.[43]

This may make us wonder, much as Engels made us wonder, why the insistence on action was there in the first place. For what this suggests is that the belief essentially consists in confidence in various hypotheticals relating possible antecedent experiences to possible consequential ones. Action then follows, guided by the belief, under circumstances which may be described roughly thus: that the agent wants some of these consequential experiences and is in a position to bring about the relevant antecedents. Why the precipitate haste to get specific habits of action into the content of the belief itself?

[41] F. C. S. Schiller: 'The Ethical Basis of Metaphysics' in *Humanism, Philosophical Essays* (Macmillan, London 1903) pp. 7—8.
[42] Peirce: *Collected Papers* 5.401.
[43] Ibid. 5.468.

Peirce is at times quite unmistakable on the point, as where he says that the content of a thought

lies in its tendency to enforce a corresponding practical maxim expressible as a conditional sentence having its apodosis in the imperative mood.[44]

Why not accept that it takes a thought plus a desire to indicate any particular line of action, and explain the content of what is thought independently of any desires the thinker may have—as Peirce sometimes appears to do? He could still maintain that it is the function of thought to produce habits of action—a fact which leads one to speculate that he may have confused the point about its function with the analytic principle about its content. Even more speculatively: perhaps this is no confusion, but the unconscious beginnings of a tendency to think of the theory of meaning very differently, in terms of a direct relationship between the sign and the way its users respond to it, the significance of any intermediate 'content' being minimised. To today's reader that will suggest a picture of thought and language also suggested by the illustration of the shopkeeper from the first paragraph of Wittgenstein's *Philosophical Investigations*. Historically this is fanciful, but one thing is not fanciful: we find in Peirce an intimacy of relationship between thought and action for which he argues very imperfectly.

It is one thing to tie meaning to habits of action, another to give this thesis an empiricist reading and insist that what is done, and upon what occasion, must be describable in observational terms. But Peirce, as we have seen, did so; and his willing espousal of empiricist criteria is also evident in his more populist contemporary, William James. But James' conception of experience, it must be noted, is far from being limited to what would normally and naturally be called the sensory; rather it includes the whole of our conscious mental life. Secondly, although James does say things like

The whole function of philosophy ought to be to find out what definite difference it will make to you and me, at definite instants of our life, if this world-formula or that world-formula be the true one.[45]

44 Ibid. 5.18.
45 William James: *Pragmatism* Lecture II (Harvard p. 30).

—so sounding as if he wanted us to embark on a programme
of empirical conceptual analysis not unlike that recommended
and practised by the logical positivists—at other times he
seems less concerned with the question of what difference the
truth of a given 'formula' will make to us than with the
question of what difference it will make to us if we believe it to
be true. This is his favoured line when the topic is religion:

> Even if matter could do every outward thing that God does, the idea
> of it would not work as satisfactorily, because the chief call for a God
> on modern man's part is for a being who will inwardly recognise
> them and judge them sympathetically. Matter disappoints this
> craving of our ego, so God remains for most men the truer
> hypothesis, and indeed remains so for definite pragmatic reasons.[46]

Thus James awakens a far stronger sense than does Peirce
that belief is, and legitimately is, a matter of human
convenience and interest; that we choose our beliefs to do jobs
for us, jobs which may range from that of accurately
predicting observables to that of making us feel at home, or
morally safe, in the world—and that we are quite right to
make our choice of belief on such grounds. Not only does he
hold that 'In our cognitive as well as in our active life we are
creative',[47] but also that the creative faculty is not exercised
disinterestedly in cognition: belief is an instrument for the
attainment of our goals.

When James speaks of creativity in this context he does not
mean that creativity of mind that is normally needed for
making discoveries, like the ability to generate a brilliant
hypothesis; his view is much more strongly constructivist than
that. Since he thinks of the real as being the object of true
belief, and of true belief as what it is ultimately satisfactory to
believe, the real is for him partially dependent on human
propensities for satisfaction. One must say 'partially', because
he does recognise certain other constraints on belief, such as
the data of phenomenal sense-experience, within which the
creative process has to work and which it cannot just set aside.
It is not that we can believe anything, provided we are keen

---

[46] James: 'The Pragmatist Account of Truth and its Misunderstanders', in *The
Philosophical Review* Vol. XVII (1908); reprinted in *The Meaning of Truth* (Harvard
p. 269n).
[47] James: *Pragmatism* Lecture VII (Harvard p. 123).

enough to do so, for certain beliefs are forced on us; James' favourite picture is rather of us operating on given raw materials:

The world stands really malleable, waiting to receive its final touches at our hands. . . . Man *engenders* truths upon it.[48]

Within these limits, it is up to us to create that system of beliefs which will afford us maximum satisfaction; and in so far as we succeed we have both grasped the real and made it. It will not then come as a surprise to find the old Image of God doctrine still maintaining at least a verbal presence:

No one can deny that such a role would add both to our dignity and to our responsibility as thinkers. To some of us it proves a most inspiring notion. Signor Papini, the leader of Italian pragmatism, grows fairly dithyrambic over the view that it opens of man's divinely creative functions.[49]

It is not only Papini— sometimes James can come very close to it himself, as in the following passage (in which, incidentally, he also sounds like a less optimistic version of Engels[50]):

The scope of the practical control of nature newly put into our hands by scientific ways of thinking vastly exceeds the scope of the old control grounded on common sense. Its rate of increase accelerates so that no one can trace the limit; one may even fear that the *being* of man may be crushed by his own powers, that his fixed nature as an organism may not prove adequate to stand the strain of the ever increasingly tremendous functions, almost divine creative functions, which his intellect will more and more enable him to wield.[51]

Whatever theological implications it may be felt to have, this picture of the investigator as constrained by the sensory input, and to some extent restricted by the corpus of belief which he inherits from his society, has much in common with that found in the work of Quine. It is also notable that there is a great deal in the pragmatists to remind one of Michael Dummett and his concern with anti-realism. What we see growing in James' writings is a version of constructivism, the doctrine that certain areas of reality are the product of the

---

[48] Ibid. Lecture VII (Harvard p. 123).
[49] Ibid. Lecture VII (Harvard p. 123).
[50] See above, Chapter 5 Section 3.
[51] James: *Pragmatism* Lecture V (Harvard p. 91).

mind. Like Dummett, James also applies this to mathematics and logic:

Their objects can be better interpreted as being created step by step by men, as fast as they successively conceive them.[52]

On the other hand, he feels the pull towards Platonism, or at least towards the doctrine that truths are not of our own making. Readers of Dummett will be keenly aware of the 'quasi-paradox':

Undeniably something comes by the counting that was not there before. And yet that something was *always true*. In one sense you create it, and in another sense you *find* it.[53]

Notoriously, constructivism leads Dummett to doubt the determinacy of reality prior to investigation. Pragmatism did just the same for F. C. S. Schiller:

The truth is that the nature of things is not *determinate* but *determinable*, like that of our fellow men. Previous to trial it is indeterminate, not merely for our ignorance, but really and from every point of view, within limits which it is our business to discover.[54]

Two other major features of James' thought demand attention. Both are of first importance in the subsequent history of philosophy in Britain and America, and not only there; and both are intimately bound up with James' insistence on the centrality of human creativity and his consequent brand of constructivism. They are his pluralism, and his claims for the autonomy of man and human experience.

Pluralism first. The Image of God doctrine had set a specific goal for man, and one that could be realised in a strictly limited number of ways. When it concerned itself with the formation of belief there was one set of beliefs, those held by God, which it was bound to regard as uniquely privileged. James' conception of the role of belief pulls in exactly the opposite direction. Belief is to satisfy needs, which for him

[52] 'James: Humanism and Truth' in *The Meaning of Truth* (Harvard p. 218).

[53] Ibid. (Harvard p. 222). It must be said that James is not actually speaking of mathematical objects in this quotation, but of constellations.

[54] F. C. S. Schiller: 'The Ethical Basis of Metaphysics' in *Humanism, Philosophical Essays* p. 12 n.

means human needs as actually felt, and their experienced satisfaction. But desires can change:

The individual has a stock of old opinions already, but he meets a new experience that puts them to a strain. Somebody contradicts them; or in a reflective moment he discovers that they contradict each other; or he hears of facts with which they are incompatible; or desires arise in him which they cease to satisfy.[55]

Sometimes James seems, in the style of Peirce, to envisage a possible end-state of investigation after which there would be no further changes in belief, though just how seriously he takes the idea is open to question.[56] Well might it be, for in view of the fact that he allows human desires and their satisfaction to be a factor that legitimately produces changes in the corpus, there is no reason why he should think of that stable state as anything more than a purely theoretical possibility which there are no grounds to expect, even at infinity. Wouldn't a stable set of beliefs need a stable set of desires? And one thing which can change our desires, after all, is boredom with our beliefs. So the stage is set for the entrance of a multiple pluralism, diachronic and synchronic, for even if human desires and needs chanced to be perfectly constant there would still be what James calls 'different types of mind', and these would find their best satisfaction in different systems of belief.[57] Besides, there is also pluralism is another, related, dimension:

Satisfactoriness has to be measured by a multitude of standards, of which some, for aught we know, may fail in any given case; and what is more satisfactory than any alternative in sight, may to the end be a sum of *pluses* and *minuses*, concerning which we can only trust that by ulterior corrections and improvements a maximum of the one and a minimum of the other may some day be approached.[58]

Until that day dawns, if ever, pragmatism must encourage a plurality of beliefs and be happy to regard them as transient.

[55] James: *Pragmatism* Lecture II (Harvard pp. 34–5).
[56] In this connection see ibid. Lecture VI: 'The absolutely true, meaning what no farther experience will ever alter . . .' (Harvard pp. 106–7).
[57] See ibid. Lecture II: '. . . individuals will emphasise their points of satisfaction differently . . .' (Harvard p. 35).
[58] James: 'Humanism and Truth' in *The Meaning of Truth* (Harvard p. 206).

To travel hopefully is a better thing than to arrive, and the true success is to labour;[59] at least, for the sake of our best satisfaction we had better believe it.

James once said that the struggle between monism and pluralism was 'the most central of all philosophic problems, central because so pregnant'.[60] What he meant, he went on, was that knowing which side of this divide a philosopher stands gives grounds for the maximum number of reliable inferences about what other positions he will take up. If that was all he meant, I shall not dispute it; but I do deny that the monism/pluralism distinction is central in the sense of being either argumentatively or psychologically primary. Argumentatively, pluralism is a natural consequence of an account of belief which makes it a tool for the achievement of human satisfaction, as we have just seen. And I cannot feel it as having any great emotional pull in its own right; but what may well have such a pull is the doctrine that belief, and hence reality, can legitimately be treated as being our creation in pursuit of our purposes. Such a philosophy promises adulthood, the age of majority for the human race; the demanding, compelling father-figure of the Absolute recedes. And from this doctrine, as we have seen, the corollary of pluralism quickly follows. There also follows, by an inferential step so short as hardly to be a step at all, the other great theme of James' metaphysic: the autonomy of man. The basic desideratum ceases to be the satisfaction of some alien criterion, set up by an external reality, but rather the satisfaction of our own inner needs. We are authorised to do, as the saying used to be, 'our own thing'; we have become again the measure of all.

This emancipatory turn was of the first importance to James, and one easily finds the tell-tale marks when he is writing of it or in its immediate neighbourhood, an intensity of style and image combined with a thinness of argumentative rigour, the 'halo effect' which we have often seen attaching to the central pillars of a philosophy. James opposes, as one might expect, a correspondence theory of truth—it would mean, after all, correspondence with an external reality, and

---

[59] R. L. Stevenson: 'El Dorado', from *Virginibus Puerisque and Other Papers*.
[60] James: *Pragmatism* Lecture IV (Harvard p. 64).

so infringe our autonomy of thought—and his treatment of this topic can provide us with a good example. One thing that James wished to account for was the 'magnetism' of truth (to borrow an expression that C. L. Stevenson later used of the concept of the good.[61]). Why do we aim at it? Why do we reverence it so? If possessing the truth were having an interior copy of reality, why should we find it so important? James gave this thought, and his answer to it, graphic expression:

A priori, however, it is not self-evident that the sole business of our mind with realities should be to copy them. Let my reader suppose himself to constitute for a time all the reality there is in the universe, and then to receive the announcement that another being is to be created who shall know him truly. How will he represent the knowing in advance? What will he hope it to be? I doubt extremely whether it could ever occur to him to fancy it as mere copying. Of what use to him would an imperfect second edition of himself in the new comer's interior be? It would seem pure waste of a propitious opportunity. The demand would more probably be for something absolutely new. The reader would conceive the knowing humanist-ically, 'the new comer', he would say, 'must *take account of my presence by reacting on it in such a way that good would accrue to us both.* If copying be requisite to that end, let there be copying; otherwise not.' The essence in any case would not be the copying, but the enrichment of the previous world.[62]

In drawing these 'humanist' conclusions about truth, James invites certain fairly obvious comments. First, he has assumed that truth must be that which, in the situation he describes, is taken to be valuable *per se*; from that he argues that it cannot be copying or correspondence— whose value would be only instrumental. But truth might be understood as the copying of reality, and then valued as a means to the mutually beneficial reactions: perhaps a correspondence between thought and reality makes the beneficial response especially likely, or especially secure. It would be possible to reserve the concepts of truth and knowledge for that kind of relation between the world and the mind, and hold of a world that was full of mutually beneficial reactions which did not arise out of such a relation that, whilst it was a most admirable world, truth and

---

[61] C. L. Stevenson: 'The Emotive Theory of Ethics', *Mind* Vol. 46. (1937) p. 16.
[62] James: 'Humanism and Truth' in *The Meaning of Truth* (Harvard p. 216).

knowledge played no part in it. James' arguments have force only against a opponent who takes the possession of truth to be a value of the non-instrumental sort, and this brings us on to a second and deeper point: it is notable that he appears quite to have lost sight of what would have struck the European philosopher of two hundred years earlier as the obvious answer, and the obvious justification for thinking of truth in that way—indeed, that he has lost sight of the answer is evident from the way in which he puts the question. It is not, for his predecessors, that they stand there and become an object of knowledge for someone else. It is God who stands there, and in adjusting their minds to copy his reality they thereby adjust them to copy him. There should be no great difficulty in seeing how, for the heirs of a tradition which regarded God's mind as the sum of all moral and intellectual perfections, this could be felt as a goal overriding every other sort of human satisfaction. The change of perspective, and its efficacy in rendering the past invisible, can be seen in the way James leaps straight over this point in spite of elsewhere having come within a hair's breadth of making it himself:

When the first mathematical, logical and natural uniformities were discovered, men were so carried away by the clearness, beauty and simplification that resulted, that they believed themselves to have deciphered authentically the eternal thoughts of the Almighty.[63]

Again, he tells us earlier in the same paper that it was because there was 'a spark of divinity hidden in our intellects' that this kind of insight was held to be possible. Indeed he came, if possible, even closer. In the very paragraph that introduces the last quotation but one, he says:

philosophy, without having ever fairly sat down to the question, seems to have instinctively accepted this idea: propositions are held true if they copy *the eternal thought* . . .[64]

In view of what we know of, for instance, Leibniz, it can hardly be judged fair comment to say that philosophy had never 'fairly sat down to the question'. As for the idea that to 'copy the eternal thought' might understandably have struck

---

[63] James: *Pragmatism* Lecture II (Harvard p. 33).
[64] James: 'Humanism and Truth' in *The Meaning of Truth* (Harvard p. 216).

a religiously engaged epoch as a primary goal, James has apparently not so much lost sight of it as just pushed it aside; such is the attraction of the idea that the purpose of belief, and of truth, must be the satisfaction of our requirements, that we are at once the labourers and the taskmasters and the arbiters of success.

James, it is true, is anxious to retain one feature of the correspondence theory: the idea that belief is somehow constrained, and that truth cannot just be allowed to any set of beliefs which we enjoy believing. For this reason he does speak of an independent reality which provides the constraints. But two points are to be noticed. First, we are not called upon to copy this reality, but to 'enrich' it to our best satisfaction; secondly, the independence of this reality just consists in the fact that we find certain judgements thrust upon us, psychologically inescapable:

That reality is 'independent' means that there is something in every experience that escapes our arbitrary control. . . . some questions, if we ever ask them, can only be answered in one way.[65]

Since these are facts about the internal nature of our experience, we can agree that there are constraints, and very restrictive ones, upon belief, whilst continuing to hold that: 'we are not required to seek [truth] in a relation of experience as such to anything beyond itself'.[66] Not only are we required to; James offers an argument to show that in any important sense we cannot. Suppose that there is an absolute standard to which all belief ought to conform. Our sole chance of conforming to it is that it should coincide with what we would be led to believe anyway by our experience and the experience of exercising our faculties. The Absolute, real or not, plays no part. That, at any rate, I take to be the import of such passages as the following:

How does the partisan of absolute reality know what this orders him to think? He cannot get direct sight of the absolute; and he has no means of guessing what it wants of him except by following the humanistic clues. The only truth that he himself will ever practically

65 Ibid. (Harvard p. 211).
66 Ibid. (Harvard p. 212).

accept will be that to which his finite experiences lead him of themselves.[67]

Evidently there is something odd about this. No one is likely to deny that my beliefs are *my* beliefs, or that my reasons for holding them are things that count as reasons for *me*. But what transforms these harmless little tautologies into a substantive metaphysical position? What we are doing (of course) is following the clues that are available to us, and that means following our experience, if the word be given wide enough scope. But this must, surely, be neutral as between James' position and the one he is attacking. It does not show that experience gives us neither ground nor motivation for believing in something beyond it; nor does it show that experience is to be followed for the sake of the satisfaction of following it, rather than for the sake of the state to which we believe it will lead, if properly followed. On these further questions the whole controversy turns, and the way in which James passes them by is a good indicator of his inner haste towards the autonomy of belief, the thesis that it is answerable only to internal and to no external standards.

Once achieved, this thesis has two faces. One of them gives a blessing to human creativity, tells us that we are now adult and subject to no decision but our own. The other tells that we are now by ourselves, bidden to make our own applause and be our own consolation—this can all too easily come to seem more like a curse. Should it do so, the pragmatist will counsel us to take to belief in the Absolute, or in a god, 'for definite pragmatic reasons'.[68] But so long as we are aware that our reasons are pragmatic nothing is significantly altered—it was an absolute Absolute that we wanted, not a pragmatic one. Very much as the ethical utilitarian might find himself in the paradoxical situation of having to reject utilitarian belief for utilitarian reasons (if, that is, it turned out to be less conducive to happiness than the adoption of some other moral theory), so the pragmatist might have to repudiate pragmatism on the grounds that belief in it did not make for our

[67] Ibid. (Harvard p. 213).

[68] James: 'The Pragmatist Account of Truth and its Misunderstanders' in *The Meaning of Truth* (Harvard p. 269 n).

greatest satisfaction.[69] The trick of enjoying the benefits of belief in the Absolute whilst holding it 'for pragmatic reasons' is not likely to work; and if it did it would involve a feat of self-deception more welcome to the Orwellian politician than the philosopher—unless, of course, 'for pragmatic reasons', those two concepts were to be merged. The Jamesian has to be prepared to accept the thesis of human autonomy for what it is, with no evasions, and try to see only its brighter face. Presumably that was the face which James wanted his readers to see when he wrote:

Humanism is willing to let finite experience be self-supporting. Somewhere being must immediately breast non-entity. Why may not the advancing front of experience, carrying its immanent satisfactions and dissatisfactions, cut against the black inane as the luminous orb of the moon cuts the caerulean abyss?[70]

But many will find this vivid image to evoke as terrifying a feeling of the trackless void surrounding human life as anything ever produced by any purveyor of existentialist *Angst*. We have seen James wondering whether man would always be able to control the instruments of his technological advance, or whether they might not instead overwhelm him.[71] We now know, much more clearly than he did, how real that threat is. But the risks inherent in the humanist philosophy, the metaphysical vision of the autonomous agent in the void, do not just lie in its close connections with the urge to technological progress that may then run amok. Quite apart from the instability of the world which it might easily encourage, it is psychologically unstable in itself. It is the philosophy of the confident man, or, as its opponents would very likely have it, the over-confident man. Should that confidence flag it offers no secure consolation. The image of the void, from being a symbol of the limitless liberty of the agent, becomes a menacing abyss waiting to engulf all his purposes and reduce him to a nullity. It may be true that

---

[69] James was well aware of the similarities between Pragmatism and Utilitarianism—see *Pragmatism* Lecture VI: '"The true", to put it very briefly . . .' (Harvard p. 106).

[70] James: 'Humanism and Truth' in *The Meaning of Truth* (Harvard p. 222).

[71] Above, Chapter 5 this Section.

'somewhere being must breast non-entity'. But that is not to say that it makes no difference to us whether non-entity is hard up against our breastbone, or whether we are allowed to interpose the stout figure of the Absolute.

James, whatever his failings on points of detail, had a rare sense of philosophical mood and the large-scale metaphysical tendencies in which it issues. The three great themes to which he gives such prominent and lively expression have, in various guises, made a fair bid for the control of philosophical thought in the twentieth century, and if one is to speak of a dominant philosophy of this period, parallel to the one which character-ised the seventeenth and early eighteenth centuries, it will surely have to be the conception of man which they define. Man is seen as a creative agent, participating in the making of reality. As such a participant he is autonomous, his creations subject to no controls or standards other than those which he himself imposes; and with this thesis of man's autonomy comes the corollary image of the surrounding, unresisting, but also unsupporting void in which he has henceforth to make his way. A few years earlier James' contemporary, Nietzsche, had also written with resonant optimism of the 'open sea' of creative possibilities that the 'news that the old God is dead' made available to us,[72] but he had a far sharper sense than did James of the strength of will that would be necessary if one was to go on saying 'Yes' to life and the world under the new metaphysical order.

5. *Nietzsche: the will to power*

Other philosophers call for a place in this chapter. Fichte's name has already been mentioned; and Schopenhauer's conception of the world as will, with its connotations of desire and activity, makes him another obvious candidate. But it is Nietzsche's voice which seems the loudest of all; he was the most vociferous champion of the cause of the concepts of agency and creativity, along with their satellite notions of drive, need, and the power to achieve satisfaction; he used them as keystones of his account of reality, truth, and knowledge, of his aspirations for man and the demands he made of the philosopher.

[72] Nietzsche: *Die Fröhliche Wissenschaft* Bk. V (para. 343).

At the very beginning of the relatively early essay *Of the Use and Disadvantage of History for Life* Nietzsche quotes Goethe:

All is hateful to me which merely instructs, without increasing my activity or immediately enlivening it.

This is to be his motto—history is there for the sake of life, for the sake of the deed, only in so far as it subserves these are we to serve it. And he goes a little further: it is not just that the inactive grasp of history is distasteful, but rather that from the purely theoretical stance history is not even to be understood; only 'as one who builds the future' can we understand the word of the past, for 'the word of the past is always like the speech of an oracle'[73]—it will bear many interpretations, and without knowledge of the present and a goal for the future the neutral interpreter is at a loss to select one.

The idea that we have some kind of creative role to play in the formation of the future is nothing very surprising, and were it not for the fact that Nietzsche makes it crucial to our ability to understand the past it would hardly be worthy of mention. But the importance which he ascribes to human activity goes far beyond this—it is the source of value, and a principle source of reality. Formerly man could look to God to infuse value into the world. Now: 'Since the belief is over, that a God directs the destinies of the world . . . human beings must set up . . . purposes for themselves.'[74] Nor is there any other seat of value in things existing independently of human modes of experience and classification: 'It is not the world as thing in itself which is so meaningful, deep, wonderful, pregnant with joy and misfortune, but the world as represented.'[75] Which Nietzsche not only tells us—he also goes to the trouble of telling us that he has told us: 'That the value of the world lies in our interpretation . . . is a theme of all my writings.[76]

What goes for the good also goes, in Nietzsche's opinion, for the true, and for its correlatives the real, the world, and

---

[73] Nietzsche: *Of the Use and Disadvantage of History for Life*, Sect. 6. See also *The Will to Power*, trans. Kaufmann and Hollingdale (hereafter WP) para. 974.

[74] Nietzsche: *Human, All Too Human* para. 25.

[75] Ibid. para. 29.

[76] Cited from: Friedrich Nietzsche: *Erkenntnistheoretische Schriften* ed.Blumenberg, Habermas, Henrich and Taubes (Suhrkamp 1968) p. 186.

knowledge. The statement of his position is complicated by the fact that he uses these terms for both what he believes in and for those cornerstones of earlier philosophies which he takes to be refuted; so that he will tell us in successive breaths that there is no truth, and what truth is—or that our cognitive equipment is not designed to produce knowledge, but something else, which on another occasion he will also call knowledge.[77] The king is dead, long live the king! This double use of the vocabulary, expressive of the energy with which Nietzsche approaches his material, need not obscure the essentially simple point. There is no truth in the sense of correspondence with a world in itself, a world distinct from the way in which those who interact with it experience it; there is no knowledge in the sense of grasp of such truths; and indeed there is no such world. In so far as there is it is not a determinate reality but something formless and ineffable:

The antithesis of this phenomenal world is *not* 'the true world' but the formless, unformulable world of the chaos of sensations . . . [78]

and so truth is the ever-changing product of

a *processus in infinitum*, an active determining—not a becoming conscious of something that is in itself firm and determined.[79]

a remark in which the reader of this book may hear a pre-echo of the passage from the pragmatist Schiller.[80] As for the idea that the cognitive process continues *in infinitum*, it seems at first sight to be an arbitrary addition to the kind of constructivism that Nietzsche affirms. But we have already seen it in Engels,[81] and its presence here may serve to confirm what was implied there, that to a philosophy which so exalts activity and the agent the admission of a goal in which investigation might come to rest would be an embarrassment; there would be difficulty in saying what it was about that goal which gave it the special status of an acceptable terminus, and what would become of us should we reach it. Nietzsche would have no such thing. He wrote:

[*On the value of 'Becoming'*]—If the motion of the world aimed at a

---

[77] See ibid. paras. 496, 503.
[78] WP para. 569.
[79] WP para. 552.
[80] Above, Chapter 5 Section 4.
[81] Above, Chapter 5 Section 3.

final state, that state would have been reached. The sole fundamental fact, however, is that it does not aim at a final state; and
every philosophy and scientific hypothesis (e.g., mechanistic theory)
which necessitates such a final state is *refuted* by this fundamental
fact.[82]

This formative activity is undertaken for a purpose. It may
be described as the purpose of coming to know the truth, but
not if that is understood as the absolutist tradition meant it.
For in that sense there is no truth, and no knowledge to be had
of it; our minds are not, and never were, designed for the
pursuit of any such chimera, nor have they ever pursued it. A
species thinks, investigates and theorises in order to preserve
itself and enhance its power. It is not just that cognition
involves creative activity, perhaps for the Kantian reason
(which Nietzsche himself adopts) that 'We can only understand a world which we ourselves have made';[83] the very point
of the activity, the criterion by which its products stand or fall,
is the promotion of further activity and the capacity to impose
one's will on everything else. The will to truth, as Nietzsche
would happily use the word, is the will to power, the urge to
truth is the urge to mastery, truth is 'the kind of error without
which a certain species of life could not live'.[84] The will to
truth in the absolutist sense, which he reviles, is the very
opposite: ' . . . *the impotence of the will to create.*'[85]

We have already seen the tendency for this style of thought
to issue in pluralism: 'power' takes various forms, life may be
'enhanced' in many different ways —Nietzsche once defined it
as 'a multiplicity of forces connected by a common mode of
nutrition'[86]—hence we may anticipate that he will recognise
many perspectives, and in consequence recommend a plural-
istic conception of truth. So he does (here in a passage which
incidentally illustrates well the double use of the vocabulary to
which I earlier referred):

There are many kinds of eyes. Even the sphinx has eyes—and
consequently there are many kinds of 'truths', and consequently
there is no truth.[87]

[82] WP para. 708, see also para. 1066.
[83] Ibid. para. 495.
[84] Ibid. para. 493.
[85] Ibid. para. 585A.
[86] Ibid. para. 641, see also para. 490.
[87] Ibid. para. 540.

And Nietzsche's pluralism is not just a conceptual point; it also has a historical and an evaluative dimension. In a paragraph headed 'Age of Comparison'[88] he describes what he calls the 'polyphony of endeavours' of his time, the copying of all styles of art, morality and culture. This polyphony, set free by the loosening bonds of tradition, yields opportunities for comparison which less varied epochs have lacked. Therefore, though there is pain in such a task, we are not to fear it; we are to sift and select, develop this, allow that to die, and so earn the gratitude of the generations that will come after. Like epistemic pluralism, cultural pluralism is to be welcomed as well as noted. So is a pluralism of individual ends and means: 'This is *my* way—where is yours? . . . *The* way does not exist'—thus Zarathustra's answer to those who ask him for guidance.[89]

Returning now to Nietzsche's picture of the real as the product of investigation, we find that there is a good deal to be added to it, even after we have said that the investigation is itself aimed at the enhancement of our power. For much that he writes seems *prima facie* to pull in a different direction. Whether, in the end, he contrives to remain consistent is a tricky question, but I shall not try to decide it—the point is the prominence of the concept of agency and its entourage in everything he says on the topic. Should that be held to have led him into incoherence, so much stronger the support for the thesis of the pre-rational attraction of the Practice Ideal.

In the first place, Nietzsche does not think that reality is exhausted by the results of our investigation, that it consists entirely of human perspectives. It is at the least the sum of all perspectives, many of which will reflect needs and requirements quite different from our own. But this expansion of the original point obviously does not disturb the basic thought, that the activity of inquiry constitutes—if in each case only in part—truth and reality. In the second place, though, comes something rather more awkward: a number of remarks suggest that some perspectives are better than others, that from the better ones we may manage to 'grasp a certain amount of reality'; and Nietzsche, having disposed of tra-

---

[88] Nietzsche: *Human, All Too Human* para. 23.

[89] Nietzsche: *Thus Spake Zarathustra* Part III Ch. 11 (Of the Spirit of Heaviness) Sect. 2.

ditional attempts to tell us how things really are, seems quite prepared to have a go himself.

When he does so, however, two things are notable: the content of his views and the apparent ease with which he assumes a right to them; both are in fullest accord with the predilections of the nineteenth-century as we have seen them. As regards content, Nietzsche's favoured category for the description of reality is that of the 'will to power' which he affirms it ubiquitously to manifest. 'Power', as he understands it, is a widely diversified idea covering a variety of phenomena; but its diversifications all overlap in the central concepts of the Agency Theory: activity, creation, the initiation of growth and change, the incorporation of other beings into one's sphere of potency, the imposition of order and form on one's material. And he prefers to think of change not as something that happens to beings, but as something which they from their own energy and resources seek and bring about. Darwin failed to appreciate this, and overestimated the effect of external circumstances, whereas 'The essential thing in the life process is precisely the tremendous shaping, form-creating force working from within . . .'[90] Here the organic is under discussion, but elsewhere Nietzsche appears to apply quite generally a doctrine of a similar kind. There are 'centres of force', and the world is their interplay:

Every centre of force adopts a perspective towards the entire remainder, i.e. its own particular valuation, mode of action, and mode of resistance. The 'apparent world', therefore, is reduced to a specific mode of action on the world, emanating from a centre.

Now there is no other mode of action whatever; and the 'world' is only a word for the totality of these actions. Reality consists precisely in this particular action and reaction of every individual part toward the whole . . .[91]

It is surprising to notice how much of Leibniz is audible—but then he also treated the agency of created things as radically as his framework allowed, though from the most contrasting motives.

Nietzsche, having no theological spur to do otherwise, treats human nature as continuous with the rest of reality; so

[90] WP para. 647.
[91] Ibid. para. 567.

it is not to be expected that it will appear as a constant, exempt from the processes of creation and change that affect everything else and lead him to speak of the world as self-making, a 'work of art which gives birth to itself'.[92] Man too is to form himself, to 'elevate himself';[93] he is called to autonomy, to '*invent* his higher form of being',[94] and here Nietzsche sees the role of the philosopher, the new kind of philosopher that he asks for and thinks he already discerns. His stance is not to be descriptive of the present order, or supportive of existing ideologies; the task is 'to create values', to be a 'commander and a legislator', to 'reach for the future with a creative hand',[95] to invent new possibilities against which man may then test his powers of self-realisation. The point, it seems, is not to understand the world but to recommend ways in which it might be changed.

I hinted at a second point, less easily demonstrated: the pull of the Agency Theory is felt not only in the content of Nietzsche's views, but just as much in the manner in which he embraces them. His enthusiasm for the all-pervasive 'will to power' far outruns the force of any arguments which he presents; it is not even clear how his own procedure escapes the bolts he casts at his opponents. We are to use man 'as an analogy', he tells us, to achieve understanding of nature. But what, in the end, is the difference between doing that and projecting our beliefs about ourselves on to the cosmos in the way which Nietzsche constantly rejects? Those projections were unacceptable to him for one or both of two reasons: that the belief in question was baseless, and that the tendency to think of the real in terms of it could be seen to originate in aspects of our psychology which, to Nietzsche, were themselves disreputable.

Now, as regards the latter, it is clear enough that the tendency to think of reality in terms of the will to power arises from feelings which are not, in Nietzsche's eyes, disreputable. But this they could hardly be, since his evaluations stem from a glorification of that very will to power; so that the crucial

[92] Ibid. para. 796; we find ourselves once again in the neighbourhood of Goethe's god!

[93] Ibid. para. 973.

[94] Ibid. para. 866—my italics.

[95] These three phrases: *Beyond Good and Evil* para. 211.

question concerns the origins of this choice of values. And as regards the former, just how compelling is the basis for thinking of man in that way?

Not very, to the antecedently neutral mind. We should be armed against the train of thought which first finds the will to power in nature, then invites us to see it in man with the remark that we are after all a species of animal, and the implication that we may therefore be taken to share the same basic characteristics. For this argument is (at best) no stronger than its first premiss, so we had better be sure that the will to power is genuinely found in nature rather than illegitimately foisted on to it. And if it is genuinely found, and this can be shown, there remains the question whether it is fundamental in the way in which Nietzsche would have it. The question is far from idle, since it is quite easy to imagine a philosopher who would regard it as derivative. Anyone who held the two (Hegelian) theses that the truly fundamental drive is that towards self-understanding, and that self-understanding comes only from the experience of confronting one's own works, would be an example. They would say that the will to power is the will to enlarge one's sphere of action, and so to enable in greater degree the creation of those conditions in which self-knowledge can advance.

Nietzsche, of course, has plenty of objections to make to Hegel: his theological assumptions, his supposition of a final state in which the dialectic comes to rest. But the 'two theses' of the previous paragraph do not require either a theological backdrop or a definitively achievable goal in order to generate the alternative, non-Nietzschean explanation. And in any case Nietzsche's reasons for denying that the basic drive can be towards stability and equilibrium are hardly such as to convince the impartial: since the world had no beginning but has existed from infinity, it would before now have reached equilibrium if such a drive were active. Quite apart from any doubts that may attach to the first step of that argument, there is the matter of the assumption that there is some such equilibrium to be attained; in a system which had no stable configuration, the unchecked urge to reach one would result in perpetual change. Besides, there is no reason to think that the will to power, let loose for all eternity, would itself never produce stasis. A game of Monopoly, after all, does eventually finish—the sated victor surveys the conquered board.

For the exponents of the Image of God doctrine the acquisition of insightful knowledge could be a joy precisely because their theological metaphysic made it a value. To Nietzsche, who was well aware of that doctrine's part in philosophy and at times went out of his way to turn it on its head,[96] there is an instinctive joy in creative activity. This 'primeval joy . . . in shaping and reshaping'[97] is what is to put the gaiety into the Gay Science. And with this glad acceptance of the active, the creative, there comes, as there must, one of Nietzsche's grand 'revaluations': the honour accorded to the static, the permanent, is now to be transferred to change and process.

Contempt, hatred for all that perishes, changes, varies—whence comes this valuation of that which remains constant?[98]

Moreover, since the changeable is all that there is, those who reject it in favour of what is permanent have no option but sheer invention:

If one is a philosopher as men have always been philosophers, one cannot see what has been and becomes—one only sees what *is*. But since nothing *is*, all that was left to the philosopher as his 'world' was the imaginary.[99]

One cannot help but be struck by the similarities that emerge between the philosophy of Nietzsche and, in particular, William James—they encourage the suspicion that James' debt to Nietzsche may have been greater than is acknowledged in his published work. They are close in their understanding of truth and the crucial part played in it by the enhancement of life, close in their scorn for the unchanging and transcendent world of the absolutist, in their emphasis on autonomy and the welcome they hold out to pluralism. Nietzsche, like James, had his image of the void, the empty spaces that now surrounded the thinker:

[96] See WP para. 15, last sentence.
[97] See ibid. para. 495.
[98] Ibid. para. 585A, see also paras. 12A and B.
[99] Ibid. para. 570.

the sea, *our* sea lies there open again, perhaps there has never yet been such an 'open sea'.[100]

Yet at the same time they are poles apart in spirit. For James' writing exudes a certain easy confidence that Nietzsche altogether lacked and could never have approved. His optimism, where it is found, is hard-won and precarious. He feels very keenly something of which James shows little awareness and most certainly does not emphasise, that the realisation that a belief is held for pragmatic purposes is half-way to its abandonment. Where pragmatism enters, 'Nihilism stands at the door',[101] and to accept nihilism and overcome it calls for a degree of inner strength far beyond the normal. Hence the force of its competitors, as Nietzsche well knew.

We see, then, how the Agency Theory tends to leave its characteristic fingerprints on the work of philosophers who are in many respects of quite diverse temperament. It would be possible to chase these themes for miles through other aspects of Nietzsche's work. But it would not be worth while to do it here in print. For the reader, once on the look-out, can no more miss them than the reader of Leibniz can miss the Image of God doctrine and its ramifications.

[100] *The Gay Science* para. 343.
[101] WP para. 1.

6

ONE WAY TO READ OURSELVES

1. *The Vienna circle—a recalcitrant experience?*

So far we have proceeded almost exclusively by attention to the work of particular philosophers. But for this final chapter, in which we turn to the philosophy of the twentieth century, I shall change tactics and think primarily in terms of the most popular doctrines and lines of approach to philosophical problems, only secondarily in terms of specific names. I hope in this way to be able to give a broader picture of the penetration of recent philosophy, and especially of recent Anglo-Saxon philosophy, by the concepts and themes of the Agency Theory.

I write for the most part of the philosophy of the English-speaking world, largely because it is better-known to me than that of the European mainland. But this is not the only reason for the choice of emphasis. Recent Anglo-Saxon philosophy, somewhat unlike its continental counterpart, has not been very forthcoming about the *Weltbilder* which it might possibly incorporate. The overwhelming tendency, in fact, has been to deny any such thing and indeed to decry the attempt to formulate, or embody in one's thought, any such kind of comprehensive vision. The implied self-image is one on which I would like to cast a little doubt: the philosophy of our own time is just as much informed by a *Weltbild* as was that of the seventeenth century. In the previous chapter we have been looking at its emergence and its flowering in the philosophies and under the disparate styles of William James and Nietzsche. I have elsewhere called it the philosophy of the Agent in the Void.[1]

To neglect the Continental scene entirely, however, would be to miss the opportunity to prick another bubble which

[1] E. J. Craig: 'Philosophy and Philosophies', *Philosophy* Vol. 58 (1983) pp. 189–201.

stands in equal need of dispersal. There has been current a myth, still vigorous, to the effect that 'Continental' philosophy and Anglo-Saxon philosophy are chalk and cheese, two wholly distinct intellectual enterprises which have a title in common largely as a result of linguistic negligence. And it has produced a reaction every bit as mythical: that only British insularity holds them apart, and that they could be reunited given a modicum of goodwill and the price of a ferry ticket. Contrary to the first I shall argue that one can find striking similarities both of general tendency and at times of detail between the two traditions: both can be seen as deeply immersed in the metaphysics of agency, and each has its variants on the doctrine of the void. James' paper 'Humanism and Truth' makes a useful introduction to Heidegger and Sartre as well as to Wittgenstein and Quine. It would not fit the plan of this book to spend much time on the refutation of the second myth; but I will at least state my opinion that the rift has nothing imaginary about it. Briefly and crudely put, it results from the fact that the one tradition was started and has been sustained by men who were at least at heart natural scientists, whereas the other was decisively influenced, in the generation after Kant, by thinkers whose inclinations and training were theological. This has led to differences both of favoured topics and doctrine, but, perhaps most importantly, on the one side to a certain suspicion of clarity—for what is clear to us poor mortals is unlikely to be very close to the truth—and a deep suspicion of unclarity on the other. The consequent gap may not be unbridgeable, but it would take a hint of schizophrenia to be happy on both sides of it. I hasten to add that I make no judgement on the question whether so mild an attack of that condition is a disease or not; the demand for thoroughgoing intellectual consistency is often heard, but it is not one that is self-evidently justified.

In this chapter we shall be looking at the effects of two factors. One is negative: the disappearance of the Image of God doctrine from the philosophical scene. The second is positive: the rise of the Practice Ideal or Agency Theory to take its place. But this statement of the position, though pleasingly concise, is inexact, especially in regard to the negative point. The Image of God doctrine does not simply disappear with the coming of the new metaphysic; it may well be doubted whether that sort of sharp discontinuity is ever found anywhere. We have already seen that, in some writers, the doctrine transfers itself explicitly to the notion of practice and creativity—we are said to be godlike in our powers of action and self-determination. Even here, though, we should remember that 'godlike' has changed its tone; there is now a feeling that we are being said to be not so much like God as a replacement for God, and a philosopher such as William James, who recommends belief, recommends it not because there is a god whom we may strive to resemble, but for the pragmatic reason that such a belief will be life-enhancing. What we are to resemble is the shadow of which Nietzsche wrote,[2] the intensional object of our former convictions. With the advance of the century, however, comes an increased secularisation of philosophical thought, and such references, even in the pragmatist's tone of voice, are found less and less in professional publications.

It is worth keeping these two aspects of the change, the positive and the negative, separately before the mind. The negative factor, the recession of the Insight Ideal, has what one might call a liberating effect: it makes possible various approaches to philosophical problems which, in the earlier climate, would at once have been felt to be so wholly unsatisfactory as not to be worth pursuing. One example, which we shall come to consider closely, is the rise to prominence of causal concepts in the theory of knowledge and the theory of meaning. But we shall also need to think of the likely effects of the positive factor, for we should like to understand why, from the newly widened range of possibilities, certain types of response emerge as dominant.

With the emphasis shifting to practice and agency, it was more or less inevitable that the 'activity' branch of the theological Similarity Thesis, detectable in Leibniz and even in Descartes,[3] should continue from time to time to haunt the scene. But at most very rarely (if I may be allowed a rash guess, never) is it found in connection with its epistemological aspect, the Insight Ideal. That is hardly surprising, since the

---

[2] Nietzsche: *Die Fröhliche Wissenschaft* (The Gay Science) para. 108.
[3] See above, Chapter 1 Sections 6 and 2 respectively.

concept of insight is in full retreat during this period—perhaps only in the *Wesensschau* of the phenomenologists does it put in an unambiguous appearance. In this century even the former paradigms of insight, logic and mathematics, have consistently been treated in ways which make them matters of decision and convention, and allow them nothing to do with insight at all.

Yet one ambivalent phenomenon stands obstinately in the foreground of twentieth-century thought: the logical positivist movement. It is not immediately clear that this school of thought has much in common with the Agency Theory. On the contrary, its basic idea, that everything meaningful is to be analysed in terms of possible sense-experience, epistemically the most secure components of our world as they were traditionally held to be, smacks rather of the Insight Ideal. Berkeley's God may be dead, but doesn't the rest of his philosophy remain? Isn't this the epistemology without the theology, the Insight Ideal without the Similarity Thesis? (much as the emphasis on practice can—and did—come both with and without the Similarity Thesis).

We shall shortly see reason to doubt that suggestion. That there is some truth in it I would not attempt to deny—that fact by itself does no damage to the hypothesis of the primacy of the Agency Theory. Any era will maintain some kind of contact with previous traditions; a perspective which made it appear otherwise would *ipso facto* deserve suspicion. Quite the reverse, in fact: it would be reasonable to expect that the most popular fashions will be those which combine aspects of the old and trusted with aspects of the new and exciting. We should remember that one of the most successful philosophical systems there has ever been, that of Kant, besides offering to smooth the ruffled feathers of the Insight Ideal by using the thought that the (empirically real) environment was the product of the active mind, also reserved a most important area for faith—and made no secret of the fact—so leaving room for an older tradition which the Insight Ideal, with its stress on the human capacity to know, threatened to submerge. And with the same stroke Kant gave the venerable tradition of scepticism its due, or at any rate its opportunity; thus he fashioned a system with points of appeal for almost every cast of mind.

What would shake our hypothesis somewhat would be the existence of a major philosophical movement which nowhere gave prominence to the central concepts and styles of thought of the Agency Theory. But it can easily be seen that the logical positivism of the Vienna Circle is not such a movement: in espousing emotivist views of the various kinds of value judgement, and conventionalist views of the *a priori*, it gave full rein to the vision of man as the source of his own standards.

One might think that, like Kant, it thus caught more than one tide. For as regards the empirical, it sought to present that 'perfection of human knowledge' which Berkeley had believed his philosophy to offer. So what we have is a scientific realism which spans both pictures: there are no evaluative or modal facts—these are human creations—but there are scientific facts, and of these we can in principle always have knowledge. So it may seem; but although positivism can be read and felt as proudly announcing that the realm of empirical reality lies wholly open to us, the fact is that its connections with the Insight Ideal are tenuous, if not actually fraudulent.

Earlier on[4] we caught Schlick jumping an enormous gap in order to arrive at the conclusion that 'in principle there are no limits to our knowledge'—conjuring, by the addition of the inability to understand to our inability to know, potential omniscience out of less than nothing. Now if we are to think in terms of an independent reality whose boundaries are claimed to coincide with the limits of our comprehension and hence, because of the link provided by the verification principle, with the limits of our knowledge, this is utter recklessness. For it to have any kind of logic at all we have to give up that picture and think instead as constructivists. We have to suppose, that is, that our investigative procedures define the real, that it is the product, or potential product, of our inquiries. Only if that were so, and we knew it to be so, could we know that reality cannot extend beyond our cognitive reach. To show that would call for an approach quite different from Schlick's, which, sad to say, amounts to this: that if there is nothing which we can think but can't know, there is nothing we can't know, and quietly ignores the possibility that there may be

<hr>

[4] See above, Chapter 2 Section 6.

some things which we can't even think. Kant had a far clearer conception of what was needed, even if not quite clear enough. It is not an accident that we nowadays have a vigorous constructivist, or anti-realist, school of thought which takes as fundamental the connection between understanding meaning and the capacity to recognise truth-conditions; such anti-realism is a very natural successor to positivism.[5]

There is another factor, having nothing to do with his aspirations for the scope of human knowledge, that tends to force the positivist into an explicitly constructivist stance: his attitude to the *a priori*. Which propositions we accept as *a priori* truths depends, for him, on certain decisions or stipulations of ours, or at least on certain properties of our minds even if it is not in our power to alter them and so exercise any degree of choice. But now the *a priori*, presumably, is also thought of as making some difference to the description of empirical fact. Our having adopted the arithmetic which we actually use, for instance, requires us to describe certain circumstances (say, in which we count three red apples, three green apples, count them all over again and make it seven apples) as involving a miscount or some other irregularity. With another arithmetic we might have spoken of a miscount had the third attempt yielded 'six'. But this means that at least some empirical 'facts', such as whether or not there was a miscount on a given occasion, are dependent on which conventions we have adopted. And the same would apply to any fact which could in a similar way be the *a priori* consequence of certain premises, and whose negation could have been the consequence of those premises, given different *a priori* conventions. That, to put it mildly, is rather a lot of facts. So positivism, if presented as taking a realist line, is unstable; its tendency is to turn into constructivism and see empirical fact as dependent for its existence upon our verificatory capacities and for its detailed nature upon our conventions. Man is hard at work again.

Of the arguments that might be used to insist on the close relationship between positivism and the Agency Theory, there is one which we must in all honesty deny ourselves. It would consist in pointing out that it is a near relative of pragmatism, as historically formulated. The pragmatists, as we have seen,

[5] As well as to pragmatism—see above, Chapter 5 Section 4.

sometimes formulated their criterion of meaning in such a way as to make it sound very like the verification principle, if not actually identical with it. Peirce certainly did this, and James followed him. This is true enough, but it does not mean that verificationism is straightforwardly a brand of practice theory. It does not mean that, because even in the writings of the pragmatists it is not clear how the principle that thought is essentially connected with action leads to the positivist-like criterion of meaning. There is a gap between Peirce's two claims that: 'What a thing means is simply what habits it involves' and: 'Our idea of anything is our idea of its sensory effects,'[6] and I know no clue as to how he thought it could be closed. One way, having some *prima facie* possibility, would start from the observation that the thought 'That is an X' is not connected with any determinate habits at all until certain purposes involving Xs are specified. So if we want an account of that thought, taken on its own in abstraction from any specific desire and consequently also in abstraction from any specific habit, we have no real alternative but to allow for it to have a role in the formation of any possible habit. That is, we will have to include anything which combined with a wish could produce a course of action. And that, it might be thought, must mean anything we are conscious of in Xs, in other words all an X's sensory effects.

Before we conclude, however, that pragmatism turns smoothly into Viennese verificationism, there is a good deal more that needs to be said. Firstly, I can quote no evidence that any positivist, or for that matter any pragmatist, actually did argue in this way—though in the literature of both movements there is plenty of room for some to exist undetected. Secondly, the argument is invalid. For what can lead me to an action involving an X is not just what I perceive about Xs—the 'sensory effects' of Xs—but what I believe about them. If I believe that they have the property F, and that things having that property are dangerous, I will tend to shun Xs, regardless of whether F is a perceptible property or not. In this context it cannot of course be replied that if F-ness is imperceptible, then I cannot believe anything to have it— that would be baldly to assume exactly what was to be

---

[6] See above, Chapter 5 Section 4.

proved. But thirdly, to complicate the position yet further, there is conclusive evidence that at least one positivist, Moritz Schlick, was attracted by just this fallacy of thinking only of what we can observe when the relevant question is what we can believe.[7]. So the invalidity of the argument is not much reason for supposing that the positivists did not use it.

The attempt to connect Peirce's two versions of the 'pragmatic maxim' by argument falls, then, into disarray. We are left with the idea that anything there can be said to be must be such as to make, at least potentially, a difference for us, plus a vague (and wholly delusive) sense that we have been shown some cogent argument for it. Without the delusion, we have a dogmatic injection of anthropocentrism. To connect it to the more specific concept of human agency calls for another twist, one which the pragmatists did and the positivists on the whole did not bother to make. But with or without the further move, the anthropocentric assumption shows a very good fit with James' picture of the void that surrounds the human agent once we have exhausted his interests, his creations and his experiences. And the fact that when we look at the logic of the situation it does appear to be an *assumption* fits well with the hypothesis of the underlying, directing role which that picture had come to play.

None of this should be taken to suggest serious doubts about the affinities between positivism and the metaphysic of agency. As a final point on this topic we may observe that the positivist doctrine of the realm of empirical fact embodies the agency theory in another, and more direct way. Physical objects, to take a particularly prominent example of the empirical, are said to be 'logical constructions' out of sense-experience. That there are such things at all means, therefore, that our experiences exhibit certain types of regular pattern. But that surely implies that regarding the world as composed of physical objects in the way we do is to some degree at least a conventional matter. There must be other types of pattern discernible in our sense-experience; and for the positivist there is no standard external to it which could even give sense to the question whether we had latched onto the 'right' patterns or

[7] Craig: 'Meaning, Use and Privacy', *Mind* Vol. XCI (1982) pp. 541–564 (this point pp. 541–545).

not—the void starts just beyond our sense-experience. The 'existence of physical objects', it seems, is just a reflection of the way we sort and categorise our experience, and that is what it remains, even if there are the strongest reasons of convenience and the most compelling psychological forces pushing us to do it thus and not otherwise. Whether or not the positivist uses the language of constructivism, it is still just beneath the surface; only one thin layer has to be removed for all the conceptual apparatus of the agency theory to stand revealed.

When we add to these considerations the obvious facts about logical positivism's treatment of value, and the *a priori*, it becomes quite clear that it is intimately and comprehensively bound up with the Practice Ideal. But we should not miss the interest of the fact that the positivists themselves were not more explicit on the point. It is hard to resist the impression that they nursed a secret hankering after some kind of scientific realism combined with a great optimism, drawn from earlier times, about our powers of cognition. Such a combination, however, was not compatible with their austere and secularised epistemology.

2. *The attack on moral realism*

An unmistakable feature of twentieth-century thought has been a strong tendency in ethical theory to move away from objectivism towards emotivist or 'projectivist' theories. We are not to think in terms of a realm of moral facts, solidly there and independent of our thought about them much like the greater part of facts of the more familiar kind, but differing from them in being evaluative whereas they are neutral. Rather we are to think of ourselves as having certain preferences, possibly including second-order preferences which relate to the ways in which our first-order preferences are formed; and then as speaking (or thinking) as if these facts about ourselves were really located in the events, states of affairs, character traits etc. which are the objects of these preferences. It is easy enough to see how this turn fits the general pattern furthered by the spread of the Agency Theory: we become the source, the creators, of ethical value.[8] But it is

---

[8] Even John Rawls, who differs from most ethical writers of the twentieth-century in that he offers a substantive moral code rather than just meta-ethical theory, still

interesting to take a closer look at the way in which this position, or type of position, is often supported.

We find arguments of two main kinds being brought to bear on the objectivist (or, as I would rather call it, realist) position. The first is epistemological; it claims that the realist's conception involves him in mysteries about how moral truth could ever be known. The second is ontological; it says that, irrespective of how (or whether) moral truth could be known on the realist account of it, the very type of fact which the realist affirms is hopelessly mysterious—how could there be facts which were in themselves evaluative? Both tend to be presented as if they stood on nothing but their own intrinsic logic; I shall suggest that they in fact draw much of their force from the metaphysical predilections of their time.

This is most clearly seen in the epistemological genus. Such arguments typically proceed by pointing out that the detection of moral fact will call for a moral sense, that there is no evidence for the existence of such a sense other than the fact that we hold moral beliefs, and that this is evidence only if we suppose, question-beggingly, that moral beliefs are acquired by scanning the moral facts. The moral realist faces other epistemological problems, of course: the nature and extent of moral disagreement does not give any assistance to the view that moral beliefs are delivered by something akin to moral vision. But that kind of consideration lies outside my present concern, which is solely with the opinion that a sense that detected evaluatory facts would *ipso facto* be too queer a thing to be admitted by a responsible thinker. There is no sign that this alleged sense has any physiology, nobody has ever found any organs of moral perception, and so on. In similar vein Crispin Wright, discussing the view that there might be some 'modal' sense with which we recognise necessity, writes:

However striking, for example, the results of a series of experiments in telepathic communication, we feel that no evidence has been provided for supposing that human beings do possess special powers of that sort unless we are confident that no more mundane explanation can be provided of the experimental findings.[9]

reaches his code by asking what *we would choose* from a certain standpoint.

[9] C. J. G. Wright: *Wittgenstein on the Foundations of Mathematics* (Duckworth 1980) p. 451.

That this brand of argument has a great deal of force I do not deny; but it should be clear that it relies upon the willing input of a great deal of philosophy. What is mundane depends heavily upon one's prior conception of what sorts of things and processes this world is likely to contain. A philosopher who confidently expects man to be informed by a quasi-divine component will not be worried by the lack of indication that it operates physiologically—for he will not suppose God to be dependent on physiology. Nor will he be much impressed by being told that he is postulating a capacity for whose existence there is no independent evidence—the theory that there is such a capacity has just as snug a place in his system of beliefs as does the view that there is not in the belief-corpus of his latter-day colleagues. Thus what set out as a point of epistemology turns out to rely on a piece of ontology; and the piece of ontology carries conviction only in the right philosophical climate.

A recent, and revealing, statement of this line of argument is provided by J. L. Mackie in his book *Ethics*, the significance of whose subtitle, 'Inventing Right and Wrong', will not be missed in the present context. He calls it the 'argument from queerness'; it has a metaphysical and an epistemological prong:

If there were objective values, then they would be entities or qualities or relations of a very strange sort, utterly different from anything else in the universe. Correspondingly, if we were aware of them, it would have to be by some special faculty of moral perception or intuition, utterly different from our ordinary ways of knowing everything else.[10]

But when, two pages later, Mackie gets round to telling us just what is so queer about these facts, the relevant paragraphs are not quite as perspicuous as his writing generally leads one to expect. Here is the kernel of the first of them:

[10] J .L. Mackie: *Ethics* (Penguin 1977) p. 38. Readers who know chapter 9 of Hilary Putnam's *Reason, Truth and History* (Cambridge 1981), especially pp. 209–11, will notice a certain similarity with the discussion that now follows. To admit that it was composed in ignorance of Putnam's chapter is almost as embarrassing as it would have been to have to admit that it was not. But perhaps similarity plus independence at least suggests truth—and perhaps my perspective helps to place Putnam's remarks in a wider setting.

Plato's forms give a dramatic picture of what objective values would have to be. The Form of the Good is such that knowledge of it provides the knower with both a direction and an overriding motive; something's being good both tells the person who knows this to pursue it and makes him pursue it. An objective good would be sought by anyone who was acquainted with it, not because of any contingent fact that this person, or every person, is so constituted that he desires this end, but just because the end has to-be-pursuedness somehow built into it.[11]

It seems that two distinct criteria are here being presented. The fact of something's being good, it is said, on the one hand 'tells the person who knows this to pursue it', and on the other hand 'makes him pursue it'. My suspicion is that the first of these requirements may not be too hard to satisfy, and that the second may be illegitimate. The first may not be too hard to satisfy, because we all believe that it sometimes happens that a certain course of action is commanded, or recommended, or suggested; and if I know that any of these is the case then I know that I am told, with varying degrees of peremptoriness, to do it. What of the second requirement? Why does an objective good have to be such that 'it would be sought by anyone acquainted with it', quite irrespective of his character? Is this meant to include the devil himself, one might ask? It would certainly take the edge off his unique ability to flout the good if we had to ascribe it to nothing more blameworthy than a total lack of the capacity to recognise it. There is, doubtless, a sense in which what one sees, all factors being taken into account, as ultimately preferable must be what one at any rate wants to do (though even then scarcely what one is thereby made to do). But that does not mean that the belief, or perception, that something is morally good must be thought of as having even that effect on its own. In certain moods I might be prepared to let morality go to hell, even at the risk of going there myself—other preferences might hold sway.

At this stage it could look as if the first requirement has been misstated. It must have been misstated, so the thought would go, if it can be met as easily as I have suggested, simply by reminding the reader that there are such things as

[11] Ibid. p. 40.

commands and recommendations. We were looking for a fact that could make something good, good independently of what you or I or our social group or our species wish, command, approve of or whatever. Just pointing out that it may be objectively true that I have been ordered to peel potatoes won't secure the possibility of that kind of fact. What is needed is some preference which is not a human preference, but rather the preference of someone or something else which, in our view of the world, occupies an authoritative position— a preference of God, or of the *Weltgeist*. Some philosophies, of course, have a place for such things, but one in which the concepts most intimately connected with agency, like will and purpose, have been removed from the world and located solely in man does not. For the supporters of such a philosophy there are no preferences beyond human preferences, no independent and authoritative evaluations, hence the force of these ontological considerations against moral realism. But it is no matter of pure, timeless logic; against a different metaphysical background the problem which Mackie's first condition poses might have looked very pale and unproblematic. That does not mean, I hasten to add, that the problem it poses for us, or any of us who lean towards moral realism, is not a genuine one. On the contrary, it shows what the true magnitude of the problem is: either to avoid positing a kind of fact quite out of congruence with the prevailing ontological framework, or to recover the congruence by changing the framework, which in this case may mean convincingly reinterpreting the world in theological or '*Geist*-like' terms. Both look very much like practical impossibilities, and the first—this is what such arguments as Mackie's really amount to—may be a theoretical impossibility as well.

But still it may seem that the conditions on moral realism have not been fully stated, and that when they are fully stated it becomes clear that even a philosophy of *Geist*, or of God, does not have the resources to satisfy them. It can of course satisfy Mackie's first requirement, since anyone who knows of a divine command to do X has been told to do X; and the second requirement, that it make him do X, appears to be spurious. But is there not a third requirement, namely that knowledge of the objective fact, whatever it is, should at least make the knower believe that X is good? If it is possible to know of the divine command, and consistently with that knowledge not believe that X is good, then the existence of the command cannot be the fact that constitutes the goodness of X. And isn't it possible? To hold something bad, or morally neutral, whilst knowing that God requires it of us is blasphemous, and may be desperately imprudent; but is it really inconsistent? To press the point in a popular way: unless we suppose that it was logically possible for him to have got it wrong, how can we regard it as a merit in God to have got it right?

Just asking these questions doesn't settle the matter. On the contrary, they lead to a discussion which is at least in outline fairly familiar. But I would like to take a slightly less familiar route and ask whether the conviction that we can coherently ask of the deity's decrees whether they are good or not might not itself need certain philosophical inclinations to sustain it. One can surely imagine a consciousness for which there was not so much 'the good' as 'the law'. It could conceive of obeying the law and of disobeying it, and the consequences of each, but it could not conceive of asking what we would express by saying 'Ought the law to be what it is?' Apart from the law itself, so such people would think and feel, what standards could there be that would give such a question sense? To think that there are any is to credit ourselves with a degree of autonomous judgement in these matters. As to the merit of the lawgiver, they would think of it in a different way: not as a matter of being good, but as a matter of the awesome magnificence of a being whose will was *ipso facto* the Law; they would not be short of cause to worship. Some may hesitate to call this consciousness a 'moral' consciousness. But that is not of great importance, since it could be just as decisive for its possessors' code of behaviour and the rigour with which they adhered to it as any other ethical outlook. If such a consciousness is possible (which I do not for a moment doubt) then it looks as if the question that was to 'reveal' the impossibility of seeing the good as constituted by the will of the deity may be one which can coherently be asked only when and where the progress of a humanistic, anthropocentric philosophy has already allowed us to think of ourselves as exercising independent moral judgement.

The kind of metaphysic which enables one to meet these

questions will be equally comfortable with Mackie's next point: how to account for the relation between the natural facts of a situation and the moral ones? He puts the problem like this:

Another way of bringing out this queerness is to ask, about anything that is supposed to have some objective moral quality, how this is linked with its natural features. What is the connection between the natural fact that an action is a piece of deliberate cruelty . . . and the moral fact that it is wrong? It cannot be an entailment, a logical or semantic necessity. Yet it is not merely that the two features occur together. The wrongness must somehow be 'consequential' or 'supervenient'; it is wrong because it is a piece of deliberate cruelty. But just what *in the world* is signified by this 'because'?[12]

The philosopher of the Image of God doctrine can make the unruffled reply that the relation in question is much like the one which relates our preferences to the natural facts. The idea is quite familiar that we abhor something because it is a case of deliberate cruelty. That it is familiar doesn't mean that there are no problems about it; but if there are, then they are just as much problems for the anti-realist line that Mackie (along with many others) favours.

In the passage just quoted Mackie mentions the concept of supervenience; but he does not develop an objection to realism which some writers[13] have seen lurking there. Moral characteristics are said to be supervenient upon natural ones, and this means that there can be no change in moral properties without a change in natural properties. If something is good, then anything which is (naturally) indistinguishable from it is good as well. The combination of this with the denial of ethical naturalism poses a problem. The falsehood of ethical naturalism consists in there being no entailment relations from natural to moral properties, so that no naturalistic description of anything entails any moral evaluation of it. The problem is to see how, in that event, the continuation of the natural properties can entail the continuation of the moral. To say that there is no entailment is to say that it is logically

---

[12] Ibid. p. 41.

[13] See S. W. Blackburn: 'Moral Realism' in *Morality and Moral Reasoning*, ed. Casey (Methuen 1971) pp. 101–124, and 'Supervenience Revisited' in *Exercises in Analysis*, ed. Hacking (Cambridge 1985) pp. 47–67.

possible that the moral property actually possessed by whatever it is should not go with a thing having exactly those natural properties. Why then should it be impossible for it to go with them on one occasion but not on another? What guarantees the consistency of distribution of goodness and badness over the world of natural objects and happenings?

The subjectivist, so the argument proceeds, finds himself at home here. What guarantees consistency, he says, is our decision that only such preferences as are consistent with respect to natural properties shall be allowed as moral preferences; all else is whim and fancy. We create the consistency just as we create the values. But this is just what the realist cannot say. For him moral properties are simply there, and if anything prevents them from being inconsistently distributed with respect to natural properties it cannot be just a decision of ours. What then? Not that the natural properties entail the moral; nor that they cause them, which would not do justice to the feeling that supervenience is a conceptual matter. So it remains—though only from the realist's point of view—a complete mystery.

Obviously there is more to be said here, and some will feel that this brisk exposition makes the realist's quandary sound deeper than it is. Without prejudice to that question I should like to take the point of the last two paragraphs for granted, and strike off in a direction by now anticipatable: it seems that whether the realist is embarrassed or not may again depend on his metaphysical stance. If it allows him to draw on the preferences of some authoritative being, then he can call on the presumed consistency of that being, and everything else in his philosophy which speaks in its favour, to guarantee the consistency of the moral with respect to natural properties. He will at once, however, need something more: if by 'natural' properties we mean only such non-evaluative properties as we can detect, then it will take more than consistency to guarantee supervenience as it is normally understood. If states of affairs have properties which we cannot detect, then states which are indistinguishable for us might be very different from the point of view of the authoritative being, which might therefore distribute its evaluations perfectly consistently, never making evaluative distinctions unless there were also non-evaluative distinctions, whilst differentiating evaluatively between states that were for us indistinguishable. It follows that our realist will need something in addition to consistency in his authoritative being to motivate belief in the super-venience of moral properties on natural properties that are in principle discriminable by us—which, I think it is fair to say, is the way in which the supervenience thesis is normally taken.

But if we survey the metaphysical preferences of the past four centuries we find them well suited to the task of delivering this additional element. One feature is the doctrine of our affinity with the source of authoritative evaluations (in other words the Similarity Thesis), which would strongly incline one to hold that its evaluations and ours must be made on the basis of the same kind of fact. Another might be the idea that God (or 'nature' or the *Weltgeist*) had a benign interest in our moral welfare, and could for that reason be relied upon not to create moral differences without providing clues to them which we could at least in principle detect.

Now there are, as I have already suggested, many who would see it as a conceptual truth that if two states of affairs are alike as regards their natural features they must also be alike in their moral properties. They might object that the realist who calls on the sort of metaphysico-theological reality that I have spoken of cannot account for this aspect of supervenience; he can perhaps cope with its truth, but he cannot cope with its modality. For he makes it dependent on something like the goodwill of a god towards his creatures, or our moral similarity to the *Weltgeist*. These sound *prima facie* contingent and are at best of somewhat obscure modal status, whereas supervenience is clearly a necessary truth.

At this point our realist would be well advised to go on the offensive. Is the principle of the supervenience of moral on natural fact really a necessary truth? Or could it be just a reflection of a particular conception, perhaps a thoroughly parochial one, of the nature of morality? It would, admittedly, be hard to see how morality could survive in a society in which it was generally believed that moral properties were randomly distributed with respect to natural ones—only a standing miracle would produce common assessments and allow co-operative action or successful prediction of the actions of others. But no such problem would be faced by a society which had its agreed norms linking the two sorts of property, and simply held that there were occasions when, perhaps by special divine decree, these links could be broken. Its members would hold that the human agent, who is obliged to rely on natural properties for his moral clues, was exposed to an ineliminable element of risk in making moral choices; now and again, it pleased the powers of the world to catch us out, even the best of us. It isn't too difficult to imagine such an approach to ethics, nor the underlying philosophy or attitude towards reality of which it might be an expression. Nor is it very hard to think of the sort of facts about life, the buffetings handed out to the apparently blameless by an apparently indiscriminating world, that could give rise to and sustain such an attitude. Perhaps the powers whose decrees determine our moral status regard luck as one of the virtues; or perhaps they do not much care for consistency. Such a perspective may, to our ears, sound a primitive note; but that does not mean that we see it to be conceptually awry, let alone self-contradictory. Making supervenience a law of logic smacks of the desire to turn our own metaphysical tastes absolute. What is really just intolerable to a certain philosophical temperament, namely that our moral worth should be beyond our control, is being made out to be flatly impossible.

It is quite comprehensible that such a thought should widely be felt threatening in an age in which the dominant philosophy increasingly tended to bring the universe, or what was important about it, into the sphere of human action and governance. The same tendencies of mind which give direct encouragement to a projectivist theory of ethical judgement also lend support, indirectly, to principles like that of supervenience, which can then be used to make it look as if something like projectivism must be true. And it should be said that, if this has any substance as an explanation of the status ascribed to the principle of supervenience, it would not be the only time that recent ethical theory has sought to dignify a currently popular way of thinking with the title of conceptual law. It has been claimed, for instance by Philippa Foot, that morality is essentially tied to human welfare. 'It is surely clear', she wrote, 'that moral virtues must [of conceptual or logical necessity, it was implied] be connected with human good and harm.'[14]. And a few years later, Geoffrey Warnock was saying:

the *relevance* of considerations as to the welfare of human beings *cannot*, in the context of moral debate, be denied. (Again, of course, we do not choose that this should be so; it *is* so, simply because of what 'moral' means.)[15]

The closing bracket seems to overlook the possibility that what 'moral' means might itself be something which we choose, in a sense; and could it be that what choice we make has something to do with our dominant philosophy? Or, to put it another way: if we take it as hard and fast that this is what 'moral' means, would it not be possible to hold that moral considerations have no special, let alone unique, importance? For there certainly have been flourishing societies with codes of behaviour which saw the good not in terms of human welfare but in obedience to the dictates of a supreme being. Some connection with welfare, not of an *a priori* but of a *de facto* kind, there would of course need to be; no society could for long tolerate a code of behaviour that was consistently inimical to their welfare in respect of the basic needs of life; though it would be perfectly possible to operate a code which was very far from maximising their happiness, or one which under certain circumstances would lead an individual or a group into great suffering or even destruction. The connection with welfare that these considerations imply is, however, altogether too minimal to underpin Foot's thesis. And in any case, there is no need for the connections, such as they are, to count in the minds of those who follow the code as the reasons why it ought to be practised. It is true that such systems are very often accompanied (indeed psychologically shored up) by a belief in another kind of human welfare, that to be enjoyed in the hereafter by those who conform to the code here and now. But two things are to be said: first, that there is no need to think of that happy state as being the grounds of the goodness of the actions which the code enjoins; indeed, it may actually be held wrong to think so—we are to

[14] Phillipa Foot: 'Moral Beliefs', *Proceedings of the Aristotelian Society* Vol. 59 (1958–9) pp. 83–104, reprinted in *Theories of Ethics*, ed. Foot (Oxford 1967).

[15] G. J. Warnock: *Contemporary Moral Philosophy* (Macmillan 1967) p. 67.

act from the love of God, not from the hope of future bliss. Secondly, that future bliss is a very different condition, dependent on very different factors, from the mundane type of welfare which Mrs Foot wished to link, and to link analytically, to morality. Her ethics are the expression of a strongly secularised, strongly pragmatic and anthropocentric worldview: morality is a matter of our bringing about the good for man. As such it has an excellent place in philosophy, especially twentieth-century philosophy; but to present it as a truth of logic is to mistake its nature and exaggerate its universality.

3. *Bad faith and how to avoid it—autonomy revisited*

One who takes a survey of twentieth-century ethical theory can hardly fail to be struck by the fact that whilst so much of it insists, explicitly or otherwise, on the human creative role in the realm of value, at the same time it has characteristically held back from giving opinions as to which values we ought to create. It may seem strange that an epoch so committed to the centrality of practice and agency should have been so widely reluctant to offer any substantive advice about what should be done. I do not believe that there is any single reason for this. One thing that lay behind it, in some quarters, was the feeling that philosophy could and should emulate the natural sciences: they might concern themselves with evaluation as a factual phenomenon, but they were not themselves evaluative. I should like to concentrate on another reason, one which is associated with existentialism. It is in itself a moral stance, and closely related to the thesis of the autonomy of man that we met with in the last chapter in the outlook of William James. It turns out, paradoxically enough, that the reluctance (or perhaps it should be called 'refusal') to say how human beings ought to act is grounded precisely in the radical insistence on the centrality of the notion that human beings are essentially agents.

In a sense, the existentialist refusal to issue first-order moral advice *is* its recognition of the autonomy of the moral agent. Vital to the ethical position of Sartre, for instance, is the tenet that one may not allow others to take moral decisions on one's behalf, and its corollary that one should not attempt to take a moral decision on behalf of someone else. There is, however, more than one level at which he takes this to be true, and more than one type of autonomy which he takes to be involved.

In the first place there is the near triviality that only I can make my decisions, as only I can perform my actions or achieve my achievements. But in the neighbourhood of this triviality is a much more contentful, and correspondingly more contentious, claim. If I turn to you for moral advice, or appeal to my society's accepted ethic, I still have to decide whether to take the advice or to spurn it, whether to follow the norms or flout them. The contentful point is that this is always a decision of mine, that is to say a choice which could have been made differently, for which I therefore have to take responsibility. If I try to tell myself that I have to do such and such, because it is what all my friends advise, or because etiquette requires it, or because it is what 'people in my position' do, then with this 'have to' I am making an attempt to off-load the decision on to others, or on to an institution. Of this attempt two things are to be said. First, it cannot succeed, and second, it is immoral of me to make it. That it cannot succeed is a consequence of the very radical doctrine of human freedom which Sartre espouses: we are never bound to do anything to which we can envisage an alternative—only the sheer inability to imagine the negative brings true compulsion. That it is immoral is the content of the central existentialist doctrine of bad faith, or inauthenticity. In bad faith we make an insincere attempt to limit the sphere of our own agency and consequent responsibility. In our heart we know that we are pretending, for our comfort, not to have a choice; so bad faith is a form of self-deceit. And we are half-trying, half-pretending, to be like things, which are truly compelled because they are unconscious and hence devoid of the power to conceive the contrary of what is; so bad faith is a denial of our humanity, a betrayal of our real nature:

This means that no limits to my freedom can be found except freedom itself, or, if you prefer, that we are not free to cease being free. To the extent that the for-itself wishes to hide its own nothingness from itself and to incorporate the in-itself as its true mode of being, it is trying also to hide its freedom from itself.[16]

[16] J.-P. Sartre: *Being and Nothingness*, trans. Hazel E. Barnes (Methuen 1958)

To issue moral advice in the spirit of seeking to influence the recipient is therefore something that the Sartrean existentialist cannot in conscience permit himself; it is to invite to bad faith. Nor can he do it in much the same spirit as that in which a mathematics teacher might tell his pupils some mathematical result, namely as a prelude to telling them, or getting them to discover, its proof, so putting them in a position to see its truth independently of the teacher and his authority. The comparison fails because there are no reliably interpersonal moral conclusions; and that because there are no reliably interpersonal moral premises. For, to start with, so Sartre maintains, no external fact can be a motive for action. Only in being seen in a certain light, as an object to be attained or overcome, can it motivate; and this is a fact about the conscious subject. Indeed, even something as 'internal' as one's own suffering cannot be a motive until it comes into consciousness and can there be assessed:

[The sufferings of the worker] are not seen in the clear light of day, and consequently they are integrated by the worker with his being. He suffers without considering his suffering and without conferring value upon it. To suffer and to *be* are one and the same for him. His suffering is the pure affective tenor of his non-positional consciousness, but he does not *contemplate* it. Therefore his suffering cannot be in itself a *motive* for his acts.[17]

But now, so Sartre at any rate declares, no fact about the subject can offer a fixed point to be the fulcrum of moral thinking or give us an unmoving premiss for moral argument. For all the facts about the subject are ultimately in the subject's decision, objects of his free choice, and, what is more, they must be so treated by him if he is avoid bad faith. It appears to follow that the most a third party can legitimately do is suggest possibilities for his consideration, which is of course a very far cry from issuing moral advice. Notoriously, Sartre had nothing to say to the young student who came to

pp. 439–440. Readers unaccustomed to Sartre's terminology should not panic. 'The in-itself' refers to unconscious things; 'the for-itself' refers to conscious beings; and when Sartre speaks of the 'nothingness' of the latter he is thinking of his doctrine that there are no facts about ourselves which we can legitimately take as a moral starting-point, since all such facts ultimately rest on our moral choices and are our responsibility.

[17] Ibid. p. 435.

him with an agonising moral dilemma—except that he should *invent* a resolution of it.[18]

For Sartre, man is morally autonomous in that he creates his own moral values. But he is also autonomous in the even more spectacular sense that, in creating them, he is beyond all constraint—or, in a different mood, beyond all help. His creativity operates in a void, nothingness, since there is nothing that can legitimately help him from without, and ultimately nothing to help him from within. The only fact about him which escapes his choice is that everything else about him is chosen, that he is fully free—and so fully responsible. That is his nature, and it is the only thing which can be said to lie in the nature of the human being; all else is our own work. The ethic of authenticity is the demand that we recognise this one truth about our nature for what it is, and keep faith with it. We have encountered, in William James, the image of the creative agent and his self-sustaining experience. Here is the radicalisation of that picture in twentieth-century moral theory, as stark as we please or, as Sartre intimates, a little starker than we please:

for human reality, to be is to *choose oneself*; nothing comes to it either from the outside or from within which it can *receive or accept*. Without any help whatsoever, it is entirely abandoned to the intolerable necessity of making itself be—down to the slightest detail.[19]

The concept of autonomy, on which such stress comes to be laid, is in its broadest terms that of self-reliance, of being independent, and this is manifestly something which comes in many types and degrees. In this and the previous chapter we have been considering two very general forms of it, independence in judgement and independence in action. In the former case what was in question was independence of prior or external fact to which our judgements might be answerable; in the latter it was independence of any kind of compulsion, however mild. We should take notice at this stage of two senses in which our judgements (if not our actions) might be called independent.

I might be said to be an independent judge of the colours

---

[18] Sartre: *Existentialism and Humanism*, trans. Mairet (Methuen 1948).
[19] Sartre: *Being and Nothingness*, trans. Barnes pp. 440–1.

and shapes of ordinary physical objects, that meaning not that
there were no independent facts about these things to which
my judgement was responsible, but simply that I had the
capacity to determine them myself with a good level of
reliability and accuracy; that I was not in principle reliant for
this sort of information on a third party, as a blind man would
be in the case of colours. But there is also a stronger sense of
independence, the one with which we have mainly been
concerned. In this sense, judgement is independent when
there is no prior fact to which it is required to conform. This
latter is the judgement of the referee, whose decision is final,
and so to speak creative of the fact; the former is the
judgement of the expert witness, who does not create the facts
but may safely be assumed to be right about them.

Now if we are thinking of autonomy as independence in the
first of these senses, then the popularity of the doctrine that
human beings are autonomous judges of at least many kinds
of truth goes back far beyond the beginnings of the period
which I have described as that of the Agency Theory or
Practice Ideal. It is also a highly typical feature of the theories
that articulate in their various ways the metaphysic of the
image of God. For it was characteristic of them to hold that
our godlike cognitive powers could give us insight into many
of the facts that made up reality, and that they rendered us
self-reliant in the enterprise. In Chapter 1, it is true, we
noticed two points which might be thought to cloud the issue.
Did not Descartes show some doubt about our self-reliance in
cognitive matters when he deemed a proof that God is the
author of our powers necessary to justify us in taking them to
be trustworthy? But there is no need to read it in that way. It
is certainly not, for Descartes, that we can acquire knowledge
only by being told; it is just that to be sure that we really do
have the capacity to acquire knowledge for ourselves calls for
a proof that our faculties are reliable. The proof, admittedly,
passes through God, but he acts as a guarantor of our abilities,
not as an authority from whom we are to hear the truth and
accept it.

The second doctrine which might on first glance be thought
to dim the light of our autonomy is Malebranche's view that
our reason, when functioning at its best, merges with the

thinking of God. But even this is not in unequivocal conflict with our autonomy as judges of truth; after all, it is very far from making us blindly dependent upon an external informant. So I think it can be said, quite generally, that cognitive autonomy in the weaker sense is a ubiquitous as well as central feature in the work of all the main philosophers of the early modern period. This is the first stage of emancipation; it goes hand in hand, of course, with the banishment of deference to authorities from the theory of knowledge. The second stage, the coming of autonomy in the stronger sense, is quite a different thing. It can appear just to the extent that human judgement is thought of as constrained not by any external reality but only, if at all, by our own experiences and values. That is why it is characteristic, almost definitive, of the last hundred years of European thought.

It can of course be found earlier, and just where one might expect to find it, at the point where the Insight Ideal began to give way. Kant is its first systematic champion; but more than a hint of it is to be found in Hume. Clearly his ethics, which locate the source of value in the feelings of the subject, form a theory of this kind, and something very similar might be said of his theory of our factual beliefs. Whether, for instance, there really is necessary connection in nature, whether there are real causes, our belief in them is generated without their assistance —regularities amongst our impressions are all that is needed—and Hume urges us to regard that belief as legitimate without regard to the question (which in any case we can barely understand) whether they exist or not. But two features dampen down the growing feeling of man's autonomy in Hume's work. First, there is the occasional tendency to hint that some of these beliefs, the psychological origins of which he describes, should strictly speaking be called mistakes. And secondly, even if he does portray man as autonomous he makes no attempt whatsoever to portray him as *sovereign*; on the contrary, the human being is a cog in the psycho-mechanism of nature. The big emancipatory effort comes from Kant, who presents us as being in large measure the source of the empirical world and so the arbiters of its contents, as well as being able to transcend its causal determinism by the spontaneity of reason, causality through freedom—the obscurity of this idea should not blind us to its existence or to its effects on the emotional tone of Kant's philosophical system. As well as empirical reality, he also thinks of us as being originators of the moral law. For although the moral law springs from reason, it is our reason that it springs from; and so it may be said that we give the law to ourselves, that the categorical imperative is 'self-addressed':[20] '[man] is subject only to laws which are made by himself. . . '.[21] Indeed, if there is to be such a thing as a categorical imperative, Kant argues (passing a trifle rapidly from 'reason' to 'the will' as he does so), it cannot be otherwise. For a categorical imperative is one which is binding on us no matter what our interests may be, and no imperative which does not have its seat in our own will can satisfy that condition:

For when [previous philosophers] thought of man merely as subject to a law (whatever it might be), the law had to carry with it some interest in order to attract or compel, because it did not spring as a law from *his own* will: in order to conform with the law his will had to be necessitated by *something else* to act in a certain way.[22]

It is not just that there is autonomy in morals; as Kant sees things, there could be no morals without it, since all imperatives would be hypothetical only.

We have already seen William James arguing for the self-sufficiency of what he calls 'human experience', and for the irrelevancy to any of our endeavours of 'the absolute' or 'pre-human standards of truth'. Let the absolute be what it will, our beliefs are the outcome of the way we react to our experience:

But is it not obvious that even tho there be such absolute sailing directions . . . that we *ought* to follow, the only guarantee that we shall in fact follow them must lie in our human equipment.[23]

There is of course a sense in which everyone, including any absolutist, will agree to this. But the pull of autonomy

[20] I borrow the expression from Bernard Williams.
[21] Kant: *Groundwork of the Metaphysic of Morals*, trans. Paton (*The Moral Law* Hutchinson 1948).
[22] Ibid. p. 100. .
[23] William James: 'Humanism and Truth' in *The Meaning of Truth* (Harvard p. 212).

makes itself felt in James' happy endorsement of the idea that we need worry about nothing but faithfully following the instructions of our human equipment; in particular, we need not worry about whether, faithfully obeyed, it will bring us to *the right* harbour. After all, *tu quoque*:

The only truth that [the partisan of absolute reality] will ever practically *accept* will be that to which his finite experiences lead him of themselves.[24]

No hint here of the fact that that is exactly what the partisan of absolute reality is worried about. But it is not only this type of conclusion that has been popular in the twentieth century. The style of argument—'whatever we were given, it would still be up to us what to make of it'—also recurs at some crucial points in recent philosophy. We have just seen Sartre championing the moral autonomy of the human agent—for there is no moral authority, and if there were, it would be bad faith merely to follow its decrees unless they happened to coincide with the values of our own free choice. Now one also finds in Sartre's writings a second argument for autonomy, this time independent of the moral principle of bad faith: even if there were a moral authority which gave us indications of its thoughts and preferences, it would still be up to us to create our own values, to decide what to do. And this is not, or not just, because we would have to decide whether to bow to its authority, but because it would be up to us how to interpret the indications that it gave us. By way of illustration Sartre tells the story of a certain Jesuit of his acquaintance. This man, who had been brought up in an institution where he had evidently experienced little human warmth, then encountered in his youth further setbacks, culminating in his early manhood with failure in his military examination. How did he react?

He took it ... as a sign that he was not intended for secular successes, and that only the attainments of religion, those of sanctity and faith, were accessible to him. He interpreted his record as a message from God, and became a member of the Order. Who can doubt but that this decision as to the meaning of the sign was his, and his alone? One could have drawn quite different consequences

[24] Ibid. p. 213.

from such a series of reverses—as, for example, that he had better become a carpenter or a revolutionary. For the decipherment of the sign... he bears the entire responsibility.[25]

Sartre's example draws much of its force from the nature of the 'sign' vouchsafed to his acquaintance: it is vague, it manifestly stands in need of interpretation and leaves much scope for it. That point might appear to obstruct the generalised form of the argument: if there were an absolute, and it made a difference to what we encounter in the world, its effects upon our experience would not be such as to single out a unique conclusion about its nature which we were obliged to draw. Would one not answer, 'First let's see the effects; there is no *a priori* reason why they should all be ambiguous, even if many of them are'?

Many readers, however, will by now be thinking of the similarity between this passage from *Existentialism and Humanism* and the notorious argument of Wittgenstein about following rules. A sign, so it runs, needs an interpretation; it does not bring its single admissible interpretation along with it, except perhaps in the psychological and relativised sense that a given interpreter may only be able to take it in one way. We saw Sartre relying on the fact that the sign in his example is obviously susceptible of any number of different responses; Wittgenstein's striking contribution was to argue that the same can with equal justice be said of those signs which, because of our training, seem to us firmly univocal, like the pointing signpost or the command 'go on adding two'. Whether his reasoning is as cogent as it is puzzling may be another question, but it is clear that he has made a particularly radical application of a thought that was in the air at the time and much to the taste of his contemporaries.

He also did something highly characteristic of recent Anglo-Saxon thought in making this application within the theory of meaning. This provides a good example of the way in which a principle can operate both in immediate contact with what the intelligent but philosophically untrained person will at once recognise as a central philosophical issue, and also in more abstract and technical areas which, though arguably more

[25] Sartre: *Existentialism and Humanism* (Methuen 1948) pp. 38–9.

fundamental, may well strike the same person as merely remote and scholastic. We shall see the same thing again in the further course of this chapter.

4. *Publicity and Popper*

The Image of God doctrine was firmly tuned to the philosophy of the individual; it was between God and each human being that the resemblance was to hold. Theology apart, one can see that its cognitive aspect, the Insight Ideal, pulls strongly in that direction, for the insight it bids us strive for is something that one cannot at all naturally imagine as distributed amongst several minds. If you know the premises but cannot draw the inference, and I see the validity of the inference but have no knowledge of the premises, there is no insight into the truth of the conclusion. A philosopher might take the step of speculatively (not to say incomprehensibly) assigning to us some kind of communal mind; but barring that unappetising morsel the philosophy of insight will have to be a philosophy of the states and powers of the individual. Be that as it may, the very different philosophical climate that replaced it has no such bias; it directed attention to activity, and whereas an individual can have projects and execute them, so of course can groups. And group action, provided the problem of its direction is solved, often has obvious advantages. The change therefore has a liberating effect, making room for lines of thought that emphasise the social, the communal, alongside lines emphasising the individual. Accordingly, we find a sharp rise in the prominence of such concepts. The reader may think at once of the Communist thinkers of the nineteenth century and their progeny, but it would be quite wrong to associate this trend exclusively with left-wing political thought, or even with political or social thought in general. Those branches of philosophy are, after all, by definition concentrated on life in society; the question is not whether, but how, they do it. Much more significant for understanding the permeation of philosophy by the Agency Theory and its ramifications is the way in which the notion of community appears in load-bearing positions at crucial points in such disciplines as epistemology and the theory of meaning, where the individual had previously ruled.

An interesting case in point is Sir Karl Popper's treatment of knowledge and scientific method. Notoriously, he attacked the 'subjectivist' approach to knowledge, that which sees it as a favoured kind of belief and belief as a state of an individual's mind. We can now see at any rate why the seventeenth and eighteenth centuries should have given it such impetus: in view of the job they wanted knowledge to do in the context of their thought, they were bound to construe it as a state of the individual—how else could it be the sort of thing which God and particular human beings had in common? Popper's attempts to dispose of this conception and replace it by that of the 'third world' of knowledge and theory, distinct from that of physical objects and from that of states of consciousness, are hardly to be taken seriously if one reads them as intended proofs;[26] but there is very good reason to believe that Sir Karl himself regarded them more as provocation.[27] His concern, it appears, was more to propose and develop an alternative than to demonstrate its necessity. In his scheme of things knowledge (and not just knowledge but everything that constitutes 'the current state of research') becomes a public object, to the construction of which any or all of us may contribute.

Popper's reader may be forgiven for thinking that he must have been very powerfully drawn by the idea of what is communal to adopt an ontology at once so weird and so unnecessary. It surely is unnecessary, for anything that Popper shows. His 'argument' really amounts to the observation that libraries are very important repositories of knowledge, and this doesn't call for the postulation of his 'third world', for in the first place libraries are composed of physical objects in various physical states, and in the second place they are only of interest in this connection because they have the power to cause certain states of mind in suitably equipped readers. But it may have been that Popper was just dramatising a rather more sober thesis, for there is another way in which he regards the scientific enterprise as being essentially public, and it is instructive to see that he treats this as a rather obvious point which can be taken for granted without a great deal of argument.

[26] Karl R. Popper: 'Epistemology Without a Knowing Subject' in *Objective Knowledge* (Revised edn. Oxford 1979) pp. 106–152 esp. pp. 107–8

[27] Ibid. p. 106.

Let us recall Popper's reaction to foundationalist theories of knowledge.[28] Such theories hold that there is a favoured type of statement which may be known non-inferentially and indubitably. But there are no such statements, Popper holds; anything can be subjected to doubt. We should be content to take as foundational, that is to say as our starting-point *pro tem*, those about which there is, *de facto*, no disagreement:

> For any basic statement can again in its turn be subjected to tests, using as a touchstone any of the basic statements which can be deduced from it with the help of some theory, either the one under test, or another. This procedure has no natural end. Thus if the test is to lead us anywhere, nothing remains but to stop at some point or other and say that we are satisfied, for the time being.
>
> It is fairly easy to see that we arrive in this way at a procedure according to which we stop only at a kind of statement that is especially easy to test. For it means that we are stopping at statements about whose acceptance or rejection the various investigators are likely to reach agreement.[29]

This passage raises a number of questions. Did Popper think that, once he had rejected intrinsically indubitable statements, his choice of replacement was the only real possibility? The speed of the transition suggests it, but nothing of the sort is the case. Instead of picking on statements about which there is unlikely to be disagreement, one might opt for a rather stronger criterion and select those about which there is, by common consent, no reasonable room for doubt. Or (even more germane to the present context) one might avoid the whole subject of consensus and agreement, and simply recommend to the individual investigator that he (provisionally) regard as basic whatever he feels to be beyond reasonable doubt—a piece of advice which has the merit that he is almost certain to follow it anyway. One thing which might be helping Popper to bypass this option without the lacuna becoming too obvious is the double use of 'we'. 'We are satisfied' can mean the same as 'one is satisfied', and so be neutral between singular and plural readings; but it is of course equally at home in contexts which are decisively plural.

[28] He calls it 'psychologism', no doubt because the foundational statements are nearly always taken to be descriptions of the mental states of the speaker—see *The Logic of Scientific Discovery* (Hutchinson 1959) ch. V.

[29] Popper: *The Logic of Scientific Discovery* p. 104.

The second paragraph from the quoted passage, with its mention of 'the various investigators', provides just such a context. I do not believe that this linguistic fact could be the cause of the jump to the social perspective; but it could assist when the will to make it was already there.

What would allow Popper to speak in terms of agreement rather than communal certainty? Surely the fact that he seeks not insight (he denies, after all, that it is even a possible aim of science to try to show anything to be true) but involvement in a process of hypothesis, corroboration and criticism, not a glimpse of the truth but participation in the activity of science. Since that is what he seeks he is at liberty to think of this activity as something carried on by a group; and for a number of people to combine in the scientific enterprise there is no need for certainties, nor even for there to be anything about which they all feel certain. All they need is a common grasp of the rules under which they are working, and the ability to agree on when a theory under test has been falsified and when corroborated. The psychology of the matter, why they agree on these things or what, in general, they think they are up to, is irrelevant; so long as the agreement is there, the collaborative effort can continue.

This is not the only way in which the quoted passage betrays its underlying allegiance to the Agency Theory and its corresponding lack of interest in the goals of the Insight Ideal. Another is its attitude to foundationalism. The foundationalist holds that there are certain statements which cannot be doubted. Popper does not actually say that anything can be doubted; he says that anything can be tested (though presumably thinking that nothing can be tested unless it can be doubted—otherwise the 'test' would be fraudulent). What test does he propose?

any basic statement can in its turn be subjected to test, using as a touchstone any of the basic statements which can be deduced from it with the help of some theory, either the one under test, or another.[30]

This is strange. What Popper has in mind is a test of the original basic statement. But if that statement has a serious claim to being basic in the sense required by the traditional

[30] Ibid. p. 104.

foundationalist, what will happen when another basic statement (the one 'deduced from it with the help of some theory') turns out to be false? In so far as these statements do have a claim to be basic, that the former is true and the latter false will not be open to doubt; the only element susceptible of genuine doubt here is the theory, and that is surely what will, and ought to, give way. So if there are any statements that are basic in the foundationalist's sense, where that implies indubitability, Popper's test will not be a test of them, but of something else. His argument in this passage, that no statements are indubitable, because all are testable, rests on the unargued, question-begging claim that there are no indubitable statements. When that claim can appear as unargued dogma the Insight Ideal has passed into history.

Let us return to Popper's use of the notion of agreement. He assumes that what is the object of general agreement must be something that it is easy to test:

It is fairly easy to see that we arrive in this way at a procedure according to which we stop only at a kind of statement that is especially easy to test.[31]

Whether that is so or not depends, surely, on how the agreement is reached. It seems perfectly possible that human beings might naturally find themselves in agreement about a number of things which it would be very hard indeed to subject to a Popperian test, and which it would be (at best) extremely hard to settle were disagreement to arise. 'There are physical objects' is a case in point. The continuation of the passage just quoted makes it clear which way Popper's thought tends: he soon stops speaking of testing and concentrates on agreement, saying that agreement at some level is a necessary condition of the very existence of science. That is not at all implausible; but the fact remains that it is agreement, not testability, which is carrying the weight of his position. Where there is agreement he is satisfied, even if, were agreement to fail, there would be no testability, no science, and no language.

Not only does agreement come before testability for Popper, but the notion of agreement determines, in part, what he is

[31] Ibid. p. 104.

prepared to count as a test. In the next paragraph, we read:

we stop at basic statements which are easily testable. Statements about personal experiences . . . are clearly not of this kind. . .[32]

How, we may ask, can that be clear, when a well-known and long-standing tradition has it that nothing is more easily and decisively checkable than these very statements? Only, it seems, if the publicity of the test is being built into the concept of testing, and the way in which Popper goes on leaves no doubt that this is what is happening: we do not stop at statements about personal experiences because the 'intersubjective' testing of them is complicated and difficult.[33] Perfectly in line with the philosophical tenor of his view he assumes, or takes for granted, that the test must be one which any member of the team can perform, a common procedure which can generate a common belief.

It appears, then, that the stress on the social character of science is shaping Popper's whole approach in this central passage. His base-line is agreement in judgement, and his attempt to distinguish this from communal dogmatism by saying that there is always the possibility of further testing turns out, in the end, to be spurious. Equally spurious is the derivation, from what might look to be a pretty basic requirement of rationality (namely, that we operate only with statements for whose truth or falsity we have some kind of test), of the view that public testing and agreement is essential and that descriptions of experience cannot therefore play the foundational role. Popper has not so much refuted the traditional foundationalist as simply overridden his conception of the goals ('in our theory there is no question of trying to prove any statement'[34]) and the nature of the business of science. And this is characteristic of what happens when a philosopher operating under the auspices of one dominant philosophy confronts a doctrine which is really at home under another.

[32] Ibid. pp. 104–5.

[33] Ibid. p. 105. When Popper uses these words he is actually quoting from Carnap; but the context is such that the point is unaffected.

[34] Ibid. p. 105. It is of course a basic doctrine of Popper's account of science that, far from trying to *prove* its propositions, we are not even trying to *verify* them, as that had previously been understood.

5. *Agency and opacity: causes and explanations*

Another pervasive feature of the philosophy of this century has been the willing acceptance of what I shall call opacity, or opaque connections. 'Opacity', as I shall use it, has nothing to do with obscurity, and if possible still less with its technical use in the theory of reference; it is more nearly related to the notion of a brute fact, that which is the case whilst being, in the sense of the term common in the eighteenth century, 'unintelligible'. This phenomenon, I shall argue, is closely linked to the prominence of the concept of agency: the emphasis on agency or practice favours the acceptability of opacity.

An agent has goals, states of affairs which he wishes to bring about, and these will not in general (unless perhaps he is God) be things which he can bring about directly. Rather he will have to seek out suitable means, find starting-points which he can directly realise and which will lead to the goals at which he is aiming. He therefore needs true beliefs of an 'instrumental' kind, beliefs of the form that if a certain state of affairs, call it A, obtains, then another state of affairs B will (or will usually) follow. To be effective as an agent he needs such beliefs, and they must be true—but his effectiveness as an agent will not be increased by his knowing why B generally succeeds A. For him, the connection may just be a brute, given fact about these two types of state; he will still be just as good at getting B as someone to whom the connection is 'intelligible'.

That thought needs a good deal of refinement. If we are thinking just of his getting B on one occasion, and that an occasion on which the generally valid rule that Bs follow upon As is going to hold, then perhaps he is just as good. But if we are thinking of his capacity day in day out to function as a generator of Bs the issue is not so simple. For now someone who knows not just that but also how Bs emerge from As may be better at dealing with the cases in which an A will not lead to a B—he may be able to tell that it won't, and so avoid useless effort; or he may be able to set about altering the situation so that, after all, it will.

This is not to be denied. But what, essentially, gives the

superior agent his advantage is the fact that he knows more
generalisations, or generalisations more consistently true,
about the relationship of A and B. Given that, he will be no
better off, as a producer of Bs, for knowing why these further
generalisations hold or how the connections work. Once
again, however, we have to observe that this is not quite right.
Our superior agent may know, for instance, that it is only
when Cs occur that Bs *invariably follow, and that* Cs usually
follow As but sometimes do not. Knowing why this is so
might, under certain circumstances, make him very much
better at producing the goal-state, B, than someone who did
not have this knowledge. For he might come to know of
something else, D, that unlike A it correlates invariably with
C, and hence also with B. So he has available a means of B-
production which is more reliable and perhaps, in the event of
Ds being easier to produce than As, more convenient to operate.

There is another way in which knowing why Bs follow upon
As may enhance the agent's powers: it may involve knowing
things which he can make use of for purposes other than the
generation of Bs. One possibility might be that the derivation
of Bs from As turns out to be merely a special case of a
generalisation which provides recipes for doing all manner of
things. But through all these variations the same theme
remains. Our agent needs true conditional beliefs. If he has
them, he will not be one whit better off for knowing why they
are true, except in so far as knowing why they are true consists
in knowing more, or more general, conditionals. For some
kind of ultimate insight into the truth of these conditionals he
has, *qua* agent, no use at all. From his perspective, what is
better than knowledge of brute fact is knowledge of more brute
fact.

Prediction is the other side of the same coin. An agent, if he
is to be able to achieve his goals, needs to be able to predict
the outcome of his doings. He also needs to be able to predict
the outcome of events not of his doing, for this may alter both
what he can realistically aim to do and how he should set
about doing it. For both these reasons an emphasis on action
will give rise to an emphasis on prediction. But once again all
that is needed is true belief, as comprehensive as possible, in
conditional statements connecting the occurrence of one state

of affairs with the subsequent occurrence of another. There is nothing to encourage an emphasis on insight into, or the intelligibility of, such connections, unless that be interpreted as simply a demand for more of the same. In any stronger interpretation they can slip from the stage, and their exit may not even be widely noticed.

The stress on activity thus encourages a tolerance of opaque connections, if we so call these links which lack intrinsic intelligibility. One of the most obvious areas in which philosophers of the twentieth century have taken advantage of this tolerance is in their accounts of causality and natural law. Every contemporary student of philosophy is more than aware of the question 'Is causality just regular sequence?'—as well as of the tendency to answer 'Yes', or as near to it as one can decently get. How near has that seemed to be, to the thought of the last fifty years? That causality is just regular sequence could not be sustained in its baldest form; for that there are too many cases of concomitance which we are not willing to regard as causal, like that famous one between the Manchester factory hooter and the behaviour of the London factory workers. So causal connections have been taken to be instances of regular concomitance of some particular kind; and the great majority of philosophers have felt that they could specify which kind without introducing notions that would make causal connections, for us, ultimately any less brute than had they been simply any old case of regular concomitance. One prominent option was to restrict the title of cause to such regularities as were supported by what might be called, in a broad sense, the 'theoretical' beliefs of whoever was bestowing the title. Thus in the clearest case, where the system of theoretical beliefs is well developed, the difference would be that between a regular concomitance which was, and one which was not, supported by what the person in question took to be natural laws. A thesis of this kind was held, for instance, by Richard Braithwaite. 'If a thing is A, it is B', when used to express a causal (or nomic) relation, may properly be asserted when 'Nothing is both A and non-B' is a consequence of 'a higher level hypothesis in a true and established scientific deductive system'.[35] . Briefly, if roughly:

[35] R. Braithwaite: *Scientific Explanation* (Cambridge 1953) pp. 296–7.

it must be a consequence of a hypothesis, many of whose other consequences have turned out true; but there is nothing here to the effect that 'What is A is B', or the higher-level hypothesis from which it follows, is possessed of any kind of necessity or even 'intelligibility', let alone that it is a potential object of *a priori* insight—it is simply a matter of its place in a scientific system which *de facto* works, that is produces true observation statements. Braithwaite also held a very similar view about how a generalisation qualifies as a natural law:

> The thesis which has been maintained is that the genuine differences between assertions of constant conjunction and assertions of natural law arise out of the way in which the propositions concerned in the assertions are related to other propositions in the deductive system used by the asserter. This thesis makes the notion of natural law an epistemological one and makes the 'naturalness' of each natural law relative to the rational corpus of the thinker.[36]

Thus Braithwaite avoids having to call on any 'nomic necessity distinct from constant conjunction'.[37] Some writers, however, were of the opinion that without the introduction of some kind of necessitation the essence of causal concepts could not be grasped. Here the plot thickens, for it may sound as if such people must be recommending an understanding of causality which makes causal connections potentially transparent to the mind. But there is no must here; they may, but equally they may not. One may hold that some form of necessitation is required, but then continue to regard it as a brute fact that a certain power, that of producing Bs, attaches to events of type A. What such philosophers are in conflict with is not the principle that the ultimate connections in the universe are, at least for our minds, brute, but rather with a certain traditional kind of empiricism: they may have difficulty, if they wish to remain within that empiricist framework, in explaining how our concept of this necessitation or power arises, and its exact content. On the other side of the coin, they may attract criticism for leaving too much room for the sceptic: how do we distinguish those cases where necessitation occurs from those where there is simply a *de facto* concomitance? But be that as it may, they do not infringe the

---

[36] Ibid. p .317.
[37] Ibid. p. 294.

Humean principle that causal connections are, for us, brute facts. That such philosophers are in recent years in a large majority over those who do still hanker after the old intelligibility of causes, is something I leave to the feeling of the experienced reader—I shall certainly not attempt to count heads. But here, to give one example, is William Kneale, opting for necessitation without the possibility of insight:

the contentions of those who oppose the necessitation theory of natural laws reduce to this: 'Since we cannot say what it would be like to know the necessity of a natural law, it is senseless even to suggest that such a law may be a principle of necessitation'. The hypothesis that something we cannot know *a priori* is nevertheless a truth of principle seems curious, I admit, but I think that it seems so only because we fail to notice the peculiarity of the concepts used in natural science.[38]

So much for causal connection. Let us now look at the topic of explanation. One's first impression might be that an interest in explanation is an interest in knowing why things happen, and so accords better with the Insight Ideal than with the Agency Theory—which ought to be satisfied with knowing that they happen and under what circumstances. So when Carl Hempel begins his well-known paper 'Explanation in Science and in History' by speaking of 'two pervasive human concerns' and characterising them as 'man's persistent desire to improve his strategic position in the world by means of dependable methods for predicting, and, wherever possible, controlling the events that occur in it',[39] and 'man's insatiable intellectual curiosity, his deep concern to *know* the world he lives in, and to *explain*, and thus to *understand*, the unending flow of phenomena it presents to him',[40] it may look as if he is speaking first of agency, and then of insight, so that for the sake of my hypothesis he ought to have gone on either to say that this insatiable curiosity seemed in our times to have become satiated, or to illustrate the fact in his own person by

---

[38] W. C. Kneale: *Probability and Induction* (Oxford 1949) p. 80.

[39] C. G. Hempel: 'Explanation in Science and History' in *Frontiers of Science and Philosophy* ed. Colodny (Allen and Unwin 1962) pp. 7–33. This quotation p. 7. Reprinted in *The Philosophy of Science* ed. Nidditch (Oxford 1968) pp. 54–79. This quotation p. 54

[40] Ibid. p. 7 (reprinted version p. 54).

proceeding to ignore it. But, on the contrary, it is just what his paper is about.

The impression of misfit disappears, however, when we examine what explanation actually is, according to Hempel. Explaining any fact consists in deducing it, or deducing that it is probable, from a statement of initial conditions plus laws. The latter may be strictly universal, or statistical in form; Hempel represents them as statements to the effect that in all cases (or with high relative frequency) certain specific conditions will result in a certain kind of occurrence. Such generalisations need to be true; but there is no sign that Hempel is searching for any intrinsic intelligibility in them. Explanation, for him, has little or nothing to do with insight in the traditional sense. But on the other hand it does show an excellent match with what, from the perspective of the Agency Theory, would recommend itself as being the ideal cognitive situation. Genuine explanation, in Hempel's eyes, exists when we have so complete a statement of initial conditions and laws as to be in a position to deduce the *explanandum* from them. Explanations as usually offered, it is true, fall short of this ideal, though mostly harmlessly; but by calling them 'elliptical' Hempel signals clearly that he regards the complete form as the true one. And the complete form is the one that can only be given by someone who grasps, besides all that is relevant about the initial conditions, laws sufficiently comprehensive to make the connection with the *explanandum* deductive—which is what the exaltation of agency will incline us to think of as the preferred state.

We can see why that should be so when we remember that the Agency Theory is interested in promoting those states of mind which make for the most efficient agent. An efficient agent needs to be an efficient predictor; and to be an efficient predictor he needs to be able to calculate, for a given initial state, the consequent state to which it will always lead. Any relaxation of this requirement will mean that there are certain circumstances under which it will not lead to this state, and unless he knows what these are—in which case he can build them into his 'law' and so restore its universality—their existence will impair his reliability in prediction and thereby also his efficiency as an agent. But if he does have knowledge of these exceptionless generalisations, Hempel's condition for genuine explanation will *ipso facto* be met; for he will know that the initial conditions are *A*, and that if *A* then invariably *B*, from which *B* is of course a deductive consequence.

6.   *Agency and opacity: knowledge*

There are two other areas of philosophical thought in which opacity, though of a slightly different kind, figures large. In the much-pursued topics of the analysis of the concept of knowledge, and the theory of meaning, we meet with doctrines that are sometimes referred to as 'externalist'. It used to be thought that the meaning of an expression resided in facts that were known, often indeed infallibly known, to its user. As was earlier pointed out, the Insight Ideal needed this, since our insight into the truth of what we say can be no greater than our grasp of what we mean by it. But recently we come across the idea that what we mean may be in part determined by facts of which we have no knowledge, even by facts which find no reflection of any kind in our consciousness. I shall return to this; first I want to draw attention to a comparable feature of contemporary analyses of knowledge.

Plato set the all too well-known scene: knowledge is true belief plus a good reason for it. Recent debate, I need hardly say, has centred on the question whether he found the right factor to add to true belief. Various alternative proposals have enjoyed some popularity: the belief must have the right kind of causal connection with the facts,[41] or it must have been formed by a reliable method,[42] or the believer must satisfy certain counterfactual conditionals (be a good 'tracker' of the fact).[43] I shall attend primarily to the 'reliable method' formulation, but my real interest is not so much in the distinctions between these alternatives as in a feature that they have in common.

The feature is this: they avoid the implication that the knower has to be aware that the third condition is fulfilled, or

---

[41] See Alvin Goldman: 'A Causal Theory of Knowing', *The Journal of Philosophy* Vol. LXIV (1967) pp. 357–372.

[42] E.g. D. M. Armstrong: *Belief, Truth and Knowledge* (Cambridge 1973) esp. ch. 12.

[43] See R. Nozick: *Philosophical Explanations* (Oxford 1981) ch. 3; closely comparable is F. Dretske: 'Conclusive Reasons', *Australasian Journal of Philosophy* Vol. 49 (1971) pp. 1–22.

even to have thought of it. The traditional analysis, by contrast, did have that implication. Arguably it need not have been read as having it, but it is evident that it was generally so understood. When the third condition was phrased as: 'S (the knower) has good reason to believe that p', or '. . . is justified in believing that p', this was seen as involving some conscious grasp of the fact on the knower's part. Having a good reason for p, it was understandably felt, is not just believing something, q, the truth of which makes the truth of p probable (at least); the subject also needed to see that this relation held. For otherwise, if I believe two things, A and B, which happen to be true, and A implies B, then I know B, even though it should never have entered my head that the two could be in any way connected. I would not, under those circumstances, have a good reason for believing B—so the traditional third condition has traditionally been taken. Nor would it do, incidentally, for me just gratuitously to believe A—if it is to give me knowledge of B I will surely need at least good reason to believe it in its turn.

Keeping for the moment to the first of these difficulties: if we give in to the argument, we are quickly led to the view that the subject must be aware that the one proposition is a good reason for the other; but 'be aware' is just a verbal variant on 'know', and the analysis is seen to be defective—either it is regressive, or it calls on a different use of 'know' which is as yet unanalysed. Without question there is a serious problem here; it is one of the pressures towards foundationalism, the view that the regress does indeed start but is then stopped by some non-evidential insight into the truth of a certain type or types of proposition. Another exit, the one we are about to take a closer look at, does not even let it start:

Rather, we should acknowledge that if we are speaking *in general* about knowledge, not only is it not necessary that the knower be able to support or ground his true belief by reference to other propositions, but it is not necessary that he be in any special state with regard to this belief at all, at least at the level of what he can consciously rehearse.[44]

Notice that this exit could not have much charm for someone

[44] B. A. O. Williams: 'Knowledge and Reasons' in *Problems in the Theory of Knowledge*, ed. von Wright (Nijhoff 1972) pp .1–11.

whose imagination is still held by the Insight Ideal. A state which consisted in believing that p (when p was in fact true) plus satisfying some further condition about which one had no conscious thought at all would not confer on its owner the slightest hint of insight into the fact that p, so that if 'knowledge' is to be reserved for the favoured relation to the facts, the one which the Ideal bids us try to achieve, it will not be analysed like this, but in some way which tries to pack the insight into the truth of p into the third condition. This may be the historical source of the dissatisfaction which, for some, still attaches to the externalist proposal. But not only is the demise of the Insight Ideal necessary before an externalist account of knowledge can seem an option to be taken seriously; one can go on to argue that externalism is positively encouraged by the rise of the concepts of practice and agency.

There are at least two perspectives from which the encouragement is visible. Earlier, we considered the point that the Insight Ideal, with its original theological motivation, would promote an infallibilist conception of knowledge, that being the state of mind which its supporters would value most. The Agency Theory, in the same way, would tend to dignify with the name of knowledge that state which would best advance efficiency as an agent. We might also ask that the knower, quite apart from his own practical potential, should be valuable as a source of knowledge for others, who equally have need of it as a guide to action. Either perspective readily leads to a kind of reliabilist thesis about the nature of knowledge, in which the third necessary condition, the one to be added to true belief, is allowed to be opaque to the knowing subject.

What state is it which best advances our efficiency as agents? The question is not straightforward; there are various levels at which one may think about the efficiency of an agent, various possible hazards which one may expect his competence to survive, various degrees of comprehensiveness which one might require of it. Basic, surely, is that his actions lead to the desired outcome; and that at once generates the further desideratum that he hold true beliefs as to what courses of action will have that effect. If we are limiting our view to the matter of his capacity here and now to produce a

B, and doing *A* will here and now have that effect (even though this might not generally, or even ever again, be the case), then it will be enough for him to believe that doing *A* will result in *B*. How he came to think this, or whether he has any reason to think it, will not affect his performance on this occasion, if it is to be judged solely on whether it attains its goal. But flukes have low practical status, which understandably stems from the fact that they mostly don't work; and once we ask of our agent that he be tolerably consistent at producing *B*s when he wants to, he will have to be good in general at telling when the needful antecedent conditions— those under which action *A* will have outcome *B*—obtain. So he will need a way of detecting those conditions which is reliable, in the sense that it nearly always, at least, yields the right answer.

These remarks relate only to how good someone is at performing a specified task. We shall rate higher an agent who is competent over a greater range of goals; and this line of thought leads to the conception of an ideal agent whose beliefs and executive capacity are such that he can produce whatever he wishes to produce under any circumstances which might obtain. Such a being would have the property that, in whatever circumstances he might find himself, he could quickly come by a mass of highly detailed information about them, as well as true beliefs linking the actions he could perform, in those circumstances, to their outcomes under those circumstances. How he comes by these beliefs doesn't matter in the slightest, so long as they are true. But if there is such a thing as the method whereby he arrives at them it will *ex hypothesi* be a reliable one. Conversely, given that there is going to be a method for arriving at beliefs, and that it is desirable that those beliefs be true, and the more of them the better, it *ipso facto* becomes obligatory that the method be reliable, and the more so the better.

All this, it will be seen, applies to a being that has to achieve its ends by operating on the given situation and transforming it in accordance with general principles. If we think of a divine agent, who merely needs to will something for it to become fact, no such train of thought arises; *qua* agent, that sort of god needs no factual beliefs at all. The Agency Theory, however, is not about God, but man. And when we consider what sort of beliefs are desirable in an agent subject to certain very general limitations—to which any natural being is subject—we find reason to say at least this: that they had better be potentially very numerous; that they had better be at least nearly all true; and that if these two conditions are to be satisfied they will have to be formed by a reliable method. And so we arrive at the broad outline of a reliabilist analysis of the concept of knowledge.

Our interest, however, was not exclusively in reliabilism *per se*; rather we began with the business of the 'opacity' of the third condition in the analysis of knowledge, the thought that, whatever this condition may be, there is no need for the knower to be aware of it as holding. This recent tendency is in accordance with everything we have seen so far—nothing about the knower's own attitude to his method of acquiring beliefs has yet emerged. But there remains the possibility that some such thing might appear, if we squeeze the notion of effective action a little harder—so we should go on trying. In fact at least two arguments worthy of the name can be mounted in support of the view that some kind of awareness of the satisfaction of a third condition will benefit the agent *qua* agent.

One might be put like this: the world being generally on the move, despatch and decisiveness will frequently be of advantage—*carpe diem*—so it will generally be good if the agent's beliefs, in so far as true, are confidently held, to minimise dithering; and for that it will be a help if he believes that these beliefs have an ancestry which gives them a high probability of truth. Concentration on the notion of effective practice therefore does encourage, after all, transparency of the third condition; opacity, it turns out, would be a disadvantage. But although this argument has some plausibility, it is in fact not very hard to resist.

We may provisionally grant that confidence is a desideratum. Still, the subject may be confident in his beliefs without that confidence resting on the second-order belief that his first-order beliefs have been acquired by reliable means. It is possible to hold many beliefs, and with great confidence, without having even considered the question whether there is such a thing as the method by which any of them were reached. What is needed is not that one hold any beliefs about the method at all, but simply that it generate beliefs that are not only true, and held, but held confidently as well. Allowing the subject to believe that the method is reliable is only one way of raising the level of confidence. Besides, is it so clear that confidence in the belief is exactly what we want? Isn't it—since quick and decisive action is the aim—something more like taking for granted? Once we start thinking of some property of a belief that needs to be shored up by awareness of the way in which the belief arose we are surely on the wrong track; for that process itself would be too deliberative an affair to be ideal for this particular job.

A second, related, argument takes its cue from Plato.[45] Given that there is practical value in having true beliefs, there must equally be practical value in maintaining true beliefs, so that anything that tends to preserve true beliefs once they are acquired and make it less likely that the subject will give them up will be indirectly, but importantly, beneficial to him *qua* agent. And having a good reason for a belief will have just that tendency: assuming that you are aware of having good reason—and of course this awareness is just what is at issue when we are thinking about the opacity of the third condition—it will take much more to get you to drop the belief if you have one than if you do not. Having a reason, then, where this implies transparency to the subject, is, practically speaking, advantageous.

This argument must be allowed some force, but in the end not very much. Its force is in the first place reduced by the fact that it speaks of the agent's competence only in a very restricted range of circumstances: we must imagine him first exposed to some influence tending to unsettle the belief in question, and then in a situation where that very belief would have been of use to him. In the second place, and to my feeling more decisively, it could be countered that although the belief that one has a good reason can provide a valuable bulwark against doubt, what is important is that there should be some such bulwark, not that it should be this one in particular. Anything that generated a high subjective certainty would do just as well; it could for instance be

[45] Plato: *Meno* 97–8.

some kind of Humean mechanism, of whose operation the subject was wholly unaware. There are no grounds for thinking that it would have to involve the subject's recognition of the fact that he had reasons; hence neither does this agent-centred approach give us any grounds to assign such recognition special status in the analysis of knowledge. It would just be one thing, amongst others, that could do the job.

So far these considerations dovetail fairly well with what we actually find in the recent literature on knowledge—as my hypothesis would lead us to expect. But another question, one that has nothing to do with this particular struggle between opacity and transparency, arises out of them: why any third condition at all? Our agent, be it granted, needs true beliefs and plenty of them, but given that he has them, why should anything about how he has come by them have any effect on his success in action? Even if we found no detectable general facts whatever about the acquisition of belief, he would still so act as to get what he wanted—and wasn't that to be the criterion? No doubt very nearly all, probably all, human beliefs can be said to have been acquired by some method or other (there don't seem to be many which are hereditary, and even if there were that might just about be called a 'method'), but why should the Agency Theory encourage us to give that fact a special position in the analysis of knowledge, any more, for instance, than the fact of possessing a central nervous system? Some writers do occasionally appear to recommend that we should stop at true belief:

there are hosts of expressions both verbal and behavioural that may be called expressions of knowledge or expressions of belief interchangeably in the same circumstances. He says 'Shush'. He tiptoes past the bedroom. Are these expressions of knowledge or belief? An idle question: call them which you please.[46]

—if the belief is true, and you *do* the same thing, there is no difference; therefore identify them.

This objection can probably not be met from our present standpoint; but I spoke earlier of two perspectives, and the second promises more assistance. Recalling that the Agency

---

[46] R. F. Holland:'Hidden Complication and True Belief', in *Aristotelian Society Supplementary Volume* LIX (1985) pp. 8–9.

Theory gives encouragement to the themes of the social and the communal, we can see that not only is it likely to focus our attention on knowledge as what every good agent needs; it is also likely to direct the mind to whatever it is that fits someone to be a source of information for others—so that they may become effective agents as well, and so that there can be co-operation. What will that be? In the first place, and unsurprisingly, we shall want a potential informant to hold true beliefs or, to put it minimally, a true belief on the matter on which we are seeking information. But that cannot be all. We need to select our informants, or decide which volunteered information to accept. So we need him to be detectable as a source of truth, which means, of course, detectable by those who do not yet know what the truth is—we are thinking not of people in the position of examiners, who already know the answer, but of inquirers who are trying to reach it by choosing a suitable informant. So we need some way of assessing his claim to be heard which does not involve our knowing the truth in advance; hence he will have to satisfy some further condition—his merely holding a true belief will not ensure that he is of use as a source of information, and so as an aid to successful practice in others.

Incidentally, it is now of interest to ask whether this approach favours any of the recently popular options in the analysis of knowledge above the others. It would seem that it does: of the three we have mentioned it offers much the fairer wind to the 'reliable method' theory. For, first, the causal analysis has as its third condition that the belief that p be causally linked to the fact that p, and this is something which our inquirer, who *ex hypothesi* does not yet know whether or not p is the case, cannot independently ascertain. Or rather, to the extent that he can, either he will be going on some other fact about the potential informant, or he must have some quite different way of finding out whether p, and then he will no longer be interested in him as a source of information. Similarly, the epistemology of counterfactuals is unfavourable to the 'tracking' option of Nozick and Dretske. If we are looking for a trustworthy informant, then someone who satisfies the tracking requirement is no doubt a person we should like to meet, but that he satisfies it is not something that we can straightforwardly detect; instead we shall have to infer it from other facts about him, facts for instance about the way in which he has come by his belief. That being so, it is the latter type of fact which is to be thought of as fundamental in conferring status on our potential informant. I shall not pursue these issues of detail here, however,[47] since my present interest is in the more general point: there will have to be some property of the informant which correlates well with his holding a true belief on the matter in question, but nothing in this line of thought suggests that the correlation, or even the correlated property, must be known to him or so much as thought of by him—it is enough that it should exist and have its effect on those who are trying to choose a reliable source of information. This aspect of contemporary work on knowledge, the feature which most decisively sets it apart from the earlier understanding of that concept, is thus in full accord with the spirit of the Agency Theory.

7.   *Opacity in the theory of meaning—and doing things with words*

At the beginning of the last section I said that opacity was also a feature of recent accounts of meaning. The Image of God doctrine, when applied to our cognitive powers, was bound to emphasise the notion of insight into truth, understood as the grasp of a reality independent of man. Accordingly, it called for a theory of thought that satisfied two conditions. In the first place, it needed to be representationalist, that is to say it had to make a thought some kind of representation of truth-conditions, a model of a putative state of reality. And secondly, it needed to make content transparent to the thinker, in other words to allow us insight into the content of our own thoughts; for there would be no value—because no real insight—in knowing that a certain representation correctly represented the real, if it were not accompanied by an insightful grasp of just what it represented. But with the passing of the demand for insight into the real there also passes the need for insight into the content of our thoughts or the meanings of our expressions. This change then liberates

---

[47] Though I hope shortly to do so elsewhere—see e.g. Craig: 'The Practical Explication of Knowledge', *Proceedings of the Aristotelian Society* Vol. LXXXVII (1986–7)

opaque theories of meaning: the speaker or thinker does not have to have any access to an incorrigibly known representation of a state of affairs. Many writers have availed themselves of this option in one form or another. It is clear in advance that there are going to be several possibilities: one will be able to drop the incorrigibility, or even the knowledge, whilst retaining the underlying representationalism, or to take the more radical line of abandoning the latter as well.

The prime example of an incorrigibilist and representationalist theory of meaning would be one which made the meaning of an expression some item, before the consciousness of the speaker and wholly transparent to it, picturing univocally and precisely the conditions under which his utterance would be true. It should be no surprise to find that the closest approaches to such a theory—and in intention at least they are very close indeed—are found in the seventeenth and eighteenth centuries. The best attempts to work it out in detail, consequently the ones which give us the clearest view of its problems, are those of the classical empiricists, especially Locke. That some such theory was right appears hardly to have been questioned in this era, which is no surprise either: the assumption could meet serious resistance only when the faith in the Insight Ideal had faded, for the programme which the Ideal generated had no prospects of success without it. A version of it, substituting somewhat obscure entities called 'propositions' for the clearer (and more clearly wrong) mental imagery of the empiricists, has dragged on into our times, where, having no deep metaphysic to sustain it, it has lost ground drastically. Items that provide a picture, fully accessible to consciousness, of the truth-conditions of sentences then said to express them are no longer required by the mainstream fed by the dominant philosophy.

It is only our own occurrent mental states that have ever been strong candidates to be the objects of incorrigible knowledge. With such knowledge no longer needed cogent arguments were soon found, by Wittgenstein and others, that made the equation of meanings (or of thoughts) with any kind of conscious state highly problematical, to say the least. With that any real chance of presenting our knowledge of our own meaning as incorrigible was gone; but some writers are happy to allow cases in which the speaker, so far from knowing incorrigibly what the truth-conditions of his utterance are, does not know what they are at all—and without, I may add, this making his speech on such an occasion in any way abnormal or improper. Thus Putnam and Dummett each favour a view on which the sense of an expression may acceptably be, and often is, unknown to most of those who use it, although all allow that the truth of what they say is to be judged in accordance with that sense. I may (and do) speak of elm trees without being able to distinguish them from many other types of tree, let alone state the distinguishing features. Yet I do not intend my statements to apply to all those trees, many of them not elms at all, which satisfy the woefully deficient description I am able to give of an elm. What 'elm' means is determined by certain standard works on botany, and may be retained in the minds of a few experts. The true criteria are not widely known, and the individual speaker does not have to do much more than agree that his utterances are to be assessed in accordance with them, whatever they are:

A particular speaker may attach only a partially specific sense to the word, but may exploit the existence of the socially acknowledged sense to enable him to use it in communication with others.[48]

And for Putnam:

the determination of reference is social and not individual . . . you and I both defer to experts who *can* tell elms from beeches.[49]

We have seen that the Agency Theory provides a natural route to the social and communal: there can be no division of insight, but there can very well be division of labour. If there is to be communication there must be a shared linguistic basis, but the task of maintaining the basis need not fall on each of us separately—it can be left in the care of an archive whose authority we all acknowledge.

It should be noticed that the threat posed to the Insight Ideal by this point about meaning is not yet very serious. The division of labour sanctioned by Putnam and Dummett is in

---

[48] M. A. E. Dummett: 'The Social Character of Meaning' in *Truth and Other Enigmas* (Duckworth 1978) pp. 420–430. This quotation p. 426.
[49] H. Putnam: *Reason, Truth and History* (Cambridge 1981) p. 18.

principle optional: any speaker could avail himself of the information in the public semantic archives and so come to an unaided grasp of the truth-conditions of what he was saying. There is no more permanent damage to the apparatus of the Insight Ideal than there was in Berkeley's observation:

it is not necessary ... significant names which stand for ideas should, every time they are used, excite in the understanding the ideas they are made to stand for . . .[50]

since for Berkeley it is still important that there be such ideas and that they can be called to mind in place of the words that were 'made to stand for them' whenever the situation requires it; the 'opacity' is temporary and inessential. But Putnam takes another step which goes a good deal further in respect of making the meaning of speech opaque to the speakers. It used to be held that the meaning of a word like 'gold' could be given in terms of a list of fairly easily detectable properties which gave the necessary and sufficient conditions for being gold, conditions which we could grasp precisely because we had selected them. But according to the view suggested by Putnam this is not the case, not even in rough outline. What really happens is that we designate certain lumps of material 'gold' and adopt the convention that gold is anything having the same physico-chemical constitution as *this*—even though we do not know what that constitution is. We allow the stuff, as it were, to set the standards, and then aim to comply with them without really knowing what they are.

Apart from locating the determinants of meaning in the publicly accessible sphere, this further step has nothing in particular to do with the alleged social character of meaning; but it does, obviously, have a great deal to do with its opacity. And it suggests an argument which tends to make the opacity even less penetrable. Suppose that research were to reveal that there are two ways in which a neutron can be made up, that in the stuff we call gold the neutrons are made up in one way, and that there is another substance otherwise exactly like gold but having its neutrons composed in the other way. Would it be gold or not? If Putnam says not, then the opacity of meaning looks like becoming very opaque indeed; for then it

[50] Berkeley: *The Principles of Human Knowledge*, Introduction para. XIX.

would seem that a new discovery of this kind, at a more minute level of composition than that previously (and provisionally) regarded as ultimate, would at any time bring about the revision of many of our previous judgements as to what was gold. It would not be just that we might use the word 'gold' without anyone's having a complete grasp of the conditions which a stuff had to meet in order to be gold, but that we were committed to using the word without anyone's ever being able to attain a position from which they could tell definitively what these conditions were. If on the other hand he were to say that this hypothetical substance would be gold, we would presumably want to know why, if this difference does not make a different substance, a difference of composition at a slightly less microscopic level should do so. It seems that Putnam is on the brink, at least, of attributing a quite radical opacity to the semantics of terms for natural kinds.

These views, then, accord progressively less and less status to the idea of the individual as master of his own meanings, and also to the idea that he can have insight into the meaning of his own speech or the content of his own thought. But they can still all be thought of as being basically representationalist theories. In each case there is some set of conditions for the application of 'elm', 'gold' or whatever; truth is achieved when the facts meet those conditions, when they fit that 'representation'. The representation in question now exists, at least partially, outside the head of the speaker, determined in the one case by the authoritative semantic archive on 'elm' and in the other by the microstructure of the stuff we call 'gold'. In either case the speaker may, typically will, and in one case even arguably must be unaware of just what these conditions are in accordance with which he agrees to use his words. But the conditions are none the less there, acting as a kind of template which we have to fit to the world if we are to think or speak truly; description is still the basic function of language. At least equally characteristic of twentieth-century philosophy of language, however, has been the move away from representationalism altogether. It frequently takes the form of an attack on the notion of a reality which is represented; thus we find a prevalence of pragmatist, coherence and in general anti-realist accounts of truth. But I shall concentrate here on a variant which works from the other direction: it looks at language, and takes its essential role to be not so much descriptive as instrumental.

Such a tendency is unmistakably present in Wittgenstein's comments on language in the *Philosophical Investigations*, where even his illustrative metaphor is tuned to bring the reader to think in these terms:

Think of the tools in a toolbox: there is a hammer, pliers, a saw, a screw-driver, a rule, a glue-pot, nails and screws.—The functions of words are as diverse as the functions of these objects.[51]

A literal appearance of the same conception opens the whole work:

Now think of the following use of language: I send someone shopping. I give him a slip marked 'five red apples'. He takes the slip to the shopkeeper, who opens the drawer marked 'apples'; he then looks up the word 'red' in a table and finds a colour sample opposite it; then he says the series of cardinal numbers—I assume that he knows it by heart—up to the word 'five' and for each number he takes an apple of the same colour as the sample out of the drawer.—It is in this and similar ways that one operates with words.[52]

Noteworthy is the very phrase 'operate with words'; but that is not all. There is a temptation—until quite recently philosophers would unthinkingly have succumbed to it—to think of the words 'five red apples' as being a description of a certain kind of complex object. The shopkeeper—so the thought would continue—understands this description, that is thinks of an object of that sort, and then puts together an object to match the thought, a group of five red apples. But nothing about descriptions, or about reality matching thoughts, features in Wittgenstein's account—just what the shopkeeper does on seeing the words. The Agency Theory is here seen at work twice: what is emphasised is the shop-keeper's behaviour (witness also the way in which Wittgenstein deals with the ensuing question in the rest of the paragraph from which the quotation is taken), and how language has been instrumental in modifying it.

---

[51] Wittgenstein: *Philosophical Investigations* para. 11.
[52] Ibid. para. 1.

Alongside Wittgenstein, the most salient example of an instrumentalist approach to language is that adopted by J. L. Austin in *How to Do Things with Words*.[53] In the first half of that book Austin investigates the distinction between 'constative' and 'performative' utterances. Constatives are such as describe, or state, facts; they are properly assessed in terms of truth and falsehood. Performatives, on the other hand, are not naturally regarded as true or false; rather, using them is best seen as carrying out a certain action (other than, trivially, that of saying something) and thereby altering— though this broad formulation will not fit all cases equally well—social relations or conventions, as when one says 'I promise . . .', or 'I bet . . .', or 'I name this ship . . .'. It is the constative use, evidently, which a representationalist theory (such as the Insight Ideal required) will take as central and prize most highly.

Austin is only too well aware that it is the constative which has been the main object of philosophical attention, though he treats the fact as if it were the outcome of oversight or carelessness, without any deeper motivation. He himself, anticipatably, puts the stress on the performative, the business of acting through speech. One might think that this emphasis is explicable simply as the attempt to redress the balance, to give an under-discussed phenomenon its due hearing; as such it would be compatible with, not necessarily even mildly hostile to, the opinion that language is primarily descriptive, and that the central semantic problems are about the notion of sense rather than force. Occasionally, indeed, Austin speaks as if he might not want to contest that view, and nowhere, to my knowledge, can he be found explicitly saying that he does. But the reader of *How to Do Things with Words* can see from his cavalier, almost negligent approach to the descriptivist position which way the wind is blowing. Consider, for instance, the following passage:

One thing, however, that it will be most dangerous to do, and which we are very prone to do, is to take it that we somehow *know* that the primary or primitive use of sentences must be, because it ought to be, statemental or constative, in the philosophers' preferred sense of

[53] J. L. Austin: *How to Do Things with Words*, ed. Urmson (Oxford 1962).

simply uttering something whose sole pretension is to be true or false and which is not liable to criticism in any other dimension. We certainly do not know that this is so, any more, for example, than, to take an alternative, that all utterances must have begun as swear words—and it seems much more likely that the 'pure' statement is a goal, an ideal, towards which the gradual development of science has given the impetus . . .[54]

For all this to be so frightfully dangerous it must, one would imagine, be the sort of thing that is liable seriously to mislead us about the nature of language as we have it—Austin is certainly not just thinking of some error about linguistic prehistory, in spite of the fact that this is the context in which the passage occurs. The great mistake that threatens must surely be that of overrating the importance of the constative use as a concept of linguistic theory. Thereupon two questions arise: first, has Austin really shown that this is a mistake?, and second, is one's view of the early prehistory of language likely to push one into the wrong camp on that issue?

As regards the second question, we may reasonably be dismissive. To be misled, one would first of all need to conflate being primary in the sense of being theoretically basic with being primitive in the developmental meaning of the word. And surely the historical error, if it is such, is far more likely to be the effect of the contemporary theoretical position than its cause? In any case, it can be said with confidence that someone who wishes to point to the descriptive, representative properties of language as uniquely central to its function has no need whatever to adopt any specific view of the earliest history of speech; and certainly nothing so absurd as that our distant ancestors had no interest in warning, but only in informing each other that a sabre-toothed tiger was in the offing; at most he will have to hold that describing is a vital component of warning. Nor is there any call for him to maintain that there are purely descriptive utterances which are not liable to criticism in any other dimension than that of truth and falsehood. Admittedly, that is the dimension on which philosophers have concentrated—and I would hope that this book may have a part to play in explaining why this has been so. But why Austin should suggest that they have

[54] Ibid. p. 72.

overlooked the fact that when one says something one's utterance may, whether true or false, be unfounded, malicious, socially inept or just off the point—this remains quite mysterious, and we have to conclude that Austin had no interest in thinking out what the descriptivist's position might actually be.

A philosopher who insists on the centrality of representation, truth and falsehood in any theoretical approach to meaning can happily accept the existence, indeed the frequency, of the phenomena which Austin locates and classifies. But he may give various reasons for favouring his own distribution of the emphasis. Were there a language (so he might argue) in which one could only utter imperatives, it would not involve constatives—a trivial truth; but it would have to have some way of representing the states of affairs which speakers commanded their audiences to bring about—or none of these imperatives would actually command anything. Likewise a language all of whose permissible utterances took the form 'I bet you that . . .'—the blanks would have to be filled by expressions representing the outcomes on which the speakers wagered. Once we accept this, it becomes hard to believe that such languages are anything more than fantasy—given that they would have to possess the necessary vocabulary (and in the second case also the syntax) for issuing descriptions, surely there would arise the practice of using them to report that what was commanded had now been done, or that what was wagered on had in fact come about.

Another attractive line would be to point out that the descriptive content, and constative force, of a sentence is very often useful for explaining how it can enter successfully into performatives in the way it does. If I say 'The bull is pawing the ground', then the state of affairs which you take that to represent and the fact that you take me to be stating that it obtains do much to explain why the utterance can so easily take effect as a warning, and be used for that purpose; but there are no prospects for a theory that makes the explanatory flow go in the other direction. Finally, our theorist might assign special status to these aspects of language because although (as a disciple of the Practice Ideal) he was pre-eminently inclined to find the solutions to his problems in man's active and creative capacities, he took himself to be offering descriptions, true descriptions, of these capacities and their roles. It is, in fact, because of what he himself is doing, somewhere between hard and impossible for a philosopher sincerely and with due consideration to downgrade the representative, fact-stating dimension of language by comparison with the active, performative dimension. Austin gives the impression of doing this sincerely enough, but without giving the impression of due consideration. Nor does he show sign of having given much thought to the resources available to his descriptivist opponent when it comes to ethical theory. Writing of the correct understanding of 'I promise to . . .', he says:

It is gratifying to observe in this very example how excess of profundity, or rather solemnity, at once paves the way for immorality. For one who says 'promising is not merely a matter of uttering words! It is an inward and spiritual act!' is apt to appear as a solid moralist standing out against a generation of superficial theorizers . . . Yet he provides Hippolytus with a let-out, the bigamist with an excuse for his 'I do' and the welsher with a defence for his 'I bet'. Accuracy and morality alike are on the side of the plain saying that *our word is our bond*.[55]

Austin speaks as if his opponent had no way of bringing moral criticism to bear on the person who promises with his lips but not in his heart. Now what can be said of this descriptivist account of promising is that according to it Hippolytus did not promise, since he withheld the inner act; but to infer that therefore he did not place himself under any obligation, or lay himself open to moral censure if he failed to carry out whatever was specified, would be premature, not to say downright mistaken. In saying 'I promise . . .' he has, on this account, intentionally made a false statement about his intentions; hence he has wilfully deceived his audience about facts highly pertinent to their confident (though deluded) expectations about his future behaviour. His deceit may well—as he easily and gladly foresees—lead them into actions which will be disadvantageous to them should he not perform

[55] Ibid. p. 10.

his part. Doesn't all this offer the stern moralist handhold enough, even if it be not literally true that a promise has been made and broken? And suppose that it has been made, as Austin's performative account tells us: does the immorality of breaking it consist in anything different? The two views differ as to whether the speaker has really and literally promised— but whether they differ on any substantial question of morals is open to serious and fairly obvious doubts. To have overlooked these doubts cannot, in Austin, be a sign of stupidity. It is rather a sign a sheer lack of interest in the alternative—thus do the prejudices in favour of activity and against representation manifest themselves.

8. *Brave new world*

In the preceding three sections I hope to have persuaded the reader to see a number of apparently separate concerns as being all of one family. The Agency Theory promotes the instrumentalist style of thought, and because of this, so I have argued, it promotes the acceptability of opacity. Thus when explanation, for instance, is thought of in instrumentalist terms it becomes possible to see it as a grasp of brute fact; when knowledge is seen from the same perspective we are led to welcome 'externalist' accounts of it. Instrumentalism, moreover, encourages the resort to the concepts of the communal and the social which we have seen in Popper, Putnam and Dummett. But it also, as one might expect, appears undisguised: our example was the attitude towards language variously articulated by Wittgenstein and Austin. So far, we have selected topics from within what might broadly be called 'academic' philosophy. But if my thesis about the dominant philosophy has substance, one would expect the effects of the metaphysic of the activity of man to be visible in intellectual life well beyond these somewhat narrow confines. In this closing section I should therefore like to mention two phenomena which indicate that this very legitimate expect-tion is not going to be disappointed.

Two of the best-known English novels of the twentieth century are Aldous Huxley's *Brave New World* and George Orwell's *Nineteen Eighty-Four*. Both are concerned directly with what has been called 'social engineering' and its effects upon the quality of human life. They investigate a theme patently close to the heart of the Agency Theory: man's control of man and the environment in which he lives, and the consequences of his exercise of that control. That Huxley is hardly enthusiastic about the life-style he portrays—for though it may be said that most of his characters are presented as being, for the most part, reasonably happy, they are happy only in proportion as their responses are superficial or infantile—and that Orwell's book is, with only the most fleeting inter-missions, deepest black from first sentence to last, is no objection here. Nor, after all, was Hume greatly taken with the Image of God doctrine, yet his writing bears witness to its strength and status in the thought of his time; the dominance of a dominant philosophy can manifest itself just as clearly in the work of its critics as in that of its supporters.

Brave New World throws down a challenge to the utilitarian. The advocates of that ethic in the nineteenth century had assumed that the goal, the happiness of mankind, was to be attained by the adjustment of social institutions to promote the satisfaction of human desires. They do not, understand-ably enough, appear to have given much thought to the alternative which Huxley illustrates, namely that happiness might be achieved by another route, that of moulding the individual's desires to fit the circumstances and institutions which he was going to encounter, so that he would find his contentment in the activities which were in any case going to be required of him. The utilitarian is called upon either to embrace the brave new world as an acceptable way of realising his ideals, or to explain to us why it does not realise them after all; neither prong of the fork is comfortable, and Huxley's 'world controller', Mustapha Mond, is moved to wish that he didn't have to think so much about happiness.[56] But the book is not just a critique of utilitarianism. It pictures a social order in which we have passed 'out of the realm of mere slavish imitation of nature into the much more interest-ing world of human invention',[57] one possible embodiment of a philosophy in which everything, outer and inner, is manipu-lated by man for man, a life therefore in which nothing is left

[56] Aldous Huxley: *Brave New World* (Penguin 1955) p. 142.
[57] Ibid. p. 22.

to struggle against, nothing is left to which we must perforce accommodate, all has been enveloped by human activity and shaped to our comfort, an order whose saviour is the inventor of mass-produced convenience, whose one sacred symbol is the 'T' of the Model T Ford.

And what if our convenience, 'the maintenance of well-being', were not the sovereign good after all? The thought, so reflects Mustapha Mond with some reluctance, though 'quite possibly true', is inadmissible, along with anything else that might lead the more intelligent to believe that 'the goal was somewhere beyond, somewhere outside the present sphere'.[58] Not just the utilitarian, but also the pragmatist is being called to account—one can almost hear William James asking us why human experience should not be self-supporting, invoking the image of the void beyond it.[59] Anyone who doesn't like the society of *Brave New World* is challenged at least to ask themselves the question, whether a philosophy which speaks only of the satisfaction of our needs can ever satisfy our needs.

In *Brave New World* society operates by taking control of the desires of its citizens and adjusting them to suit the circumstances they will encounter; that of *Nineteen Eighty-Four* operates primarily by taking control of truth—given the right beliefs, acceptance of the social order will follow, however profound the dissatisfaction that is felt. And the philosophy with which this is justified is a kind of anthropocentric idealism in which the doctrine that man is *fons et origo* of the universe is taken to the extreme: there is nothing outside human belief, therefore whoever controls that may be said to control the facts—the void beyond human experience gives unlimited scope to the agent within it. Human imperialism now expands to take in everything; even the past becomes a pliable construct. Winston Smith, feeling the ground of historical objectivity buckling under him, asks himself the question: if both the past and the external world exist only in the mind, and if the mind itself is controllable—what then?[60] The answer he is to learn in the closing chapters: what follows is the invincibility of the party, as O'Brien, the official entrusted with his 'rehabilitation', tells him:

[58] Ibid. p. 141.
[59] See above, Chapter 5 Section 4.
[60] George Orwell: *Nineteen Eighty-Four* (Penguin 1983) p. 73.

Nothing exists except through human consciousness . . . Before man there was nothing. After man, if he could come to an end, there would be nothing. Outside man there is nothing.[61]

The void is prepared, now enter a malevolent agent:

We control matter because we control the mind . . . We make the laws of nature.[62]

And then the rule of the party, the rule of pain and hatred, can last for ever:

We control life, Winston, at all its levels. You are imagining that there is something called human nature which will be outraged by what we do and will turn against us. But we create human nature. Men are infinitely malleable.[63]

The philosophy of human creativity, we are grimly warned, had better set itself limits; and it had better not get into the wrong hands.

The tendency for the Agency Theory to come to the surface in matters theological is as old as the theory itself,[64] but of late its effects have become evident in the public pronouncements of certain dignitaries of the church, so that it can claim at least a semi-official position within the Christian establishment. Views expressed, for instance, by the present Archbishop of York, Dr John Habgood, about the formation of religious belief and practice bear a distinct resemblance to those adopted by Sir Karl Popper in respect of the progress of science. Habgood sees, and welcomes, a plurality of churches involved in a process of constructive mutual criticism; the community of researchers is seen edging towards Peirce's 'final opinion':

in an ideal ecumenical environment churches should be able to do what each does best, without pride or competitiveness, yet able to learn from one another, and correct one another, and move towards a greater Christian wholeness.[65]

When, in an interview given a few days before his enthrone-

[61] Ibid. pp. 228–9.
[62] Ibid. p. 228.
[63] Ibid. p. 232.
[64] We have seen it, for instance, in Pascal—above Chapter 5 Section 2.
[65] John Habgood: *Church and Nation in a Secular Age* (Darton, Longman and Todd 1983) p. 175.

ment, Habgood was asked a question about the Church of England's stance on a major issue of public moral concern, he replied in a similar spirit: the Christian was not so much bidden to take up any particular position on the matter; rather he was called to debate, to inquiry, his duty was to wrestle with moral issues, to engage in the activity of search. Was the Archbishop Elect merely being diplomatic? I think not; for that his remarks harmonise a little too well with his more general opinion as I have just quoted it. Besides, what he said bears a striking resemblance to something which David Jenkins, Bishop of Durham, wrote a little later of the traditional conception of Christian belief. It was, he said, 'an alarmingly static and limited view of God'.[66] Now anyone's view of God may, I suppose, be limited without thereby ringing episcopal alarms; but what of 'static'? If there is an unchanging object corresponding to the view, then one who believes himself to have reached truth about it might be expected to want to stay put. He might, in so doing, lay himself open to a charge of complacency, or of slothfully stopping well short of the limits of his powers. But there would be nothing wrong with having a static view of God as such; for static is just what the right view of God ought to be—unless perhaps God is a shifting phenomenon, more akin to a human projection than a transcendent reality. Is this to read Jenkins' words too literally, and take him to be alarmed by the very thought of a static opinion when his complaint really lies only against the stasis of particular people's minds? Possibly, but again I hardly think so. He also wrote: '. . . to believe is to question, and . . . to have faith is to be under a divine compulsion to explore'.[67] These words, quite apart from the way in which they link with those of Habgood, give a strong suggestion that an underlying value has changed. No longer is there, even for each separate individual, such a thing as *the* right view which we are to aim at achieving and holding fast; value now resides in sincere and committed participation in the activity of religious thought.

A lay writer has offered an opinion as to what the object of

[66] David Jenkins: 'The Pathology of Fear in a Search for Truth' The *Guardian* Monday 17 December 1984 p. 12.

[67] Ibid.

such thought should be. Religion, he said, 'addresses the problem of human adaptation'. And from this highly pragmatist premiss he drew the following consequence:

Instead, therefore, of verification or falsification, religious hypotheses give rise to a negotiated settlement: between sun and moon, man and woman, individual and state, and so forth. And religion is therefore an activity—seeking the hypothesis, constructing the settlement, and keeping it in repair . . .[68]

in which we hear not only the Agency Theory (religious belief has become a continuing activity of adjustment), but even perhaps an echo of the far-off romantic quest for the re-unification of opposites.

The symbol of faith was formerly a rock. Now, as viewers of a recent television series will know, it is a sea.[69] And the moon that pulls its tides hither and thither is made up, it seems, of human requirements and human experience. It is the same moon, surely, as the one which William James saw, breasting non-entity, cutting the caerulean abyss.

[68] Charles Plouviez: 'Beyond the Faith of Our Fathers', The *Guardian* Monday 25 February 1985 p. 8.
[69] See Don Cupitt: *The Sea of Faith* (BBC, London 1984).

INDEX

Absolute 181, 266, 269–72, 275, 280, 307–9

Absolute Idea, the 253–4

aesthetic experience 149–52

agency (activity) 22, 32, 49, 53–7, 149–50, 160–1, 197–8, 200, 206, 225–345 *passim*
- of God 28, 32, 180, 202, 225
- of man 25–7, 33, 36, 50, 52, 80, 133, 136, 150, 174, 181, 198–205, 221, 225–345 *passim*
- of mind (thought, spirit) 112, 154, 161–2, 181, 188, 192, 195, 199–219, 226–7, 235–43 *passim*, 256, 262–6, 272–8, 287, 289, 297, 304–8, 342–4
- of Reason 149, 153, 160–1, 198–205

Agency Theory (=Practice Ideal) 10, 229–31, 235, 240, 256, 258, 276–8, 281–7, 290, 305, 310, 313, 320–1, 324–5, 328–9, 335, 340–1, 343, 345

Agent in the Void, 271, 282

agnosticism 76, 108–10, 113, 115, 236, 247, 252

agreement 312–15

akrasia 56

Alexander, H. G. 31 n.

alienation 162, 164, 194

analytic philosophy 4–5, 41, 213, 219–20

analytic statements, analysis 40, 60–2, 75, 86, 129, 237, 262, 322, 328

analytical (=meaning–theoretical) 75–6, 90–129 *passim*, 261

ancestor-worship 14

Angst 271

animals 31, 74, 245, 259, 279

Ansich, the (Hegel) 196–8

anthropocentrism 289, 295, 301, 342

anthropomorphism 28, 44–5, 73

anti-realism 263, 287, 296, 334

a priori 60–2, 82–3, 88–9, 93, 96–7, 100, 117, 122–3, 286–7, 290, 319

argument from design (teleological argument) 34, 72–4

Aristotle 16–17, 176

arithmetic 19, 47, 61, 77, 287

Armstrong, D. M. 322 n.

Arnauld, A. 51

art 133, 145, 149–51, 175, 181, 226, 276, 278

assumptions 23, 42, 48, 54, 63, 187–9, 196, 238, 254, 289, 315, 331

Aufhebung 151, 171, 208

Austin, J. L. 336–40

authenticity 302, 304

authority 16–17, 22, 28, 65, 121, 202, 294, 297–8, 303, 305–6, 308

autonomy 162, 174, 255, 264, 266–7, 270–2, 278, 280, 295, 301–8

Bad faith 301–4, 308

Baldwin, T. R. vii

Barnes, H. E. 302 n., 304 n.

basic statements 312–15

beauty 149, 151, 161, 166, 181–3, 268

becoming 274, 280

beer 76

Being 208

Beissner, F. 164 n., 180 n.

belief 75, 81, 84–120, 125, 133, 199, 233–6, 240–2, 251–2, 260, 262–6, 269–70, 288–9, 291, 306–7, 311, 315–17, 322–30, 342–3

Bennett, J. F. vii, 43

Berkeley 14, 30, 32–5, 40, 42–3, 55, 59, 78–9, 225, 231, 251, 285–6, 333

Bernouilli, J. 80

Beutler, E. 157 n.

Blackburn, S. W. vii, 296 n.

Blumenberg, H. 273 n.

Braithwaite, R. B. 318–19

brute fact 20, 37–8, 43, 224, 242, 316–20, 340

Cambridge Platonists 67

Carnap, R. 315 n.

Cartesian circle 27

Cartesian demon 29, 30, 34, 60

Casey, J. 296 n.

categorical imperative 307